# History of
# AFRICAN
# AMERICANS

# History of
# AFRICAN AMERICANS
## *Exploring Diverse Roots*

Thomas J. Davis

 GREENWOOD™

An Imprint of ABC-CLIO, LLC

Santa Barbara, California • Denver, Colorado

**Library of Congress Cataloging-in-Publication Data**

Names: Davis, Thomas J. (Thomas Joseph), author.
Title: History of African Americans : exploring diverse roots / Thomas J. Davis.
Description: Santa Barbara, California : Greenwood, an imprint of ABC-CLIO, LLC, [2016] | Includes bibliographical references and index.
Identifiers: LCCN 2016025200 (print) | LCCN 2016025540 (ebook) | ISBN 9780313385407 (alk. paper) | ISBN 9780313385414 (ebook)
Subjects: LCSH: African Americans—History. | African Americans—Race identity. | Racism—United States—History. | African Americans—Social conditions.
Classification: LCC E185 .D265 2016 (print) | LCC E185 (ebook) | DDC 973/.0496073—dc23
LC record available at https://lccn.loc.gov/2016025200

ISBN: 978-0-313-38540-7
EISBN: 978-0-313-38541-4

20 19 18 17 16    1 2 3 4 5

This book is also available as an eBook.

Greenwood
An Imprint of ABC-CLIO, LLC

ABC-CLIO, LLC
130 Cremona Drive, P.O. Box 1911
Santa Barbara, California 93116-1911
www.abc-clio.com

This book is printed on acid-free paper ∞

Manufactured in the United States of America

To
Alice, Laura, Mollie, Margaret, Magdalene, Uarlee, Ida, Ada
Brenda,
Lula, Gail, Ann, Suewan, Sonja, Catherine, Ethel, Alicia
and all the African descended
mothers, grandmothers, wives, sisters, daughters, aunts, and nieces
who gestated, nurtured, bled, cried, and sweated
in travail and triumph
to give the dream breath and life, hope, and stamina
with stern and encouraging example and voice
saying and showing that
"life for me ain't been no crystal stair"

# Contents

# Preface

Over the centuries black peoples in America have nurtured distinctive attitudes, beliefs, characters, folkways, and manners. They have shared common circumstances and conditions that have distinguished them in America beyond reference to the continent of their ancestral origins or their physical appearance. Yet African Americans have never been singular in experience or outlook. They have ever been diverse peoples. Time, temperament, talents, opportunities, place, and interpersonal relations, among myriad elements of life, have invariably set blacks apart from one another as individuals and as groups, even as pronounced racial distinction and discrimination have invariably set blacks as a group apart from others in America.

African American history is thus not singular or simple; it has many facets and layers; it spreads across time and place and personalities. Within diverse African American experiences, however, a shared core has persisted in spirit and structure as a complex core of black community and culture has continually risen and reconstituted itself to exult in blacks' humanity and contribution to their immediate and broader communities.

This book focuses on fundamental and pivotal experiences of peoples of African descent in their quest to forge fulfilling lives with personal and community identities since their earliest encounters with the colonial forebears of the American nation. It covers events from the 1500s into the 2000s. It opens not with the common focus on English America in the 1600s but with a focus on the earlier arrival of Africans with the Spanish in the 1500s on lands that would become the United States of America.

The narrative to follow focuses on what black people did in and with their lives, what they hoped and what they thought, what they feared and what they hated, what they loved and what they longed for. It focuses on points in the past but emphasizes the change over time that forms the essence of history as a field study. It emphasizes trends, following tendencies emerging over time. And in doing so, following the tendencies of a legal historian and lawyer, it inclines toward issues of public policy and practice. It reflects blacks' responses to others as well as others' responses to blacks. The sweep of time brushes aside most in-depth analysis of individual events in favor of developing ongoing themes, for condensing so much into so little space omits much. Every chapter, every page, and every paragraph that follows introduces only bits and pieces of plentiful materials and experiences, making this work a bare survey. And in the march of time the multiplicity of more recent event quickens in places to little more than listings.

The chapters that follow foreground blacks so as to focus on events, experiences, and influences important in blacks' lives, development, and participation in American society. Whatever their circumstances and conditions, blacks never could be less or more than human. The law of slavery could declare them property. The lash of slavery might demean them as animals. The very horror of American Negro slavery itself, however, ineluctably drew attention to blacks' humanity. By its very attempt at exclusion, the American apartheid of segregation emphasized blacks' humanity in simultaneously recognizing yet denying their claims to the same chances and choices as whites. In perhaps peculiar contrast, the efforts to dehumanize blacks have testified to blacks' humanity. Racial slavery and segregation posed African Americans as the internal "Other" in American life as blacks have stood historically as the other side of America—the side white supremacist ideology craved to exclude.

Any historical survey such as this owes much to others. To start, this African American history owes an irredeemable debt to the women and men whose lived experiences made the history treated here. It owes the recorders, preservers, keepers of the artifacts and documents, and scholars who have made that history available. It owes the pioneers and promoters who developed African American history as a recognized and rich area of scholarship. Carter Godwin Woodson, rightly praised as the "father of Negro history," and his cadre at the beginning of the 20th century pioneered the methodical, organized digging that opened the lode of historical detail and pointed the directions to rich sources of information about and insight into the black world. Many have continued to excavate and to explain the ongoing findings.

This work stands on the broad shoulders of giants. It pretends to offer few, if any, first-hand discoveries. Much of the outline and substance to follow will be familiar to experts in the field. This work is not aimed for them. It aims to provide a synthetic survey for students and general readers seeking an introduction and overview. It borrows much from many and reflects gratitude to writers of other surveys, particularly Mary Frances Berry, Ira

Berlin, John W. Blassingame, Darlene Clark Hine, John Hope Franklin, Thomas C. Holt, Nell Irvin Painter, Colin A. Palmer, and Benjamin Quarles.

My personal thanks go to Laura D. Martinez, Brenda M. Brock, Mary M. Staten, Henry Earl Cobb and Thelma M. Cobb, the Schomburg Center for Research in Black Culture, the New York Public Library, the Moorland-Spingarn Research Center at Howard University, the Library of Congress, Arizona's Maricopa County libraries, and the libraries of the Arizona State University, Tempe, especially the interlibrary loan staff. Also I thank senior editor Kim Kennedy-White for her encouragement and patience and media editor Ellen Rasmussen and project manager Gordon Hammy Matchado for their production work. My repeated and profound thanks go to Brenda M. Brock for being my researcher, sounding board, proofreader, and editor, extraordinaire.

## BRIEF NOTES ON DATES, DATA, AND TERMS

The text here uses New Style (NS) calendaring to render dates before 1752, when Great Britain shifted from the Old Style (OS) Julian calendar in which years began on March 25. That sifts the year for dates falling between January 1 and March 25. For example, the Virginia law decreeing hereditary slavery for children born of enslaved women is commonly dated as March 1661, but that follows OS dating. Beginning the year on January 1, the text here dates the act as March 1662.

Unless otherwise indicated in the text, U.S. Census population data for 1790 to 1960 come from or are computed from the Historical Census Browser from the University of Virginia, Geospatial and Statistical Data Center, available at http://mapserver.lib.virginia.edu/collections/.

The text renders documents created as writings as they appeared in their original form, signaling with brackets any changes made. Transcriptions of interviews and oral testimonies where transcribers reported sounds rather than words in seeking to reproduce dialect, however, are rendered in standard English.

African American, Afro-American, black, colored, and Negro, appear as synonyms throughout the text. All of the terms carry baggage. *African American* predominates at the moment as the commonly preferred term of address for the U.S. population of African descent, although all blacks in the Americas literally fit within the term. Afro-American more specifically identifies a U.S. population, as Afro-Brazilian, Afro-Canadian, Afro-Cuban, or Afro-Mexican identify respective national populations of African descent. *Black* is the most general term encompassing peoples of African descent. *Negro* is a long-used historical term arising from the Spanish word for *black* and predominated polite usage in the United States through the 1960s, when *black* rose as a more preferred term. *Black* is the most common term used throughout this text.

# Introduction

African American history started with the arrival of peoples of African descent in what came to be called the Americas. The narrative here starts there and moves to the transatlantic slave trade that over more than four centuries joined Africa and the Americas. That traffic memorialized as the "Middle Passage" introduced the bulk of peoples from Africa into the Americas from the 1500s through the 1800s. That forced migration made blacks part of the colonial forebears of the American nation. Their part did not begin in Virginia. Nor did it begin in 1619. The black presence on lands that became the United States of America began with the Spanish, not with the English. It began in the 1500s in Florida and in colonial Nueva España, in what would become parts of the U.S. Southwest, West, and Gulf Coast.

The black presence appeared in early America in various forms reflecting social relations predominant in an early modern world where obligation defined personal position in hierarchical structures. Individuals owed service to others as a duty arising from circumstance or condition. For most blacks with the Spanish in North America in the early 1500s, their service most often arose from capture and sale. That defined them in the status of slave, but it did not describe their services. They were explorers, expeditionaries, laborers, body servants, and more. Most served for a term of years before being released. A shift occurred in the 1550s as gold and silver mining in Mexico down through Central America to Colombia and Venezuela produced increasing demands for captive labor drawn from Africa's Upper Guinea region.

The narrative to follow moves in time with the rhythm of collective African American developments. It does not run exactly the same course as American history. Necessarily, watersheds of black life in America converge

with points in the developing American nation. The War for Independence
(1775–1783), the Civil War (1861–1865), World War I (1914–1919), or
World War II (1939–1945), for example, marked transitional points for
blacks as well as for the American nation. Yet signal events in African
American history have not merely mirrored those in American history.
Marked changes for blacks collectively occurred outside common American
history divisions. Markers such as presidential administrations or eras such
as the Gilded Age have often had little, if any, resonance in African American
history. And even eras marked as antebellum, Reconstruction, Progressive,
or the Roaring '20s, for example, identify years that carry meanings in the
collective experience of African Americans very different than those for the
American nation as a whole.

To start, the flow of peoples from Africa into North America ran in a
different stream from that of immigrants from Europe. The bulk of blacks
in early America arrived in a foul commerce. They served as property in
law and social practice, but their humanity was unmistakable. They made
themselves more than articles of commerce. They proved their worth as
people. They made their services indispensable. And beyond their interaction with those who enslaved them, blacks created their own public and
private spaces, cultivating their own personal and group identities within
and outside slavery.

Blacks became a predominantly African American—that is, an American-
born—population in the mid-1700s, scores of years before America's white
population became American-born and sooner than any other population
of African descent in the Americas. The prevalence of black women made
the difference as females early and long outnumbered males in the black
population in North America. Black women's strength and nurture produced generations who were African and American by birth and grew to
be a majority of the U.S. black population even before the United States
outlawed its transatlantic slave trade. That closing began in the 1770s with
the American Revolution's nonimportation agreements and finished with
the 1807 ban on importing slaves after January 1, 1808. That prohibition
did not completely shut the foreign slave trade, but it stemmed the inflow
of blacks born outside the United States, and without that immigration,
African Americans became more and more a largely homegrown people.

The developing plantation cultures of the Chesapeake region drew the
overwhelming bulk of blacks in developing American Negro slavery. But
blacks served as chattel everywhere in the English colonies on North America. Beginning with the Dutch, the area that became New York led sites
in slaveholding north of Maryland. New Englanders grew rich trafficking
in Africans as commodities. Indeed, blacks became part of the foundation
everywhere in English North America. Slavery dominated early black life,

but increasing numbers worked their way free from the law of bondage that Virginia and Maryland began to codify in the 1660s and that in its latter stages became "the Peculiar Institution" with its strictures of hereditary, lifelong subjugation based on African ancestry.

Whether in or out of slavery, blacks everywhere struck against their shackles. They joined with others to attack the structures and system subjugating them, as seen in their joining in Bacon's Rebellion in Virginia in 1676. Their individual resistance ranged across the gamut of imagination. Events such as the 1712 slave uprising in New York City, the 1739 Stono Rebellion in South Carolina, and the so-called Great Negro Plot in 1741 in New York City illustrated early black collective resistance. The greatest black uprising in the 1700s came during the War for Independence (1775–1783). For many blacks it was a war for *their* liberation. By the tens of thousands they marched their way out of slavery. Thousands left the self-proclaimed United States. Some went to Africa, others to Canada or the Caribbean; a few went to England or Europe.

Within the freshly minted United States of America, blacks embraced the self-declared principles of an egalitarian liberty and a government based on consent of the governed. They became primary advocates of the American creed, while decrying the nation's failure to practice what it preached. Outside of slavery blacks organized communities and institutions to sustain and advance their lives and their liberty, coming together to forge communities with institutions devoted to self-help and personal and group uplift. They established churches and schools and mutual benefit societies to attend their sick, to support their widows and orphans, and to bury their dead.

As thousands had in shouldering arms for the Patriot cause, blacks rallied to the nation's defense in the War of 1812 as they would in all U.S. wars. Although officially excluded and often discouraged from formal enlistment until the darkest hours of military necessity, blacks unfailingly rallied for the nation. Only after World War II would the nation lift barriers to black enlistment and advancement as formal segregation faded away in the U.S. armed forces. Blacks shed lives and limbs, blood and sweat, for the nation in the persistent hope of being recognized fully as American and not marginalized as black. They fought for light to banish the shadow of slavery that cast an overarching racial segregation over black life everywhere in the nation as an enduring element of American character.

How deep-seated racial separation was showed clearly as blacks stood free from slavery in New England, Pennsylvania, New York, and other states north of Maryland that outlawed slavery in the wake of the American Revolution. Public policy and practice excluded blacks or isolated them in public and in private. Protests in the 1840s against separate railcars and schools for blacks and whites in Massachusetts illustrated the antebellum segregation outside the South. African Americans fought such exclusion as extensions of slavery as they made unflagging protest against racist denial of equal rights the most consistent theme in their history.

Wrestling slavery's tentacles engaged blacks daily as their individual and collective resistance persisted. Running away was the most visible mode of individual resistance, and ads for recapture filled American newspapers. So-called fugitive slaves became a national problem as tens of thousands "stole themselves from slavery," as a phrase of the time put it. Also blacks threatened white social sensibilities and stability with looming collective violence. From the anxieties of the Haitian Revolution (1793–1804) onward, episodes such as Gabriel's Rebellion in and around Richmond, Virginia, in 1800; the 1811 German Coast Uprising in Louisiana; Denmark Vesey conspiracy in and around Charleston, South Carolina, in 1821–1822; and Nat's Rebellion in Virginia's Southampton County in 1831 repeatedly impressed on local slave communities and the slave nation, itself, slaves' determination to be free. Without cease, blacks filled antebellum America with agitation against slavery, refusing to be silent or sedate.

Blacks rushed to enlist in the ultimate cataclysm over American Negro slavery that developed in the Civil War. At least 200,000 shouldered arms in uniformed service against the Confederate slave power. Hundreds of thousands of others exerted their efforts outside of formal service. Blacks' immediate and irresistible common purpose was to end slavery. They witnessed that process officially unfolding throughout the war as Congress and then President Abraham Lincoln moved to end slavery. But they did not await word from Washington. By the tens of thousands they embraced the opportunity of war to make their own "actual freedom," in the terms of the 1863 Emancipation Proclamation.

The general emancipation from slavery the Thirteenth Amendment to the U.S. Constitution pronounced in 1865 in outlawing slavery "within the United States, or any place subject to their jurisdiction" engendered jubilee. But no magic moment materialized. Blacks' efforts would necessarily persist beyond generations as they encountered and surmounted successive barriers to realizing actual freedom. Moving into the immediate post–Civil War era called Reconstruction (1865–1877), formerly enslaved blacks confronted the sustaining structures of white supremacy. They faced fresh legal systems substituting for slavery as so-called Black Codes immediately extended the entrenched segregation of bondage.

Braving terrorism aimed to perpetuate their subordination, blacks moved to construct personal, family, and community lives. They coped with the challenges of flagging federal policies announced to ensure "equal protection of the laws," in the words of the Fourteenth Amendment ratified in 1868. They eagerly packed schools to learn how better to advance as individuals and as a community; and they built institutions from churches to civic organizations and economic cooperatives to nurture their self-help. They pushed against both law and popular practice that sought to exclude them in private and in public. They fought restrictions on where they could live, work, buy and sell, go to school, and enjoy and entertain themselves. With the backing of Congress, starting in 1867 they voted some of their own into public office with an aim of reforming law from hindering to helping them. Beginning in 1870 they sent blacks to Congress. Two would serve in the U.S. Senate and 20 in the U.S. House of Representatives before 1900, when Jim Crow slammed the doors against them.

Finding their dreams deferred with little give-and-take in the 15 states collectively called the South that had maintained slavery in 1860, many blacks moved. Thousands of so-called Exodusters set off from Louisiana and Mississippi on the way to Kansas at the end of the 1870s. More and more black Southerners streamed North and West. World War I (1914–1919) stimulated their trek into what some called "the Great Black Migration." In two broad waves between 1910 and 1970, about 6.6 million blacks would move from the South. That represented a bit more than two-thirds of the nation's 1910 black population of 9.8 million. By 1970 only 53 in every 100 blacks lived in the South, contrasted with 95 in every 100 blacks in 1870.

Blacks found no escape from the color line, as segregation dominated life in America, as slavery had. Whether South or North, East or West, blacks met exclusion from equal access to the full range of American life stamped in law and public practice. But a "New Negro" was emerging in the 1900s. Soldiering to "make the world safe for democracy," in the words of the U.S. World War I campaign, mustered increased fervor for democracy at home. In politics and popular culture the New Negro surged across the nation. New York's Harlem, Chicago's Bronzeville, and other urban concentrations of blacks, particularly north of Washington, D.C., thrummed with black creative activity and agitation that some titled the New Negro Renaissance. Fresh power was rising as blacks relocated to the North voted to return their own to public office and even back to Congress, beginning in 1928. Their crusade to vote everywhere in the nation symbolized much of blacks' battles to gain recognition and acceptance as U.S. citizens with full civil rights.

Blacks seized on national and global conditions, particularly with World War II (1939–1945), to insist increasingly on the "equal protection of the laws" the U.S. Constitution guaranteed as policy but which had never been American practice. Black demands for equal public education became a cutting edge against post-1945 segregation, and in 1954 the unanimous U.S. Supreme Court decision in Brown v. Board of Education vindicated their protests. The Court's holding that "separate educational facilities are inherently unequal" and thus violated the Fourteenth Amendment's Equal

Protection Clause marked the beginning of the end of Jim Crow's de jure racial segregation.

Blacks found that their struggles to strike racial segregation from U.S. law over the course of more than 100 years almost immediately paled against the challenges of rooting out segregation as an actual practice in American life. De facto segregation marred much of the U.S. landscape from housing to jobs to education, to say nothing of the broad range of social interaction. Massive white resistance to implementing *Brown* signaled more than problems in the 17 states that in 1954 legally mandated separate public schools for whites and nonwhites. Decades of desegregation remedies failed to change many realities. By the beginning of the 21st century, racially separate schools were more pronounced than ever, and the quality of public education for blacks had not markedly improved.

Despite the quagmire of public schools, much change for blacks was broadly afoot by the beginning of the 21st century. The black frustration that spilled into America's private and public spaces in the 1950s and 1960s with the label "The Black Revolution" produced fresh opportunities for blacks. Mass protests made the black presence felt nationally from boycotts and nonviolent marches throughout the South in the 1950s to blacks taking to the streets in the North and West in urban rioting in the 1960s. That pressure pushed affirmative action to open new opportunities for blacks in the public and private sectors with enforcement of the antidiscrimination policies of the Civil Rights Act of 1964. Also black voters made remarkable differences following the Voting Rights Act of 1965: only 103 blacks held elected public office in the United States in 1964; 30 years later the count neared 8,500. Yet blacks often continued to remain in positions of being last-hired-and-first-fired.

Moving into the 21st century, blacks had clearly arrived at a better place in their long haul from slavery and Jim Crow segregation. American law had changed. Many blacks enjoyed unprecedented positions and success. They filled much of American popular culture, although often in unfavorable images. While never a singular people, their images had become even more diverse, with more and more multiracial persons identifying as black and with a surge of Caribbean and African immigrants. Yet blacks continued to trail whites in almost every measure of quality of life. They had shorter life expectancies, higher rates of chronic and endemic diseases, lower rates of educational attainment, and poorer labor market outcomes with substantially higher rates of unemployment. So necessarily their struggles to achieve "the equal protection of the laws" persisted, as evidenced in the Black Lives Matter movement. Their needs have persisted furthermore to change the popular American mind-set that has continued to stereotype blacks and relegate them in American life as they have continued to push to pursue life, liberty, and happiness the same as any other daughters and sons of America.

In the end, as in the beginning, African Americans have been peoples in the making, never singular, always diverse. Like most other Americans, their identities have ever been a work in progress. They began not with blacks among the English, but with blacks among the Spanish. They have ever persisted with diverse cultures, and their cultural productions have permeated America from cooking to cuisine, from language arts to performance and plastic arts, and throughout popular culture. African American rhythms and rhymes have flowed throughout America's cities and countrysides. Much of the music characterized as American around the world since the early 1900s has been black music. Suppressed but never submerged, blacks have succeeded against the odds in America's hostile environments to shoulder their burdens and brave tides of white supremacist oppression and terrorism to stand with their challenges, dreams, and hopes foremost among the peoples called simply Americans.

# Chronology of Key Dates in African American History

| | |
|---|---|
| 500 BCE | Artifacts suggest pre-Columbian contact between Africa and the Americas. |
| 1440s | West African peoples encounter Portuguese on the Atlantic coast, and trading in captives begins a slave trade. |
| 1492 | Pedro Alonso Niño arrives among the 18-member crew of the *Niña* in Christopher Columbus's first landfall in the Americas; and from 1493 to 1498 others of African descent come to live and work in Columbus's post at La Isabela on Hispaniola. |
| 1502 | Juan Garrido sails to the Caribbean and joins in the exploits of the Spanish conquistadors in Cuba, Puerto Rico, California, and Mexico, where he dies in 1547. |
| 1527 | Estevanico joins explorations from Hispaniola to Cuba to Florida and along the Gulf Coast from Tampa Bay to Galveston in what became Texas, before later pressing into Southwest and dying in 1539 in what becomes New Mexico. |
| 1565 | Africans are among the founders of the Spanish colony of St. Augustine in Florida, the first permanent European settlement in what later becomes the United States of America. |
| 1613 | Jan Rodrigues enters what comes to be called New York Bay and settles among Native Americans on Long Island. |
| 1619 | Dutch traders sell English settlers in Virginia a coffle of "20. and odd Negroes." |
| 1620s | African Americans are born in Virginia. |

| | |
|---|---|
| 1626 | The Dutch land 11 African captives on Manhattan Island in the colony of Nieuw Nederland that later becomes New York. |
| 1640 | Virginia's Council confirms lifelong servitude for blacks in the case of *re John Punch*. |
| 1643–1662 | Africans in so-called half freedom become recorded landholders on Manhattan. |
| 1650s | Anthony Johnson, Emanuel Driggus, and other Africans gain their release from slavery, buy property, and create an enclave in Northampton County on Virginia's Eastern Shore. |
| 1662 | Virginia confirms hereditary slavery for blacks under the Latin rule *partus sequitur ventrum*, directing that a child's status follows that of its mother. |
| 1664 | Maryland outlaws marriage of black men and white women. |
| 1667 | Virginia closes Christian baptism's possibility of releasing blacks from slavery. |
| 1676 | Blacks join in Bacon's Rebellion in Virginia. |
| 1691 | Virginia requires blacks manumitted from slavery to remove from the colony or resume the status of slave. |
| 1691–1750 | Virginia, Massachusetts, North Carolina, South Carolina, Delaware, and Georgia follow Maryland's lead to outlaw coupling or marriages between blacks and whites. |
| 1710 | Blacks outnumber whites in South Carolina. |
| 1712 | Blacks in New York City rebel, setting fires and killing 8 and wounding at least 12 other whites; 19 blacks suffer execution. |
| 1720s–1770s | Most of the blacks imported into English North America arrive. |
| 1730s | Blacks establish an independent settlement in Florida at Gracia Real de Santa Teresa de Mose. |
| 1739 | Blacks just north of the Stono River in South Carolina stage the largest black uprising in colonial British North America, killing at least 40 whites and suffering a like number of deaths during nearly a week of skirmishing. |
| 1741 | Thirteen blacks burn at the stake and 17 are hanged in New York's so-called Great Negro Plot. |
| 1777 | Outlawing slavery, Vermont initiates the movement called the First Emancipation that releases from slavery most blacks in the North by 1830. |

| 1780 | Pennsylvania enacts a gradual emancipation program that abolishes hereditary slavery and releases blacks born after November 1 from service on their 28th birthday. |
|------|------|
| 1781–1783 | Thousands of blacks evacuate with the British to maintain their freedom from slavery as the U.S. War for Independence concludes. |
| 1784 | Connecticut and Rhode Island enact gradual emancipation programs. |
| | Prince Hall and other blacks establish the first Black Masonic Lodge that the Grand Lodge of England charters as African Lodge No. 459. |
| | Blacks establish the benevolent New York African Society for communal self-help. |
| 1787 | Blacks in Manhattan working with the New York Manumission Society establish the African Free School. |
| | Richard Allen, Absalom Jones, and other blacks in Philadelphia form the Free African Society. |
| 1790 | The U.S. Census counts 757,208 blacks as 19.3 percent of the U.S. population, with 59,150 blacks counted as not enslaved. |
| | Blacks in Charleston, South Carolina, form the Brown Fellowship Society. |
| 1793 | Blacks become subject to the first federal Fugitive Slave Act. |
| | Connecticut inventor Eli Whitney produces an improved cotton gin. |
| 1793–1804 | The Haitian Revolution stirs unrest among U.S. blacks. |
| 1794 | Richard Allen and other blacks in Philadelphia establish "Mother Bethel," which becomes the core of the African Methodist Episcopal (AME) Church. |
| 1795 | Blacks in Pointe-Coupée, Louisiana, plan an uprising that results in 23 being executed. |
| 1799 | New York enacts a gradual emancipation program. |
| 1800 | The U.S. Census counts 1,002,037 blacks as 18.9 percent of the U.S. population, with 108,435 blacks counted as not enslaved. |
| | Gabriel Prosser and other blacks in and around Richmond, Virginia, organize a thwarted uprising; 27 suffer execution. |
| 1810 | The U.S. Census counts 1,377,808 blacks as 19.1 percent of the U.S. population, with 186,446 blacks counted as not enslaved. |

1811            Blacks in the German Coast area of the recently acquired
                U.S. territory stage what some call "the great Louisiana
                slave revolt"; 44 blacks suffer execution.

1812–1814       Blacks join in U.S. armed forces fighting the Anglo-American
                War of 1812, providing especially notable service in the Bat-
                tle of New Orleans.

1815            The African Methodist Episcopal (AME) Church officially
                organizes.

1816–1818       Blacks ally with Native Americans in the First Seminole War
                against U.S. incursions into then Spanish-held Florida.

1820            The U.S. Census counts 1,771,656 blacks as 18.4 percent of
                U.S. population, with 233,504 counted as not enslaved.

1821            Blacks in New York protest the new state constitution deny-
                ing them equal suffrage.

1822            Denmark Vesey and fellow blacks plan an uprising in and
                around Charleston; Vesey and 36 other blacks suffer execution.

1827            *Freedom's Journal* appears as the first black-owned and
                edited U.S. newspaper in anticipation of New York's Gen-
                eral Emancipation Day on July 5.

1829            David Walker publishes *An Appeal to the Colored Citizens
                of the World* calling for armed resistance to slavery.

1830            The U.S. Census counts 2,328,842 blacks as 18.1 percent
                of the U.S. population, with 319,599 blacks counted as not
                enslaved.

1831            Nat and other blacks in Virginia's Southampton County stage
                an uprising, killing as many as 60 whites while marauding
                for two days; 57 blacks suffered execution.

1832            Black women in Salem, Massachusetts, organize the Female
                Anti-Slave Society, the first U.S. women's antislavery society.

1834            The African Free Schools become part of New York City's
                fledgling public school system.

1840            The U.S. Census counts 2,873,648 blacks as 16.1 percent
                of the U.S. population, with 386,293 blacks counted as not
                enslaved.

1841            The U.S. Supreme Court in the *United States v. Amistad*
                declares free 53 Africans held aboard a Spanish slaver seized
                off the U.S. coast and brought into port at New London,
                Connecticut, in 1839.

| | |
|---|---|
| 1842 | The U.S. Supreme Court in *Prigg v. Pennsylvania* invalidates so-called personal liberty laws providing blacks due process against recaption as fugitive slaves. |
| 1845 | *The Life and Times of Frederick Douglass* appears in its first edition. |
| | Macon B. Allen passes the bar in Massachusetts to become the first black admitted to practice law in the United States. |
| 1846–1848 | Blacks join in U.S. armed forces fighting the War with Mexico. |
| 1847 | Frederick Douglass begins publishing *The North Star* newspaper in Rochester, New York. |
| | Dred and Harriet Scott file freedom petitions in Missouri. |
| 1848 | Frederick Douglass and other blacks join in the Women's Rights Convention at Seneca Falls, New York. |
| 1849 | Blacks join in the California Gold Rush. |
| | Harriet Tubman begins conducting her Underground Railroad runs to rescue enslaved blacks. |
| | Blacks in Massachusetts lose challenge to racially segregated public schools in *Roberts v. Boston*. But the notoriety of decision prompts the legislature in 1855 to outlaw racial segregation in the state's public schools. |
| 1850 | The U.S. Census counts 3,638,808 blacks as 15.7 percent of the U.S. population, with 433,807 blacks counted as not enslaved. |
| 1851 | Fighting off slave catchers' attempt to seize fugitive blacks in Christiana, Pennsylvania, results in arrest and trial of 37 blacks and 1 white for violating the federal Fugitive Slave Act of 1850. |
| 1852 | Martin R. Delany publishes *The Condition, Elevation, Emigration and Destiny of the Colored People of the United States*. |
| 1856 | Wilberforce University opens near Xenia, Ohio, as a black-owned and operated institution under the direction of the AME church and with Bishop Daniel A. Payne as its president. |
| 1857 | U.S. Supreme Court in *Scott v. Sandford* denies Dred and Harriet Scott's freedom petitions and rules that blacks have never been nor can ever be U.S. citizens. |

| | |
|---|---|
| 1859 | Five blacks join radical abolitionist John Brown's band of 20 men in a plan to seize the federal arsenal at Harpers Ferry, Virginia, and arm slaves in an insurrection. |
| 1860 | U.S. Census counts 4,441,830 blacks as 14.1 percent of the U.S. population, with 488,070 blacks counted as not enslaved. |
| 1861–1865 | The Civil War. |
| 1862 | U.S. Congress abolishes slavery in the District of Columbia and in U.S. territories, and authorizes black enlistments in the U.S. Army. |
| | President Lincoln issues the preliminary Emancipation Proclamation; it becomes final in January 1, 1863, declaring legally free all held in slavery in areas then in rebellion. |
| 1863 | Blacks in New York City suffer violent attacks in the four-day long so-called Draft Riots. |
| 1865 | The Thirteenth Amendment outlaws slavery in the United States. |
| | U.S. Congress establishes the Bureau of Refugees, Freedmen, and Abandoned Lands, popularly called the Freedmen's Bureau. |
| | Blacks in coastal South Carolina, Georgia, and Florida receive grants from 400,000 acres of abandoned lands under U.S. Army General William T. Sherman's Special Field Order No. 15, prompting talk of former slaves receiving 40 acres and a mule from the federal government. |
| 1866 | U.S. Congress overrides President Andrew Johnson's veto to pass the first federal Civil Rights Act. |
| | Blacks in Memphis, New Orleans, and other southern cities suffer riots from white civilians and police. |
| 1867 | U.S. Congress overrides President Andrew Johnson to enfranchise adult black males in the District of Columbia and later in U.S. territories. In the Reconstruction Acts, Congress further enfranchises adult black males in the former Confederate states. |
| 1868 | The Fourteenth Amendment confirms blacks' right to federal and state citizenship. |
| 1870 | U.S. Census counts 4,880,009 blacks as 12.7 percent of the U.S. population. |

| | |
|---|---|
| 1872 | Charlotte Ray admitted to practice law in the District of Columbia, becoming the first black female licensed to practice law in the United States. |
| 1872–1873 | Lieutenant Governor Pinckney Benton Stewart Pinchback acts as governor of Louisiana for 35 days, the first black to sit as a state governor. |
| 1875 | U.S. Congress enacts a Civil Rights Act to outlaw racial discrimination in public accommodations. The Supreme Court in 1883 held the act unconstitutional in the *Civil Rights Cases*. |
| 1879 | So-called Exodusters begin a black migration about 6,000 strong from Louisiana and Mississippi to Kansas. |
| 1880 | U.S. Census counts 6,580,793 blacks as 13.1 percent of the U.S. population. |
| 1881 | Tennessee mandates Jim Crow segregation of railroad passenger cars; 12 southern states follow that lead by 1907. |
| 1890 | U.S. Census counts 7,488,676 blacks as 11.9 percent of the U.S. population. |
| 1895 | Booker T. Washington delivers his Atlanta Compromise Address. |
| 1896 | U.S. Supreme Court in *Plessy v. Ferguson* sanctions racial segregation on railroad passenger cars, announcing what becomes known as the Separate but Equal Doctrine. |
| | Mary Church Terrell leads formation of the National Association of Colored Women. |
| 1897 | Rev. Alexander Crummell and other leading blacks form the American Negro Academy. |
| | The National Ex-Slave Mutual Relief, Bounty and Pension Association receives its corporate charter. |
| 1898 | Black U.S. Army regulars and volunteers fight in the U.S. war with Spain, during which five receive the Congressional Medal of Honor. |
| 1900 | U.S. Census counts 8,833,994 blacks as 11.6 percent of the U.S. population. |
| 1900 | First Pan-African Conference opens in London, UK. |
| 1905 | W.E.B. Du Bois, W. Monroe Trotter, and other leading blacks organize the Niagara Movement. |
| 1908 | Blacks in Springfield, Illinois, beset by race rioting. |

1909        The National Association for the Advancement of Colored
            People (NAACP) organizes.

1910        The National Urban League organizes.

            Following Baltimore's lead several southern cities pass ordi-
            nances requiring racially segregated neighborhoods; the U.S.
            Supreme Court in *Buchanan v. Warley* (1917) will hold such
            ordinances unconstitutional.

1914        World War I begins in Europe, and the Great Migration of
            blacks from South to North accelerates.

1915        Carter G. Woodson founds the Association for the Study
            of Negro Life and History (ASNLH), the forerunner of
            the Association for African American Life and History
            (ASALH), publisher of the *Journal of Negro History*, later
            the *Journal of African American History*.

            U.S. Supreme Court in *Guinn v. United States* outlaws
            grandfather clauses used to disenfranchise blacks.

1916        Marcus Garvey opens a branch of his Universal Negro
            Improvement Association (UNIA) in New York City.

1917        The United States enters World War I, and 370,000 blacks
            join the U.S. armed forces, with 107 being awarded France's
            highest military honor, the *Croix de Guerre*.

            Blacks beset in East St. Louis, Illinois, race riot.

            Black U.S. Army troops in Houston, Texas, become
            embroiled in a race riot.

1918        November armistice ends World War I fighting.

1919        The so-called Red Summer flows with blood from at least
            25 race riots across the United States. The most noted riot
            occurs in Chicago.

1920        U.S. Census counts 10,463,131 blacks as 9.9 percent of the
            U.S. population.

            The Nineteenth Amendment makes women eligible to vote.

            Baseball's National Negro League organizes.

1921        The Tulsa Race Riot destroys the city's Greenwood section
            with its district called "the Black Wall Street" because of its
            business enterprises.

1923        The Rosewood Massacre in Florida destroys the black
            town.

| 1925 | Howard University professor Alain Locke publishes his *The New Negro* anthology, signaling what many call the New Negro Renaissance. |
|---|---|
| | The National Bar Association organizes for black lawyers, as the American Bar Association (ABA) excludes blacks. |
| 1926 | Carter G. Woodson establishes Negro History Week in February, which later becomes Negro History Month. |
| | Black Puerto Rican bibliophile Arturo Schomburg's collection on black history and life becomes the basis for the Schomburg Center for Research in Black Culture in New York City. |
| 1928 | Republican Oscar De Priest wins election to Congress from Chicago. |
| 1929–1939 | The Great Depression. |
| 1930 | U.S. Census counts 11,891,143 blacks as 9.7 percent of the U.S. population. |
| 1931 | The nine Scottsboro Boys are arrested in Alabama on charges of rape and rushed to convictions with sentences of execution, prompting mass black protests. |
| 1935 | Blacks riot in New York City's Harlem section on rumors of police brutality. |
| | Mary McLeod Bethune leads creation of the National Council of Negro Women. |
| 1936 | National Negro Congress (NNC) convenes in Chicago. |
| | Track and field star Jesse Owens wins four gold medals at the Olympic Games in Berlin. |
| 1937 | Joe Louis becomes world heavyweight boxing champion. |
| 1938 | Democrat Crystal Bird Fauset wins election to the Pennsylvania House of Representatives from a Philadelphia district as the first black woman to serve in a state legislature. |
| 1939 | World War II begins in Europe. |
| 1940 | U.S. Census counts 12,865,518 blacks as 9.8 percent of the U.S. population. |
| 1941 | A. Philip Randolph's March on Washington Movement pressures President Franklin D. Roosevelt to issue Executive Order 8802 banning discrimination in war production plans. |

U.S. Navy messman Dorie Miller mans an antiaircraft gun during the Japanese attack on Pearl Harbor, Hawaii, earning the Navy Cross for heroism.

U.S. entry into World War II stimulates a new wave in blacks' Great Migration.

**1942**       James Farmer Jr. and others organize the Congress of Racial Equality (CORE).

**1943**       Race riots break out against blacks across the country in places such as New York's Harlem, Mobile, Alabama, and Beaumont, Texas. The worst of the rioting hits Detroit.

**1945**       World War II ends with approximately 1,000,000 black men and women serving in the U.S. armed forces.

**1947**       Jackie Robinson and Larry Doby break the color barrier in Major League Baseball.

**1948**       President Harry Truman's Executive Order 9981 orders the U.S. armed forces to desegregate.

**1950**       U.S. Census counts 15,044,937 blacks as 10.0 percent of the U.S. population.

**1953**       Blacks launch the Baton Rouge Bus Boycott.

**1954**       U.S. Supreme Court decides in *Brown v. Board of Education* that laws requiring racially separate public schools are unconstitutional. And in 1955 in *Brown II* (1954) orders public schools to desegregate "with all deliberate speed."

**1955–1956**  Blacks organize the Montgomery Bus Boycott.

**1956**       U.S. Supreme Court sanctions the Montgomery Bus Boycott in *Gayle v. Browder*, outlawing legally mandated segregation in local public transportation.

**1957**       Civil Rights Act creates the U.S. Commission on Civil Rights.

The Little Rock Nine desegregate the Arkansas capital's Central High School under the protection of U.S. Army troops.

**1960**       U.S. Census counts 18,871,831 blacks as 10.6 percent of the U.S. population.

**1961**       CORE launches its Freedom Rides to test desegregation of public transportation in the South.

**1963**       The March on Washington for Jobs and Freedom masses hundreds of thousands in the nation's capital to demonstrate for stronger federal action on civil rights. Reverend King delivers his "I Have a Dream" speech.

|      | White terrorists bomb the black Sixteenth Street Baptist Church in Birmingham, Alabama, killing four girls aged 11 to 14. |
|------|---|
| 1964 | Civil Rights Act of 1964 overhauls U.S. law in the field, creating the Equal Opportunity Employment Commission among other things. |
|      | Economic Opportunity Act advances the "War on Poverty" with programs such as Head Start and Upward Bound. |
| 1965 | Gunmen in New York City assassinate Malcolm X. |
|      | "Bloody Sunday" in the Selma-to-Montgomery March advances the landmark Voting Rights Act of 1965. |
|      | Immigration and Naturalization Act opens surge of black immigration from the Caribbean and Africa. |
|      | Police brutality amid oppressive conditions ignites the Watts Uprising in a black area of Los Angeles, California. |
| 1966 | Huey P. Newton and Bobby Seale found the Black Panther Party for Self-Defense. |
|      | Edward Brooke (R-MA) becomes the first black elected to the U.S. Senate. |
| 1967 | U.S. Supreme Court in *Loving v. Virginia* outlaws statutes against interracial marriages and in the process finally overturns *Plessy v. Ferguson*'s Separate but Equal Doctrine. |
| 1968 | Civil Rights Act of 1968 outlaws discrimination in housing rentals and sales. |
|      | Shirley Chisholm (D-NY) elected as the first black woman in the U.S. Congress. |
| 1970 | U.S. Census counts 22,580,289 blacks as 11.1 percent of the U.S. population. |
| 1971 | Congressional Black Caucus organizes. |
| 1972 | National Black Political Convention convenes in Gary, Indiana. |
|      | Shirley Chisholm (D-NY) campaigns for the Democratic presidential nomination. |
| 1977 | Randall Robinson and others form TransAfrica to lobby for greater U.S. support to Africa. |
| 1978 | U.S. Supreme Court in *Regents of the University of California v. Bakke* sanctions race as a "diversity" factor in public higher education admissions. |

| | |
|---|---|
| 1980 | U.S. Census counts 26,482,349 blacks as 11.8 percent of the U.S. population. |
| 1983 | U.S. Congress establishes a federal holiday to honor Martin Luther King Jr. to be first celebrated in 1986. |
| 1984 | Jesse Jackson campaigns for the Democratic presidential nomination, as he does again in 1988. |
| 1989 | Democrat L. Douglas Wilder in Virginia becomes the first black elected a U.S. governor. |
| 1990 | U.S. Census counts 29,986,060 blacks as 12.1 percent of the U.S. population. |
| 1992 | Rioting in Los Angeles follows acquittal of LAPD officers who brutalized black motorist Rodney King in a videotaped traffic stop in 1991. |
| | Carol Moseley Braun (D-IL) becomes the first black woman elected to the U.S. Senate. |
| 1994 | Trial of former NFL star running back O. J. Simpson for double murder in Los Angeles becomes a media spectacle. |
| 1995 | NOI minister Louis Farrakhan leads the Million Man March in Washington, D.C. |
| 1996 | California referendum Proposition 209 outlaws affirmative action statewide. |
| 1997 | Black women organize a Million Woman March in Philadelphia. |
| | President Bill Clinton apologizes for the scandalous U.S. Public Health Service medical malpractice in the Tuskegee Syphilis Study carried on from 1932 to 1972. |
| 1998 | Black historian John Hope Franklin heads the President's Commission on Race. |
| 2000 | U.S. Census counts 34,658,190 blacks as 12.3 percent of the U.S. population. |
| 2001 | Colin Powell becomes U.S. secretary of state, and Condoleezza Rice becomes national security advisor, the first blacks in either post. |
| 2003 | U.S. Supreme Court in *Grutter v. Bollinger* upholds affirmative action admissions policy at the University of Michigan law school, but in *Gratz v. Bollinger* strikes down an undergraduate affirmative action policy at the University. |
| 2004 | Barack Obama (D-IL) wins election to the U.S. Senate. |

| | |
|---|---|
| 2005 | Condoleezza Rice becomes the first black woman U.S. secretary of state. |
| 2006 | Deval Patrick (D-MA) wins election as governor. |
| 2007 | U.S. Supreme Court in *Parents Involved in Community Schools v. Seattle School District No. 1* and *Meredith v. Jefferson County Board of Education* outlaws race as a factor in assigning students to public schools. |
| 2008 | Lieutenant Governor David A. Paterson (D-NY) becomes the first black governor of New York State on former governor's resignation. |
| 2009 | Barack Obama (D-IL) becomes the first black president of the United States. |
| 2010 | U.S. Census counts 42,020,743 blacks as 13.6 percent of the U.S. population. |
| 2012 | President Barack Obama wins reelection. |
| 2013 | Tea Party favorite black U.S. Representative Tim Scott (R-SC) wins appointment to the U.S. Senate to fill an unexpired term and wins election to a full term in 2014. |
| | Black Lives Matter movement organizes. |
| 2014 | Blacks riot in the Ferguson suburb of St. Louis, Missouri. |
| | Mia Love (R-UT) becomes the first black woman elected to the U.S. Congress as a Republican. |
| | Will Hurd (R-TX) becomes the first black Republican elected to the U.S. Congress from Texas. |
| 2015 | Charleston, South Carolina, Mother Emanuel African Methodist Episcopal Church pastor and parishioners murdered by a white supremacist. |

_____ *Chapter 1* _____

# Voyage to These Shores

They came before Columbus. They came with Columbus. They came after Columbus. Long before 1492 people from Africa came to what became known as the Americas. Artifacts such as stone carvings and other figures in pre-Columbian Middle America displayed African images. Coins and other objects scattered in the Caribbean and Central America also have revealed pre-Columbian transatlantic exchange with Africa. Animals and plants such as the banana, its cousin the plantain, maize, and tobacco have further indicated the Americas' pre-Columbian ties to Africa.

And with the Genoa-born Cristoforo Colombo, exploring for Spain from Palos de la Frontera in August 1492, came Pedro Alonso Niño, a mariner of African descent. DNA evidence recovered from unearthed human remains in Hispaniola shows Niño was not a lone son of Africa on Columbus's voyages. Relics from the colony Columbus established at La Isabela on the north coast of Hispaniola during his second voyage in 1493 showed a significant African presence before the settlement's demise in 1498.

That blacks sailed from Spain with Columbus was not surprising. People from North Africa had a long presence in Spain and its western Iberian neighbor, Portugal, when Columbus sailed to the New World. The seven-century-long Moorish occupation in Spain, following the Islamic invasion of 711, had entrenched people from Africa in Spain's culture and society. And fresh people from Africa had arrived in Iberia beginning in the mid-1400s as Portuguese forays pressed southward along West Africa's coast. Blacks grew into a significant presence in and around Lisbon, Portugal's principal city and major Atlantic port. They appeared also in Spain as captive labor. Collectively labeled *bozal* in Spanish, the recent arrivals from Africa refreshed the current of black blood in Spain and its enterprises as it entered its *Siglo de Oro* or Golden Age that stretched from 1492 into the 1650s.

The black conquistador Juan Garrido exemplified the presence of people of African descent in early European colonization of the Americas. Born in West Africa around 1480, he found himself in the traffic up the Atlantic to Portugal and then to Spain. Illustrating something of the social integration of blacks, he accepted Christian baptism, dropped his birth name, and called himself "Juan Garrido." Perhaps renaming himself the equivalent of "John the handsome" was tongue in cheek or reflected his ego. Or he may have adopted the family name of a household in which he served in Spain, a practice common there and elsewhere, then and later, among servants and slaves who considered themselves part of a *familia*—a term of old Roman origin encompassing all in a household, not simply blood relations.

By the beginning of the 1500s Garrido was on his way to the Americas. He sailed from Seville, which the Spanish crown designated as the sole port of entry and exit for Spanish trade with the Americas. In 1503 Garrido was in the Caribbean's second-largest island (after Cuba): the Spanish called it La Española, but it became more commonly known by its French name, Hispaniola. Bases Columbus set up there in 1492 and 1493 grew into the colony of Santo Domingo, which served as the staging point for Spanish expeditions to Central, North, and South America.

Garrido distinguished himself among the conquistadores Hernán Cortés led to invade Mexico in 1519. He served further in Spanish assaults throughout

Juan Garrido and other blacks were among Spain's early conquistadors and expeditionaries in the Americas, exploring Florida, the Gulf Coast, the Southwest, and California. (DEA/G. Dagli Orti/De Agostini/Getty Images)

the 1520s, marching through western Mexico and reaching the Pacific coast with forces Antonio de Caravajal led in 1529 and going further into Baja California with Cortés in 1533.

Garrido married and settled in what developed into Mexico City, siring at least three children there. Other blacks also served as Spanish expeditionaries and auxiliaries. Some joined with Garrido in assaults against the indigenous Aztecs and Tarascans in the 1520s. Others such as Estevanico—also called Esteban the Moor and Esteban de Dorantes—marched in later Spanish excursions into southeastern and southwestern North America that would become parts of the United States. Records showed Estevanico traveling in expeditions from Hispaniola to Cuba to Florida and along the Gulf Coast from Tampa Bay to Galveston Bay in Texas in the 1520s and disappearing in the 1530s in what became New Mexico, as the Spanish pressed northward from Mexico.

Garrido wrote himself into history. He detailed his exploits for the Spanish crown, submitting in 1538 a *probanza* or proof of service in hope of garnering a pension or reward for his service. He referred to himself as "*de color negro*"—black in color. His self-reference used the term *Negro* as descriptive, not as a label of identity as it would become for people later labeled "Negro."

Garrido presented himself as a valiant servant of the king, showing no modesty in testifying to being present with Cortés "at all the invasions and conquests and pacifications which were carried out." He testified further to participating in campaigns and expeditions in Cuba, Puerto Rico, and even into islands off Mexico's Pacific coast. He did all without salary or allotment "or anything else," he swore. Further, he claimed he was "the first to have the inspiration to sow maize here in New Spain and see if it took." What he called "maize" was probably a strain of wheat rather than the corn later associated with maize. "I did this and experimented at my own expense," Garrido emphasized (Alegría 1990, 6, 127–138).

Garrido's writing found deep within the accounts in Spain's New World archives in Seville rescued him from the anonymous and impersonal bulk of blacks in Spain's early forays into the Americas. Others rescued, by name at least, have included Juan Bardales, Juan Beltrán, Pedro Fulupo, Juan García, Antonio Pérez, Juan Portugués, Miguel Ruíz, and Juan Valiente. Their names, like that of Estevanico, appeared in the annals with some indication of their birth in Africa or their parentage or status showing their descent from Africa. Without such written records, such blacks would have been forever lost as individuals in history, like millions of their brothers and sisters.

Blacks explored the Americas with others besides the Portuguese and Spanish. Serving on Danish, Dutch, English, and French ships that came to explore the Americas in the 1500s and 1600s, they garnered little notice among the motley crews common at the time. In the early years of sailing exploration from Europe and later, seamanship appeared more important than appearance or birthplace. Columbus, himself, illustrated that. He was not a Spaniard, after all, although he led Spain's exploration of the Americas. Born in Genoa, like Columbus, the mariner named at birth Giovanni Caboto sailed into history as John Cabot for his North American voyages in the 1490s for England. Similarly, although born in the Chianti region of central Tuscany, Giovanni da Verrazzano sailed for France when he explored North America's East Coast in the 1520s, reputedly becoming the first European to enter what became known as New York Bay.

Garrido, Estevanico, and others of African descent joined Verrazzano, Cabot, and Columbus in illustrating something of the shifting sense of geopolitical identity in the 1400s and 1500s. Nation-states were then only beginning to emerge in Europe. Nationality was not what it would become, nor was ethnicity. Columbus, Cabot, and Verrazzano, for example, were born in the geographic area of Italy when there was no Italian nation-state or nationality to claim them as they sailed away to the Americas. Only later would such persons be known generically as Italians.

Men like Columbus, Cabot, and Verrazzano elevated to greatness in history have secured their individuality and escaped the generic labeling that has obscured the identity and personality of the masses. Men such as Garrido, Estevanico, and others of African descent among the early explorers in the Americas were individuals in their own right and among their contemporaries. Yet the ordinary passing of time submerged their individuality, as it did that of the masses of humanity in history. And the transatlantic slave trade further submerged them. It plunged people of African descent into a generic pit. They became increasingly indistinct and interchangeable as others designated them simply as Africans, blacks, Negroes, or slaves.

The identities of peoples from Africa became lumped in the far-reaching human trafficking that followed European exploration of the Americas in the 1500s. They became a major part of a complex world-changing movement that buried the record of their individuality in the second-largest wave of human migration in all history. As the principal part of that wave until the 1850s, they became prime builders of a New World, an Atlantic World, where they served as the muscle and sinew of commercial and cultural exchange. They became prime connectors in a new orientation for Africa, the Americas, and Europe, developing a New World outlook that transformed their identities, and not theirs alone.

African Americans arose as a New World people. The seeds of their birth were sown and resown in European colonization of the Americas and in the burgeoning transatlantic slave trade that persisted through the middle of the

1800s. They descended from the primary immigrants to the Americas from the 1500s through the mid-1800s, when peoples from Africa far outnumbered peoples from anywhere else as arrivals in the Americas. Before the 1820s about four Africans landed in the Americas for every one European, as the estimates indicated about 8.4 million arrivals from Africa and only about 2.4 million immigrants from Europe (Eltis 1983, 278).

The Americas were the crib of African American nativity and nurture. Created by the circumstances and conditions of their presence in the Americas, they came to life as a people in formation. Garrido, Estevanico, and others of African descent among the early explorers in the Americas stood as forebears. They arrived at the dawn of African American history, signaling change in the offing. They were not themselves the change; they were forerunners and forefathers. The mass of their fellows who followed from Africa would walk different paths, as would their children for generations ever after. The early pioneers of African descent served to introduce something of the variety of black experience in the Americas, pointing to the fact that what would become the United States of America encompassed more than the lands the English colonized on the Atlantic coast.

Garrido, Estevanico, and their fellows illustrated that African American history did not begin in 1619 or in the English colony called "Virginia." It was not a matter of the first blacks to appear on what would become U.S. soil. Nor was it a matter of the lineage of blacks in the Americas reaching to fabled kingdoms of medieval Africa such as Ghana, Mali, and Songhai. It was a matter of complex interactions emerging in the mid-1400s to create an Atlantic World as ancestral societies in Africa furnished generations of its daughters and sons in a rich legacy of achievement and contribution to human history. Africa was, after all, a birthplace for humankind. Peoples across the continent produced creative, sophisticated, and spectacular developments in various dynamic cultures and civilizations. Those elements supplied rich human capital among the peoples taken from Africa. Yet African societies did not produce African Americans. Africans in the Americas gave birth to African Americans—a new people in a New World.

The transatlantic slave trade bridged Africa and the Americas. Its continuous traffic kept African blood flowing into the soil of the Americas over almost four centuries. More than trafficking in people, the business of slaving built a world of connections, an Atlantic World that became central to modern history. It reoriented Africa, the Americas, and Europe, changing much of the known world and the lives of many of the peoples there then and for ages to come. It transformed the peoples snatched to the Americas and changed the lives of many African peoples touched by but not taken in the traffic to the Americas.

Before the Portuguese forays along Africa's west coast in the mid-1400s, the Atlantic was Africa's backwater. The mainstream of most commercial activity in Africa was not actually a waterway: it was the Sahara. The desert served as West and Central Africa's inland sea, as its main commercial channel. North Africa also had the Mediterranean Sea. East Africa had the Red Sea and the Indian Ocean, which also served southern Africa. No main currents ran to the Atlantic.

Most African networks before 1500 looked east or northeast. That was easily visible in the extensive trading connections north of the equator where expansive political entities grew along eastward-looking commercial and cultural routes. Islam had expanded the eastward outlook as it reached the West African Kingdom of Ghana in the late 900s and in the early 1300s became the state religion of Mali under Mansa Musa. Islam's expansive political power shimmered in the wide area of Songhai in the 1500s. Those major medieval kingdoms all ranged inland, spreading their reach to the east, where commercial nodes centered. The Atlantic marked the periphery—until the Portuguese and other Europeans arrived and offered fresh alternatives.

Africa's goods and services were well known and well regarded in Arabia, the Far East, Near East Asia, and Europe long before Portugal's West African forays. Indeed, coastal, tropical forest, and savanna societies in West Africa eagerly supplied part of the trans-African commerce, with sea and land networks reaching around the Mediterranean into Asia as far as China. The Muslim geographer and historian Al-Bakri, born in Andalucia in southwest Spain in the 1000s, detailed the trans-Saharan trade in his *Kitāb al-Masālik w'al-Mamālik* or *Book of Highways and Kingdoms*, extending work under similar titles from the 800s by the Persian geographer ibn Khordadbeh and others.

African caravans traded various commodities. They carried gum, hides, and cloth, chiefly cotton and silk, joining in the fabled Silk Road to China. They carried foodstuffs such as dates and peppers, but mostly grains such as millet, rice, and sorghum. They carried salt, a scarce and vital commodity in arid or sultry climes. They carried ivory and tropical hardwoods, and they traded heavily in gold. The Wangara in the area of the Volta River watershed with its colorfully named three tributaries—the Black, Red, and White Volta—were renowned as gold merchants. Arabic chronicles such as Abd al-Sadi's *Tarikh al-Sudan* or *History of the Sudan* of the mid-1600s echoed the Wangara's repute. Their gold produce and prowess brought the area of the Gulf of Guinea, centered in what would become the nation of Ghana, the label "Gold Coast."

The caravans trafficked also in slaves. The traffic in humans was old in Africa. It was old around the globe. It grew from imbalance as supply and demand created the market. Wherever war existed or raiding occurred, captives were bought and sold. An ancient alternative was slaughter. Some traded in the traffic were not captives to start. They were prisoners of social circumstances. Some societies lacked the wherewithal to sustain all the people they had. Other societies had the wherewithal to expand their production and consumption by taking in more people to work. The same was true of households. Some could not feed all the mouths or care for all the bodies they had. Selling members that circumstances made marginal allowed some households to sustain their core, sometimes selling some members to feed and shelter others or to pay debts. Some sales were grudging; some were not. Criminals and other troublemakers were sold to rid their societies of their burden. The buying and selling developed in various ways and for various reasons. And it varied in meaning, for the concept of property was not the same everywhere. Indeed, what was being bought and sold in the human traffic was not always the same.

The status or social position of persons bought and sold as slaves varied as the term *slave* covered diverse conditions. The word itself differed. The English word *slave* developed from practices in Eastern Europe. As Germanic peoples pushed eastward, capturing and forcing into labor Slavic peoples, the Slavs' subordination became a byword—*slavery*. The term fit with the Latin *sclavus*. But the ancient Latin word for *slave* was *servus*, which denoted *serf* as well as *personal servant*. What the position meant in practice differed by circumstances, time, and place, but everywhere it distinguished from others those called slaves.

Simply put, *slavery* did not mean exactly the same thing in every time and place. It everywhere meant serving others, but in much of the premodern, pre-cash-driven world of developing societies, even into the 1900s and later, serving others was the essence of personal standing and social relations. Social structures depended on personal service. Indeed, personal service determined social identity. A web of personal service joined almost everyone in premodern society. Only outlaws and deviants stood unconnected in prescribed personal relations of duty. So service did not set slaves apart from others. Even the terms and conditions of service did not everywhere distinguish slaves from others. Moreover, distinctions changed over time. Like much else, especially after 1500, slavery existed amid an ever-more rapidly changing world and was changing with it.

Africa's traffic in slaves flowed north and eastward for the most part, before the Portuguese incursion of the mid-1400s. A trans-Saharan trade to North Africa, Arabia, and the Near East prospered by the time of Islam's birth in the early 600s. By the 1500s the traffic bore an annual average of 10,000 persons Arabs called *abeed*, indicating *slave*, and the term became a derogatory stereotype for black Africans. That trade spun off increased

numbers of slaves kept within sub-Saharan Africa for local uses. Yet the
scale of such slavery remained marginal until the mid-1650s. Then it grew
as the slave trade expanded with accelerating transatlantic demand.

Before the 1600s slaves from West Africa's Atlantic coast went mostly
to Europe and islands off Africa's Atlantic coast. The Cape Verde Islands,
about 350 miles off the coast of Western Africa and about 1,200 miles from
Portugal, received increasing number of slaves and became a way station for
slavers as the traffic up the Atlantic from West Africa grew from about 600
captives a year to 1,700 by 1525 when Portugal lost its exclusive control
of the business. The Canary Island archipelago off North Africa's Atlantic
coast, about 1,000 miles southwest of Portugal, also drew increasing numbers of enslaved Africans to attend to its expanding sugarcane cultivation in
the late 1400s and 1500s.

Portuguese and then other traders strewed captured Africans along
Europe's Atlantic shores from the late 1400s through the 1500s. Spain took
a considerable part. England also got a share. Indeed, by the late 1500s the
numbers of Africans in the region of the Thames alarmed some. England's
Queen Elizabeth in 1596 complained to London's Lord Mayor that "there
are of late divers Black-moores brought into this realme, of which kinde of
people there are allready here to manie." She further declared her "good
pleasure to have those kind of people sent out of the land" and suggested
"to transport them into Spaine and Portugall" (Bartels 2006, 305). The
Good Queen Bess appeared to have wanted to send the Africans in and
around her capital back where they came from in her view.

The transatlantic traffic to the Americas ticked up only in the 1600s.
Before then about 1,000 Africans on average reached the Americas annually.
Almost exclusively they went to Iberian possessions. No other significant
European bases then existed in the Americas. Spanish possessions received
about 60 percent of the approximately 125,000 African arrivals in the
Americas before 1600. Of that 75,000, northwestern South America—the
area that would become Venezuela, Colombia, and Peru—took 45,000
(36.0%). Mexico and Central America took 23,000 (18.4%). The Spanish
Caribbean got 7,000 (5.6%). The Portuguese enterprise in Brazil got the
remaining 50,000 (40.0%) (Manning 1993, 280; Elbl 1997, 31–75).

The Iberians had started slavery in the Americas even before they
imported significant numbers of captives from Africa. Columbus had forced
into labor those he called "Indians" as he seeded Spanish outposts on Hispaniola in the 1490s and early 1500s. He shipped some captive Taino—the
majority of the native Arawak peoples indigenous to the Caribbean—to
Spain for display and drudgery. The Spanish in Hispaniola and elsewhere
put to work in fields and mines most Taino on whom they could lay hands,
and the captivity and contact devastated the Taino, as it would many other

indigenous peoples of the Americas. Disease killed many, as did brutality. Within 20 years of first contact with the Spanish incursion, only about one-tenth of the Taino population in 1490 remained alive.

Bent on extracting as much as they could as quickly as they could in the Americas, the Spanish and Portuguese scavenged for additional labor. The Iberians were, for the most part, soldiers, auxiliaries, and administrators. They were not field-workers or miners. At best they were supervisors for the hard, routine work of extracting the earth's riches. What's more, they disdained doing manual labor as such drudgery existed outside their self-image, even if they could have coped with the exhausting demands they pressed on their captives.

The apparent devastation of indigenous peoples horrified some of the clergy dispatched to the Americas in the announced tripartite mission dedicated to "God, Gold, and Glory." Various Catholic clergy in the colonies repeatedly recommended reforms to the crown. Writing from Hispaniola to Spain's King Charles I in 1518, Bernadino de Manzanedo, a friar of the order of San Jerónimo, recommended that "all the Indians of this island be set free entirely, so that no Spaniard might employ their labor except by their own free will" (Parry and Keith 1984, 334–335). Among his final reports before resigning as bishop of Santiago de Cuba in 1544, Diego de Sarmiento complained of his fellow Spaniards' terrifying treatment of Indians on the Caribbean's largest island.

Bartolomé de Las Casas became known as "protector of the Indians" for his advocacy against his fellow Spaniards' brutal treatment of them. The one-time settler born in Seville but turned Dominican friar and reformer railed against the "forms of killing labor" Spaniards forced on Indians. Las Casas's 1561 *Historia de las Indias de Nueva Espana y islas de Tierra Firme*, or *History of the Indies of New Spain, the Islands and Mainland*, and other writings became a historical indictment of Spanish inhumanity to indigenous peoples in the Americas.

The drive for wealth in the Americas was not to be derailed, however, by humanitarian sensitivities. If Indians were unavailable to do the drudgery that produced fortunes, then others would be forced to do it. To fill their desires in the Americas, Iberians turned to West Africa as a familiar source of captive labor. Blacks had accompanied them to the Americas from the start in the 1490s. After a royal dispensation in 1518, Spaniards began more wholesale importing of blacks from West Africa. A temporary halt occurred in 1522 when enslaved black Muslims revolted in Hispaniola, killing nine Spaniards. A similar suspension followed in 1537 after a plot in Mexico. The captives' resistance would persist, yet the passion for riches drove Europeans to accelerate their trafficking of Africans to the Americas.

West Africa responded to increasing demand for captives in the first half of the 1600s. The Iberian possessions in the Americas continued to demand the bulk of the traffic that before 1640 began to average about 11,000 annual African arrivals. Brazil took 160,000 (34.4%) of the estimated 439,000 Africans arriving in the Americas between 1600 and 1640. All but 19,000 (4.3%) of the remainder were distributed in Spanish possessions: 135,000 (30.7%) in Venezuela, Colombia, and Peru; 70,000 (15.9%) in Mexico and Central America; 44,000 (10.0%) in the area that became Argentina and Bolivia; and 20,000 (4.5%) in the Spanish Caribbean (Manning 1993, 280; Elbl 1997, 31–75).

But exporting captives was not West Africa's main business, not in the beginning nor at the ending of the transatlantic traffic. Africa always was more than a warehouse of captive labor. From the mid-1400s through the mid-1600s gold rather than slaves dominated West Africa's exports. Even as the transatlantic slave trade accelerated, West Africans maintained a considerable basket of various other exports such as ivory, palm oil, and spices. They were not exclusively or simply in the slaving business. Nor were they for the most part in the business of selling their own.

Much has been made of Africans selling Africans as if captors and captives were one and the same, a people feeding upon themselves, as it were. Africans were not, however, a single people any more than Europeans or Asians or indigenous Americans were a single people. At the opening of the era of the burgeoning Atlantic World, the peoples of West Africa and all of Africa, for that matter, much resembled the fragmented, scrappy peoples of Western Europe in vying for place, position, power, and wealth. They had their own military and religious ambitions, and commerce and greed drove them no less than others. They differed considerably from society to society and in their economic, political, and social organizations and outlooks. They had differing technologies and resources, varying beliefs and rituals. They had internal contentions, external rivalries, and settled agendas, and the arrival of Europeans on the Atlantic coast fed those agendas and traditional competitions.

The commercial demands on Africa's Atlantic coast from the mid-1400s onward insinuated themselves throughout West Africa and around the continent. The Portuguese intrusion began on Africa's bulge into the Atlantic. It focused on the coastal area called Senegambia. It started at a spot that came to be called Saint Louis, where the 1,110-mile-long Senegal River flowed from Africa's interior northwest into the Atlantic. It went south past Dakar on the Atlantic peninsula that formed Africa's westernmost projection, down to where the 700-mile-long Gambia River spilled westward into the Atlantic. The traffic spread further southward through the Bight of Benin and the Gulf of Guinea down to Angola. In its latter stages it reached around the Horn of Africa to Mozambique and Madagascar. Also it spread into the interior, to the Kongo and the Sudan, where horsemen engaged in raiding and rounding up captives for the transatlantic traffic.

Indigenous traders along the Atlantic coast opened their societies to Portuguese and other Europeans with an eye on profits. Shrewd dealers engaged in no one-sided transactions; they saw immediate income and political advantage in dealing with Europeans, and they long restricted and controlled European access to their markets and resources. When the Oba of Benin opened his kingdom to Portuguese commerce in the 1470s, for example, he granted only a limited license, dictating who could buy and sell what, when, and where. Other African rulers followed the strategy of limiting Europeans to trading posts some called "factories," indicating a place where foreign commercial agents conducted transactions.

Trafficking in captives became big business along with other commodities, and it had deep consequences. As the expanding logistics of raiding, transporting, and confining captives for market moved further and further inland from the Atlantic coast, the traffic changed the shapes and structures of local economies and societies. It wedged a growing divide between predators and prey, captors and captives, and perhaps most of all, it more and more drained population from deeper and deeper in Africa's heart. It stunted overall population growth in Africa from the mid-1500s to the mid-1700s. The crest of transatlantic traffic in the 1700s went further: it plunged West Africa into stagnation with actual population decline from 1750 to 1850 (Manning 1990, 8–85). That decline and changes in trafficking in Africa and across the Atlantic affected who arrived from Africa into North America and, thus, who would become African Americans.

## PROFILE: ESTEVANICO (CA. 1500–1539)

Born in North Africa around 1500, Estevanico joined in the Spanish exploration of Florida, the Gulf Coast, and what became the U.S. Southwest. He was known by various names in varied spellings such as Estebanico, Esteban de Dorantes, and Esteban the Moor. Some English translations offered his name as "Little Stephen" or "Stephen the Black." Some have identified him by the Arabic name Mustafa Zemmouri. He came to the Spanish via Portuguese slavers and joined in the expedition Pánfilo de Narváez in 1527 led from Hispaniola, through Cuba, to Florida, along the Gulf Coast, into the Southwest, and down into Mexico.

Estevanico proved among the hardier on the near nine-year-long expedition, as he was among a mere handful of survivors from the initial 300-man group to finish the journey to Mexico City. His trek attached him to the leading Spanish explorers of the Southwest—Álvar Núñez Cabeza de Vaca,

Andrés Dorantes de Carranza, and Alonso del Castillo Maldonado. After reaching Mexico City in 1536, his earlier experience positioned Estevanico to become a guide for other expeditions into the Southwest.

The Franciscan friar Marcos de Niza hired Estevanico in 1539 for an expedition into what became Arizona and New Mexico in search of Cibola, a Zuni complex described as seven cities and said to rival Mexico City in size but to surpass it in wealth. Estevanico reportedly made it into Cibola, but he alone of the group. Fray de Niza stopped at a distance, only glimpsing what he took to be the fabled Zuni settlements. He returned to Mexico City to relate the adventure in *Descubrimiento de las siete ciudades* (1539), which contained the last word on Estevanico, for nothing more was heard of him after he entered among the Zuni. Estevanico became a legend based on the fact of his being a black among the early Spanish explorers of North America and particularly of what became the U.S. Southwest (Logan 1940, 305–314).

## REFERENCES

Alegría, Ricardo E. 1990. *Juan Garrido, el Conquistador Negro en las Antillas, Florida, Mexico y California, c. 1503–1540*. San Juan, P.R.: Centro de Estudios Avanzados de Puerto Rico y El Caribe; reproducing at 127–138 Juan Garrido's Petition of Proof of Merit, dated September 27, 1538, Archivo General de Indias, Seville, Grupo de México 204, f.1.

Bartels, Emily C. 2006. "Too Many Blackamoors: Deportation, Discrimination, and Elizabeth I." *Studies in English Literature, 1500–1946*, no. 2 (Spring): 305–322; quoting Queen Elizabeth to the Lord Mayor et al., July 1596, *Acts of the Privy Council of England*, 26 (London: H.M. Stationery Office, 1596–1597), 16–17.

Elbl, Ivana. 1997. "The Volume of the Early Atlantic Slave Trade, 1450–1521." *Journal of African History* 38, no. 1: 31–75.

Eltis, David. 1983. "Free and Coerced Transatlantic Migrations: Some Comparisons." *American Historical Review* 88, no. 2 (April): 251–280.

Logan, Rayford. 1940. "Estevanico, Negro Discoverer of the Southwest: A Critical Reexamination." *Phylon* 1, no. 4 (4th Qtr.): 305–314.

Manning, Patrick. 1990. *Slavery and African Life: Occidental, Oriental and African Slave Trades*. New York: Cambridge University Press.

Manning, Patrick. 1993. "Migrations of Africans to the Americas: The Impact on Africans, Africa, and the New World." *History Teacher* 26, no. 3 (May): 279–296.

Parry, J.H., and Robert G. Keith, eds. 1984. *New Iberian World: A Documentary History of the Discovery and Settlement of Latin America to the Early 17th Century*. New York: Times Books.

_____ *Chapter 2* _____

# Coming to America

African Americans came to life as New World peoples. They were not Africans. They were the children of Africans. They were born of African descent in North America. They were first the offspring of the likes of Juan Garrido and others of African descent in Spanish North America, for the early African presence with the Spanish produced a significant population on lands to become part of the United States of America. They were early along the Gulf Coast and in the Southwest and West. Spanish Florida, which ranged north and west of the peninsula, hosted several black communities. Perhaps most notable was that at Gracia Real de Santa Teresa de Mosé about two miles north of St. Augustine, commonly noted as the oldest continuously occupied European-established settlement in the continental United States (Landers 1990, 9–30).

Economic demands concentrated Spanish attention south of the Rio Grande with a slow but steady flow of Africans from the early 1500s that by the mid-1650s amounted to 275,000 in central Mexico. An American-born Afro population grew early from African men such as Garrido who fathered children most often with Indian women, as relatively few women from Africa arrived in early Nueva España. Indeed, early on few women from the Old World came to the New World. They certainly were not among expeditionaries such as Garrido. Yet the black population in Nueva España became important elements in an expanding commercial economy, and by the end of the 1500s, Mexico City hosted the largest community of African descent in the Americas.

The African presence along the Atlantic coast commonly identified as the initial ancestral cohort for African Americans developed later and more slowly than that in Spanish Florida and the Southwest. What distinguished it and produced what would become the most numerous population of African descent in the Americas were women from Africa. The English colonies on North America drew a higher ratio of captive African females than other places in the Americas, and that fated much of the future.

The bulk of the 10 to 16 million Africans landed in the Americas in the transatlantic slave trade from the 1500s through the 1800s went to South America and the Caribbean where burgeoning plantation economies paid premiums for male captives aged 14 and 25 years. Buyers in North America rarely outbid buyers to the south for such captives. Generally, they had to content themselves with captives not earmarked for the Brazilian and Caribbean markets, and they managed overall to get only about 6 in every 100 African captives landed in the Americas. But they got relatively more females than elsewhere, and in the long run that relatively large number of females made all the difference in producing the largest American-born population of African descent.

The English colonist John Rolfe's oft-noted comments in January 1620 on the arrival of African captives in Jamestown, Virginia, reflected the degree to which the Atlantic slave trade was early almost an afterthought along North America's East Coast. Writing his patron Sir Edwin Sandys, treasurer of the Virginia Company of London that owned the Jamestown enterprise, Rolfe noted that "about the latter end of August, a Dutch man of Warr of the burden of about 160 tunnes arrived . . . [and] brought not any thing but 20 and odd Negroes, which the Governor [Sir George Yeardley] and Cape Marchant bought for victualls." Rolfe cast the swap of the captives for food and other provisions as nearly a giveaway, describing the deal as "at the best and easyest rates" for the governor and the colony's chief purchasing officer (Kingsbury 1933, 3: 243).

The Dutch delivery at Jamestown in August 1619 was not necessarily the first of African captives to Virginia. It was simply the first noted in preserved records. A February 1624 "List of the Livinge and Dead in Virginia" showed at least 22 blacks living in the colony for at least five years. Most went nameless, described as "one negar," "A Negors Woman," or simply "negors." A 1625 Virginia listing counted 12 black males and 11 black females, a balance among the sexes atypical elsewhere in the Americas. Among the blacks listed were four of note—two men and two women. The two women were Mary and Isabell. The two men were listed as "Antonio a negro" and "Antoney negro." The implications of the balanced sex ratio for the emergence of an African American population soon emerged, for Antonio and Mary and Antoney and Isabell became mates in notable families that produced the first African American children in England's colonies on North America.

Enslaved Africans landed at Jamestown, Virginia, in 1619, and joined the flow of captives that until the 1840s brought more Africans than Europeans to the Americas. (D.H. Montgomery. *The Leading Facts of American History*, 1910)

Antonio Anglicized his name to Anthony, took for himself and family the surname Johnson, and distinguished himself on Virginia's Eastern Shore as he negotiated his own and his family's release from slavery. Using energy and ingenuity, he made himself something of a patriarch on Pungoteague Creek off the Chesapeake Bay, gaining land he called "myne owne ground," livestock, and slaves. Johnson secured standing among the early generations of Virginians, but his struggles and successes highlighted the capricious course of black life developing in English North America, for openings he seized to establish himself as an independent proprietor closed within a generation (Breen and Innes 1980, 3–7).

Emanuel Driggus and other blacks on Virginia's Eastern Shore in the mid-1600s further illustrated aspects of the shifting character of life for blacks in early America. Francis Payne, Tony Longo, and other Africans in Virginia in the mid-1600s did much the same, moving from captivity to free labor and land owners. Like Anthony Johnson, they came to Virginia as slaves, but they did not die as slaves. Driggus appeared in Virginia's Northampton County court records in 1645. He was then unfree but he soon enough bought his release. He married an English woman and ran his own farm. Like Anthony Johnson, Driggus illustrated that Africans in early Virginia enjoyed opportunities different from African Americans born in captivity, whose lives would begin and end in slavery.

Being captives forced to labor made Driggus, Johnson, and their cohort from the first slaves in practice. No formal law initiated their slavery. Their status arose from "custome," as Virginia acknowledged in March 1662 in enacting among its labor laws what essentially was its first slave code. Treating those in "service . . . by custome or indenture," the Virginia legislature distinguished between what it referred to as "Christian servants" indentured for a fixed term of years and "Negroes who are incapable of making satisfaction by addition of a time" (Hening 1823, 2: 116–117).

Driggus, Johnson, and their cohort did not have to die in slavery to be slaves. Lifetime service was never an indelible mark of slavery. Duration determined little, if anything, about slavery's essence. Whether for a day or for a lifetime, coercion, unlimited conditions, and segregated status stamped slavery. Those were the essential elements, persisting while practices varied with time, place, personalities, and other circumstances. Captivity enslaved Africans from the first, as heredity developed to enslave later generations. Serving an indefinite term of years did not shift Driggus, Johnson, and their cohort from being slaves to being servants. Their captivity, as heredity would later, answered the difference between being a slave and being a servant. They were liable to service for life, for their term of service was indefinite, as the Virginia legislature indicated in its pronouncement about "Negroes who are incapable of making satisfaction by addition of a time." The fact that Driggus, Johnson, and their cohort served for less than life in no way altered their having been slaves, not servants, from their captivity until their release.

Some blacks in early Virginia did hold the status of servant. They did not enter Virginia as captives. They appeared among the children of the first generation of captives. One example was Edward Mozingo. He was apprenticed between 1642 and 1644 on an indenture that ran 28 years, notably longer than the five years the law allowed white indentures unless they were aged 16 years or younger, in which case their indenture ended when they turned 21. Nonetheless, when Mozingo's term expired, he had to sue for his release and rebut the presumption that because he was black he was a slave, not a servant. He won his case, *Negro Mozingo v. Stone* (1672), but as an exception to the rule emerging to equate black with slave.

The relatively relaxed atmosphere of the 1630s, 1640s, and even early 1650s in which Driggus, Johnson, and their cohort had negotiated their release and rescued their children from slavery was not the atmosphere of the 1660s and 1670s when the presumption of color cast blacks solely as slaves. A contemporary of Driggus and Johnson's called John Punch made his name a historical footnote on the question of whether Africans in early Virginia were ordinarily liable to service for life.

Punch sought to break free from his captivity in 1640 by running away to Maryland with two white indentured servants. Authorities caught all three, and the Virginia Governor's Council ordered that the three "shall receive the punishment of whipping and to have thirty stripes apiece." The council further sentenced the two white men to an added year of service to the holders of their indentures and then "to serve the colony for three whole years apiece," but it sentenced Punch to "serve his said master or his assigns for the time of his natural Life here or elsewhere" (Catterall 1926, 1: 77).

In the case titled *Re Negro John Punch* (1640), the Virginia Council referred to the convicts as "three servants," which some later commentators used to argue that Punch and his fellow African captives were in fact indentured servants, not slaves in early Virginia. Punch and his two companions were without question in servitude and in that broad sense were servants. But his two white companions had volunteered and agreed to enter service. Punch and his fellow blacks were not volunteers. Their position arose from neither consent nor contract.

Captivity brought Punch and his fellow blacks to Virginia. They were put to labor with indentured servants, but in no way were they indentured servants. They may all have been *servants* in a general sense, but even amid often interchangeable use of terms, early Virginians understood the difference between *slave* and *servant* as easily as they understood the difference between black and white. Slaves were black; servants were white. What became known as American Negro slavery was not a matter of semantics; it was a matter of custom, pattern, and practice. It was part of a developing system of racial dominance and subordination, a system of segregation built on white supremacy.

Punch's sentence to "serve . . . for the time of his natural Life" added no liability to his condition as a captive. What it did was to deny him a possibility Driggus, Johnson, and others in their cohort were able to seize to great advantage. Punch's sentence condemned him to never being legally capable of not being a slave. The sentence stripped him of any capacity for release, and negotiated release from slavery became rarer and rarer as time ticked—not only in Virginia or among the English.

Captive Africans in the early 1600s in the Dutch colony of Nieuw Nederland had experiences similar to those of blacks like Anthony Johnson, Emanuel Driggus, and others on Virginia's Eastern Shore. Jan Rodrigues, for example, entered what would become New York Bay with Dutch explorers in 1613. From sailor the man of African descent went to being something of an expeditionary. Set ashore on the tip of southwestern Long Island's Rockaway Peninsula, he was befriended by Native Americans called

Lenape and married into the tribe. Learning the language and customs, he became an important intermediary who in time advanced connections with the settlement the Dutch West India Company (WIC) established in 1625 on a smaller island to the northwest called Manhattan.

Rodrigues's children became the first African Americans in the area that became New York. The bulk of blacks arrived on Manhattan at the WIC post called Nieuw Amsterdam as captives. The initial group in 1626 numbered 11, and they were not dropped off as an afterthought as were the "20. and odd Negroes" in Jamestown in 1619. The 11 arrived as part of a studied business proposition. Imported and maintained as company property, they were on hand to serve company needs. The women mostly did domestic and personal service for WIC officers. The men mostly did heavy labor, working on construction projects such as building Fort Amsterdam, which was finished in 1635. But they did not succeed as well as the early black Virginians, for they won only partial release in what too many commentators have incongruously labeled "half freedom." They and their children remained WIC property, and the WIC retained rights to their labor on demand. Also the WIC required annual payments, essentially a quit rent, for what it titled "land of the blacks" in the hilly and swampy wilds north of the fort, between the Dutch settlers and increasingly unwelcoming Indians. So half freedom was not release from slavery; it was an outsourcing, a repositioning of service to save the company money and to protect its interests by setting blacks out to sustain themselves and serve further as a buffer against attack.

The Manhattan blacks' names suggested their origins and also illustrated the significant presence of black women and couples, as well as foreshadowing the rich mix of blacks of Spanish heritage and others from the Caribbean who would people the future of Manhattan and the larger area that became New York on the English takeover in September 1664. The names identified Angola and the Congo as points of origin for Anna D'Angola (widow of Andries), Anthony Congo, Assento Angola, Paula D'Angola, and Simon Congo. Others had names associating the person with a more specific place, such as Pieter San Tome, pointing to the island in the Gulf of Guinea, or Anthony of the Bowery, identifying him with the old footpath area on lower Manhattan.

The names also indicated the Spanish background of many of the blacks such as Domingo Angola, Domingo Anthony, Francisco Cartagena, Francisco D'Angola, Gracia D'Angola, Jan Francisco, and most obviously "Manuel the Spaniard." There was also "Anthony Portuguese." Descriptive names also appeared, as with Anthony "the Blind Negro," Cleyn (Little) Anthony, Gleyn (Little) Manuel, or Manuel Groot (Big Manuel). Widowhood was recognized as with Anna D'Angola (widow of Andries), Catalina

Anthony (widow of Jochem), and Marycke (widow of Lawrence). Then there were also Bastiaen Negro, Claes Negro, and Jan Negro. All of these named blacks became recorded landholders on Manhattan between 1643 and 1662 in the WIC program to outsource blacks it had enslaved.

The English takeover in 1664 brought the developing Anglo-American structure of racialized slavery that already surrounded what became New York. English settlers on Eastern Long Island, up along the Connecticut Valley, through Massachusetts, and elsewhere in New England held captive Africans and their offspring from the late 1600s onward. There, too, a few blacks such as Abijah Prince and Lucy Terry—who became Mr. & Mrs. Prince—negotiated their release from slavery. To exercise their independence, however, they removed from the site of their bondage in western Massachusetts and moved to less settled areas that became New Hampshire and Vermont, where they became landholders, but were still beset with difficulties from their being black in an ever-encroaching white world (Gerzina and Gerzina 2008, 1–8).

Blacks throughout North America had increasingly few openings to escape slavery as the 1700s lengthened. That was particularly so among the 13 British colonies, but it was so, also, in Louisiana under the French and Spanish, and elsewhere in Spanish America as the 1700s brought larger and larger waves of Africans to the Americas. More than half of the approximately 500,000 Africans landed in the slave trade to North America arrived between 1720 and 1780. White responses to the increasing numbers of blacks hardened the segregation separating blacks and whites, distancing blacks from all others while increasing the restraints and restrictions of slavery.

Nowhere were whites much interested in blacks other than as slaves. Segregation everywhere was stark. Interracial sex particularly became taboo to keep clear who was who. Punishments Virginia early meted out in *Re Davis* (1630) and in *Re Sweat* (1640) illustrated the growing concern. Both Maryland and Virginia moved in the 1660s to outlaw marriages between blacks and whites. Similar statutes appeared in Massachusetts (1705), North Carolina (1715), South Carolina (1717), Delaware (1726), and Georgia (1750). The term *miscegenation* would arise in the mid-1860s to describe interracial coupling, but the English colonies on North America long before then had enacted what would be called antimiscegenation laws against what many considered to be "dangerous liaisons" (Robinson 2003, 4).

Laws against black–white sex exhibited racialized eroticism, but they were about more than stirred passions or even general concerns about socially acceptable sexual conduct. They made visible the developing conundrum of race as a long contentious issue of personal identity. Mixed race long represented a horror to many. What was to be the social identity of the child of a black–white union? Virginia answered the question in *Re Mulatto* (1656) by identifying only the black lineage and ignoring the white lineage in ruling the mulatto to be a slave like other blacks.

The law of identity followed a practice that became known as *hypodescent*. It excluded any middle ground and in the developing ethos of white supremacy, it stamped a person as either white or not white. So children of any black–white union were automatically assigned the identity of the subordinate parent. In Anglo-America that meant being identified as black. And that meant such children were likely to be slaves, as identity generally determined status. To clarify any doubt on status, the Virginia legislature in March 1662 adapted to slavery a traditional English property law treating livestock. Known by the Latin phrase *partus sequitur ventrem*, the rule identified offspring as following the condition of the mother.

If the mother was a slave, then her child was a slave. The law recognized no paternity. Carving out a gross exception to Anglo-American patrilineal rules, American slave law simply ignored fathers of children born of enslaved black women. That denial of paternity fit with the denial of personal rights to mate, marry, or form legally protected families. With damnable effects on patterns and structures of black family formation, that early denial of paternity in many ways set up the black female-headed household.

Not only were blacks stripped of family identity; they were stripped also of the protection of Christian identity. Reflecting the primacy of religion in many Western European worldviews, entering the 1600s being or becoming a Christian served often as a shield against slavery. Yet as the commerce in slaves increased during the 1600s, Christianity faded as a distinction between slave and free. Race rather than religion emerged more and more to distinguish status. Maryland codified the point in 1664 and Virginia followed in 1667, declaring that "the conferring of baptisme doth not alter the condition of the person as to his bondage or ffreedome" (Hening 1823, 2: 260). But English colonists in North America were hardly alone in taking that position. The *Code Noir* Louis XIV promulgated in 1685 to regulate relations with blacks in France's colonies also pronounced baptism no basis for blacks' release from slavery (Goetz 2012, 1–34, 86–111).

The hardening of slavery developed with the tobacco boom that began sweeping Virginia in the 1620s. At its start blacks and whites worked side by side in the fields. As the cash crop grew, positions shifted. In 1649 Virginia counted only 300 blacks, who amounted to about 1 in 50 of all the colony's residents. By 1710 enslaved blacks numbered about one in four of all Virginians. And their growing number ranked Virginia consistently as the largest slaveholding colony and state in America. It had almost 293,000 enslaved blacks in 1790, more than twice those in the second-place state—South Carolina with 107,000. It would still lead the United States on the eve of the Civil War with more than half a million blacks—491,000 enslaved and 58,000 unenslaved. That was more than 80,000 greater than second-place Georgia in 1860.

Blacks fought against the leaching away of their personal standing. Moving was one recourse, as Anthony Johnson illustrated in the 1660s in taking his family from Virginia to Maryland. A series of Virginia suits in the 1670s, including *Moore v. Light* (1673), *West v. Negro Mary* (1674), and *Negro Angell v. Mathews* (1675), further illustrated court battles. But blacks appeared to vanish as suitors in Virginia courts after the 1670s. The denial of rights cut so sharply as to prompt protest from a lawyer at the British Board of Trade that supervised colonial affairs. "Altho' I agree that Slaves are to be treated in such a manner as the proprietors of them (having a regard to their number) may think necessary for their Security, yet I cannot see why one *Freeman* should be used worse than another merely upon account of his complexion," objected Richard West in 1723 on reviewing Virginia restrictions on blacks. "It cannot be right to strip all free persons of Black complexion, from those rights which are so justly valuable to any freeman," argued West (Neill 1875, 295–296).

Blacks' fate became sealed. American Negro slavery had begun as a work in progress, and it would continue as such. As it grew with increasing numbers, however, the system of degrading subordination also grew. At the start, few European settlers—whether English, Dutch, French, Spanish, or others—had experience with slavery, certainly not the slavery of captive Africans, and certainly not in the numbers increasingly brought to the Americas from the 1600s forward. From relatively simple captive labor, the system became more organized and complex in the struggle for control over labor, position, and power in which blacks and whites would long engage.

Labor was the key to wealth in the New World. And wealth was what the New World was all about. It was what drew most settlers. It was certainly the object of imperial schemes that sponsored colonizing. Captive Africans and their descendants became the primary New World laborers. Drafted to fill demand, blacks became 8 in 10 of all immigrants to the Americas before 1820. Controlling their labor became the key to wealth production in most of the colonial Americas, for the richest parts were plantation economies built on large-scale production of export staples. Sugarcane led all other commodities. It was the fabulously lucrative product of the Caribbean and Brazil. On the North American mainland, it gained a foothold only in Louisiana and Florida. Tobacco and rice and, later, cotton occupied most black labor in North America, and the requirements and rhythms of producing those commodities dominated the lives of blacks in America for generations.

## PROFILE: ANTHONY JOHNSON (CA. 1601–1670)

He arrived listed as "Antonio a negro." The *James* delivered him in 1621, but the English ship had probably picked him up from Dutch or Portuguese slavers treating with the Kingdom of the Kongo at its port of Luanda on Africa's South Atlantic coast. The Portuguese influence there would account for what he was called. Entering Virginia as a captive, he was sold to work on a tobacco plantation on the south side of the James River. He did well enough over the years to negotiate his own release from slavery and that of another captive African, "Mary a negro woman," whom the *Margrett and John* had delivered to Virginia in 1622.

Preferring to call himself "Anthony," he took the surname "Johnson," in tune with the English around him, and moved from where he had slaved, across the Chesapeake Bay to Virginia's Eastern Shore. He and Mary married, and in time had at least two sons and two daughters. He became the owner of what he called "myne own ground" along the Pungoteague Creek, and using the headright system Virginia adopted in 1618 to stimulate settlement, he claimed 50 acres each for six captive Africans he purchased as imports.

Johnson prospered as a small plantation owner and slaveholder, but not without difficulties. Whether from accident or arson, fire destroyed much of his holdings in 1653. He moved his clan north from Virginia to Maryland in the 1660s, probably reflecting Virginia's intensifying hostility to blacks who were not slaves. Resettling in Somerset County with his wife and children, including his two married sons, John and Richard, Johnson continued as a landholder until his death 1670. His grandson John Jr. would memorialize Johnson's African origins in naming his own 44-acre Maryland farm "Angola."

Anthony Johnson's legacy faded from history with dwindling family notice as American Negro slavery rose to overshadow blacks throughout English colonial America. He became later noted for his success in negotiating his release from slavery and prospering as both a landowner and slaveholder, representing a moment in early America before slavery had so solidified as to virtually exclude blacks from the opportunity to live life on their own terms, as it trapped the bulk of blacks in lifelong bondage.

## REFERENCES

Breen, T. H., and Stephen Innes. 1980. *"Myne Owne Ground": Race and Freedom on Virginia's Eastern Shore, 1640–1676.* New York: Oxford University Press.

Catterall, Helen Tunnicliff, ed. 1926. *Judicial Cases Concerning American Slavery and the Negro.* 5 vols. Washington, DC: Carnegie Institution of Washington, 1926–1937; reprint, New York: Octagon Books, 1968.

Gerzina, Gretchen, and Anthony Gerzina. 2008. *Mr. and Mrs. Prince: How an Extraordinary 18th Century Family Moved out of Slavery and into Legend.* New York: Amistad.

Goetz, Rebecca Ann. 2012. *The Baptism of Early Virginia: How Christianity Created Race.* Baltimore: Johns Hopkins University Press.

Hening, William Walter. 1823. *Hening's Statutes at Large: Being a Collection of All the Laws of Virginia from the First Session of the Legislature, in the Year 1619.* 13 vols. 1819–1823. Vol. 2: New York: R. &. W. & G. Bartow, 1823. Vol. 3: Philadelphia: Thomas Desilver, 1823. Vol. 4: Richmond: Franklin Press, 1820.

Kingsbury, Susan Myra. 1933. *The Records of the Virginia Company of London.* 4 vols. Washington, DC: Government Printing Office.

Landers, Jane. 1990. "Gracia Real de Santa Teresa de Mose: A Free Black Town in Spanish Colonial Florida." *American Historical Review* 95, no. 1 (February): 9–30.

Neill, Richard D. 1875. "Rt. Hon. Richard West, Lord Chancellor of Ireland." *New England Historical and Genealogical Register* 29: 295–297.

Robinson, Charles F. 2003. *Dangerous Liaisons: Sex and Love in the Segregated South.* Fayetteville: University of Arkansas Press.

_____ *Chapter 3* _____

# A People in the Making

Lifelong hereditary slavery became the overwhelming lot of blacks in North America from the mid-1600s to the mid-1800. Captives transported to the mainland directly from Africa or transshipped from the Caribbean entered into what became known as American Negro slavery—an assortment of active and changing patterns of relations that subordinated blacks as depersonalized property legally accounted as chattel. It incorporated practices in Spanish North America from Florida across the Gulf of Mexico into the Southwest and West and also in French Louisiana. Its core resided in the British colonies where approximately 190,000 enslaved blacks landed in the 1700s, more than half (62.6%) from 1726 to 1775. They boosted the black population as slavery grew in all 13 British colonies such that by 1750 blacks formed at least 2 percent of the population in each colony and about 20 percent of the total population of those colonies—about the same percentage blacks would constitute in the population of the new American nation at the end of the 1700s.

Blacks numbered about one in five of all Americans in the second half of the 1700s in part because of the growth of a new people: *African Americans*, daughters and sons born in America of parents from Africa, almost all born as slaves by law. Even while imports remained in the tens of thousands, it was the birth of these new people—blacks born in America—that contributed most to blacks growing almost 10-fold from about 13 per 1,000 inhabitants of English colonial America in the 1620s to about 201 per 1,000 by the beginning of the 1800s.

Growing in number and stature, American-born blacks rivaled and then outnumbered their African-born forebears in number and influence in the patterns and practices of black life in what became the United States of

America. Becoming a self-sustaining, native-born population extended, rather than extinguished, black Americans' African roots. The captive Africans who became the first generations of enslaved blacks in North America laid a foundation of enduring experiences to navigate the perils of removal, relocation, and subjugation. The generations fresh from Africa became living bridges, connecting their native continent and its peoples with the Americas and its peoples, and with Europe and its peoples. Their continuing passage into the Atlantic created a cultural basin awash with changes to new physical and social environments.

The Chesapeake became the cradle of black America. It was not simply that "20. and odd Negroes" landed in 1619 at Jamestown, Virginia, as perhaps the most noted group of early captive Africans in North America. The slave South began there, and the center of black population long remained there. Virginia and Maryland together had 61 of every 100 blacks in the British colonies in 1750. And in both Chesapeake colonies blacks by 1750 formed a substantial portion of their total population: 43.9 percent in Virginia and 30.9 percent in Maryland. In South Carolina, blacks notably formed a majority (60.9%) of the 1750 residents.

North of the Chesapeake, blacks in New York formed the largest population in the mid-1700s, as slavery had taken early hold in what would become the Empire State. The estimated 11,000 blacks there in 1750 were 14.3 percent of New York's colonial residents. They had grown notably as the English expanded use of captive Africans after seizing Nieuw Nederland from the Dutch in 1664. By the early 1700s, enslaved blacks lived in at least 42.0 percent of the households in colonial New York's capital on Manhattan Island. Their number on the eve of the War for U.S. Independence in 1775 ranked New York City second only to Charleston, South Carolina, among urban populations of enslaved blacks in North America. Colony-wide, New York's black population during the 1700s ranged between 12 and 14 percent of the total population (Davis 1984, 134–136, 142, 144).

Across from New York, about 1 in 13 (7.6%) of New Jersey's population in 1750 was black. In New England blacks were fewer. The 4,100 in Massachusetts were the most in the region and formed about 1 in 25 (2.2%) of the colony's population in 1750. The 3,000 blacks in Connecticut formed much the same proportion (2.7%) as in the Bay colony. Blacks formed a larger portion of the population in Rhode Island with its deep connections to transatlantic slave trafficking from Africa: they were nearly 1 in 10 (9.9%) of the colony's population in 1750, and they would peak at about 1 in 7 (15.0%). Blacks were moving west also with the general population of the British colonies on North America. Pushing the frontier from Virginia, for example, blacks in 1775 were about 1-in-6 (17%) of the persons in the areas that would become Kentucky and Tennessee (Lemon 1987, 123).

Where blacks concentrated long depended on slavery, for until the Civil War in the 1860s, enslaved blacks dwarfed blacks commonly called "free Negroes." The few unenslaved blacks in Britain's North American colonies or later in the early United States nowhere reached a tenth of the overall population. At the first U.S. Census in 1790, no state had a free black population larger in proportion than Delaware's 6.6 percent. But even there almost 7 in 10 (69.5%) blacks were enslaved. More than 8 in 10 of the blacks in New York (81.9%) and New Jersey (80.2%) were enslaved in 1790. More than half (51.1%) the blacks in Connecticut and about 1-in-5 of the blacks in New Hampshire (19.9%) and Rhode Island (21.6%) also were enslaved.

The largest number of blacks in 1790 labeled "other free persons," following the language of the U.S. Constitution, were in Virginia, but they amounted to only 1.7 percent of the state's population. In contrast, nearly 4 in 10 (39.1%) of Virginia's approximately 750,000 residents were enslaved blacks. South Carolina led the nation, with more than 4 in 10 (43.0%) of its population being enslaved blacks in 1790. Like Virginia, fewer than 1 in 50 (1.7%) of its blacks were not enslaved. Overall, only about 8 in 100 (7.9%) of the approximately 750,000 blacks counted in the 1790 U.S. Census were free of slavery.

Blacks in Massachusetts had the distinction in 1790 of living in the only state listing all its blacks as free persons. The Bay State's neighboring territory of Maine and the territory of Vermont also listed all their resident blacks as free. Together the blacks in those three areas amounted to about 1 in 9 (10.5%) of all unenslaved blacks then in the nation, but fewer than 1 in 100 (0.9%) of all blacks. Indeed, the relatively few blacks in Massachusetts and its New England sisters buoyed protest against slavery there even while wedging few openings against segregation.

The relative decrease in black population north of Maryland and its relative increase south of Pennsylvania grew in national significance and in meaningful differences in black life. The divide that traditionally marked the Pennsylvania–Maryland border came to be called the Mason–Dixon Line. Blacks north of the divide were becoming increasingly unshackled as the 1700s closed, although they remained in the shadow of slavery with segregation ruling their lives. South of the divide, the shackles of slavery tightened as the nation's black population grew from about 750,000 in 1790 to more than 4 million in 1860, with nearly 9 in 10 of those blacks being enslaved.

With the bulk of blacks in shackles, American Negro slavery dominated black life. Regardless of where they lived or what status they held, blacks everywhere in America in the 1700s had to feel the oppression of slavery. And for those in shackles, their slavery weighed on all they did. It forced

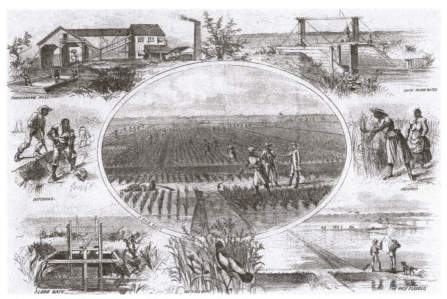

Blacks did all manner of labor in colonial America. They were the primary agricultural laborers, particularly in the South, and also mainstays among artisans and craftsmen. (Library of Congress)

work to take precedence over all else in their life, for from the perspective of slaveholders, the enslaved lived to work. From the perspective of the enslaved, work was what they did to live. They slaved to survive.

Early and late, enslaved blacks worked the land as did most people in North America, for agriculture was the leading economic sector until the early 1900s. Early generations of enslaved blacks almost everywhere engaged in the backbreaking, ground-clearing, earth-turning spadework of establishing viable settlements. And they continued such work throughout the 1700s and well in the 1800s as settlement moved westward from the Atlantic coast, laboring to transform the land from wilderness to ground readied for planting and producing crops. They bent to cutting back forests to clear land for planting and also to provide timber for framing and finishing buildings from forts to houses to barns to commercial structures in rough homesteads and towns. In many places they were the primary engines of development.

Blacks cultivated and produced crops and raised livestock, including beef, dairy and oxen cattle, horses, hogs, sheep, and poultry. Most of all, south of Pennsylvania they grew the plantation cash commodities of tobacco, rice, sugarcane, indigo, and cotton, as well as a variety of food and fiber crops such as wheat, corn, oats, flax, and hemp. But they toiled also in almost every line of labor, and the diversity of their work expanded with economic development. Typically, they carried few titles of craftsmanship or, if any, their titles customarily differed from whites doing the same or similar tasks. Black midwives, root doctors, and traditional healers often did the work of physicians. And they worked as assistants to white physicians and surgeons. They worked with artisans across the range of crafts and skills. Few, if any, type of smithy had no black practitioners. Pennsylvania's early iron industry employed enslaved blacks to a degree that ironmasters there in 1727 petitioned to import more slave labor to maintain and expand their iron smelters and forges.

Black craftsmen were prominent in American Negro slavery's urban regime. Indeed, few, if any, crafts existed in which no enslaved blacks worked, for holders early and often trained or acquired skilled black bondsmen to augment artisanal enterprises. Such blacks usually worked alongside their holders who were bakers, blacksmiths, boatmen, carpenters, cobblers, coopers, masons, silversmiths, wainwrights, and more. Frequently, too, they were jobbed or rented out by slaveholders. When examined in terms of who did the actual work rather than who got the credit or made the profit, enslaved blacks proved primary producers of much urban craftwork in many places in early America. And that relationship persisted for black labor in and out of slavery, although often obscured by an occupational hierarchy that had more to do with who appeared in charge than with knowledge of the work to be done or the skill in doing it—to say nothing, again, of who did the actual work.

Enslaved black craftsmen so challenged white artisans in colonial New York City in the early 1700s that the latter complained bitterly to the point that acting Governor George Clarke took up their petitions in the 1730s. "The artificers complain with too much reason of the pernicious custom of breeding slaves to trades," he reported to officials in London in 1737. "The honest and industrious tradesmen are reduced to poverty for want of employ. And many of them are forced into other countries," Clarke lamented (Davis 1985, 32).

Skilled blacks became objects of white animosity in many places, not merely in colonial times but down through American history. Competition for jobs hardened black–white segregation as white workingmen insisted on privileging their color to exclude blacks from worksites or, at least, to confine blacks to low-paying, low-status jobs. The antagonism heard against black artisans in colonial New York echoed especially in the urban regime of slavery prominent in colonial cities from Boston to Charleston. It long operated as a prominent feature of southern cities from Baltimore to Richmond to Charleston to Savannah and New Orleans. And it extended into the 20th century across America.

Competition for jobs and rank in workplaces long embittered black–white relations. Whites early and late insisted on distinguishing their labor and status from blacks. White indentured servants in the Chesapeake in the mid- and late 1600s illustrated the tendency, leaving fieldwork as the virtual province of blacks alone. And the tendency persisted from fields to factories. Not doing work blacks did became a badge of distinction for successive generations of European immigrants eager to claim whatever edge they could in advancing their life in America. Where they could corner labor markets or niches so as to exclude black labor, they did. Such segregation grew as a pronounced part of America's socioeconomic structures. It long relegated blacks to being low persons on the totem pole regardless of their abilities or aptitudes.

Enslaved black women were perhaps most prominent in slavery's urban regime. They did most of the domestic service in smaller holdings, busy with what was deemed women's work. They did everything imaginable to keep a household functioning. They were the labor-saving additions of the

Enslaved black women did multiple duties inside and outside households, from nursemaids to childcare, to cooking, cleaning, laundering, sewing, spinning, personal service, and field labor. (Library of Congress)

day for those who could afford them when almost every household task was a chore. In a world without indoor plumbing, electricity, or appliances, almost all that needed to be done to maintain a household had to be done from scratch, and in the gendered division of labor of the day, most of those tasks fell to females.

Little was simple: for example, water for food preparation and all other uses had to be hauled from neighborhood wells. Then there were all the other household tasks from laundry to garbage disposal to scrubbing and dusting to emptying chamber pots. There were spinning and weaving and sewing and more, including personal service from hair-dressing to wet nursing and other childcare. It was endless work, and as domestics almost always lived in the household where they slaved, they were almost always at the beck and call of their holder. At night some even slept outside their holder's bedroom so as to be ready if called for service.

Enslaved blacks in the urban regime typically were not simply units within a slaveholding; they were members of their holder's household. They tended to live in the same structure as their slaveholder or in an outbuilding. They usually had daily, extended, face-to-face contact with their holder and their holder's family. Theirs was an intimate setting. Personal and social distance existed, but little physical distance. Also as slaveholding marked a degree of wealth, enslaved blacks in the urban regime tended to live in the better households, indeed in some in the best, because of the correlation between wealth and slaveholding.

Relatively few enslaved blacks in the urban regime got to live together in family units. Most enslaved couples lived apart, with enslaved women in one holding with their children, while their mates lived in separate households. That occasioned not merely longing over separation but trouble as unrest flared where slaveholders refused or overly restricted black men's conjugal or familial visits. Such holders or constables faced resentful black men thwarted from visiting their mates. And black women prevented from seeing their mates were no less resentful. Thus, the prevalent pattern of slaveholding in the urban regime that separated slave mates provoked continual consternation and frustration. The situation was among the many that made black men on city streets at night suspect.

Young black men frequently appeared as threats away from their own household or workplace. Watchmen and constables everywhere were alert to the presence of black men individually and, particularly, in groups, frequently stopping them on the streets to check who they were and why they were where they were, day and night, especially. They were considered dangers in neighborhoods where they were not personally recognized. While the relative density of urban environments cloaked others with benefits of anonymity, black men frequently found relatively few places where they could be unnoticed and free from having to identify themselves. Where they were not immediately individually recognized, they were liable to be cast in the indistinct stereotype of the troublesome black male.

Records from early New York and other colonial cities and from slavery in antebellum southern cities showed the frequent policing of black males and the high disproportion of their arrests, jailings, and punishments for what whites considered being in the wrong place at the wrong time. Apprehensions about their behavior combined with objections to the labor competition they created to make black males, whether in slavery or out increasingly unwelcome in American cities, and their presence in the urban regime dwindled relatively over time.

For slaves on family farms, the homestead was their hub. For most enslaved blacks, in fact, their hub was their workplace as their daily and seasonal activities centered on their work. And in small holdings, whatever their locale, work included the dynamic of more direct and frequent interaction between slaves and slaveholders, for small holdings tended to collapse the space between enslavers and enslaved, blacks and whites. Also it collapsed the space enslaved blacks had to themselves. The close space exposed them more immediately to white dictates and directions and prompted them to learn the patterns and patois of the dominant culture of the household where they slaved. Their speech and manners reflected the lessened distance, as the greater distance between enslaved blacks who worked and lived in large holdings remote from large numbers of whites fostered stronger persistence of autonomous black patterns of acting and speaking.

The Gullah and Geechee of the coastal plains and sea islands of South Carolina, Georgia, and Florida perhaps best illustrated blacks persisting with their own customs. They spoke their own language—a creole vernacular mixing English they heard from whites with vocabulary, syntax, and grammar from African languages. Their beliefs, customs, foods, cooking and eating patterns, crafts, and much else resembled those in West and Central Africa.

Work dominated slave life, whatever the regime. Yet learning to negotiate slavery meant more than learning about work. Captive blacks landed directly from Africa almost always arrived old enough to be put directly to work. What they were put to do often required training but not always, for blacks did not arrive on American shores ignorant. Few were babes. They arrived with cultural identities and intelligence, and with practical lessons. Most came from agricultural societies. They knew crops and cattle. They knew rice, other grains, and tobacco, for example. Indeed, many were imported for skills they possessed.

Rice planters in South Carolina learned early to appreciate the expertise of rice growers from Africa and sought to import blacks from rice-growing areas. Indeed, South Carolina shared similar climate and natural features with the lowland plains of coastal West Africa between the Niger and Volta Rivers. The peoples there were experienced with the crop white South Carolinians hoped to make their staple, and so they paid a premium for such peoples in the slave traffic.

Also the slave traffic brought to North America from the West Indies captive blacks who had undergone a process called "seasoning." The term arose from the process some slavers used to make captives appear more profitable by cleaning and oiling their bodies for presentation at market. "Seasoning" was also called "breaking in," as it was a process of disciplining captives, suppressing their resistance and building their obedience to commands. Slaveholders and overseers viewed the process as akin to training horses or other domestic animals as it accustomed captives to the demands and routines of slavery.

Captives were to learn to submit to white authority and comply with whatever was required of them. Their learning often began with their naming, for slaveholders often presumed to name their slaves, identifying what they considered their property; and they used names to segregate blacks, distinguishing them with names not commonly used for whites. The names blacks may have answered to at their slaveholders' call was not, however, the only names they carried. Many used their own names among themselves, as famously illustrated in the battle of the African who insisted on his name "Kunta Kinte" rather than "Toby," as his slaveholder insisted on calling him in Alex Haley's 1976 epic *Roots: The Saga of an American Family*. Calling himself by whatever he chose asserted an independence.

Classical and place names dominated among names of slaves in colonial New York in the mid-1700s. A list of blacks jailed in the early 1740s illustrated the pattern among black males. Among common classical names were Caesar, Cato, Othello, Pompey, and Scipio. Among place names were Albany, Bridgewater, Burlington, Curacoa Dick, Cambridge, Dundee, Dublin, Galloway, Hanover, Jamaica, London, Scotland, and York. Jupiter and Mars made appearances also.

Some names appeared for characteristics such as Brash, Fortune, and Venture. Spanish blacks appeared to retain Spanish names such as Antonio, Diego, Emanuel, Juan, Pablo, and Pedro. Also enslaved black men carried diminutives or shortened forms of common English names such as Ben, Bill, Dick, Frank, Jack, Tom, or Will. Diminutives appeared also in names for enslaved black females such as Lizzie or Sally. The naming pattern suggests more emphasis on distinguishing black men from white men rather than in distinguishing black women from white women.

African names also appeared perhaps most prominently in the persistence of the Akan day-naming pattern common in West Africa. Variants such as

Cudjoe (Monday), Kobe and Kobi (Tuesday), Quaco (Wednesday), Kwaw and Aba (Thursday), Cuffe, Cuffy, and Kofi (Friday), Quame and Quamina (Saturday), and Kwesi and Quashie (Sunday) dotted lists of blacks in colonial and later America.

Whatever their names, enslaved blacks were called to work. The pattern of their activity differed by time and place and by the requirements and whims of their slaveholders. Except in the most general terms, no single standard stretched across North America over the centuries. The day-to-day content of slaving shifted, as did the site and the slaveholder. Yet whatever the workplace was remained crucial, for it was where most slaves developed their closest contacts and adopted their work habits, where they learned what to do and what not to do and when; it was where they publicly displayed their daily attitudes and behaviors. It was the main place to display their public face.

Their work identified slaves in many ways, as it classified, distinguished, and in some cases associated or isolated them. Their work connected and disconnected them from their fellow blacks and also from whites. It influenced how long, where, with whom, and how they lived; it influenced how, when, and where they formed communities, families, and societies. It molded attitudes with both rewards and resentments, shaping aspects of individual and group character and creating conditions for personal and cultural developments. Few, if any, aspects of their life escaped the reach of their work, as for many work constituted their life from sunup to sundown, from can-see-to-can't-see.

What they produced determined most of the work enslaved blacks did. The details differed by place and time, but several general regimes described most slave labor in North America, and those turned on the dominant crop. Tobacco, rice, and sugarcane grew to lead all cash crops by 1750. Production of each had undergone something of revolution from the mid-1600s to the mid-1700s: tobacco in the Chesapeake, rice in the Carolina Lowcountry, and sugarcane in Louisiana. Their rising market demand drove slavery, propelling an ever-more expansive plantation regime to rule black life and setting the stage for the ascendancy of "King Cotton" in the 1800s.

Yet life for enslaved blacks was more than a commercial production; it was also a cultural production. It was a negotiation that extended Atlantic World cultural exchanges in the works since the late 1400s when Portugal led Europe's expansion to Africa's Atlantic coast. European contact triggered transformation in Africa, and the African peoples trafficked to the Americas over more than 400 years became carriers and creators of transformation. They became the forebears of new peoples and cultures emerging in North America. In the 1600s and 1700s they were peoples of many languages. They came speaking in a variety of tongues, and in the Americas they became speakers of whatever languages were spoken where they were as they came to understand and make themselves understood in the languages of their enslavers. They added to the polyglot, speaking Dutch, English, French, Spanish, Portuguese, and native African languages. They developed various pidgins, mixing tongues to create common languages to communicate at least basic ideas with speakers of diverse languages.

And as with language, blacks learned to integrate themselves into developing North American societies, extending their lives in families and communities and in striving for recognition of their identities and respect for their autonomy. They extended their labors to work against slavery and segregation and the degrading, dehumanizing stereotypes that sought to make them outcasts in what was increasingly the land of their birth.

## PROFILE: FODIO (1688–1749)

Memorialized with a headstone at her segregated gravesite a bit more than a mile north and west of the main harbor in New London, Connecticut, the woman whose name was Fodio has lain as a symbol of millions snatched from Africa to the Americas in the transatlantic slave trade. She arrived in bondage between 1700 and 1710 in an area that in light of harsh sectional struggles leading to the Civil War worked to scrub away marks and memories of the American Negro slavery it maintained in its colonial and early national years.

She was bought for training as a luxury appliance, as something to ease the household drudgery of her merchant slaveholder's wife, for her lot was time-consuming domestic tasks that were woman's work. Her slaveholders called her by other names but she preferred her own—Fodio, with its reach to her African birthplace. The name pointed to the Hausa area of West Africa and the ethnic Fula, sometimes called Fulani. Islam's inroad in the area accounted for the name *Fodio* arising from a family name for a jurist, called *fuwdi* in Arabic. Fodio appeared to cling to that as her own, and perhaps privately to Islam itself, as also she clung to her husband called "Hercules." Only through him did memory of her linger, for she was buried with a marker reading simply "In Memory of Fodio Hercules Wife of Hercules Governour of the Negroes." His honor as the local black community leader raised her to notice from the dark shadows of forgotten memory where were lost millions of her black sisters in America.

## REFERENCES

Davis, Thomas J. 1984. "'These Enemies of Their Own Household': A Note on the Troublesome Slave Population in Eighteenth Century New York City." *Journal of the Afro-American Historical and Genealogical Society* 5, nos. 3 & 4 (fall and winter):133–147.

Davis, Thomas J. 1985. *A Rumor of Revolt: The "Great Negro Plot" in Colonial New York*. New York: Free Press.
Lemon, James T. 1987. "Colonial America in the Eighteenth Century." In *North America: The Historical Geography of a Changing Continent*, ed. Robert D. Mitchell and Paul A. Groves, 121–146. Totowa, NJ: Rowman & Littlefield.

# Chapter 4

# Strike a Blow and Steal Away

Blacks resisted being enslaved from the outset proving themselves anything but docile. They responded to slave catchers in Africa with fight and flight. In coffles marched in chains and penned for shipping and then as human cargoes, some embraced death rather than being enslaved. Particularly as slave catchers moved deeper into Africa's interior, captives recognized their trek to the sea as a death march. At least one in four captives by the 1790s died in coffles on the way to the coast. At times the death toll reached half or more. Crossing the ocean was also deadly. Shipboard riots added to the toll of abominable conditions on the so-called Middle Passage. And although sick, starved, and weak when landed in the Americas, many remained recalcitrant. The brutality of the so-called seasoning process for "outlandish" blacks—as imports were called, particularly if they entered directly from Africa—attested to blacks' refusal to submit meekly to capture and forced labor. Such behavior developed into a legacy that cast blacks as defiant, insubordinate, obstinate, and stubborn.

Enslaved blacks provoked slaveholders to complain incessantly about blacks' refusing to work and, especially, about slaves' absenting themselves from work. If forced labor was slavery's primary substance, then refusing to labor was slaves' primary resistance, and its most common and dramatic form emerged in slaves' flight. Runaways were a common phenomenon throughout the Americas as flight was blacks' most public and regular act of rejecting slavery. Captivity created their condition; escape released them. If property they were, they resorted to stealing themselves, reclaiming their persons for themselves.

Runaways among the first generation of captive Africans provoked anxieties as the relatively sparse population of early America allowed blacks to escape into unsettled areas. Refuge loomed in remote spaces such as the

Great Dismal Swamp, stretching in the marshy coastal plain from southeastern Virginia into what would become northeastern North Carolina. Black runaways early established maroon communities there that became the stuff of legend, but black refugee communities enjoyed at best fleeting success in North America, unlike in the Caribbean and South America where they persisted for multiple generations as independent settlements. Borderland areas in North America allowed fugitive slaves some extended success—not so much as maroons but as adoptees among Native Americans. Blacks in the colonial South eyed escape into Spanish Florida, for example. The Muscogee Creek who dominated the southeast from what would become North Carolina to Florida and into Alabama harbored runaways, and the Seminole in northern Florida became noted for incorporating black fugitives.

The areas and avenues for black maroonage closed, however, as white settlement pushed west and south. Yet increasing settlement also brought increasing numbers of blacks that increased chances of escape by blending into a blackening background. The more blacks there were, the less blacks stood out. Particularly by the end of the 1700s, as areas above Maryland gradually released blacks from slavery, fugitives gained a wider area for escape as they could hide among blacks living free in states turning away from slavery.

Not all runaways headed for permanent escape. Their rebellion had less long-term goals. Some simply fled for a break from drudgery. Absenting

Aside from day-to-day defiance, fleeing was the most persistent and effective resistance to American Negro slavery. Stealing themselves in a flight to freedom, hundreds of thousands of enslaved blacks liberated themselves over the years. (Library of Congress)

themselves for a few days, they were more truants than escapees and turned themselves in after their break. Some truants ran not for a break but for a reunion. Separated from loved ones, they dashed off for forbidden visits. They were more absent without leave than truants. Closest to escapees were so-called outliers who fled hoping for escape but finding no way to reach refuge lingered in the local area as long as they could before recapture.

Black males between 15 and 30 years of age proved over time most likely to run away. Indeed, they were the most likely suspects whatever the misbehavior. They also were the most prone to violence, and it was violence, even more than the volume of runaways, that most worried slaveholders and governmental authorities from slavery's beginning to end. Worries heightened particularly at times of larger political and social discontent, for many whites worried that blacks would collaborate with their enemies. The reality of such concerns showed early in colonial America when blacks eagerly took up arms in Virginia in 1675–1676, when blacks joined with upstart planter Nathaniel Bacon to set fire to the colonial capital at Jamestown and send Gov. William Berkeley fleeing in September 1676. But the governor also enlisted blacks with promises of freedom, and he prevailed with a contingent of English troops dispatched to quell the rebels. No count appeared of the number of blacks on either or both sides who won their release from slavery in Bacon's Rebellion, but the numbers who rallied were enough to demonstrate blacks' readiness to fight for freedom.

Black rebels differed in their plans and paths. Some were painstaking in devising detail over months or longer with goals of attacking and escaping slavery. Perhaps less cautious, others were more ready to attack immediately and destroy as much as they could with hope of escaping slavery but with no set plan to achieve that goal. Others rose on impulse, seizing a situation to vent their frustration: they had no plan or clear goal other than doing as much damage as they could, retaliating as best they could by inflicting on their enslavers whatever pain and suffering they could. They did what they could with what they had at hand, willing for the moment to suffer the consequences of venting their impulses.

Blacks in arms or suspected of plotting violence in the 1700s repeatedly struck terror in communities from New York to the fresh colony of Georgia. Slaves growing into a black majority made South Carolina especially a repeated scene of insurrection anxiety. In 1700, for example, authorities there crushed a plot among enslaved blacks and Indians. In September 1702 the Carolina assembly heard testimony about a reported black plotter "threatening that he and other negroes would Rise and Cutt off the Inhabitants of this Province" (Aptheker 1963, 168).

Fears hit north of the Carolinas in 1709 where "greater numbers of ye said negroes and Indian slaves," according to a colonial Virginia special court of investigation were "concerned in a Late Dangerous Conspiracy . . . for making their Escape by force from ye Service of their masters, and for ye Destroying and cutting off Such of her Majesties Subjects as Should oppose their Design." While discovered in 1709, the plot was not completely crushed, for in April 1710 officials in Surry and James City counties continued to report on plotters planning an Easter Sunday attack (Aptheker 1963, 169–170).

Black insurgence was hardly confined to the South. Early in the 1700s, the New York assembly publicly lamented that "the Number of slaves in the City of New York and Albany, and also in other Towns within this Province, doth daily increase" and "have been found oftentimes guilty of Confederating together in running away, or other ill practices." Enslaved blacks' behavior on Long Island prompted New York Royal Governor Edward Hyde, Lord Cornbury, to issue a proclamation in July 1706 warning "that several negroes in Kings County have assembled themselves in a riotous manner" (New York 1894, 1: 519–520).

Cornbury authorized local authorities to arrest blacks if there were "reason to suspect them of ill practices or designs," and he further authorized that "if any of them refused to submit themselves, then to fire on them, kill, or destroy them." Blood in Long Island streets in February 1708 proved the reasons for official worry. Enslaved blacks and Indians, men and women, rose up to kill seven whites in Queens County's Newtown, stretching between the East River and Flushing River. Authorities burned at the stake a black woman and hanged two black men and one Indian man for their rebellion. But the episode proved only a prelude (Ostrander 1894, 1: 171–172).

The most notable black uprising at the opening of the 1700s occurred across from Long Island in Manhattan, which was then the whole of New York City. Early in April 1712 slaves "put us into no small consternation the whole Town being under Arms," a contemporary reported to Boston's *Weekly-Newsletter*. The insurgents numbered more than two dozen. The bulk were identified as fresh captives from West Africa called "Coromantees" because they were shipped from Fort Kormantine on the Gold Coast region of what would become the late 20th-century nation of Ghana. The core were young male Ashanti-speakers, whose rites of manhood introduced them to warrior culture. They were ready to fight and to die rather than to continue enslaved. And they were not alone. Blacks called "Spanish Negroes" because of their names and capture aboard Spanish ships joined the plot, as did enslaved Indians. The insurgents included women too.

For at least three months, the New York blacks planned their 1712 uprising, reportedly "tying themselves to secrecy by Sucking ye blood of each

Others hand." Organized to attack and destroy as much as they could, they set fires to several outbuildings just after midnight on April 6 and lay in ambush, armed with pistols, knives, clubs, and axes. They pounced on white townsmen as they responded to the blaze, killing 8 on the spot and critically wounding at least 12 others. The fighting and fire alarmed New York Royal Governor Robert Hunter enough for him to dispatch troops from his seat at nearby Fort George and to fire cannon to rally townsmen to defense (Aptheker 1963, 172–173).

Their surprise ended with the alarm sounded against them, the black insurgents fled northward to the Harlem woods. The dark of night covered their flight, but daylight brought white vengeance. Militia joined royal troops in a dragnet that reached northward into Westchester and widened to question hundreds of blacks. "Tis feared that most of the Negro's here (who are very numerous) knew of the Late Conspiracy to murder the Christians," a townsman reported (Davis 1985, 54–55).

At least 70 slaves languished in city jail by the closing weeks of April. Prosecutions condemned 27, and 19 faced whites' wrath in execution, with what one witness described as "the most exemplary punishment inflicted that could be possibly thought of." Perhaps most horrific, one black suffered whipping and then was chained to starve in public, lingering for three days before dying. Another black man died while being roasted for 8 to 10 hours over slow fire. Two burned at the stake. Fourteen other slaves were hanged (Aptheker 1963, 173; Davis 1985, 55).

Memory of the 1712 mayhem long haunted New Yorkers. And not them alone. News of the death and destruction swept the colonies as the April events and aftermath circulated from Boston to Charleston, adding to anxieties among whites about blacks' growing number and disposition, which exposed a dilemma for some, a predicament for others. The economic benefits of enslaving blacks were undeniable in the wealth they produced as laborers and as commodities. No small part of New York commerce reached to Africa as it joined Boston and Newport as major North American slaving ports. But making money from black bodies reduced little, if any, mistrust of blacks. Suspicions of misbehavior lurked wherever blacks appeared in number, and they were appearing in ever larger numbers with growing profits from slavery throughout colonial America.

Tensions only grew as the 1700s unfolded with the enslaved continuing to rebel. Their plans to free themselves from slavery by raining death and destruction on whites incited notable scares in Virginia in 1722, Pennsylvania in 1734, and Maryland in 1739. And the alarms they triggered spread beyond British North America, as shown in French Louisiana in 1730. But nowhere in North America did blacks occasion more alarm and anxiety than in South Carolina. Throughout the 1720s and 1730s and into the 1740s, the growing black majority in South Carolina put whites in continual panic with plots and outbursts of violence.

The most spectacular slave rebellion in colonial North America erupted in South Carolina in September 1739. The core in South Carolina was described as "Angolan," as the core of black rebels in 1712 New York was described as Coromantees. About 20 followed a leader some called "Jemmy" and others "Cato" to seize pistols, muskets, powder, shot, and other weapons from a store off the tidal channel called the Stono River south of Charleston. So armed, the band marched southward, reportedly headed for St. Augustine in Spanish Florida, 300 miles away. They set off beating at least two drums and flying banners in files, suggesting some sense of military experience. They tripled their number as other blacks rallied to the marchers shouting "Liberty!" They torched seven plantations in their progress and killed at least two dozen whites. Along the way, the Stono rebels sent scurrying South Carolina Lieutenant Governor William Bull and a mounted party of a half dozen or so who unexpectedly came upon the group.

Bull's startled party scampered to muster local planters and militia. Their efforts took a day. But on September 11 about 100 heavily armed local whites and militia caught up with the rebels, then numbering perhaps 80, at the North Edisto River about 25 miles south of the Stono. The rebels acquitted themselves well, displaying military savvy and discipline. Although heavily outgunned and wholly disadvantaged against the mounted whites, the blacks fought to a standoff. They killed at least 20 whites but suffered heavy casualties themselves, losing about half their number. Retreating from the battle, surviving rebels scattered and a cadre continued southward for almost a week before trailing militia converged to rout them. Most of the rebel remnant were killed in battle or executed, although a captured few were sold into exile in the West Indies.

The audacity of the Stono rebels elicited more than retaliation. After their first encounter with rebels on September 11, whites decapitated captured blacks and mounted the severed heads upon stakes to point up their view of what black rebels should expect. Whites wanted all blacks on notice not to think escaping slavery possible. Governor Bull offered bounties to local Indians, mainly Chickasaw and Catawba, to hunt scattered rebels, and the South Carolina legislature overhauled its slave code in May 1740, mandating stricter controls on blacks whether enslaved or not. Its neighbors followed suit.

Events in New York City in 1741 soon again bared the continual tension rebellious blacks created as a series of eight fires in 10 days terrified many. The conflagrations began in mid-March with a spectacular blaze that burned much of the colonial capital at Fort George. Suspicion fell on slaves for setting the fires. In fact, authorities fingered Quack, the frustrated husband of the governor's cook, for setting the blaze at the fort out of resentment at being banned from visiting his wife. Further investigations and prosecutions that stretched into August exposed many blacks' seething anger and much of a dark side of slavery to which many preferred to turn blind eyes so as not to see the social disorder and danger enslaving blacks created. Hysteria engendered a witch hunt that left 13 blacks burned at the stake and 17 blacks and 4 whites hanged.

The episode sparked argument about the increasing number of blacks in New York City and particularly about the rapid rise of black males between 15 and 30 years old, consistently identified as the most dangerous and difficult to control. And changes followed, not only in stricter surveillance of blacks but in a lull in importing slaves. It proved momentary in South Carolina as planters soon shook off what one contemporary described as "the great risque we run" in enslaving so many blacks. But it proved more significant in New York, where in a decided turn the city moved away from increasing the number of black males and toward a more female-dominated domestic slavery (Wax 1982, 136; Davis 1984, 133).

More changes were coming with King George's War (1739–1748), the French and Indian War (1754–1763), and the War for U.S. Independence (1775–1783), which proved pivotal in the life of many blacks in America, for in the fighting they found fresh opportunities—as would repeatedly prove true throughout American history. Little better illustrated such opportunities than the War for Independence. In the battle of arms and of ideas, thousands of blacks seized their chances to end slavery. They early exploited the revolutionary rhetoric of republican liberalism based on individual rights spouted by those styled "Patriots" to advance their incongruous position, pushing for their own liberty and self-determination. Notably blacks in Massachusetts issued four petitions between January 1773 and January 1777 to press their case against slavery and segregation (Davis 1989, 248–263).

Blacks did much more than petition. Crispus Attucks was famously among the five hailed as martyrs in the March 1770 incident called "the Boston Massacre," which radicals propagandized as a display of British troops' brutal policing of Americans. And when the war commenced, blacks joined the ranks. Peter Salem and Salem Poor distinguished themselves in June 1775 at the Battle of Bunker Hill, and tens of thousands of other blacks joined them in shouldering arms. Further, as they had 100 years earlier in Bacon's Rebellion, blacks rallied to both sides from 1775 to 1783, joining where they saw their best chance to liberate themselves.

Blacks joined in the failed British assault on Hampton Roads in late October 1775, the first of the War for Independence's battles south of Massachusetts. Indeed, thousands joined the British to free themselves from their colonial American enslavers. Virginia's Royal Governor John Murray, Earl of Dunmore, exhorted blacks to his side in November 1775 with the promise of emancipation. In what became known as Lord Dunmore's Proclamation, the governor declared "all indented Servants, Negroes, or others (appertaining to Rebels) free that are able and willing to bear Arms, they joining His Majesty's Troops as soon as may be" (Holton 1997, 183).

In a sequence foreshadowing a proclamation of emancipation fourscore-and-eight years later, Dunmore had threatened rebels with losing their slaves if they refused to "return to a proper sense of Duty, to His Majesty's Crown and Dignity." That hint of promised emancipation drew enslaved blacks to the British, and on the issuing of the proclamation, thousands joined. Mustered into what was dubbed "Dunmore's Ethiopian Regiment," blacks with the words "LIBERTY TO SLAVES" emblazoned across their uniformed chests did battle alongside loyalists and British troops.

When the fight was in the offing, white Patriots under fire welcomed blacks willing to expose life and limb along with them. Thus, Prince Estabrook suffered wounds with the Minutemen at Lexington in April 1775, when flew "the shot heard 'round the world." Similarly, at Bunker Hill in June 1775 blacks such as Alexander Ames, Seymour Burr, Titus Coburn, Blaney Grusha, Cato Howe, and Barzillai Lew manned the earthworks and trenches of Breed's Hill against the British, even while the Massachusetts Committee of Safety in May 1775 had declared that "no slaves be admitted into this army upon any consideration what ever." Patriot commander George Washington in July 1775 banned blacks from enlisting in the Continental Army. Only reluctantly did Patriot forces officially open their ranks to blacks.

Yielding to both logistics and ideology, the self-proclaimed independent new states and, in time, the Continental Army itself not simply enlisted but recruited blacks to serve their cause as military necessity trumped racial exclusion. In October 1780 Maryland became the largest slaveholding state to enlist bondsmen in the Patriot cause. North Carolina also mustered blacks in its Continental Line. New York—a slaveholding state then rivaling Georgia and still largely in the grip of loyal forces—in March 1781 also moved to recruit slaves to its rebel forces. The major slaveholding states of Virginia and South Carolina persisted in refusing to enlist blacks, preferring them only as slaves: in fact, they used slaves as bounties, promising to pay them out to white recruits.

With or without official sanction, at least 10,000 blacks joined in the war as soldiers, sailors, spies, couriers, guides, and more. And they fought their own war in spots, unattached or only loosely attached to either the rebel Americans or the British and loyalists. The escaped slave titled "Colonel Tye" became perhaps the most notorious of black revolutionary guerrillas. He led a contingent known as "the Black Brigade" on raids in central Jersey and along Jersey's Atlantic shore and helped defend the British position at the Battle of Monmouth in June 1778. On Tye's death shortly after being wounded in September 1780, the Black Brigade merged into the Black Company of Pioneers, an offshoot of the Ethiopian Regiment that served in British General Henry Clinton's command up and down the Atlantic coast from New York to Charleston.

Seizing the opportunity at hand, blacks throughout British North America made the War for Independence the largest armed black campaign for liberty in America before the Civil War. They were rebels in their own right fighting for their lives, their freedom, and their posterity. By the tens of thousands, blacks reveled in achieving a fresh life from formal emancipation or simple escape in the revolutionary fighting. And what they did on and off the battlefields, in arms, in flight, and in protest had immediate and continuing effects.

Joining in rebel cries for "Liberty," blacks continually pointed up the glaring inconsistency of slavery among people adhering to principles announced in the 1776 Declaration of Independence. The incongruity bore most immediate fruit in New England as the handful of blacks in Vermont could in 1777 boast of living in the first American republic to outlaw slavery in its fundamental law. In Massachusetts, New Hampshire, Connecticut, and Rhode Island, blacks petitioned and sued to end slavery and pointed also to the new states' constitutions as a basis for their freedom.

While most of the documents of the era carried men's names, black women were fully engaged as rebels for liberty—as they were from the first and would be to the last. Elizabeth Freeman, as she came to call herself, illustrated black women's striving in the forefront of liberty. Many in western Massachusetts preferred to call her "Bett," "Mum Bett," or "Mumbet." She was by all accounts a no-nonsense woman who worked without servility. If she was a slave, it was by title not by temperament. And after Massachusetts adopted its Bill of Rights in 1780, she joined in a series of freedom suits that led in August 1781 to the case of *Brom and Bett v. Ashley*.

Bett's case in the Berkshire County Inferior Court of Common Pleas set her free and also set the stage for Quock Walker's Massachusetts suits from 1781 to 1783 that won not only his freedom from slavery but that of others throughout the state as it fixed as a point of law in America a precedent set in England's Court of King's Bench in 1772 in *Somerset v. Stewart*. William Murray, England's Lord Chief Justice Mansfield, ruled there that without a specific statute sanctioning it, slavery was illegal. So in *Walker v. Jennison* in 1783 Bay State Supreme Judicial Court Chief Justice William Cushing noted that no legislation had ever established slavery in Massachusetts. Further, Cushing echoed the decision in Bett's case in ruling that the 1780 state Bill of Rights providing "that all men are born free and equal—and that every subject is entitled to liberty" made "the idea of slavery . . . inconsistent with our conduct and Constitution" (Massachusetts 1783).

Blacks in Pennsylvania witnessed the first direct legislation against slavery in the United States with the March 1780 "Act for the Gradual Abolition of Slavery." It was not, however, a true abolition act in the sense of instantly eradicating slavery. Rather, it aimed to end slavery over time by letting it die out as slaves died off. To that end it closed Pennsylvania to new slaves, shutting off importation, and it stopped natural increase by reversing the slave-by-birth rule of *partus sequitur ventrem*. Enslaved mothers in Pennsylvania could then rejoice that their children born in the state on or after November 1, 1780, would no longer be born in slavery. But the act also muted such joy, for it declared children of enslaved mothers, although born free, bound to serve their mother's holder until age 28 years.

Despite its promise for future generations, Pennsylvania's 1780 act hardly heartened blacks. For while reaching to the future, it left the present untouched as it released no slave from bondage. Blacks then enslaved were to remain enslaved. Moreover, the act brought backlash from disgruntled slaveholders who resisted what they viewed as interference with their rights. To recoup what they saw as their due, some such slaveholders resorted to shipping pregnant slaves to places outside Pennsylvania where children could be born slaves. And some sold mothers, too, as fertile black women fetched better prices in places where not only they but their offspring could be enslaved for life. Some Pennsylvania holders sought to sell their entire slaveholding outside the state. Thus, the 1780 act set off a boom in domestic slave-trading that put blacks even more on edge (Nash and Soderlund 1991, 194–206).

Blacks in Rhode Island had a flash of hope of something better than Pennsylvania had provided in 1780. The Ocean State in 1784 provided an act for actual "manumission" rather than simply for "gradual abolition." Moving not simply to wait for slaves to die off, it encouraged their immediate release. Indeed, the assembly accepted the cost of supporting emancipated blacks. The state's relatively small number of slaves lessened any public burden, for Rhode Island in the 1780s had only a bit more than half Pennsylvania's 6,000 slaves. Yet proportionally, the 3,300 blacks in Rhode Island were almost 5 percent of the state's population compared with 1.5 percent in Pennsylvania. Still white voters in Rhode Island rebelled against accepting any cost to release blacks from slavery. In October 1785, voters repealed the 1784 provisions beyond abolishing *partus sequitur ventrem*.

Also in Connecticut blacks found no public will to act boldly against slavery. It, too, abolished *partus sequitur ventrem* but went further only to encourage manumission by removing both public and private liability to support former slaves. Throughout what came to be called the "First

Emancipation," blacks witnessed whites' resistance to making blacks special public beneficiaries, as they viewed it. For many whites then and long after, blacks' condition in or out of slavery was a private matter to be handled by private action, not by public policy and certainly not at public expense.

Blacks' difficulties in securing public action to end slavery showed most clearly in New York, home of the largest slave population north of Maryland during the revolutionary era. Businesses and households throughout the state relied on enslaved blacks. Manhattan alone held more than 2,000 slaves and would account in 1790 for a bit more than 1 in 10 (11.2%) of the state's enslaved population. The Long Island counties of Kings, Queens, Nassau, and Suffolk held almost another quarter (23.1%) of the state's slaves. The core of New York's slaveholding lay, however, along the Hudson Valley: the counties of Westchester, Dutchess, Columbia, Ulster, and Albany held 11,500 slaves, a bit more than half (54.5%) of the state's total in the 1780s. In key places then, strong economic interests weighed against losing slaves as investments and as laborers.

Yet forces were at work against slavery in New York. Perhaps the most powerful force was growing waves of European immigrants that between the 1780s and 1800 enlarged the population of the state (72.3%) and city (82.7%). Many whites fresh to New York's shores swarmed against slavery and blacks in general, bristling for their jobs. Somewhat ironically then, black New Yorkers witnessed many who meant them no good advancing their cause against slavery while also pushing to exclude blacks altogether wherever they could. Antislavery efforts succeeded in March 1799 to pass an act providing for children to be born free after July 4, 1799, but binding them to serve their mother's slaveholder until age 25 years if female and 28 years if male.

Blacks saw the First Emancipation end with New Jersey's providing for free birth after July 4, 1804, and reducing the age of service to age 21 years for females and 25 years for males. That was hardly the end of slavery for which blacks hoped. Distant release from bondage could only have limited appeal, and for those destined to die as slaves, it could have no appeal. Letting slavery die out by letting slaves die off was not what blacks had hoped for from the American Revolution. Hearing from others or even seeing gains blacks had made changed little. If a revolution had changed America, blacks saw that it had not changed enough to alter their position. Instructed to wait for a better day, they had more work ahead.

## PROFILE: PHILLIS WHEATLEY (CA. 1753–1784)

Hailed as the first published black female poet in America, Phillis Wheatley was born in West Africa around 1753 and snatched into slavery. Taken when she was about seven years old, she was one of millions from Africa whose birthname and birthplace became lost memories. Merchant John Wheatley bought her in Boston in 1761 and named her "Phillis"—the name of the slave ship on which the child had arrived in Massachusetts. Quick and pleasant, the child endeared herself to her slaveholders. Wheatley's teenage daughter Mary virtually adopted Phillis as her protégé and experimented with the child's abilities to learn, fascinated by her brightness. Soon reading and writing under Mary's tutoring, Phillis progressed as an avid reader and became something of a novelty at home and away, where the Wheatleys displayed her as a shining example of the capacity of her race and of the Wheatleys progressive philanthropy. Advancing to read Greek and Latin classics, such as works by Homer, Horace, and Virgil, Phillis also read more recent English writers, such as John Milton and Alexander Pope. Their poetry particularly attracted her, as did the rhyme and rhythm of the King James Bible.

At 14 Phillis produced her own verse, a poem titled "To the University of Cambridge, in New England," paying notice to Harvard. Gifted as she was, she became a curiosity at home and abroad. People wanted to see for themselves whether she truly was as intelligent as she was touted as being. Taken to London, she impressed the city mayor and was invited for an audience with King George III, having praised him in a 1768 poem, "To the King's Most Excellent Majesty." She also wrote a 1775 poem of praise titled "To His Excellency, George Washington," and visited with Washington in Cambridge when the War for U.S. Independence brought him to the Boston area.

Among Phillis's most noted poems was "On Being Brought from Africa to America," which sounded a note of gratitude but also carried a note of criticism. "Twas mercy brought me from my Pagan land/Taught my benighted soul to understand/There's a God, that there's a Savior too," she wrote in her characteristic iambic meter with couplets rhyming aabbccdd. "Remember, Christians, Negroes, Black as Cain,/May be refin'd, and join th' angelic train," she closed in illustrating her oft-repeated themes of Christian, classical, and biblical reference. She there also referenced her own success as a note on the potential of her fellow blacks and as a caution on Christian duty.

Her 1773 book published in London as *Poems on Various Subjects, Religious and Moral* by Phillis Wheatley, "Negro servant to Mr. John Wheatley, of Boston, in New England," displayed her talents and themes. But life turned hard for her as her patrons, John and Mary Wheatley died. John's will freed Phillis but she lost the shelter the merchant's wealth had provided. She married black grocer John Peters but struggled in poverty, particularly after her husband's imprisonment for debt in 1784. She bore two children and died at 31 in childbirth with the third, a son who lived barely four hours. Her legacy was her challenge to the stereotype of Africans not only as ignorant but as incapable of intellectual refinement.

## REFERENCES

Aptheker, Herbert. 1963. *American Negro Slave Revolts*. New York: International Publishers.

Davis, Thomas J. 1984. "'These Enemies of Their Own Household': A Note on the Troublesome Slave Population in Eighteenth Century New York." *Journal of the Afro-American Historical and Genealogical Society* 5, no. 3–4 (fall and winter): 133–147.

Davis, Thomas J. 1985. *A Rumor of Revolt: The "Great Negro Plot" in Colonial New York*. New York: Free Press.

Davis, Thomas J. 1989. "Emancipation Rhetoric, Natural Rights, and Revolutionary New England: A Note on Four Black Petitions in Massachusetts, 1773–1777." *New England Quarterly* 62, no. 2 (June): 248–263.

Holton, Woody. 1997. "'Rebel against Rebel': Enslaved Virginians and the Coming of the American Revolution." *Virginia Magazine of History and Biography* 105, no. 2 (spring): 157–192.

Massachusetts. 1783. *Walker v. Jennison* (unreported), notes accessed at http://www.mass.gov/courts/court-info/sjc/edu-res-center/jn-adams/the-quock-walker-case.html.

Nash, Gary B., and Jean R. Soderlund. 1991. *Freedom by Degrees: Emancipation in Pennsylvania and Its Aftermath*. New York: Oxford University Press.

New York. 1894. *The Colonial Laws of New York from the Year 1664 to the Revolution*. Albany, NY: James B. Lyon.

Ostrander, Stephen M. 1894. *A History of the City of Brooklyn and Kings County*. Brooklyn, NY: by subscription.

Wax, Darold D. 1982. "'The Great Risque We Run': The Aftermath of Slave Rebellion at Stono, South Carolina, 1739–1745." *Journal of Negro History* 67, no. 2 (summer): 136–147.

Wheatley, Phillis. 1773. *Poems on Various Subjects, Religious and Moral*. London: A. Bell.

# Chapter 5

# Keep on Keeping on

Blacks broadened the foundation of their individual and collective liberty during the American Revolution. The War for Independence had brought them choices that tens of thousands seized to change their circumstance and condition. Tens of thousands of blacks came to realize release from slavery as the so-called First Emancipation took hold north of the Mason–Dixon Line to allow the states that came to be called "the North" to revel unduly in being free of slavery. Yet the region did become one of refuge and opportunity for blacks as their populations shifted during the years after 1800 from being mostly enslaved to being mostly free of slavery.

South of the Mason–Dixon Line, blacks overwhelmingly remained enslaved until the Civil War, for in the region that came to be called "the South," abolition—whether gradual or otherwise—found no stronghold. Yet some blacks enjoyed the air of liberty blown on the winds of the Revolution. The most notable examples were the approximately 500 blacks Robert Carter III manumitted, beginning in 1791 and at his death in 1804. Carter's would be the largest private release of slaves in the United States. Carter's fellow Virginian George Washington also provided in his last will and testament to manumit nearly 125 slaves at his estate at Mount Vernon.

Blacks in Delaware and Maryland experienced manumission more than those in any of the other states that would maintain slavery by law until the Civil War. In 1790 nearly one in three (30.5%) of Delaware's blacks lived outside of slavery. And the proportion would grow such that by the end of the 1790s Delaware was the lone state of the South to have more blacks (57.3%) outside of slavery than in slavery. Maryland lay a distant second, although it upped the percentage of its black population living outside of slavery from 7.2 percent to 15.6 percent during the 1790s. By 1860 more than 9 in 10 (91.7%) of Delaware's blacks were not in slavery, as were almost half (49.1%) of Maryland's blacks. The area became something of a middle ground for American Negro slavery (Fields 1985, 1–2).

Perhaps most telling of the policies adopted in the 1780s for blacks was the Northwest Ordinance of July 1787. With it the new nation adopted antislavery in its unsettled territory north of the Ohio River. Foreshadowing policy adopted for the entire nation almost 80 years later, the Ordinance's Article 6 provided that "there shall be neither slavery nor involuntary servitude in the said territory, otherwise than in the punishment of crimes whereof the party shall have been duly convicted." The Ohio River thus became akin to the River Jordan as blacks would come to sing of crossing it as entering into what the Bible described in the books of Genesis and Deuteronomy as a promised land of redemption. The provision laid a basis also for a notable series of freedom suits culminating in the notorious Dred Scott case in 1857.

Yet when the new nation adopted its Constitution in 1788 blacks could hardly have been buoyed by its provisions protecting slavery. Apparently abashed by slavery's presence under its jurisdiction, the fresh statement of fundamental law nowhere used the words *slavery, slave,* or *slaves.* It infamously referred to the enslaved as "three fifths" of legally recognized persons and provided for protecting property interests in them. It provided for all states to uphold legal title to the enslaved as property and commanded that all states deliver up slaves described as fugitives from "service or labor in one state, under the laws thereof, escaping into another." Further, it pledged the support of the nation in suppressing any uprising of slaves. And it held the nation open for at least 20 years to transatlantic trafficking in blacks as slaves.

Blacks would learn over the generations to wield the Constitution as a weapon for their liberation, but they found little favor in the early law of the land and took other avenues to advance their initiatives. With increasing public voice, they added to the growing outcry against slavery and the international slave trade. Their early published writings held up the hypocrisy of communities and individuals touting themselves as Christian while enslaving blacks. Recognized as the first African American poet, the Long Island–born Jupiter Hammon's lines, like prevalent slave songs, embodied a protest for release and circulated themes of rebellion that would long characterize much black literature and music from early America to the Jazz Age and on to hip-hop and beyond.

With Christian themes similar to Hammon's, the African-born Phillis Wheatley became the first black female poet published in British North America. But she added more pointed social commentary to her writing and came to stand for some as an exhibit, even an experiment, to show blacks' capacities given favorable conditions of life. Like Wheatley, blacks writing as individuals would long, if not forever, be caught in the context of their color, situated as instruments for or against some cause, seen as advancing or retarding black struggles for liberation and equality. They would be caught in someone's imagination, someone's vision, as part of a problem or part of a solution, but seldom as individuals struggling for their individual self-expression. Their identity as blacks would trump all else in referencing their work. They would continually be understood only within the framework of their race, and they would be accepted and rejected on that basis and too often appropriated for racial purposes, not as commentary on the writer's humanity but on the writer's blackness.

Writing for different purposes at different times, individual writers such as Jupiter Hammon offered different voices. His September 1786 "Address

AN

# ADDRESS

TO THE

## NEGROES

IN THE

## STATE OF NEW-YORK.

BY JUPITER HAMMON,

Servant of JOHN LLOYD, jun. Esq. of the Manor of Queen's Village, Long-Island.

"Of a truth I perceive that God is no respecter of
" persons:
" But in every Nation, he that feareth him and work-
" eth righteousness, is accepted with him."—

*Acts* x. 34, 35.

NEW-YORK:

Published by SAMUEL WOOD, No. 362 Pearl-street.

1806.

The enslaved Jupiter Hammon urged his fellow New York blacks to shoulder communal self-help and sobriety to advance their liberation in the growing First Emancipation movement of the American Revolution. This movement shifted northern states away from slavery, beginning in the 1780s. (Everett Collection Inc./Alamy Stock Photo) to the Negroes in the State of New York," delivered to the African Society of New York City when he was 76, emphasized blacks' responsibility for themselves. His theme would lay at the center of much discussion about blacks' individual and community accountability. Much would be made over the years about individual blacks being a credit or discredit to their race, about the degree to which individual blacks had a duty to be mindful of how their behavior affected or reflected on other blacks. And the duty weighed by degrees such that those with more advantages or who were more fortunate were obliged to do more, not only to benefit themselves but uplift blacks generally.

Hammon's focus in 1786 fell on blacks already free from slavery amid the First Emancipation that the Revolutionary Era was ushering in. He noted, albeit indirectly, the continuing debate about the capacity of blacks to live in the United States profitably outside of slavery. The argument touched many points, among them the feasibility of blacks and whites living in harmony in the same society. Hammon offered nothing on that point, but many others at the time did memorably. Virginia slaveholder Thomas Jefferson, for example, saw no satisfactory place for blacks in the United States outside of slavery.

In his *Notes on the State of Virginia*—written in 1781 and 1782 and first published in 1787—Jefferson declared that the "real distinction which nature has made; and many other circumstances will divide us into parties, and produce convulsions, which will probably never end but in the extermination of the one or the other race." He concluded then that it was at best improvident to "retain and incorporate the Blacks into the state" if they were released from slavery (Jefferson 1788, 147).

Hammon urged blacks to demonstrate that they did belong and could be more than self-sufficient. He urged his brethren already free from slavery to counter "one great reason that is given by some for not freeing us . . . that we should not know how to take care of ourselves, and should take to bad courses." He implored blacks to defy the stereotype that "we should be lazy and idle, and get drunk and steal." He concluded by returning to the onus to be borne by those who strayed from the straight and narrow. "Now all those of you, who follow any bad courses, and who do not take care to get an honest living by your labour and industry, are doing more to prevent our being free, than any body else," he warned (Hammon 1787, 18–19).

Hammon addressed his 1786 remarks to the African Society of New York City. Founded in 1784, the society led the formation of mutual aid associations among blacks in Manhattan and across the river in Brooklyn. Together, the two communities then housed the largest black urban population north of Maryland. Significantly, the founders referred to themselves and their constituency as "African." What they would call themselves collectively would persistently arise as a question among peoples of African descent in the United States. Early Iberian transatlantic slave traffickers had labeled their captives by color as *Negro*. Others followed suit, translating the color to their own tongue. So in English the term became *black*. Whether to refer to themselves by the terms others used to identify them or to refer to themselves by a term they chose for themselves would develop as a recurring political question among blacks. Preferences would shift over time to include *African, African American, Afro American, black, colored*, and *Negro*. *African* was a common term of self-identification in the 1780s.

For the founders of the 1784 society, their choice of *African* exerted the power of self-identification and recognized their common origin as a point of shared identity, as well as a framework for their relations. It recognized also the substantial African-born population in New York. Continuing transatlantic slave trafficking would keep a considerable African-born population in the United States even as birth within the new nation raised African Americans as the predominant portion of the population. The choice of *African* connected not only people in the present; it connected past, present, and future in community with cultural heritages and traditions and institutional purposes. Further, it joined the society's founders and their constituency as equals with others in America at the time identifying themselves by place of ancestral origin, narrowly and broadly, as Irish or German or French or, simply, European. Designating their society as *African* staked blacks' claim to a recognized position on America's unfolding map.

The African Society of New York City brought to flower the roots of black brotherhood reaching back to New York's Dutch settlement in the 1620s, and it seeded the growth of black voluntarism that grew over the decades and centuries not only in and around New York City but in African American communities throughout the United States. Others would follow it, as it had followed the African Union Society that the African-born Occramer Marycoo—who took on the name Newport Gardner while enslaved—led blacks to form in Rhode Island in November 1780. It was a first as a black institution organized formally in full public view to uplift blacks individually and as a community. The Newport blacks organized for "the welfare of the colored community by providing a record of births, deaths and marriages; by helping to apprentice Negroes; and by assisting members in time of distress." Both the Newport and the New York City societies conveyed an organic voluntary tradition of self-help similar to collectivist traditions in Africa and also common sense imperatives to organize for shared public and private interests or perish (Porter 1971, 5).

Blacks in Philadelphia in April 1787 founded their own Free African Society. Absalom Jones and Richard Allen led the formation. The two zealous converts to 18th-century English evangelist John Wesley's Methodism hoped initially "to form some kind of religious society." Their primary desire, however, arose from "a love to the people of their complexion whom they beheld with sorrow, because of their irreligious and uncivilized state." Committed to improving that state, the pair joined with others of "like concern" but who "differed in their religious sentiments" to form a society "without regard to religious tenets . . . in order to support one another in sickness, and for the benefit of their widows and fatherless children," as they declared in the society's preamble (Douglass 1862, 15).

Black Freemasons formed another early branch of publicly organized black brotherhood. The Boston black leather-worker Prince Hall led the effort. Apparently attracted by the Masonic pledge of mutual support and protection and its professed love of God and all mankind, Hall pressed persistently for membership in a Masonic Lodge to no avail until March 1775 when he and 15 other blacks gained initiation into Lodge No. 441 of the Grand Lodge of Ireland. Hall and his fellows then formed African Lodge No. 1, with him as Grand Master, but with degraded status and powers. In September 1784, however, Hall and his fellows received a full charter from the Mother Grand Lodge of England. Black Freemasonry then spread to a lodge in Philadelphia and then to Providence, Rhode Island, in 1797 (Hall 1936, 411–432).

Such voluntary associations stressed morality. They insisted on their members' following strict standards of conduct and generally accepted the duty Jupiter Hammon had observed to be "true and faithful citizens," as Boston's African Society proclaimed in its rules, so as to be good examples for their fellow blacks and in the eyes of the community at large. Temperance was foremost in the codes for members. They were not necessarily what would come to be called teetotalers, but they did expect sobriety. They featured common purposes, beginning with fraternity. They offered members the mutual support of friendship for self-improvement and protection of themselves and their families against the ordinary misfortunes of life such as sickness and death, "assisting members in time of distress," as the Newport society promised. When members were "sick, and not able to supply themselves with necessaries suitable to their situation," the groups pledged, in the Boston society's words, to "tender to them and their family whatever the Society have, or may think fit for them" (Porter 1971, 5, 10). The groups paid funeral expenses. Indeed, some organized themselves as burial societies for that specific purpose. Education also was a primary purpose of the various groups, for their members, families, and wider communities.

Blacks would organize themselves over time into countless groups, large and small, to share and pursue interests and purposes. Their existence and effects, however, have too often been overshadowed by the organizations commonly considered the centers of black community throughout the 1800s and 1900s—black churches. But black worship centers seldom, if ever, were the sole organized group in black communities, certainly not in black communities outside of slavery. Granted, they stood in many black communities as their principal communal space. Indeed, historically black churches may be best understood as umbrella organizations providing a common meeting place to coordinate and shelter various groups, denominational and nondenominational, and also decidedly secular, as in Philadelphia's Free African Society.

Black churches were just that, plural not singular. There was no *the* black church. Geography at times located a single black church in a remote area. And black churches were more likely to stand at a distance from each other in the countryside than in the city, in the South than in the North, all before modernizing transportation shrank social distances. Moreover, black churches were never static. Like their communities, they were in motion. They changed over the generations, developing to fulfill their congregations' needs in changing circumstances and conditions. They came in many places at many times to represent their black communities, but they were seldom solitary representatives. For even when they served as nuclei of black communal life, black churches were no more than parts of black communal activity. Many other black institutions served as cultural, economic, political, and social centers and extensions.

Black churches arose primarily as institutions of people free of slavery, developing during the First Emancipation era. An African Baptist church, sometimes referred to as the "Bluestone Church" because of its proximity to the Bluestone River in southwestern Virginia, held services on one of William Byrd III's plantations, beginning about 1758. But blacks' attending a church did not necessarily make the church a black church: autonomy characterized institutions called black churches. Enslaved blacks early in colonial America attended churches with their slaveholders, and some even continued attending after manumission. At best they were marginal to such congregations, and in the segregation of which slavery was a part, blacks typically found themselves unwelcome as independent congregants. So they moved to their own separate churches.

The Virginia-born, ex-slave George Lisle (also spelled Liele or Leile), reputed as the first African American licensed minister, helped organize The First Colored Church in Savannah, Georgia. He preached there until 1782 when, fearing slaveholding American Patriots would take away his freedom, he evacuated with the British and removed to a missionary ministry in Jamaica. The Savannah congregation Lisle left changed its name to The First African Baptist Church and, dating its services from 1777 and 1778, claimed the title of the oldest black church in North America. The First Baptist Church of Petersburg, Virginia, dating its services from 1774, would dispute the Savannah congregation's claim. Both notably adhered to the Baptist denomination which, with various Methodists, would traditionally lead black church membership.

The Baptists and Methodists pioneered among blacks in and out of slavery during the Great Awakening of the 1730s and 1740s. Their revivals opened to all a membership based on belief rather than on any hierarchy of knowledge, accepting all as equal in Christian faith. Emphasizing personal experience, feeling, and even visible emotion, rather than abstract dogma or doctrinal professions of faith, their revivals attracted blacks. Also with their autonomy of local congregations, both denominations would in time further appeal to blacks who wanted an independent church answerable only to its own congregation and voluntary membership, allowing them freedom to choose and develop their own worship forms, sacred songs, music, and even theology.

While the Great Awakening swept North and South and the early Baptist congregations in Petersburg and Savannah attested to the revival's extended southern influence, it was in the North that the denominations developed their early institutional bases among blacks. For in the major cities above the Mason–Dixon Line, blacks found their white Baptists, Methodists, and other coreligionists not above racial segregation. Indeed, discrimination became so pronounced in the 1790s that in both Philadelphia and New York City blacks formed separate congregations.

In Philadelphia in 1794 Richard Allen realized his hope "to form some kind of religious society" among his "African brethren, who had been a long forgotten people," in his view. Moving from St. George's Methodist Church, where blacks had become increasingly unwelcome, Allen, Absalom Jones, and other blacks received sanction from Methodist Bishop Frances Asbury to form their own congregation in full fellowship with the Methodist Episcopal Church. That congregation became "Mother Bethel," the origin of the African Methodist Episcopal Church (AME) that Allen would organize in 1816 to incorporate various black Methodist congregations.

Similarly, finding themselves less and less welcome, blacks in New York City separated from the John Street Methodist Church in 1796 to form their own congregation. It became the seed from which would grow the African Methodist Episcopal Zion Church (AME Zion). The name "Zion" reached back to the Hebrew of the Bible's Old Testament "World to Come" and distinguished the sect from their Philadelphia-based coreligionists (Hood 1895, 6–10).

Other black congregations followed. Blacks organized the Abyssinian Baptist Church in New York in 1804. They organized the Joy Street Baptist Church in Boston in 1805. The Colored Methodist Church started in Wilmington, Delaware, in 1806. In Philadelphia in 1807 they organized the First African Presbyterian Church and about 1809 the First Colored Methodist Church. They came together investing in community ownership and creating community property. Their church buildings and annexes announced

Richard Allen, a founder of the African Methodist Episcopal (AME) Church, preached for blacks to organize for collective self-determination. He worked from Philadelphia, Pennsylvania, to build a major denomination to minister to the full range of black communal and personal needs. (Daniel Alexander Payne. *History of the African Methodist Episcopal Church*, 1891)

their communal presence and stood as symbols of communal pride. In their church membership, they showed themselves as people of property and standing.

The black churches that emerged in the 1790s and early 1800s expressed long existing black spirituality that arrived with the first Africans in America. Such an ethos was inherent in traditional African societies. Moreover, the penetration of both Christianity and Islam in Africa spread their black adherents to America in the transatlantic slave trafficking. While many blacks became converts in America, particularly to Christianity, perhaps tens of thousands arrived having already been baptized.

Similarly, while submerged in the dominant Christian current, black Muslims had an early and persistent presence in America. Africans captured in the trans-atlantic trafficking, particularly from the Atlantic coastal area from the Senegal River to the Niger valleys and down to the Bight of Biafra, from the mid-1600s onward arrived in North America having in their view been purified through the word of Allah as members of the *ummah* or community of believers.

The appearance of Islamic names attested to the presence and persistence of its adherence and traditions, as Akan day names illustrated theirs. The common appearance of the name "Sambo" and its use as a generic term in the South, for example, inadvertently evidenced an Islamic presence. *Sambo* stemmed from *Samba*, meaning "second son" among the Islamic Fulbe. Other corruptions also appeared. "Bullaly," for instance, reached back to the Islamic *Bilali*, meaning "chosen one" or "smart one." "Bocarrey" represented *Bubacar*, a reference to Abu Bakr, "Companion of Muhammad." "Fatima" appeared among black female names, reaching back to Prophet Muhammad's cousin Fatimah bint Asad, who was among early converts to Islam. The name "Mamado" arose from *Mamadu*, a form of *Muhammad*, the name of the Prophet. "Mustafa" appeared, too, with its meaning of "chosen or lucky one." "Walley" connected to *Wali*, meaning "custodian" or "protector" (Gomez 1994, 671–710).

Naming patterns did not, of course, prove adherence to Islam; but they did attest to continuing connections between Africa and America and to continuing influences. Such practices appeared mostly among larger slaveholdings, where blacks had a degree of separation that allowed for insulated interaction: they could call each other what they wanted and practice what they pleased outside of white oversight.

The latitude blacks had for social interaction and for public and private relations differed very much by their locations. Remote countrysides were very different from crowded cities and towns. As the number and proportion of enslaved blacks fell north of Maryland and Delaware and increased to the south from the 1790s on, the two sections became very different for blacks. Both North and South, they suffered racial segregation, but fewer and fewer blacks in the North would be in slavery each year moving out of the 1790s, while more and more blacks in the South would be in slavery moving toward 1860. For most blacks, indeed for millions, the difference between the sections moving from the adoption of the U.S. Constitution to the U.S. Civil War yawned as the distinction between night and day. Blacks looked to the North as something of a promised land. In contrast, they viewed being "sold South" or sold "down river" as being sent to a netherworld, an occasion for great tears of anguish and grief.

## PROFILE: BENJAMIN BANNEKER (1731–1806)

What Phillis Wheatley was to arts and letters, Benjamin Banneker was to math and science for blacks in early America—a clear demonstration of intellectual capacity that challenged prevailing stereotypes. Born free on November 9, 1731, in Baltimore County, Maryland, Banneker had little formal schooling. Mostly he learned from reading, observing, and experimenting.

With loaned equipment and books he began serious study of the stars' motions and positions, and within a year he calculated a solar eclipse with precision enough to win work in 1791 on the initial surveying of the federal capital district on the Potomac River. His work interested him in clocks and devices such as an ephemeris to locate objects in the sky at any given time, and for six consecutive years beginning in 1792 he published an annual *Almanack and Ephemeris.*

Banneker's publications drew attention to him for his scientific merit but most of all for his race. Notable contemporaries called attention to his genius. Antislavery advocates invoked Banneker's work to illustrate blacks' capacities and to condemn slavery for suppressing those capacities. Banneker himself denounced slavery and called for its end. Notably he engaged Thomas Jefferson in an exchange of letters, pointedly underscoring Jefferson's hypocrisy in holding slaves, for by his own declarations "you should at the same time be found guilty of that most criminal act, which you professedly detested in others," Banneker charged (Allaben 1892, 67).

Like Phillis Wheatley, Banneker offered himself as an example of blacks' God-given talents. To show what blacks could do, Banneker sent Jefferson manuscripts of advanced calculations in his own handwriting. He apparently anticipated Jefferson's clinging to his views of blacks as wanting in "talents equal to those of the other colours of man," as Jefferson had insisted notoriously in his 1784 *Notes on Virginia.* Nevertheless, Banneker pressed the urgency of ending slavery as arising from natural rights, Christian duty, and national conscience to practice what it preached. "It is the indispensable duty of those who maintain for themselves the rights of human nature and who profess the obligations of Christianity, to extend their power and influence to the relief of every part of the human race, from whatever burthen or oppression they may unjustly labor under," Banneker insisted (Allaben 1892, 66).

Banneker's protests to end slavery yielded little, but his example paid handsomely in establishing a scientific legacy of African American development and invention that would include Thomas Jennings, who in 1821 became the first black patentee, for his dry-cleaning process; Norbert Rillieux, developer of evaporators; Judy W. Reed, developer of an improved dough kneader, and the first black woman to hold a U.S. patent; Lewis Latimer, developer of carbon filaments for light bulbs; Daniel Hale Williams, open-heart surgery pioneer; Sarah E. Goode, developer of the cabinet bed; Miriam Benjamin, patentee of an early chairlift; George Washington Carver, agricultural and botanical sciences pioneer; Garrett Morgan, inventor of the traffic signal and gas mask; Ernest Everett Just, pioneer in cell research; Alice Augusta Ball, developer of treatments for leprosy; and Charles Drew, pioneer in blood storage techniques. Inventor and engineer

Elijah J. McCoy with his 57 U.S. patents, including mechanical lubricators key to the railroad industry and often connected with the phrase "the real McCoy," stands as another example of the often unsung contributions of Banneker and his creative progeny.

## REFERENCES

Allaben, Frank. 1892. "Banneker's Appeal to Jefferson for Emancipation." *The National Magazine: A Monthly Journal American History* 17, no. 1 (November): 65–69.

Douglass, William. 1862. *Annals of the First African Church in the United States of America Now Styled the African Episcopal Church of St. Thomas, Philadelphia*. Philadelphia: King & Baird Printers.

Fields, Barbara Jean. 1985. *Slavery and Freedom on the Middle Ground: Maryland during the Nineteenth Century*. New Haven, CT: Yale University Press.

Gomez, Michael A. 1994. "Muslims in Early America." *Journal of Southern History* 60, no. 4 (November): 671–710.

Hall, Prince, et al. 1936. "Documents Relating to Negro Masonry in America." *Journal of Negro History* 21, no. 4 (October): 411–432.

Hammon, Jupiter. 1787. *An Address to the Negroes in the State of New-York*. New York: Carroll & Patterson.

Hood, J. W. 1895. *One Hundred Years of the African Methodist Episcopal Zion Church*. New York: A.M.E. Zion Book Concern.

Jefferson, Thomas. 1788. *Notes on the State of Virginia*. Philadelphia: Prichard & Hall.

Porter, Dorothy, ed. 1971. *Early Negro Writing, 1760–1837*. Boston: Beacon Press.

_____ *Chapter 6* _____

# Under the Lash

Blacks struggled against slavery with increasing intensity from the U.S. War for Independence through the Civil War. North of Maryland their struggle took form in developing associations and institutions of a people increasingly released from slavery but fighting the segregation of which slavery was a part and fighting to release the millions remaining in slavery, understanding they could not be fully free until all were fully free. In the South their struggle took form primarily in the continuing day-in-and-day-out individual resistance of the enslaved, in their flight, and in their repeated acts of collective rebellion.

The precedent of rising up in arms lingered among blacks from the War for Independence. The Haitian Revolution reinforced its effects. The blacks who won their release from slavery fighting among and against the rebel Americans called "Patriots" showed the effectiveness of taking up arms. Yet blacks' successes in the fledgling United States paled against the nearby blacks' achievements in the western portion of Hispaniola. Less than 100 miles from Cuba and 600 miles from Florida to the northwest, blacks in Saint-Domingue—the richest colony in the Americas—not only ousted the colonial power, as had occurred in the United States, but also abolished slavery.

The black violence in Haiti encouraged enslaved blacks in the United States to weigh possibilities of winning their freedom through wide-scale collective action. The spillover hit Louisiana first as it ran awash with Haitian refugees. Slaveholders, slaves, and free people of color flowed by the thousands into New Orleans and its surrounding area. The influx frightened Louisiana slaveholders to press for stricter policing of blacks. And their anxieties were confirmed in April 1795 with what became known as the Pointe-Coupée conspiracy.

Displaying the depths of both whites' anxieties and enslaved blacks' plotting to free themselves, the planning centered on Julien Poydras's sugar plantation off the Mississippi River about 100 miles northwest of New Orleans.
Blacks seasoned in the West Indies, some perhaps having done a stint in
Saint-Domingue, formed the reported rebel core. Their leaders reinforced
many Louisiana planters' belief that West Indian blacks were the most
dangerous slaves. Such planters preferred to enslave blacks directly from
Africa, whom they called *bozales*, asserting that they were more manageable
although not as good workers as blacks born in slavery in Louisiana and
sometimes referred to as "creole blacks." Such enslaved African Americans
tended in planters' eyes to be less fractious and not given to running away
as much as others, restrained by ties of kinship and community.

And, in fact, the Pointe-Coupée blacks divided among themselves along
lines of birthplace—as did others elsewhere from time to time in and out of
slavery. Reciprocated condescensions and suspicions swirled between blacks
born in North America and those from the West Indies and those fresh from
Africa. The Africa-born appeared the most likely to run away in the bay-
ous and backwaters of Louisiana to form maroon communities the Spanish
called *cimarrones*. Those identified as West Indian blacks appeared more
ready to stand and fight rather than run, as they showed in taking the lead
in Pointe-Coupée.

The reported rebels never got to put their intentions into action in
Pointe-Coupée. An informant alerted planters, who immediately formed a
dragnet, interrogating and arresting scores of slaves. Prosecutors had 23
slaves hanged and their heads cut off and nailed to posts along the Mississippi River from Pointe-Coupée down to New Orleans as displays to daunt
would-be black rebels. Thirty-one other convicted blacks were flogged and
deported to hard labor at Spanish garrisons in Cuba, Florida, Mexico, and
Puerto Rico (Din 1997, 5–28).

Neither the prosecutions nor the punishments quieted Louisiana's
enslaved blacks. Slaves in Opelousas, not 30 miles west of Pointe-Coupée,
also were reported restless in 1795. And in March 1796 rumors surfaced of
blacks caching weapons in the Mississippi east bank settlements of Augs-
burg, Hoffen, Karlstein, and Mariental—collectively called the German
Coast to reflect its early settlers' origins. The area about 60 miles northwest
of New Orleans would in 1811 be U.S. territory and the location of what
some called "the great Louisiana slave revolt" (Paquette 2009, 72; Davis
2012, 58–63).

To lesser degrees U.S. port cities and their nearby communities from
Savannah, north to Charleston, Baltimore, Philadelphia, and New York City
suffered disquiet with the influx of Haitian refugees. Suspicions attached to
the rising Francophone presence, especially as Franco-American relations

turned tense with shots fired at sea in the so-called Quasi-War from 1798 to 1800. Racial tensions also attached to the influx, as they had in Louisiana. But it was in and around Richmond, Virginia, from 1798 into 1800 that blacks in the United States organized an uprising under the banner "Death or Liberty."

The enslaved blacksmith called Gabriel on Thomas Henry Prosser's tobacco plantation in Henrico County, Virginia, led the uprisings' planning. His name would become attached to the episode called "Gabriel's Rebellion" or "Gabriel's Uprising." The 24-year-old recruited hundreds of blacks and whites also, including Frenchmen, considered "friendly to liberty." The plotters fixed the last Saturday in August 1800 as the day for their coordinated attack. Their plan was to muster that night at a site near Richmond and then march on the capital. They aimed to capture Gov. James Monroe and to seize the arsenal and the state treasury, arming and fortifying themselves for a siege. In basic strategy, their plan resembled Bacon's Rebellion in 1676. They expected not only blacks but also whites disgruntled at the planter-dominated society to rally to the cause of "liberty, equality, and fraternity," adopted from the French Revolution slogan.

Heavy rains on launch day delayed Gabriel's attack, but what doomed it was informants. Snitching to white authorities would long be a problem in black communities. The mentality that produced those whom many called turncoats or worse was sometimes complicated and sometimes simple. Sometimes it was simply betraying information for personal gain. Sometimes it was done out of some sense of saving the community from something more terrible, such as indiscriminate white retaliation. In any case, collaborating or cooperating with officials to police black behavior bedeviled black collective activities before and beyond Gabriel's doings. His two chief betrayers were slaves named Pharoah and Tom, whom Virginia's General Assembly later rewarded with release from slavery.

Virginia executed 27 conspirators in all. They were no riffraff. Like Gabriel, they tended to be artisans. They were not fresh off the boat from Africa or the Caribbean. They appeared American-born, assimilated in the Richmond area's burgeoning metropolitan market economy, literate, and informed on regional and national politics and international affairs enough to weigh and consider their actions in those contexts. They were not looking to escape from Virginia; rather, they were looking for more equal entree into the Virginia their labors were enriching (Egerton 1993, 186).

Gabriel's plan and its attraction revealed the continuing complexity of what was labeled as "slave rebellion." The complications were similar to those attached to understanding the American Revolution. Both had multiple facets with their different aspects that attracted varying adherents. The rebels called Patriots were not all of the same mind, nor were rebellious slaves. They shared a demand for self-determination, but means and methods, strategy, tactics, and timing split black rebels no less than rebel Patriots who, while agreeing on home rule, disagreed on who should rule at home and how.

Multiple constraints channeled black defiance and discontent. The weight of their oppression during and after slavery turned some black rebels toward destruction or rejection as they despaired of achieving the place they wanted in America. Gabriel and his cohort sought acceptance. They wanted an end to the slavery and segregation that barred them from enjoying the position and profit to which their labors and skills entitled them in their view, but that required a radically different America, one without racial and capitalist competition that sustained white supremacy.

Gabriel's execution in October 1800 hardly quieted black unrest. Blacks privy to his plans continued to plot. In south-central Virginia, more than 100 miles from Richmond, a Halifax County slave named Sancho carried the conspiracy up and down the James and Roanoke Rivers from the fall of 1801 to the spring of 1802 in what became known as the Easter Plot. It became so unwieldy that it broke apart under its own weight. Blacks' eagerness to join in such schemes alarmed Virginia officials to the extent that the state legislature from 1801 to 1805 seriously considered schemes to remove, or at least reduce, Virginia slave population through gradual emancipation tied to colonization.

Virginia was hardly alone in its scares of collective slave violence. No slave state escaped alarms about unruly slaves during the 1800s. And such fears were hardly new. They had rippled through colonial North America. They were common throughout the Atlantic World. The Caribbean and South America suffered, too, for having slaves meant being frightened of slaves. Lingering fears became concentrated into explosive concoctions when extensive slave plans for violence surfaced. The so-called New York conspiracy in 1741 had dramatically illustrated how pent-up fears of slaves could expand angrily into mass executions. Exposure in 1822 of a plot in and around Charleston, South Carolina, again illustrated the explosive combination of white fears and black ambitions.

The plot in South Carolina featured a common outline. Like the 1741 plot in New York City and Gabriel's plot in Richmond in 1800, blacks shaped their plan around capturing, or at least attacking, the capital city. As in Richmond, the leader of the Charleston plot was a black artisan, a carpenter named Denmark Vesey. Unlike Gabriel, Vesey was already free of slavery when his plot appeared. He had won a $1,500 lottery that allowed him to buy himself in 1799. He knew, however, that being free of slavery was not being free. He also knew his own condition depended on his fellow blacks' condition. None would be truly free unless all were truly free.

Vesey reportedly recruited close to 1,000 blacks. Incredible speculations put the number as high as 9,000. Like Gabriel in 1800 and also blacks in New York City in 1741, Vesey reportedly had white accomplices. Indeed, prosecutors in South Carolina in October 1822 would convict four white men for "inciting Slaves to insurrection" with Vesey's plan. Four whites had also been convicted and executed as black insurrectionary accomplices in New York in 1741. As in Gabriel's plot, informers gave the plan away before it unfolded.

Vesey was about 55 years old when his plotting came to light in June 1822. He reportedly had set July 14 as the launch day for his planned attack. The date was the 33rd anniversary of Bastille Day, celebrated as the start of the French Revolution. While authorities described the plot as Vesey's plan, it was not his alone. As in New York City in 1741 and Richmond in 1800, more than one person molded the design and, indeed, more than a single vision or plan of action was afoot. Prosecutors and a credulous public concocted a more closely knit grand design than blacks had prepared. Yet even such prosecutors appeared to fail at grasping the sole fact that the common cause of slave unrest was slavery, as the common cause of black unrest was being relegated by race.

Vesey and his cohort died as symbols representing very different impulses to blacks and whites, to slaveholders and slaves, and to the public at large. Many slaveholders took Vesey's reported plan as a sign for stricter policing of blacks in and out of slavery, particularly in a place like Charleston with so heavy a black majority. The county population in 1820 included nearly 61,000 blacks, 57,000 of them enslaved, and 19,000 whites—a more than 3 to 1 ratio. Anxious slaveholders pressed along with a shocked white public for exemplary punishment, as usual in response to such black unrest. Vesey was hanged on July 2, 1822, after a two-day trial. In all, South Carolina executed 35 blacks and exiled 32 others after a dragnet yielded 131 black arrests, including house slaves of Gov. Thomas Bennett Jr. (Egerton 2004, xvii–xx).

To further inhibit blacks' activities, the South Carolina legislature in December 1822 passed "an act for the better regulation of free negroes and persons of color, and for other purposes." The statute's title displayed the prevalent suspicion that slave unrest did not arise among slaves by themselves but was incited by others, particularly unenslaved blacks. And primary on the list of black inciters were outsiders such as black seamen who sailed into South Carolina with foreign news and notions. South Carolina's legislators targeted them in section 3 of the 1822 statute, which itself became infamous as "the Negro Seamen Act" (South Carolina 1822, 561).

And, indeed, black ship hands had long been and would long be purveyors of news, notice, and other information, as were blacks employed elsewhere in transportation. Simply, they got around and passed around what they heard and saw. In the late 1700s and early 1800s, black sailors enjoyed and exuded degrees of liberty distant from their landlubber brethren. Harsh as crew conditions could be, seafaring imposed close and confined interactions that tended to force reciprocal respect for ability, regardless of race, which had moved many black men early to the sea as a way of life.

The 1822 Negro Seamen Act almost immediately created a furor and an international incident when Charleston Sheriff Francis G. Deliesseline arrested black seaman Henry Elkison, a crewman on the British ship *Homer*, out of Liverpool. The British government protested and sued to release Elkison and to forbid the act's seizure of British subjects. U.S. Supreme Court Justice William Johnson, himself a South Carolinian, heard the case on circuit as *Elkison v. Deliesseline* in August 1823. He declared the act "unconstitutional and void," and South Carolina legislature modified it in December 1823 (United States 1823, 496). It was not Justice Johnson's decision, however, but the weight of the British government negotiations that secured Elkison's release. Indeed, Johnson's decision said nothing about blacks' rights; rather, it rested on the federal government's exclusive authority over interstate and international commerce. Black rights were nowhere a priority in U.S. law.

Blacks, themselves, in and around Charleston protested the dragnet and the backlash to the Vesey plot. But they were on the downside of a descending slope of tolerance in the slave South. Coming changes in law and practice would only further degrade what was allowed or available to them. White blood blacks shed in Southampton, Virginia, in 1831, along with growing agitation outside the South against slavery sealed worsening conditions for blacks in the slave states.

The Southampton County event became noted as the deadliest slave insurrection in U.S. history. At its end, blacks had killed as many as 60 whites, marauding for two days from farmstead to farmstead along a path from outside a place then called Jerusalem (later Courtland), about 70 miles due west of Norfolk, onward southwest across the Nottoway River in southeastern Virginia, just above its border with North Carolina. Blacks were 6 out of 10 (59.1%) of the county's population that tended to general farming with a concentration on tobacco.

The 30-year-old enslaved black named "Nat" during his childhood with slaveholder Benjamin Turner led the uprising. In interviews after his capture, he gave local attorney Thomas R. Gray what was published as *The Confessions of Nat Turner*, purportedly detailing his life and thinking and describing the unfolding of his rebellion. Nat said his core group gathered on Saturday night, August 20. Then about 2:00 a.m. on Sunday, they entered the house of Joseph Travis, Nat's then slaveholder, killed him and his family,

Nat and fellow Southampton, Virginia, insurgents in 1831 planned and executed the bloodiest slave uprising in U.S. history. (New York Public Library)

and launched their house-to-house attacks, gathering more blacks as they marched.

The rebels would number at least 60. Their rampage set off alarms that dispatched local militia and eventually federal troops. Confronted by militia on their second day at large, the rebels—equipped mostly with knives, hatchets, and other cutting weapons rather than firearms—suffered heavy casualties and 48 were captured. Nat escaped, however. He knew the neighborhood. As with many who spent their entire life in the same area, he had explored it early and often, and he managed to remain at large for more than two months.

Enraged whites immediately wreaked revenge on blacks at random, slaughtering perhaps 200. The state executed 57 other blacks, including Nat who was captured on October 30, put on trial on November 5, and executed on November 11. His corpse was flayed, beheaded, and drawn and quartered in the fashion of the old English law punishment for treason that disemboweled the victim and then severed the limbs. He became a legend and to some a messianic figure called "Prophet," a seer trying to deliver his people; to others he was a reviled devil, a wanton butcher of women and children.

Nat's actions provoked wide-ranging argument about blacks' release from slavery and served as a midway point of sorts between the First Emancipation of the American Revolution era and the general emancipation to come with the Civil War. The release from slavery prompted by the Revolution's Enlightenment ideals of equality or by religious conviction had largely worked its way through the states north of Maryland by 1830. The 2,254 enslaved blacks then remaining in New Jersey gave it the largest slave population north of the Mason–Dixon Line. Pennsylvania still harbored 403 enslaved blacks and New York had 75, despite its General Emancipation Day proclaimed for July 4, 1827. Only 54 other enslaved blacks lingered among the remaining original states in the North.

For blacks in the North, Nat's rampage presented a quandary. Many condemned violence as evil in itself or saw slave uprisings as either destined to failure or as a sure means of inviting extermination. Others at least accepted black violence against slavery as a necessary evil. The question on both sides was whether black violence would advance or retard black liberation.

David Walker was one who embraced violence as necessary. Born of a free black mother in North Carolina in 1785 and residing in Charleston before moving to Boston, Walker in 1829 penned a volatile *Appeal to the Coloured Citizens of the World*. His near 90 pages bluntly surveyed blacks' condition in the United States, reaching most of the major issues of the day concerning blacks and at least condoned, if not counseled, violence as a manly response to subjugation. He appeared to adopt a motto popular in the French Revolution: *Vivre Libre ou Mourir* (Live free or die).

Walker refrained from directing slaves to rise up, but he did not flinch from the prospect. He foresaw occasions of black violence and advised "if you commence, make sure work—do not trifle, for they will not trifle with you—they want us for their slaves, and think nothing of murdering us in order to subject us to that wretched condition—therefore, if there is an attempt made by us, kill or be killed," he urged. Calling out blacks who got comfortable outside of slavery and drifted away from their still-enslaved brethren, Walker repeated his admonition that blacks in America stood alike in the same condition, even while their material circumstances may have differed. "Look into your freedom and happiness, and see of what kind they are composed!" Walker taunted such blacks, bidding them to move from their perch, "if any of you wish to know how FREE you are" (Walker 1830, 29–30, 33).

Walker further weighed in on a topic circulating with increasing heat since the First Emancipation—blacks' place and prospects in America. The recurring question was whether blacks would be better off elsewhere. Getting free of American Negro slavery regularly carried a note of escape, and the great escape of thousands of blacks who evacuated with the British after the War for Independence rather than trust their fate in the fledgling United States resoundingly declared elsewhere was better than here. Yet thousands of blacks also relieved of slavery during and after the war decided that here was better than elsewhere. To go or stay was long a question for blacks in America.

Movements to go gained momentum as blacks in the late 1700s and early 1800s viewed prospects of ever enjoying equal opportunity in America. As they considered relocating to a place they could make their own, Africa beckoned to some as a return to the continent of their birth. For few could it be a return to their homeland. Even for those who could locate it, the place of their birth was unlikely to have survived the changes slaving wrought. Yet Africa was to many a place to settle and live with self-determination.

The British resettlement of blacks in what would become Sierra Leone boosted what would long be known as a back-to-Africa movement. It early beckoned the likes of entrepreneurial sea captain Paul Cuffee. Indeed, the successful businessman of African and Native American parentage helped fund the Friendly Society of Sierra Leone and several times visited the fledgling British colony. Cuffee promoted black settlement in the colony and personally funded scores of black settlers, advocating that blacks who wished to leave America should be allowed to do so. For him it was a matter of choice, and while he chose to help others exercise their own choice, his choice was to continue to live in Massachusetts, where he died in 1817.

While Cuffee and other blacks sought to facilitate colonization as an exercise of black choice, by the time of his death colonization had very much become a design by whites to rid the United States of blacks who were not enslaved. Some whites, in fact, coupled colonization with emancipation. They were willing to release blacks from slavery on condition that such blacks went elsewhere to live. The idea was part of making America a white man's land. The American Colonization Society (ACS)—its full official title was "The Society for the Colonization of Free People of Color of America"—took the idea as its mission when founded in 1816. For the ACS colonization was about whites' choice, at least that was the view David Walker and other outspoken blacks took.

Walker derided what he termed "the colonizing trick" (Walker 1830, 76). He was not against blacks' moving to better conditions. He had moved from North Carolina to South Carolina to Massachusetts to find a better place for himself and his wife and son. Others, too, were ready to move within the United States, even to unsettled parts. Noticing Congress's chartering of the ACS, William Bowler and other blacks in Richmond, Virginia, petitioned Congress in January 1817 "to grant us a small portion of their territory . . . that may seem to them most conducive to the public good and our future welfare." But they rejected leaving the United States. "We prefer being colonized in the most remote corner of the land of our nativity, to being exiled to a foreign country," Bowler and his fellows declared (Aptheker 1951, 1: 71).

The issue for Walker and others who opposed the ACS was choice, whether blacks decided for themselves whether and where to move. He and others emphasized blacks' stake in America and their right to remain, as a January 1817 meeting of blacks in Philadelphia made clear. "Whereas our ancestors (not of choice) were the first successful cultivators of the wilds of America, we their descendants feel ourselves entitled to participate in the blessings of her luxuriant soil, which their blood and sweat manured," the meeting at Bethel church resolved. "[A]ny measure or system of measures, having a tendency to banish us from her bosom, would not only be cruel, but in direct violation of those principles, which have been the boast of this republic," the meeting declared (Aptheker 1951, 1: 71).

Moreover, the Philadelphia meeting denounced colonization schemes for stigmatizing free people of color as "a dangerous and useless part of the community." Walker put it more bluntly: "Do they think to bundle us up like brutes and send us off," he sneered (Walker 1830, 77). Blacks were just as American as any other Americans and with better claim of place from their exploited labor, the Bethel meeting emphasized. And further the black Philadelphians confronted colonization as a scheme to divide blacks. "We never will separate ourselves voluntarily from the slave population in this country," the meeting resolved. Pledging unity in the cause of black liberation, the Bethel meeting described enslaved blacks as "our brethren by the ties of consanguinity, of suffering, and of wrong" and pledged to continue "suffering privations with them" rather than succumb to "fancied advantages," as no blacks could truly enjoy freedom while slavery persisted (Aptheker 1951, 1: 71).

## PROFILE: SOJOURNER TRUTH (CA. 1797–1883)

Born of West African parents around 1797 among the Dutch remnant in the Hudson Valley community of Swartekill, Isabella Baumfree grew to be one of the most influential African American women in history. She was among the last-generation of blacks in New York born into slavery, for the state in 1799 provided that all persons born there after July 4 that year would be born free. Children born of slave mothers after that remained bound to service until age 28 years, if male, and 25 years, if female.

Coming-of-age while slavery was waning in New York, the girl called "Belle" experienced growing resentments among blacks on both sides of the July 4, 1799, divide. Lifelong slavery appeared to lay ahead for blacks like Baumfree born before the date; and those born after the date begrudged their years of forced servitude. Isabella's own grievances grew as she was sold at auction away from her birthplace and family at age 9. She was sold at least twice more by 1810, and none of her situations improved on the last. She saw more than typical cruelty and violence. Especially wrenching for her was having her first true love, a neighboring slave named Robert, so brutally beaten by her slaveholder for trespassing to visit her that he died from his injuries. That murder forever haunted her.

Isabella married in time and bore five children. The first named James may have been conceived with Robert: he died in childhood. She had a daughter Diana in 1815, two later daughters—Elizabeth (1825) and Sophia (1826)—and in 1821 a son named Peter. Because she was a slave, all her children were born into involuntary servitude, but New York in 1817 had changed its law to provide for general emancipation on July 4, 1827. After that date all residing in New York State would be deemed legally free of slavery or involuntary servitude. Isabella lived for that day for herself and her children.

Angry at losing what they thought of as their rights to service, more than a few New York slaveholders illegally sold blacks outside the state to cash in on what they saw as property the state was taking from them for nothing. One of the blacks so sold was Isabella's five-year-old son Peter. Isabella not only walked off from slavery with her infant daughter Sophia before the formal release date of July 4, 1827, but she went to court to sue her former slaveholder John Dumont for illegally selling her son to slavery in Alabama. It took until 1828, but Isabella succeeded in recovering Peter.

Her thanksgiving spilled over into Christian devotion that deepened on encountering several evangelists in New York City, where she had moved in 1829 with Peter and Sophia. The city exposed Isabella to quickening pulses that changed her attitudes about the world and also about herself. Reflecting notable change, in 1843 she renamed herself "Sojourner Truth," feeling a spirit calling her to tell what her life had revealed. Her insistent themes were antislavery, Methodism, pacifism, and women's rights. Her 1850 autobiography, *The Narrative of Sojourner Truth: A Northern Slave*, spread her fame, but her 1851 speech "Ain't I a Woman?" at the Ohio Women's Rights Convention in Akron elevated her to lasting notice.

Much in demand for the power of her plain-speaking, Sojourner Truth continued through the Civil War and after to preach the righteousness of abolition and equal rights regardless of race or gender. She died at home in Battle Creek, Michigan, on November 26, 1883 (Painter 1996, passim).

## REFERENCES

Aptheker, Herbert. 1951. *A Documentary History of the Negro People in the United States*. 2 vols. New York: The Citadel Press.

Davis, Thomas J. 2012. *Plessy v. Ferguson*. Santa Barbara, CA: Greenwood Press.

Din, Gilbert C. 1997. "Carondelet, the Cabildo, and Slaves: Louisiana in 1795." *Louisiana History* 38, no. 1 (winter): 5–28.

Egerton, Douglas R. 1993. *Gabriel's Rebellion: The Virginia Slave Conspiracies of 1800–1802*. Chapel Hill: University of North Carolina Press.

Egerton, Douglas R. 2004. *He Shall Go Out Free: The Lives of Denmark Vesey*. Lanham, MD: Rowman & Littlefield.

Painter, Nell Irvin. 1996. *Sojourner Truth: A Life, A Symbol*. New York: Norton.

Paquette, Robert L. 2009. "'A Horde of Brigands?' The Great Louisiana Slave Revolt of 1811 Reconsidered." *Historical Reflections/Réflexions Historiques* 35, no. 1 (Spring): 72–96.

South Carolina. 1822. "An Act for the Better Regulation of Free Negroes and Persons of Color, and for Other Purposes," 7 S.C. Stat. 561 (December 21).

United States. 1823. *Elkison v. Deliesseline*, 8. F. Cas. 493 (C.C.D.S.C. 1823) (No. 4,366).

Walker, David. 1830. *Walker's Appeal, in Four Articles; Together with a Preamble, To the Coloured Citizens of the World, but in Particular, and Very Expressly, to Those of the United States of America, Written in Boston, State of Massachusetts, September 28, 1829*. 3rd ed. Boston: revised and published by David Walker.

_____ *Chapter 7* _____

# Lift That Bale

Relatively few blacks engaged in cotton production before the 1790s. Indeed, few in the 1790s lived where cotton would boom in the 1800s, as those areas were then largely outside the settled United States. Enslaved blacks in the 1790s clustered mostly in the Upper South: Virginia (42.0%), Maryland (14.8%), and North Carolina (14.5%) together contained almost 7 in 10 (71.1%) of the new nation's enslaved blacks in 1790. But that changed momentously with Eli Whitney's "cotton gin."

The lives and fates of millions of blacks fell victim to changes triggered by Whitney's hand-cranked wooden drum lined with roller hooks that pulled cotton fiber through wire mesh fine enough to strain away seeds. The machine broke a production bottleneck as it allowed a single cotton picker to jump from producing 1 pound to 50 pounds of cotton a day. The technology exploded beyond the machine Whitney patented in 1794, and U.S. raw cotton production jumped seven times from 10,449 bales in 1793 to 73,145 bales in 1800. By 1820 U.S. raw cotton production stood at 334,378 bales. In 1860 it was 10 times that at 3,837,402 bales (Gray and Thompson 1941, 1026).

Enslaved blacks grew in demand and market value as U.S. cotton production grew, for enslaved blacks formed the backbone of U.S. cotton production. Indeed, they were the mainstay of the South's antebellum economy. Their market price increased on average about fourfold from a low of about $200 in the first decade of the 1800s to a peak of about $800 by 1860. The income value of enslaved blacks' labor reflected in the market prices paid for them by 1860 approached half (48.2%) of the South's wealth (Williamson and Cain 2015, figure 2 and table 4).

Enslaved blacks paved the road to wealth. They were not simply symbols of wealth; they were engines of wealth—for others. Their poverty supplied

profit beyond their reach, for their labor in cotton fields enriched not simply the South: Their production fueled Atlantic World industrial growth.
Moving from hand-cranked machines to operate horse-powered and then
steam-powered cotton gins, enslaved blacks fed the textile manufacturing
that led the Atlantic World's Industrial Revolution that started in Britain.
Textiles led all British exports into the 1800s, and the U.S. South supplied
not only Britain's mills but most of the world's mills as it grew 60 percent of
the world's marketed cotton by 1840 (Lakwete 2003, 47–71).

As it had shared lustily in the profits of transatlantic slave trafficking,
the U.S. North also partook heavily in the wealth generated from the
slave-driven cotton economy. Bankers, merchants, and shippers from Philadelphia north through New York City and into New England paid homage
to King Cotton by funding the slave enterprise and by carrying, buying,
selling, and insuring its products. Also drawing on southern cotton, New
England textile mills expanded to the Waltham or Lowell systems that created New England fortunes.

Cotton led all U.S. merchandise exports by value by the 1820s. In 1825,
for example, the United States exported about $67 million in value; of that,
cotton accounted for $37 million (55.2%). In 1860 of $316 million in U.S.
merchandise exports, cotton accounted for $192 million (60.8%). Cotton
income contributed significantly to growing interregional interdependence
between the North and South and to the growth of overall U.S. national
income (United States 1975, 885, 899).

While cotton succored others, it was no benefactor to blacks. Slaves
groaned under the growing demand that translated into increased pressure
for them to produce more and more. If work dominated their life before,
cotton came to define their life in slavery—not for all, but for most. Many
could join with Sylvia Witherspoon in her recollection of being "plum
wore out from chopping cotton" (Witherspoon 1936–1938, 1: 429). The
demands of the crop with its booming economy disrupted patterns of black
life long established for many since the 1600s. Cotton transformed the site
and substance of black life as it shifted where most blacks would live and
what they would do during much of the 1800s. Soaring market demand
and prices for slaves intensified pressures for them to produce and also
propelled them to fresh fields as cotton production continually expanded
to new territories.

More than ever, cotton made blacks in North America a people on the
move. From their clustering around the Chesapeake, the black population
increasingly moved further south and west from the 1790s to 1860 when the
Cotton States held about 6 in 10 (59.8%) of all enslaved U.S. blacks. Virginia remained the largest holder of enslaved blacks with 490,865 (12.4%
of all U.S. slaves) in 1860, but close on its heels with more than 400,000

Enslaved blacks at work on an antebellum cotton plantation where few were too young or too old for toil. Approaching the U.S. Civil War, American Negro slavery became virtually synonymous with cotton production, the leading U.S. export and mainstay of the South's economy. (New York Public Library)

enslaved blacks were in fresh cotton-growing states—Georgia (11.7%), Mississippi (11.1%), Alabama (11.0%), and South Carolina (10.2%).

Enslaved blacks were enriching America, as they had since the 1600s, yet that was not endearing them to other Americans. As engines of wealth, enslaved blacks were in demand wherever they could be had, especially wherever cotton bloomed. For that reason many demanded to hold slaves and many demanded also to be rid of slaves. More than ever, enslaved blacks stood as objects in the eyes of too many in America. They were both welcome and unwelcome as slaves, and outside of slavery few other Americans took an interest in blacks as other than objects.

As illustrated during the First Emancipation and earlier, many whites who were against slavery were not for blacks. Some saw slavery only as an evil corrupting slaveholders and the society that sanctioned slaveholders. Many such persons looked to end slavery so as to purify America, to make it what they called "a white man's land," one defined in their view with the mantra "free soil, free labor, free men." And *free* men, as distinguished from *freedmen*, were defined as white men. A relatively small group of whites did oppose slavery because of what it did not only to whites but also to blacks; some viewed blacks as objects of salvation deserving Christian benevolence; and some interested themselves in blacks as human beings, believing them equals—but they were the few.

For the most part, in and out of slavery, blacks could rely only on themselves to have their own interests at heart. Most appeared to recognize that whether they were in or out of slavery, they shared being despised as a people; they recognized their undeniable common interests. Some released from slavery, however, moved to distance themselves from blacks who continued in slavery. They feared being associated with slavery and thus feared associating with slaves. The First Emancipation thus further engendered class division among blacks, splitting those released from slavery from those remaining in slavery.

Not all succumbed, of course, to the specious sense that blacks whether in or out of slavery did not share in suffering the same oppression of racial segregation white supremacy imposed, albeit to different degrees. And then there was also the yawning divide between blacks North and South. The reign of King Cotton increasingly distanced blacks North and South. But neither forgot or forsook the other. Many blacks in the North worked as the most ardent abolitionists, giving aid and comfort whenever and wherever they could to the first-line fighters of slavery, those blacks who stole themselves away and sought refuge in the North. And blacks in the South looked upon their brothers and sisters in the North as illustrations of life beyond slavery.

Increasingly for blacks the North was that part of the United States outside of slavery, and the South was that part in slavery. It was true, nevertheless, as the escaped slave Frederick Douglass noted, that no place in the United States was truly "north of slavery," for whether enslaved or not all blacks in the United States lived in the shadow of slavery. And that would continue even after 1865 when the United States outlawed slavery. Yet the fact was that by 1860, when about one-half million blacks were free of slavery, nearly 4,000,000 were in slavery in the District of Columbia and the 15 slave states known collectively as "the South."

Particularly in what was called the "Lower South" or "Deep South," stretching westward from South Carolina across Georgia, Alabama, Mississippi, and into Arkansas and Louisiana, millions of enslaved blacks bowed and scraped under cotton's weight. Their load reached also into East Texas and North Florida. The area also carried the title "Cotton States," and the antebellum black population concentrated there. In fact, a 20- to 25-mile swath stretching from eastern, south-central Alabama into northwestern Mississippi became known from the 1820s on as the "Black Belt," first because of its rich, dark soil that attracted cotton growing and then as an area with a majority black population. The area drained by the Alabama, Black Warrior, and Tombigbee Rivers developed important sites in African American life. Alabama places such as Demopolis, Mobile, Montgomery, and Selma would come to bear historical markers in black history.

Black life in the 1800s concentrated in the Cotton States and, especially, on plantations there. About half of all enslaved blacks from the 1820s on lived in plantation settings with groups of 20 or more collectively housed in slave quarters (Webber 1978, 4). The cotton regime was not alone in the South's plantation economy, for other staple export crops—primarily rice, sugar, and tobacco—held sway in different localities with their own large slaveholdings. Indeed, at American Negro slavery's height on the eve of the Civil War, the largest U.S. slaveholding was that of rice planter Joshua John Ward. It numbered more than 1,000 slaves distributed throughout South Carolina's Georgetown County in an area that accounted for about half of all antebellum U.S. rice production. Seven other South Carolina rice planters held between 500 and 999 slaves in 1860, as did four sugar planters in Louisiana. The two states led the nation in holdings numbering 100 or more slaves, and had 12 of the 15 holdings of 500 or more slaves in 1860; Mississippi, Georgia, and Arkansas each had one holding of 500 or more slaves.

Enslaved blacks in such large holdings typically sprawled across several sites, rather than being concentrated in a single place or set of quarters. Their distribution among such sites created commonalities among slaveholdings ranging upward from 20 or more and allowed for such holdings to form a related regime with distinct routines determined by crop—for each crop had its own labor demands. Yet the clustering of 20 or more slaves brought such holdings to share key characteristics as black communities.

The group setting of larger holdings shaped their social structures and constructed the backdrop of blacks' personal interactions. It was where enslaved blacks learned to work and behave; for it was a place of both general education and vocational schooling, teaching both master–slave and black–white etiquette, as well as black-on-black behavior. It was a place for socialization and for socializing, a place for bonding with other blacks, and a place for learning how to survive slavery and white supremacy.

Little on North America ever matched the extensive sugar plantations in the Caribbean and Brazil. And size did matter. The extent of the slaveholding enterprise made big differences in the organization and operation of labor and in relations between and among slaves, slaveholders, and black and white workers. The more blacks there were, generally, the fewer whites proportionally worked directly with them. The segregation represented in slavery cleaved a world of black and white in labor relations as it did in social relations as the lines hardened. The increasing concentration of

enslaved blacks further sharpened black–white separation with distinct geographic dimensions as the size of slaveholdings made itself increasingly felt
over time in mainland North America and made the sprawling antebellum
plantation the standard image of American Negro slavery.

In large holdings a division of labor existed among enslaved blacks, but
mainly most worked in the field. What they did depended on the crop and
on their capacity. Males in the prime age range of 14 to 35 years led field
hands, followed by females in the same age range. The young and the old
fitted in where they could. The scope of operations in large holdings reduced
many slaves to cogs from the perspective of slaveholders and overseers. As
long as they meshed with others in the production process, enslaved blacks
on larger holdings tended to have a bit more stability in their lives as they
were less likely to be sold than slaves in smaller holdings. And thus they
tended to have more stability in their work lives and in their personal lives.
Lower rates of sales meant lower rates of family separation; that also meant
more persistence within their surrounding slave community.

Yet large slaveholdings tended also to produce isolation that inhibited
external interaction. So, for example, slaves in larger holdings tended to
form families later than those in smaller holdings, in part because the tendency to specialization and scattered worksites in large holdings separated
and confined slaves, restricting their choice of mates. Again, depending on
the commodity being produced and the mode of production, slaves in large
holdings could find themselves more or less socially isolated without much
opportunity for family or community or, in contrast, more or less socially
insulated with broad opportunities to develop family and community.

Enslaved blacks in large slaveholdings tended also to have less mobility
in terms of moving off or beyond the lands they worked. But chances did
exist to change jobs or at least to alternate tasks as larger holdings typically
tried to be self-sustaining communities constructed to supply most of what
their plantations needed. That required blacks to work at various skills, a
tendency that cut across crops. Blacks working rice and sugar, for example,
exhibited a similar range of skills as those working tobacco.

Tobacco lent itself less well to single large holdings, as reflected in North
Carolina and Virginia—early the leading tobacco producing areas, followed
in time by Kentucky. Together tobaccoland in 1860 had only 24 holdings of
more than 200 slaves. Of holdings of 100–199 slaves, North Carolina had
118, Virginia had 105, and Kentucky had 6. Holdings ranging from 10 to
30 slaves became the most typical by 1860 in tobaccoland where they were
23.2 percent in North Carolina, 22.6 percent in Virginia, and 16.5 percent
in Kentucky. Yet blacks working tobacco were continually on the move as
the broadleaf was notorious for depleting soil and pushing planting to new
ground or pushing slaves elsewhere. Indeed, enslaved blacks moved south

and west in an outflow from the Chesapeake and eastern seaboard numbering at least 800,000 between 1790 and 1860.

Other commodities also forced mobility. Enslaved black lumbermen, for
example, tended continually to be on the move to fresh woodlands. And
those working in producing naval stores derived largely from pine sap were
similarly on the move. In an era of sail, high demand existed in wooden
shipbuilding and maintenance for materials such as cordage, paint, pitch,
rosin, turpentine, varnish, and tar—all derived from pine sap.

What they produced determined most of the details of the work enslaved
blacks did. If they worked a crop, the rhythm of their life followed the crop's
seasonal pattern. By task, putting the crop in and taking it out demanded
the most intensive labor. Between planting and harvesting, the cycle of
seasons varied. Moreover, different crops showed different sensitivity and
temperamentality. For example, if not processed quickly, sugarcane spoiled
rapidly once ripened; so it had to be taken out of the field and got to the
mill as fast as possible. That made harvesting a harrowing time for enslaved
blacks in Louisiana and Florida fields, with their cane knives or machetes
cutting perhaps as much as half a ton of cane hourly or six tons daily. Time
marched as a terrible enemy assaulting with unrelenting force to crush the
stalks for their juice. Slaves strained under the weight of the month-long,
day-and-night, pressing process in the last and most intense stage after till-
age, planting, and harvesting.

Slaves working tobacco had a more consistent but less intense regime.
Their crop required constant year-round attention. It was tedious toil that
started with seed beds covered with wood ash or animal manure, then
transplanted in holes with pegs, and routinely inspected for insects before
harvest. The work was slow and steady without the crushing peaks of sugarcane production, opening slaves in tobaccoland to doing various jobs in
addition to attending tobacco.

After the early colonial years of establishing tobacco as a staple, slaves
in Virginia and Maryland moved also to growing wheat. They prepared
new fields and generally tidied the estate and its equipment when not working their primary and secondary crops. They had time to tinker as the
enslaved black called Stephen did in the 1830s in Caswell County, North
Carolina. He hit on a quick curing process that used intense heat to produce what became known as "bright leaf" tobacco. The discovery advanced
by Stephen's slaveholder, Abisha Slade, sparked a fresh boom in tobacco
production that made a fortune for Slade and boosted North Carolina to
dominance in late antebellum tobacco production.

Enslaved blacks working in the rice fields tended also to split their work
time as their crop, while demanding continual attention, allowed for attention to other work. Instead of working for a duration, they had to-do

lists. When they finished a task, they went to another. They had choice in their schedule and a level of individual self-direction uncommon in gang labor systems in other fields. Nevertheless they also did heavy lifting. Blacks enslaved early in South Carolina did the backbreaking work of primary field preparation, laying the foundation for what would become routine processes. Rice workers leveled and graded land for flooding, and built dikes to hold water and sluices to channel and drain water; and they seeded, with planting typically in early spring. Upland rice required no flooding but continuously moist soil, which often meant more labor for workers. During the four- to five-month rice-growing season, slaves patrolled irrigation waters to keep levels fairly constant and to keep out pests. In late summer they drained the fields and when dry harvested the two- to three-feet-high rice plants with their grain heads. They then dried the grain for milling and shipping.

The rice-growing season left perhaps half the year to other tasks, and as in the Chesapeake, where wheat grew to complement tobacco, in South Carolina rice-growing areas, indigo grew as a complement. The woody multi-stemmed plant, with featherlike leaves valued primarily for dying, grew to become colonial South Carolina's second-leading cash crop, accounting for more than one-third of the colony's exports by value in the early 1770s.

At least some captive Africans knew varieties of indigo as an herbal anti-inflammatory used to soothe toothaches, insect stings, and even snakebites. As with other enslaved blacks, they made their own uses of what they produced, following their own customs to meet their own needs, suit their own tastes, and promote their own values. Many mastered both white ways and their own ways as they negotiated their own needs in the context of their slaveholders' demands. Their degree of isolation made a difference. The less interaction blacks had with whites, the more distant they remained from white ways, as the Geechee and Gulllah of the Atlantic sea coast and Sea Islands illustrated.

Whether working cotton, sugarcane, or rice, blacks in large slaveholdings lived in circumstances unlike those in small holdings. While the core of oppression dominated black life everywhere, differences of circumstances were notable. The labor was not the same for everyone, everywhere, all the time. Age and sex made a difference, but the biggest difference makers were when and where the enslaved did what they did. The crop dictated much, but time and place each created distinctive differences in black life and development. Slavery was not the same experience for every slave, even in the same place and time. Nor was slavery the same across time and place. The organization and regulation of slavery changed as customs, practices, and laws changed. The institution was dynamic, ever a work in progress.

Coercion stayed its core, yet slavery took on distinct characteristics as it moved across time and space.

Away from large slaveholdings and sprawling landed estates, early and late, the fact was that most slaveholdings were small. At slavery's height in 1860, more than 60 percent of all slaveholdings—except in South Carolina (57.0%)—numbered nine or fewer slaves. In fact, more than half (54.1%) of all slaveholdings in the nation in 1860 numbered five or fewer enslaved blacks. Further, in every state the largest category of holding in 1860 was a single slave, ranging from 40.4% in Delaware down to 14.1% in South Carolina. Overall in 1860 about one in five (19.2%) of all U.S. slaveholdings was of a single slave. Such smaller holdings had characterized American Negro slavery from its beginnings, distributing the enslaved in mixed services regimes where they worked at crafts, in households and shops, or on family farms with crops and livestock. Thus, two contrasting images of American Negro slavery developed—that of whites with a typical small slaveholding and that of blacks in a typical large slaveholding.

Wherever they were, work was what slaves did. It identified them and much of the substance and structure of their individual and communal lives. Reputation, rewards and punishments arose from their work. What they produced notched their value and frequently their values. It set their market price. But, more, it set them in relation to their slaveholders, their overseers, and their fellow workers. Being valuable brought benefits as slaveholders and overseers usually favored slaves who produced most, often allowing them liberties denied to others. Such favors often included being less severely treated, escaping brutality that might damage high productivity and market value.

Slavery was in large part a business proposition. Holding or letting go a slave, early and often, was a matter of dollars-and-cents, and immediate payments were often weighed against long-term returns. Slaveholders generally held slaves for what they could get from them. But it was not all dollars-and-cents. Emotions also played a role. Slaves and slaveholders were, after all, human, so their feelings figured into their interactions. From revulsion to affection, from the strongest feelings to the feeblest, all the emotions imaginable affected their relations. Love, fondness, fury, hate, anger, resentment, rage, all were present at some time in some place among slaveholders and slaves.

Some slaves and slaveholders were kith and kin, as white fathers held as slaves their sons and daughters sired with women they held as slaves. And children of the same white father of slave children persisted in holding as slaves their half brothers and half sisters, their nieces and nephews. Rarely did whites sharing common paternity with slaves consider them blood relations. Ruling social norms ignored such relations, rejecting shared blood in dictating accepted lines of consanguinity and descent. Property relations prevailed over personal relations, as old English property law, not common paternity, determined status in connection to a common father. So children white men sired of enslaved black women became less than bastards, for the law in no way recognized them as persons but only as property. Thus, the ideology of white supremacy embedded in American Negro slavery denied the common heritage of blood. Yet common humanity surfaced from time to time in negotiations between slaves and slaveholders. White fathers did, on occasion, release their enslaved mates and children or otherwise assure favored treatment of them.

Release from slavery in the form of manumission could be a father's gift, but it could also be a matter of negotiation. If a slave was able to offer more than his slaveholder could otherwise get immediately in labor or at market, then he might negotiate for manumission, gaining release from slavery. But the give-and-take over the terms and conditions of the slave's work was usually for less than the prize of release from slavery—particularly in the antebellum plantation regime. Most often the tacit negotiation focused on contested concerns about how much of what work would be done, where, at what time, for how long, with what other workers, with what tools, and with what oversight. The contest over control of work extended beyond the workplace as it reached matters of rewards and punishments.

Slaves' hands-on control of the processes of production gave them some leverage against slaveholders and overseers. They could slow down or speed up what they were doing; they could do their tasks properly or poorly. They could neglect parts of their task or their tools. They could sabotage processes, making their tools, their draft animals, or even themselves unfit for work. And they could leave work altogether. Slaves could and did feign illness so often that their malingering became a common complaint among slaveholders. Also some slaves absented themselves from work, leaving for a day or two or more to express their displeasure or to seek the pleasure of change or companionship away from their assigned place. And in the ultimate act of absenting themselves, tens of thousands of enslaved blacks fled their workplaces and their slaveholders altogether, and in ever-increasing numbers. The flow of such fugitives produced a crisis in relations among the states and contributed heavily to the crisis of disunion in the United States in the 1850s. "Getting gone" or "stealing themselves away," as some styled slave flight, represented one response in enslaved blacks' ongoing struggle. It ended negotiations as the enslaved sought to opt out of the system entirely. It was the ultimate quitting.

For slaveholders, selling slaves was often the end of their negotiating, for they had primary leverage. They could bestow incentives. Most of all, they could inflict punishments, including the terrible lash and torture, both physical and psychological. For underneath all else, slavery was a system of terror. Coercion and intimidation forced slaves constantly to fear for themselves, for their kith and kin, for all their loved ones. They had little, if any, security. Law was not their protector; it was an intimidator and more. It was a device to ensure blacks' subordination and white domination; it aided and abetted the racial system of discipline and punishment that was American Negro slavery.

Yet slaveholders were dependent on slaves. Indeed, interdependence existed. There could be no slaveholders without slaves nor slaves without slaveholders. And that implicated the larger society, for it was not simply those who held title to slaves who were slaveholders; the society was the ultimate slaveholder, for it pronounced and protected the notion of property rights in human beings titled as slaves. Its governmental power supplied slavery's ultimate stability and sustained its coercion and violence, its intimidation and threat.

The mutuality between enslavers and enslaved extended to America's foundational principle of distinguishing blacks from whites by position and privilege, by the special treatment the society accorded each. The advantages, benefits, and rights the society bestowed on whites existed largely by contrast with the disadvantages with which it burdened blacks. The contrast was basic to the definition of American society, for whites could not be whites without blacks being blacks. Freedom became the other side of slavery. No privilege of race existed absent exclusion by race. And it was more than slavery. It was segregation inherent in America's ruling sense of itself that most whites accepted as their heritage and most blacks rejected as their deprivation.

## REFERENCES

Gray, L. C., and Esther Katherine Thompson. 1941. *History of Agriculture in the Southern United States to 1860*. Washington, DC: Carnegie Institution.

Lakwete, Angela. 2003. *Inventing the Cotton Gin: Machine and Myth in Antebellum America*. Baltimore, MD: Johns Hopkins University Press.

United States. Department of Commerce, Bureau of the Census. 1975. *Historical Statistics of the United States: Colonial Times to 1970*. Washington, DC: GPO.

Webber, Thomas L. 1978. *Deep Like the Rivers: Education in the Slave Quarter Community, 1831–1865*. New York: W. W. Norton.

Williamson, Samuel H., and Louis P. Cain. 2015. "Measuring Slavery in 2011 Dollars." *MeasuringWorth*, available at www.measuringworth.com/slavery.php

Witherspoon, Sylvia. 1936–1938. WPA Slave Narrative Project, Alabama Narratives, vol. 1. Federal Writer's Project, United States Work Projects Administration (USWPA); Manuscript Division, Library of Congress, Washington, DC. DIGITAL ID: mesn 010/435429.

_____ *Chapter 8* _____

# The Way They Do My Life

American Negro slavery cast an ever-present shadow that dogged blacks everywhere in the advent of the U.S. Civil War. They could not escape or ignore it, nor could their fellow Americans. Slavery engendered sectional, national, and local tensions. Nearly all blacks lived with those tensions in the stress of their everyday life, whether in or out of slavery.

In slavery, blacks lived under the law of the lash. The coercion was clear, ever-present, and terrifying. Keeping together body and soul was a primary concern, and no less distant was keeping kith and kin close. Family was a foremost concern for blacks, as a simple human desire. Yet family life proved precarious as slaveholders controlled important aspects of slaves' personal interaction—buying and selling, denying visiting, courting, and marriages, separating parents and children and siblings. Even so enslaved blacks maintained their own kinship traditions, albeit not to the extent of their African standards. Their relations differed also from European models as the segregation slavery imposed kept most slaves from idealized mother-father-children nuclear family households. Resilient as they were, however, enslaved blacks made do as best they could with variegated forms. Their families became patchworks in places, taking on their own rhymes, reasons, and rhythms.

Outside of slavery, blacks early grasped the monogamous household when it was in reach. As elsewhere in American society, that model symbolized both sobriety and stability. It stood as a mark of achievement, and for many blacks it became a coveted badge. Black communities nurtured family formations as part of their institutional development, for church and family coupled for mutual support. Indeed, in many eyes family and religion fused to represent black progress. And the combination was not some simple aping of Christian or European forms. Family was a centerpiece of African traditions, and Christianity preceded Atlantic World slavery in African life.

Black Christianity was no mere dark copy of white forms. From early on blacks adopted a teleology and theology of redemption, and they criticized the hypocritical Christianity of the dominant white society that maintained slavery. Blacks made Christianity work for them, filling its rites and rituals with their own sense, signs, and substance. They shaped it in their own patterns. In and out of slavery, blacks wielded Christianity as a weapon against their subjugation. Outside the slave South, they made their churches centers of antislavery.

North of the Mason–Dixon Line, blacks organized themselves, and joined with others, to do whatever they could to protect themselves from slavery and to release from slavery whomever they could. They networked as neighborhood watchers to warn of predators called "Blackbirders." For as the First Emancipation released more and more blacks from slavery in the North, blacks there found themselves more and more exposed to Blackbirders, especially after the federal Fugitive Slave Act of 1793 authorized any slaveholder "his agent or attorney . . . to seize or arrest [any] fugitive from labor" (United States 1793, 302). The phrase fugitive from labor was code for slave—a term U.S. statutes long shunned. Indeed, the U.S. Constitution itself deliberately avoided the terms *slave* or *slavery* until 1865, when it abolished its legal sanction.

As the presumption of color fixed early in American law to stamp every black person as a suspected slave, any black person without proof he or she was *not* a slave became suspect as a fugitive slave and thus liable under the 1793 act to be seized where found and removed to where the claim the person was a slave could be upheld. The black New Yorker Solomon Northup famously illustrated the practice in his 1855 narrative *Twelve Years a Slave*, telling the tale of his kidnapping and rescue from a Red River cotton plantation in Louisiana.

Blackbirders' snatching blacks in the North to slavery in the South prompted northern blacks to be ever wary and to push for what became known as "personal liberty laws" to provide state protection. Pennsylvania led the way, as it had with gradual emancipation. New York, Massachusetts, Ohio, and Wisconsin also would be prime movers over time. They offered blacks safeguards of basic legal due process, but those existed on paper. On the streets, in the alleys, and along the docks where blacks were being simply snatched, such safeguards by themselves offered no physical protection. At best they might invoke intervention from sympathetic local law enforcement. Likely blacks had only themselves and their friends and neighbors as physical safeguards. So they banded together against Blackbirders and others called "slave catchers."

Blacks in New York City led the way in organizing defenses. With the indomitable David Ruggles as a primary figure in the 1830s, they formed the New York Committee of Vigilance. Members went beyond being a neighborhood watch. They went on guard to block Blackbirders. They engaged in what were called "rescues" which became notable public disturbances, particularly after the Fugitive Slave Act of 1850. The bloody 1851 battle at Christiana, Pennsylvania, showed the depth of radical resistance to releasing runaways back to slavery. Other remarkable rescue events included that of William Henry, who called himself "Jerry," in Syracuse, New York, in 1851, those of Anthony Burns in Boston and Joshua Glover in Racine, Wisconsin, both in 1854, and that of John Price in Oberlin, Ohio, in 1858. Ruggles and his fellows were militant antislavers willing to put their bodies on the line for black liberty. They not simply sheltered fugitives; they saved victims from slave snatchers' hands. Among those Ruggles personally assisted was a 20-year-old Maryland runaway named Frederick Douglass.

Taking in runaways such as Douglass and guiding them to safe haven put Ruggles and the New York Committee in the forefront of an expanding network that came to be called the Underground Railroad. It served as a primary conduit that helped thousands of slaves in their flight to freedom. The routes ran in all directions away from the slave South: They ran from countryside to city, from city to countryside; they went north to Canada, south to Mexico, and west to the territories. Yet theirs was not a single, far-flung system. It was a series of local cells loosely connected by word of mouth that identified a person here and a person there willing to lend a helping hand, to open a barn for a night, or to provide a wagon ride or a meal.

Moral commitment enlisted most to the cause. Members of the Religious Society of Friends, commonly called "Quakers," were notable in supplying consistent connections. But the links had to remain secret, for they were illegal. The Fugitive Slave Act of 1793 made "any person who shall knowingly and willingly" aid any "fugitive from labor" liable to a fine of $500 (United States 1793, sec. 4). The Fugitive Slave Act of 1850 made such assistance "subject to a fine not exceeding one thousand dollars, and imprisonment not exceeding six months" (United States 1850, sec. 7).

Those who helped in the Underground Railroad and many who operated in vigilance committees did so covertly. Members of the Vigilant Committee of Philadelphia, for example, operated as a secret arm as the Vigilant Association of Philadelphia under the leadership of the wealthy South Carolina–born abolitionist Robert Purvis, the son of an English immigrant and a free woman of color. Their sympathies were usually open secrets, yet they sought to shield themselves from legal liability. They sought also to shield themselves from retaliation.

David Ruggles on several occasions suffered assaults, and even home invasions, at the hands of armed men angry at his antislavery activities. He cost slave catchers who worked as bounty hunters significant sums. Further, his outspokenness in his own semi-monthly journal *The Mirror of Liberty* that he began in July 1838 irked many who were proslavery and also many who wished to hear no more about the slavery matter. But he continued to rub salt in proslavers' wounds with his incessant abolitionism till his death in 1849.

Ruggles was one of a cadre of blacks deemed radicals. Few major northern black communities lacked such men and women. New York City, Philadelphia, and Boston frequently headlined the action, but black public campaigning was not exclusive to them. Lexington and Nantucket in Massachusetts, Newark in New Jersey, Troy and Rochester in Michigan had active black antislavery societies. In the gender segregation of the day, women formed their own, as illustrated by the Clarissa Beman-led Colored Female Anti-Slavery Society of Middletown, Connecticut. And black youth had junior societies such as the Pittsburgh Juvenile Anti-Slavery Society. Yet larger communities had more resources and garnered more attention. They were easier to get to and easier to be heard from and hosted more frequent activities. Their churches were routine meeting sites and their pastors leading spokesmen. In Philadelphia, for example, AME Bishop Richard Allen at "Mother" Bethel, Rev. Absalom Jones at St. Thomas Episcopal, and Rev. John Gloucester at the African Presbyterian Church stood in the forefront of black activism. Such men and their churches formed their own networks of black activists.

While David Ruggles and in time Frederick Douglass were powerful leaders in black causes with their journalism and other agitation, black ministers formed the front ranks in advancing black causes for most of the 19th century and into the 20th century. As religious ministers generally led much social development in early America, so it was among African Americans. As they moved beyond merely answering the call to preach to being formally trained and ordained, black ministers emerged among the most highly educated and respected members of their communities. Their congregations provided platforms for their outreach and activism, so they unsurprisingly held leadership positions.

More than their positions distinguished the leading antebellum black ministers. They were men of talent and tenacity. In New York City, for example, Peter Williams Jr. became the second ordained black Episcopal priest. His Revolutionary War veteran father, Peter Williams, had emphasized education to his son, enrolling him in the African Free School the New York Manumission Society set up in 1794. In addition to Williams Jr., the African Free School graduated such notables as the actor Ira Aldridge

Rev. Henry Highland Garnet exhorted enslaved blacks to "strike for your lives and liberties," controversially arguing that violence alone would end American Negro slavery. (Library of Congress)

and James McCune Smith, who would graduate also from the University of Glasgow in Scotland in 1837 as the first U.S. black to hold a medical degree. The Reverend Williams tutored Smith and helped send him to Glasgow.

The militant orator Henry Highland Garnet and the pioneering pan-Africanist thinker Alexander Crummell also graduated from the African Free School and pursued the ministry. Ordained as an Episcopal priest, Crummell studied at Cambridge University in England and became a missionary in West Africa before returning to the United States after the Civil War to found St. Luke's Episcopal Church in Washington, D.C. Graduating from the Oneida Theological Institute in Whitesboro, New York, the Reverend Garnet pastored the Liberty Street Presbyterian Church in Troy, New York. He became a leading figure in the National Negro Convention Movement (NNCM) that from 1830 through 1869 brought blacks together to express their common aspirations and grievances.

Much in demand as a speaker, Garnet was by turns vilified and hailed for his August 1843 "Call to Rebellion" at an NNCM session in Buffalo, New York. Formally titled "An Address to the Slaves of the United States

of America," Garnet's speech echoed elements of David Walker's 1829
*Address.* "Brethren, the time has come when you must act for yourselves,"
Garnet exhorted enslaved blacks. He praised Nat Turner and Denmark
Vesey and other rebels against slavery such as Toussaint L'Ouverture and
Joseph Cinqué leader of the *Amistad* revolt. "Brethren, arise, arise! Strike
for your lives and liberties. Now is the day and the hour. Let every slave
throughout the land do this and the days of slavery are numbered. You
cannot be more oppressed than you have been—you cannot suffer greater
cruelties than you have already. Rather die freemen than live to be slaves,"
Garnet declared (Garnet 1865, 44–51; Barnett 2003, 33–36).

Notable black ministers ranged across the antebellum North. Reputed the
first black student at Yale University, James W. C. Pennington pastored at
Talcott Street Church (later called Faith Congregational Church) in Hart-
ford, Connecticut. He wrote *The Origin and History of the Colored People* (1841) touted as the first history of blacks in the United States, and he
received an honorary doctorate from the German University of Heidelberg.
One of Pennington's fellow ministers in Connecticut was Amos G. Beman
at the Temple Street African Church in New Haven. Reputed the first
black student at Wesleyan University in Middletown, Connecticut, Charles
B. Ray pastored in New York City at the Crosby Congregational Church
and Bethesda Congregational Church. His daughter Charlotte E. Ray in
1872 became the first female graduate of the Howard University School of
Law and was admitted to practice law in the District of Columbia in 1872,
becoming the first female African American attorney. Her younger sister
Florence Ray also became an attorney.

Black ministers wore many hats and had their hands in most major community activities. The Reverend Ray, for example, owned and edited *The
Colored American*, a weekly newspaper begun in 1838. Rev. Samuel Cornish, pastor at the First African Presbyterian Church in Philadelphia and
then at Emmanuel Church in New York City, led the black movement into
newspapers. Cornish and John B. Russwurm edited the first black-owned
and edited newspaper in the United States, *Freedom's Journal*. Rev. Peter
Williams Jr. was a cofounder of the weekly that dedicated itself to "the
moral, religious, civil and literary improvement of our race." Its inaugural
issue of March 16, 1827, declared, "Too long have others spoken for us."
As with many black entries in the press, *Freedom's Journal* was relatively
short lived. It lasted only two years. Cornish followed it in May 1829 with
another short-lived weekly titled *The Rights of All.*

Following blacks in New York City, other black communities moved to
have their own newspapers. In 1828, for example, blacks in Philadelphia
produced the *African Journal* and in Boston the *National Philanthropist.*
Moving West blacks in Columbus, Ohio, in 1839 published the *Palladium*

*of Liberty*, and in 1855 the black press would reach California with Melvin Gibbs's *The Mirror of the Times* in San Francisco. The Civil War would bring the black press South with the colored Creole publication of the French language *L'Union* in September 1862 and then in 1864 the nation's first black daily, the *New Orleans Tribune*, which published English and French editions. In common the publications advocated radical abolition and equal rights. They promoted education and literacy and sought to keep their readers abreast of local, regional, national, and world news. Emphasizing black achievements and contributions, they preached moral uplift and battled against black stereotypes *Freedom's Journal* termed misrepresentations.

The most influential antebellum black newspaper was Frederick Douglass's *North Star*. Begun in Rochester, New York, in December 1847 and continued after 1851 under the title *Frederick Douglass' Paper*, the four-page weekly extended the reach of the most famous runaway slave in U.S. history. His story became an American classic with the publication in 1845 of the best-selling *Narrative of the Life of Frederick Douglass, an American Slave*. The paper gave Douglass a hearing beyond the lecture circuit, where he was in much demand. It circulated throughout North America, in the West Indies, and in Europe and gave him a platform to express himself on wide-ranging political topics. Abolition was his lead subject, but social justice and reform were by and large his message. Douglass became the dominant voice, if not the face, of antebellum black America and beyond. He became the most recognized black of the 19th century.

Prominence anointed Douglass and gave his views cachet. Much of his thinking repeated others, however. He was hardly the first or alone to crusade against American Negro slavery and the segregation white male supremacy imposed. David Ruggles early demonstrated the benefits of direct action for him, and Henry Highland Garnet impressed radicalism on him, for example. And the words and work of forceful women also taught him lessons reflected in part in the *North Star*'s motto: "Right is of no Sex—Truth is of no Color—God is the Father of us all, and we are all Brethren." He stood at the 1848 Seneca Falls convention to second Elizabeth Cady Stanton's resolution demanding women's suffrage.

Sojourner Truth and Harriet Tubman provided powerful examples for Douglass's day and beyond of black women as public figures in their own right. Like Douglass, both women escaped from slavery, and both became powerful characters of self-creation. All three named themselves in their personal growth and self-empowerment. Harriet Tubman labored in different fields from Sojourner Truth and Frederick Douglass. While Truth and Douglass climbed antebellum daises, Tubman worked behind the scenes. Out of public view she no less captured popular imagination by practicing the gospel "to proclaim liberty to captives" in a most direct way that

Harriet Tubman, dubbed the "Moses of her people," escaped from slavery
and returned repeatedly to lead scores of others from bondage. Runaways
persistently bedeviled the slave regime, costing the system time and money
and aggravating tensions between the North and South to hasten the Civil
War and general emancipation. (Library of Congress)

garnered her in time the moniker "Moses of her people." She became the
most recognizable persona of the Underground Railroad.

Tubman and Truth both suffered remarkable physical abuse at the hands
of enslavers. Abuse was, of course, the nature of slavery, but black females
like Tubman and Truth suffered especially as sexual prey. Black boys and
men also were abused sexually, yet as a group black males were not as sexually vulnerable and horribly exploited as black females. Routinely, if not
characteristically, enslaved black females fell victim to rape and domestic
violence. They lived with the constant threat of sexual assault and defended
themselves as best they could.

Their struggles and lack of protection showed clearly in the 1855 case of
Celia. Widowed Missouri slaveholder Robert Newsom bought the 14-year-
old as a slave in 1850 and over the years routinely raped her. She bore him a
son and in 1855 was pregnant again. She begged Newsom "to quit forcing

her" at least during her pregnancy, and she implored his two daughters to intervene on her behalf. To no avail. On the night of June 23, 1855, when Newsom insisted on having his way with her, Celia clubbed him to death and then burned his corpse in her slave cabin fireplace, scattering his ashes in the yard and burying his unburned bones (McLaurin 1991, 1–32).

Arrested and prosecuted for murder, Celia pled self-defense. Missouri Circuit Court Judge William Hall refused to hear such a defense or to let the jury consider it. He ruled in short that as a slave Celia had no will of her own and no right to resist her slaveholder. She was his to do whatever he wished. Following Judge Hall's instructions, the jury found Celia guilty of first-degree murder. Hall sentenced her to hang but stayed the execution until she delivered her pregnancy. Any child born, after all, was valuable property of Newsom's estate and not to be destroyed without compensation by law. When Celia did deliver, the child was stillborn, and Celia herself died on the gallows four days before Christmas in 1855.

Harriet Jacobs's 1861 *Incidents in the Life of a Slave Girl: Written by Herself* further illustrated the terror of sexual assault and the resilience of enslaved black women's resistance. To thwart her slaveholder's attacks, Jacobs ultimately hid out for seven years, refusing to be totally cut off from her children whom she could see and hear but not touch or tell them she was near and watching. She thereby refused to be raped at her slaveholder's will. Like the prosecutors and much of the public in Celia's case who wanted to hear nothing of self-defense, many on hearing Harriet Jacobs's story refused to believe it. Some even criticized her as a mother who abandoned her children, as if her proper role as a mother or as a slave was to stay and submit sexually to her slaveholder.

Some black women did submit sexually in and out of slavery, to slaveholders and others, to white men and black men. The male domination of the patriarchal society and the white supremacy of slavery and segregation combined in the plight they had to deal with as American society constructed their constrained personal and gender identities. As slaves they were objects and as women they were objects.

But if society cast them as objects under the power of others, black females demonstrated beyond all measure their independent power to construct and represent themselves as themselves. They lived severely limited by views of what was culturally and socially permissible for them. Yet Sojourner Truth, Harriet Tubman, Celia, Harriet Jacobs, and uncountable hosts of other black women demonstrated their individual and collective competence and power to succeed within and outside the boundaries others drew for them.

Black women were foremost as slaves suing for freedom. The male-dominated legal order put Dred Scott in the forefront of the most infamous U.S. Supreme Court decision on slavery or for blacks' rights generally, for that matter. But his wife Harriet Robinson Scott was no less a force in the action and the likely prime mover. She brought her own case for freedom in 1846, overshadowed as she became "Mrs. Dred Scott." Her life before and after her marrying Dred exhibited too seldom considered aspects of American Negro slavery (VanderVelde and Subramanian 1997, 1033–1122).

Rather than the typical antebellum slave scene of the plantation South or that earlier in the North, Harriet's early life opened on what was then the western frontier. She exhibited much of the life of slaves on the move, living in the Upper Mississippi region that became Minnesota and areas of the old Northwest Territory, and down along the Mississippi River. Her successive slaveholders were U.S. Army officers with whom she moved from post to post, living in areas such as Illinois and the Wisconsin territory where federal and local law prohibited slavery. She used her residence in such slave-free areas as one of the bases for her suit, as did many of the hundreds of petitions called "freedom suits" filed in high-traffic and transition areas such as St. Louis, Missouri, and Washington, D.C. (Schweninger 2014, 35–62).

Not every place allowed blacks to challenge their slave status in court. The presumption of color usually left blacks no place to start in the American legal system, for in most places they had no legal standing to be heard in court. No notion of wrongful enslavement commonly attached to blacks where slavery was settled. Yet there were unsettled areas, and the agitation of the American Revolution opened spaces for blacks to petition for freedom, as illustrated by collective petitions in Massachusetts and Connecticut in the 1770s. Blacks such as Pomp in Norwalk, Connecticut, in 1779, and Ned Griffin in Edgecombe County, North Carolina, in 1784 petitioned to recognize their claims to freedom. But those were legislative petitions. Going to court was a different matter after entry closed in the late 1600s when American Negro slavery began its first growth spurt.

Following the First Emancipation, the growing gap between states with increasing slave populations and states with decreasing slave populations opened avenues for blacks to get court hearings. Congress expanded the divide with its compromises to split U.S. territories by prohibiting slavery in some areas and permitting it in others, as it started with the Northwest Ordinance of 1787 and would continue in 1820 with the Missouri Compromise treating the Louisiana Purchase territory.

The split over slavery allowed increasing questions about which blacks were slaves and which were not. The possibility of such doubt gave rise to thousands of petitions from the early 1800s to the Civil War. Courts in St. Louis received more than 300 freedom petitions and at least 500 arose in Washington, D.C., during that time. Hundreds of other suits arose in Delaware, Maryland, Virginia, North Carolina, Kentucky, and

Tennessee—collectively referred to as the Upper South. Louisiana also had manifold freedom petitions with its rich mixed-race heritage.

Black women led the way in these freedom petitions. Early on, for example, Mima Queen made it to the U.S. Supreme Court, and a black woman named Winny would have her petition be the first the Missouri Supreme Court ruled on, opening a line of cases that would lead to Harriet Robinson Scott's 1846 petition in St. Louis. Winny won her case on the fact that her slaveholders had before moving to Missouri resided with her for three or four years in Illinois, with its local and federal prohibitions against slavery.

Who could testify to what in freedom petition cases was a controlling question. Enslaved blacks typically had no documents proving their status as free. Usually those challenging their status had only testimony typically ruled inadmissible as hearsay, as in Queen's case in which Chief Justice John Marshall noted that " 'hearsay' evidence is in its own nature inadmissible." Queen lost on Marshall's hearsay ruling. But her case elicited a pointed dissent. Arguing for a long-standing rule in his home state of Maryland, Justice Gabriel Duvall offered the progressive and controversial pronouncement that "it will be universally admitted that the right to freedom is more important than the right of property" (United States 1813, 298–299).

Harriet Robinson Scott made use of the line of freedom petition cases along with her husband, Dred. She had been taken in and out of residences in territories where the United States had declared "neither slavery nor involuntary servitude shall exist." By Winny's rule some of Harriet's residences had released her from slavery. Also Harriet had a claim that her slaveholder's consent to her wedding Dred in a recorded civil ceremony was a tacit manumission. Her status was crucial in its own right for her personal liberty. It was even more pressing on her as a mother, for her status descended to her daughters, Eliza and Lizzie. If she were free of slavery, so were they. And so they were according to a St. Louis Circuit Court jury and judgment. But that was not the last word. The matter continued to the Missouri Supreme Court and then to the U.S. Supreme Court, and the Scotts lost in both venues where Harriet and her daughters found their personal identities submerged in the single male identity of Dred Scott.

The Scotts' loss was hardly remarkable. What made the case titled *Scott v. Sandford* a landmark for blacks was Chief Justice Roger Brooke Taney's scornful language declaring that members of "the African race" had never been recognized as U.S. citizens and could never be recognized as U.S. citizens. Blacks were, Taney said, "a subordinate and inferior class of beings . . . and, whether emancipated or not . . . had no rights or privileges but such as those who held the power and the Government might choose to grant them" (United States 1857, 482, 404–405).

Blacks railed against the Taney decision announced on March 5, 1857. For some it was a note of despair, signaling an ultimate abandonment that made African Americans a people without a country or at least a people who owed no allegiance to the nation where they lived. While no less decrying Taney's decision, others took it as a rallying point. Frederick Douglass notably cast the Taney decision as a signal for advance. Noting the rumblings to dissolve the Union, he suggested that the coming Civil War would resolve that "liberty, the glorious birthright of our common humanity, will become the inheritance of all the inhabitants of this highly favored country" (Douglass 1857, 27–46).

And, in fact, the Civil War came, but not with sure liberation or civil rights for blacks.

## PROFILE: HENRY HIGHLAND GARNET (1815–1882)

Fleeing slavery in Maryland with his parents as a nine-year-old, Henry came to New York City, where at the African Free School he joined others destined for fame. Garnet stood in the forefront of black youth pressing the cause of abolition from the time he attended the First Colored Presbyterian Church Rev. Samuel Cornish established in 1821 with an insistent antislavery congregation. Joining in 1834 with David Ruggles and William H. Day, Garnet organized the Garrison Literary and Benevolent Association to advance antislavery ideas William Lloyd Garrison was controversially publishing in his Boston-based weekly *The Liberator*. The teenage radical went on to study at Noyes Academy in Canaan, New Hampshire, and at Oneida Theological Institute in Whitesboro, New York. He managed much of his studies through pain, for at age 15 he ruined a knee that tormented him until his lower leg was amputated in 1841. He persisted without complaint, becoming ordained as a Presbyterian minister, marrying, and becoming a father of three—although only one child lived to adulthood.

Garnet catapulted to national notice with what became popularly known as his "Call to Rebellion" address at the August 1843 National Negro Convention in Buffalo, New York. "Brethren, arise, arise! Strike for your lives and liberties. Now is the day and the hour. Let every slave throughout the land do this, and the days of slavery are numbered," Garnet exhorted. "You cannot be more oppressed than you have been—you cannot suffer greater cruelties than you have already. Rather die freemen than live to be slaves," he urged.

Garnet's call marked him as radical, and that was the character of his life. An insistent abolitionist, he became an emigrationist also, working with the American and Foreign Anti-Slavery Society and supporting blacks moving from the United States to Liberia, Mexico, or the West Indies, where in the 1850s he served as a missionary in Kingston, Jamaica.

The Civil War buoyed Garnet's hopes for the United States to become a more welcoming place for blacks. The three-day July 1863 New York City Draft Riots convinced him his boyhood home was then no place to be, however. He moved in 1864 to Washington, D.C., to pastor the Fifteenth Street Presbyterian Church and became the first black to preach in the U.S. Capitol, offering a sermon in the chambers of the U.S. House of Representatives.

After serving briefly in 1868 as president of Avery College in Pittsburgh, Garnet returned to New York City to pastor his boyhood church that had become Shiloh Presbyterian. The disappointments of Reconstruction inclined Garnet to continue to consider life in Africa, and in 1881 he realized an opportunity to return to the motherland when President James A. Garfield appointed him U.S. minister to Liberia.

Garnet died on February 13, 1882, within two months of reaching African soil, at age 66.

## PROFILE: HARRIET TUBMAN (1822–1913)

The woman born Araminta Ross in Dorchester County on Maryland's Eastern Shore around 1822 became one of the most fearless and accomplished antislavery agents in U.S. history. Not only did she free herself from slavery by running from Maryland to Pennsylvania, but she repeatedly returned South to lead others from slavery, beginning with her parents and siblings.

Traveling by cover of night, she used secret refuges known as "stations" among antislavery sympathizers willing to pass along fugitives in the informal network that came to be called the Underground Railroad. She earned the title "conductor" for transporting runaways and proudly noted that "I can say what most conductors can't say—I never ran my train off the track and I never lost a passenger."

Tubman's identity became no secret during her forays South. Amid the heated argument over slavery in general and runaways in particular that produced the federal Fugitive Slave Act of 1850, slaveholders targeted her as "wanted dead or alive." The rewards for her multiplied to more than 10 times the $100 offered in October 1849 when an ad in the Dorchester County *Cambridge Democrat* newspaper said she was called "Minty," put her age at about 27 years, and described her as "of a chestnut color, fine looking, and about 5 feet high." She was reported as escaping with two of her brothers, 25-year-old Ben and 19-year-old Harry.

During the Civil War, Tubman joined forces with the Union army to battle slavery however she could, even leading armed expeditions and raids. In the wake of slavery's abolition, she turned her attention to advocating for equal rights and particularly women's suffrage (Clinton 2004, passim).

Recognizing her contributions to the nation, the U.S. Treasury announced Tubman as the first woman to have her portrait on U.S. currency, replacing Andrew Jackson on the U.S. $20 bill.

## REFERENCES

Barnett, Alex. 2003. *Words That Changed America: Great Speeches That Inspired, Challenged, Healed, and Enlightened.* Guilford, CT: Lyons Press.

Clinton, Catherine. 2004. *Harriet Tubman: The Road to Freedom.* Boston: Little, Brown.

Douglass, Frederick. 1845. *Narrative of the Life of Frederick Douglass, an American Slave: Written by Himself.* Boston, MA: The Anti-Slavery Office.

Douglass, Frederick. 1857. *Two Speeches by Frederick Douglass.* Rochester, NY: C. P. Dewey.

Garnet, Henry Highland. 1865. *A Memorial Discourse.* Philadelphia: J. M. Wilson.

McLaurin, Melton Alonza. 1991. *Celia, a Slave.* Athens: University of Georgia Press.

Missouri. 1824. *Winny v. Whitesides*, 1 Mo. 472 (1824).

Missouri. 1852. *Scott v. Emerson*, 15 Mo. 576 (1852).

Missouri, St. Louis Circuit Court, Office of the Circuit Clerk. 2004. "Freedom Suits Case Files, 1814–1860," St. Louis Circuit Court Records Project, a collaboration between the Missouri State Archives, the St. Louis Circuit Court Clerk's Office, the American Culture Studies Program, Washington University, and the Missouri Historical Society (St. Louis, MO), 2004. Accessed at http://www.stlcourtrecords.wustl.edu/about-freedom-suits-series.php.

Northup, Solomon. 1855. *Twelve Years a Slave: Narrative of Solomon Northup, a Citizen of New-York, Kidnapped in Washington City in 1841, and Rescued in 1853.* Auburn, NY: Miller, Orton & Mulligan.

Schweninger, Loren. 2014. "Freedom Suits, African American Women, and the Genealogy of Slavery." *William and Mary Quarterly* 71, no. 1 (January): 35–62.

United States. 1793. "An Act Respecting Fugitives from Justice, and Persons Escaping from the Service of Their Masters" (Fugitive Slave Act). 1 Stat. 302 (February 12, 1793).

United States. 1813. *Queen v. Hepburn*, 11 U.S. (7 Cranch) 290 (1813); aff'ing *Queen v. Hepburn*, 20 F. Cas. 130 (C.C.D.C. 1810) (No. 11,503).

United States. 1850. "An Act to Amend, and Supplementary to, the Act Entitled 'An Act Respecting Fugitives from Justice, and Persons Escaping from the Service of Their Masters,' Approved February Twelfth, One Thousand Seven Hundred and Ninety-Three." 9 Stat. 462 (September 13, 1850).

United States. 1857. *Scott v. Sandford*, 60 U.S. 393 (1857).

VanderVelde, Lea, and Sandhya Subramanian. 1997. "Mrs. Dred Scott." *Yale Law Journal* 106, no. 4 (January): 1033–1122.

# Chapter 9

# There's a Change Coming

Like other Americans, African Americans could not be sure what the Civil War would bring. Like others, they saw it coming. Some hoped for it. Ardent abolitionist Frederick Douglass welcomed it as an opportunity for black liberation and elevation. He foresaw thousands of blue-coated Union men marching into slave states after the firing on Fort Sumter in April 1861. He knew President Abraham Lincoln insisted at the war's outset that its purpose was to restore federal authority, not to free slaves. Yet Douglass saw also that enslaved blacks would seize the opportunity to free themselves in unprecedented numbers, as enslaved field hands Frank Baker, Shepherd Mallory, and James Townsend did in May 1861 to become the first erstwhile fugitives local Union commander Major General Benjamin F. Butler received as what he deemed "contraband of war."

Learning of Baker and others at Fort Monroe eventually drew thousands of African Americans to the place they dubbed "Freedom Fortress." They spread to create in its shadows a self-contained black community called "the Great Contraband Camp." It housed as many as 10,000 ex-slaves by April 1865. It was the first of perhaps 100 such camps for fugitive blacks that developed during the war as their presence pressured the federal government to make practical arrangements and formal policies to deal with them.

Thousands of blacks scrambled also to Washington, D.C. Their very presence confronted federal policymakers with the urgency of accommodating their need for food, clothing, and shelter. Camp Brightwood opened in Northwest D.C. under U.S. Army direction in late 1861 to provide for those being called "contrabands." Blacks made their own accommodations east of the Anacostia River, near Battery Carroll and Fort Greble.

At the onset of the Civil War, blacks enslaved in the South fled to Union lines where they became known as "contrabands." They seized their opportunities to end slavery for themselves and built their own transient communities under U.S. Army protection. (Library of Congress)

The fugitives made clear the federal government's need to deal with slavery as a matter of war, if nothing else. Harriet Tubman explained the issue simply in the winter of 1861. "[T]his Negro can tell Massa Lincoln how to save money and young men. He can do it by setting the Negroes free," advised the woman who had fled slavery herself in 1849. "God won't let Massa Lincoln beat the South until he does the right thing," Tubman instructed (Nies 2002, 52). *Douglass' Monthly* in May 1861 concurred. "Any attempt now to separate the freedom of the slave from the victory of the Government, . . . any attempt to secure peace to the Whites while leaving the Blacks in chains . . . will be labor lost," Douglass insisted.

President Lincoln preferred to leave to their own devices fugitives and, for that matter, slaves, too. "I have not meant to leave anyone in doubt," he wrote famously in August 1862 to reiterate his position. "My paramount objective in this struggle *is* to save the Union, and is *not* either to save or to destroy slavery. If I could save the Union without freeing *any* slave I would do it, and if I could save it by freeing *all* the slaves I would do it; and if I could save it by freeing some and leaving others alone I would do that also," he declared in a letter to *New York Tribune* editor Horace Greeley in August 1862.

While Lincoln resisted the reality, blacks embraced the war as a struggle against slavery. And while those looking to escape slavery welcomed helping hands, they were not looking for handouts. They were ready to work to support themselves, their kith and kin. Indeed, many were ready to fight for freedom, but U.S. policies and practices barred them. The U.S. Army, for example, long refused black enlistments but employed black men as civilian labor in construction and maintenance; and individual soldiers personally paid blacks for services such as laundry. Black blacksmiths, boatmen, and nurses found jobs more easily, but there was not enough work to go around, nor was the pay much.

Blacks' largest self-supporting effort behind Union lines during the war developed in what became known as the Port Royal Experiment. It arose not from black fugitives but from white fugitives who fled the South Carolina Sea Islands after the U.S. Navy's victory at the Battle of Port Royal in November 1861. Blacks remained to work the lands where they had slaved, turning toil to their own benefit and self-sufficiency. The U.S. military essentially acquiesced as it lacked the wherewithal to do anything else with the more than 10,000 blacks on Port Royal Island and its environs located about halfway between Charleston and Savannah. Missionaries, teachers, and others from freedmen's aid societies assisted by starting schools and providing some medical care. Working approximately 195 abandoned long-staple cotton plantations, the former slaves within two years developed a thriving economy and created their own town at Mitchellville on Hilton Head Island. What they did not get was legal title to the lands they worked, which in time created its own issues and their dispossession.

Most of the near 4 million blacks enslaved in the 11 Confederate states remained beyond Union lines until late in the war. They had limited opportunities to escape until Union forces arrived. They did what they could, given their place and time and circumstances. They suffered privations from war, as the South itself suffered from Union blockades and the siphoning off of manpower. Some slaves enjoyed less supervision as the war drew away masters and overseers. Some suffered more spiteful supervision, as masters and overseers reacted angrily against blacks for rebel setbacks or any sign favoring the Yankees. Sixteen-year-old Mattie Jane Jackson recalled how her slave master on finding in her mother's room a newspaper clipping with a picture of Abraham Lincoln "knocked her down three times" and gave her "a month of punishment." Mattie added that in the course of war, "the days of sadness for mistress were days of joy for us" (Jackson 1866, 11–12).

Envisioning approaching freedom was sometimes nerve-racking for blacks in combat areas. They might well be elated at the arrival of Union troops only to be deflated as the formation moved on. And Yankee troops were not always welcome sights, as blacks suffered along with rebel whites when bluecoats sacked and plundered southern locales. Cornelia Robinson recalled "the Yankees was a hurricane" coming through the environs of

Opelika in east-central Alabama in 1864 and 1865. The town was an important local transportation hub warehousing Confederate supply depots. It was a target for Union destruction, and the troops were "up to the task," Cornelia reported from her childhood memories. "Child, them Yankees come through and cleaned out the smokehouse; even left the lard bucket as clean as your hand," she reported. "[T]hey tore up everything they couldn't take with them. They poured all the syrup out and it run down the road like water," she added (Robinson 1936–1938, 331).

For blacks in remote areas like West Texas or other places distant from focal battlefronts, the approach of freedom remained distant. Congress provided in July 1862 that slaves of rebels who came under Union control "shall be forever free of their servitude, and not again held as slaves" (United States 1862c, 589). But release from slavery by Union authority arrived only after the Confederate surrender at Appomattox in April 1865 formally ended the war, as was so, too, with the liberation President Abraham Lincoln's Emancipation Proclamation authorized.

Issued in September 1862, the president's proclamation gave rebels 100 days to surrender or lose their slaves. Its force depended on Union arms, but once those arms prevailed, its promise also prevailed. For the president had ordered and declared "that all persons held as slaves within said designated States, and parts of States [in rebellion on January 1, 1863], are, and henceforward shall be free." That freedom was not immediate. The black holiday that would come to be celebrated in West Texas and elsewhere as "Juneteenth" represented the proclamation's delayed reach in June 1865. Until then blacks in rebel hands continued to slave much as they had in the antebellum years and earlier.

The first to enjoy legal freedom amid the twists and turns of war were blacks enslaved in the U.S. capital. Their presence had impressed on the nation its commitment to slavery since the creation in 1790 of the federal district along the Potomac River. Their presence during the Civil War early created consternation among those eager to distinguish Union freedom from Confederate slavery, and in April 1862, on the first anniversary of the rebel slaveholders' firing on Fort Sumter, Congress signaled the developing U.S. position that slavery needed to be abolished.

Consistent with most earlier U.S. law, the District of Columbia Emancipation Act refused to use the term *slave*. Rather it addressed "certain Persons held to Service or Labor," mimicking the Constitution of 1787. It provided that "all persons held to service or labor within the District of Columbia by reason of African descent are hereby discharged and freed of and from all claim to such service or labor." Further, it previewed language to be etched into the U.S. Constitution by providing that "from and after the passage of this act neither slavery nor involuntary servitude, except for crime, whereof the party shall be duly convicted, shall hereafter exist in said District" (United States 1862a, 376).

The official count of blacks released from slavery in the District of Columbia was 2,989. That was the number for whom the law paid up to $300 in compensation to former owners loyal to the Union. The full number freed was larger as it included blacks whose slaveholders could not prove their loyalty and also blacks who had fled to D.C. and declared themselves free by virtue of being there when the act became law. They took advantage of the haven, for who was to distinguish among blacks as to who was free at one time or another after slavery was abolished. And so it was that reaching the District of Columbia proved a journey of freedom for most of the 25,000 blacks who crowded in by war's end. Whether they camped among the refugees at Duff Green's Row on First Street, between East Capitol and "A" Street SE, at Camp Barker at 12th Street and Vermont Avenue NW, at Camp Brightwood, or lived elsewhere, they were no longer legal chattel.

Blacks in U.S. territories also enjoyed release from slavery as Congress in June 1862 committed itself to no longer allowing "slavery nor involuntary servitude in any of the Territories of the United States now existing, or which may at any time thereafter be formed or acquired by the United States, otherwise than in punishment of crimes whereof the party shall have been duly convicted" (United States 1862b, 432). As with the release of slaves in the District of Columbia, the official number of blacks enjoying release from slavery in U.S. territories was relatively small. But blacks understood the congressional actions were no small things, for as the *New York Daily Tribune* anticipated when Congress abolished slavery in D.C. in April 1862, it meant that "in the domain hitherto exclusively under Federal law Slavery exists no longer."

As with thousands of black fugitives who risked life and limb to seize their freedom from slavery when war erupted, thousands of black men reached out to take federal arms against slavery. "Whites-only" was the formal rule in the U.S. military since the Militia Act of 1792 restricted enrollment to any "free able-bodied White male citizen . . . of the age of eighteen years, and under the age of forty-five years." And no change appeared in the offing as the war first raged, as Secretary of War Simon Cameron noted in 1861 in declaring that "this Department has no intention at present to call into the service of Government any colored soldiers" (DC.gov, n.d., n.p.).

African Americans long railed against U.S. policies and practices preventing their formal enlistment to fight against the Confederacy. Only in July 1862 did Congress authorize the president to enlist blacks, but even then he hesitated. In apparent irony, the Confederacy beat the Union to having blacks bear arms under its colors. The *Charleston Mercury* in April 1861 reported on the parade of Confederate troops in Augusta, including a black company from Nashville. On the western side of Tennessee, the *Memphis Avalanche* and *Memphis Appeal* reported the organizing of "a volunteer company composed of our patriotic freemen of color." Similarly, in the South's largest and wealthiest free black community, colored men rallied to the Confederate call as illustrated by a regiment of more than 1,100 parading in New Orleans in April 1861, proclaiming themselves "defenders of the native land." The *New Orleans Picayune* in February 1862 conceded that "we must also pay deserved complement to the companies of free colored men, all very well drilled and comfortably equipped" (Fleetwood 1895, 6).

Colored volunteers in the South saw themselves fighting for hearth and home, for their way of life, for sharing fidelity for the place of their birth. They had social positions to defend, and like their brethren on the Union side, they wanted not to be found wanting in the eyes of their already suspicious and often hostile white neighbors. They enlisted in the cause to show their local loyalty. Some were grateful to those who earlier had released them from slavery. Some went to war hoping their service would bring freedom from slavery. And although still enslaved, some felt gratitude for what they considered good treatment. Colored volunteers for the Confederacy identified with the society where they were born and bred: they were Southerners. They saw themselves as fighting for what they knew and against what they feared, as some accepted rebel cant that Yankees were devils and would destroy the only world they knew. And hundreds of the colored men who rallied to the Confederate cause did so to maintain slavery, as they were themselves slaveholders, especially in Louisiana, South Carolina, and Virginia: perhaps as many as 3,000 colored persons in Louisiana in 1860 owned slaves.

The bulk of blacks who saw Civil War armed service wore Union blue. Viewing the war as an opportunity to destroy slavery, black men early volunteered to fight even as federal policy rejected them. That refusal further irked blacks. It insulted their abilities, particularly their masculinity. They had led the fight against slavery from its beginning. This last fight, as they hoped it to be, was theirs at least as much as anyone else's. They wanted to own part of it. They wanted to be full participants, but they were not welcome. "Why does the Government reject the negro?" Frederick Douglass objected in *Douglass' Monthly* in September 1861. "Is he not a man? Can he not wield a sword, fire a gun, march and countermarch, and obey orders like any other?" Douglass pressed.

Blacks' fight to shoulder arms against slavery was also a fight against inferiority. Blacks wanted to prove themselves in the eyes of their fellow Americans and the world. They saw being excluded from the U.S. armed forces as an extension of slavery, as imprinting on them a lack of fitness to stand as competent human beings and as men. Blacks understood the white

Black men clamored to go to war against slavery. The thousands who freed themselves as "contrabands" were among the first to enlist when the U.S. Army lifted its ban on blacks and organized the 4th U.S. Colored Infantry and other colored troops. (Library of Congress)

prejudice that wished to relegate them, that denied them equal status and reputation, and that refused to believe blacks could stand and fight as well as whites or, in fact, do anything as well as whites. Getting in the fight, then, became more than an act of pride; it was a step to validate black humanity and manhood.

Blacks insisted on joining the fight against the southern slaveocracy. Rebuffing federal policy, they fought as irregulars. They spied, they guided, and they supported Union troops as burial and labor details and in various other ways. Yet they hankered for the first ranks rather than behind-the-scenes work to which bias typically relegated them. They wanted to wear the uniform and be recognized as regulars. Their increasing presence in Union lines and the Union need for manpower in the ranks put blacks in U.S. Army uniforms, but not as regulars: They were segregated, as they long would be, and shouldered arms as United States Colored Troops (USCT) the War Department created with General Order No. 143 in May 1863 (Berry 1977, x).

Blacks in South Carolina were the first to formally don U.S. Army attire. In the state with the largest black majority (59%) in the nation, they early swelled Union lines, particularly in the Sea Islands and coastal areas, rallying in the spring of 1862 to U.S. Army Major General of Volunteers David Hunter's enlisting them in the 1st South Carolina Volunteers. The nation's first recognized black unit caused a stir and prompted a congressional inquiry into General Hunter's authority to enlist black troops, but the winds of war soon diffused that controversy.

Blacks' performance in the field resoundingly answered the questions of whether they could and would fight. In a weeklong battle along the Georgia–Florida coast in November 1862, the 1st South Carolina distinguished itself to the degree that N.Y. infantry Lieutenant Colonel Oliver T. Beard officially reported that "the colored men fought with astonishing coolness and bravery. I found them all I could desire, more than I had hoped. They behaved gloriously, and deserve all praise" (United States 1880–1901, ser. 20, 192).

Colored Troops repeatedly proved themselves in the field. The Battle of Fort Pillow in April 1863 saw their low point. On garrison duty about 40 miles north of Memphis, Colored Troops in the 2nd and 6th U.S. artillery along with the 14th Tennessee Cavalry faced down a Confederate force about three to four times their number. They fought valiantly, but the rebels under Confederate Major General Nathan Bedford Forrest overran the Union defenders and refused them any quarter, slaughtering the black troops in what became known as the Fort Pillow Massacre. The recognized rule from that butchery was that rebels would not honor black troops as prisoners of war. That instructed blacks to fight all the harder, to prevail or die.

Blacks' determination in the field showed itself again and again at other sites in the Union campaign to control the Mississippi River. As part of the Union siege of Vicksburg, for example, the 9th and 10th Louisiana and 1st Mississippi USCT in June 1863 repulsed Confederate attacks on the Union supply depots and hospital at Milliken's Bend, Louisiana. And from May through July 1863 in the final push for Union control of North America's chief river, Colored Troops in the 48-day siege of the Confederate bluff redoubt at Port Hudson, Louisiana, about 20 miles upriver from Baton Rouge, so distinguished themselves in "the most awful ordeal" that a June 11, 1863, New York Times editorial declared, "It is no longer possible to doubt the bravery and steadiness of the colored race."

At Olustee, the largest Civil War battle in Florida, the 54th Massachusetts Volunteer Infantry and the 35th USCT in February 1864 repulsed Confederate attackers near the Georgia border in northeast Florida, covering the Union retreat to Jacksonville, 60 miles to the east. The 54th Massachusetts was the first black regiment mustered north of the Mason–Dixon Line. Frederick Douglass's oldest son, Lewis, served as sergeant major in the regiment. And before Olustee, the 54th had distinguished itself in July 1863 in the Union assault on Fort Wagner on Morris Island in the federal offensive to capture Charleston, South Carolina. The 54th led in storming the parapets and got so far as engaging rebel defenders in hand-to-hand combat before being repulsed. The prize-winning 1989 film *Glory* with noted black actors Denzel Washington and Morgan Freeman focused on the 54th and its valiant attack that left one in three of its troopers wounded or dead.

In all about 179,000 black men served in the U.S. Army and another 19,000 in the U.S. Navy during the Civil War. The Army enlistments formed 138 infantry regiments, 14 heavy artillery and 1 light artillery regiments, 6 cavalry regiments, and 5 regiments of engineers. Louisiana (24,052), Kentucky (23,703), Tennessee (20,133), and Mississippi (17,869) provided the bulk (48.5%) of black enlistments. By the end of the war, about 1 in 10 of the men who served in the Union Army were black. Black women also formed about 1 in 10 of the female relief workers on the Union side (Fleetwood 1895, 16–17)

An estimated 36,000 black men in the USCT died. Their mortality rate was about 1 in 5 (20.5%), the highest among federal forces as the rate among U.S. Volunteers was about 1 in 7 (15.2%), and among regular U.S. Army troops the rate was about 1 in 12 (8.6%). Such service and sacrifice of black men brought at least grudging respect over time. The nation awarded 16 black Civil War soldiers the Medal of Honor, its highest military distinction (Aptheker 1947, 10–80).

Such recognition was hard won. Initially the U.S. Army paid its black soldiers about half of what it paid its white soldiers. White enlistees got $13 per month, with clothing furnished by the government. Black enlistees got only $10 per month from which the government deducted $3 for clothing—a net pay of $7. Only in June 1864 did Congress authorize equal pay for U.S. Colored Troops. Acknowledging the indefensible and intolerable discrimination, Congress made equal pay retroactive to blacks' initial enlistments.

The U.S. Navy paid blacks equal wages from the start, but it restricted blacks—who formed about 16 percent of its sailors—to the lowest ranks. Only future South Carolina congressman Robert Smalls gained a naval commissioned rank with what was essentially a battlefield promotion to captain of the *Planter*, a Confederate ship he commandeered. The U.S. Army similarly restricted blacks in rank. Martin R. Delany did reach the rank of major, and he stood atop about 110 other black men who served as commissioned officers (Salter 2014, appendix 1).

As with earlier U.S. wars, blacks' service in arms contributed mightily to meeting public needs but received at best grudging acknowledgment. It hardly dented the discrimination inherent in the segregation of which slavery was a part. Popular white attitudes persisted in holding blacks inferior and excluded. Even many who clamored to abolish slavery did so more to bring down the rebel South's slave oligarchy than to elevate slaves, to say nothing of blacks, generally. Indeed, moving the nation to end blacks' enslavement proved not so simple.

Only after years of heated debate did Congress manage to propose what became the Thirteenth Amendment. It arose in part to give constitutional sanction to congressional confiscation acts and President Lincoln's Emancipation Proclamation and to outlaw slavery everywhere in the United States. The Senate adopted the proposed amendment by a vote of 38–6 in April 1864, but the House balked. It took another nine months to muster by two votes (119–56) the two-thirds required to submit the proposal to the states for ratification. And the states did not all rush to ratify. New Jersey initially refused, and it was not until the 1900s that Delaware (1901), Kentucky (1976), and Mississippi (1995) ratified the amendment that became part of the Constitution in December 1865.

The U.S. declaration that "neither slavery nor involuntary servitude, except as a punishment for crime whereof the party shall have been duly convicted, shall exist within the United States, or any place subject to their jurisdiction" moved blacks to Jubilee. American law after centuries of refusal had finally recognized that neither blacks nor any other persons could be held or used legally as slaves and that U.S. law would no longer sanction or tolerate slavery.

But to declare slavery illegal was not the same as eradicating it. Moreover, the law was unclear on exactly what slavery was. That fact glimmered in the amendment's connecting "slavery" with "involuntary servitude" and in the congressional and popular discussion that resolved the amendment to meaning simply that human beings could not be chattel. That view made American Negro slavery a matter of property relations alone; it considered nothing of interpersonal relations and social circumstances and conditions.

Frederick Douglass warned in 1865 that the Thirteenth Amendment marked a beginning not an end. "I hold that the work of Abolitionists is not done," he cautioned. The amendment released blacks from the status of slave but conveyed no other status. It conferred no rights other than a right not to be held in "slavery nor involuntary servitude," whatever that meant. "What advantage is a provision like this Amendment to the Black man, if the Legislature of any State can to-morrow declare that no Black man's testimony shall be received in a court of law? Where are we then?" Douglass warned. Leaving blacks at the mercy of state law was to leave them vulnerable to the same power that enslaved them.

"Slavery is not abolished until the Black man has the ballot," Douglass insisted. Only when blacks had equal rights would their true liberty be at hand. Till then slavery would persist. "They would not call it slavery, but some other name. Slavery has been fruitful in giving itself names," Douglass cautioned. Urging those who wanted truly to end slavery to push on in a battle for full black civil rights, he advised vigilance to "wait and see what new form this old monster will assume, in what new skin this old snake will come forth" (Foner 1999, 578–579).

## PROFILE: MARTIN R. DELANY (1812–1885)

Born free of slavery in western Virginia, Martin Robison Delany proved himself a black renaissance man, becoming the U.S. Army's first field grade officer, a physician, a journalist, and an advocate of black nationalism and emigration.

Delany's mother Pati moved him and his siblings to Pennsylvania, and at age 19, he moved on to Pittsburgh. He studied at Trinity A.M.E. Church and at Jefferson College while working as a laborer and barber. He became a physician's assistant in 1832 during a national cholera epidemic. He also published a newspaper in 1843 called *The Mystery* and went on to join Frederick Douglass in producing *The North Star* newspaper.

Fascinated by medicine, Delany in 1850 applied to Harvard Medical School in Cambridge, Massachusetts, and won admission with two other blacks, although protest from white students prompted the three to be soon dismissed. The rebuff provoked Delany to denounce blacks' future in the United States in his 1852 black nationalist classic *The Condition, Elevation, Emigration, and Destiny of the Colored People of the United States, Politically Considered.*

The grandchild of West African tribal peoples and regaled from infancy with stories of the motherland, Delany looked to Africa and also to the West Indies and South America as places more hospitable than the United States for black development. He led the National Emigration Convention in Cleveland in 1854 and further showed his lost faith in America by moving with his family to Canada from 1856 to 1859, yet he persisted in agitating to end U.S. slavery and segregation.

Working to make a practical plan for his emigration ideas, Delany in May 1859 sailed to Liberia and for 11 months scouted sites for settlement. He returned stateside late in 1860 as the Civil War was in the offing. He shared many blacks' hopes that the war would bring blacks a new day, and in 1863 when U.S. Army enlistments opened to blacks, he joined and became the highest-ranking black as a major. After the war he was seconded to the Freedmen's Bureau in South Carolina and stayed on to run unsuccessfully in 1874 for lieutenant governor. He served as a trial judge in Charleston but trumped up charges forced his removal, although he was later pardoned and reappointed. But the rise of white Redemptionists ended his term.

Delany joined with others in 1877 to form the Liberia Exodus Joint Stock Steamship Company in Charleston, which in 1878 bought a ship named

*Azor* to transport blacks from America to Africa. *Azor* enjoyed a successful maiden voyage, sailing 260 blacks from Charleston to Monrovia, Liberia. But its future proved limited, and Delany turned full-time to medical practice, moving from Charleston, to Boston, and ultimately to Xenia, Ohio, home of Wilberforce College, where he died on January 12, 1885, at age 72 (Delany and Levine 2003, passim).

## REFERENCES

Aptheker, Herbert. 1947. *Negro Casualties in the Civil War*. Washington, DC: Association for the Study of Negro Life and History.

Berry, Mary Frances. 1977. *Military Necessity and Civil Rights Policy: Black Citizenship and the Constitution, 1861–1868*. Port Washington, NY: Kennikat Press.

DC.gov. n.d. "Emancipation." Accessed at http://emancipation.dc.gov/page/ending-slavery-district-columbia.

Delany, Martin Robison, and Robert S. Levine. 2003. *Martin R. Delany: A Documentary Reader*. Chapel Hill: University of North Carolina Press.

Fleetwood, Christian A. 1895. *The Negro as a Soldier*. Washington, DC: Published by Prof. Geo. Wm. Cook.

Foner, Philip S., ed. 1999. *Frederick Douglass: Selected Speeches and Writings*. Chicago: Lawrence Hill Books.

Jackson, Mattie J. 1866. *The Story of Mattie J. Jackson: Her Parentage, Experience of Eighteen Years in Slavery, Incidents during the War, Her Escape from Slavery: A True Story*. Lawrence, MA: Sentinel Office, 1866.

Nies, Judith. 2002. *Nine Women: Portraits from the American Radical Tradition*. Berkeley: University of California Press.

Robinson, Cornelia. 1936–1938. "De Yankees wuz a harricane." In WPA Slave Narrative Project, Alabama Narratives, Vol. 1. Federal Writer's Project, United States Work Projects Administration (USWPA); Manuscript Division, Library of Congress. DIGITAL ID: mesn 010/337331.

Salter, Krewasky A. 2014. *The Story of Black Military Officers, 1861–1948*. New York: Routledge/Taylor & Francis Group.

United States. 1862a. "An Act for the Release of Certain Persons Held to Service or Labor in the District of Columbia" (D.C. Emancipation Act). 12 Stat. 376 (April 16, 1862).

United States. 1862b. "An Act to Secure Freedom to All Persons within the Territories of the United States." 12 Stat. 432 (June 19, 1862).

United States. 1862c. "An Act to Suppress Insurrection, to Punish Treason and Rebellion, to Seize and Confiscate the Property of Rebels, and for Other Purposes" (First Confiscation Act). 12 Stat. 589 (July 17, 1862).

United States. 1880–1901. *The War of the Rebellion: A Compilation of the Official Records of the Union and Confederate Armies*. Washington, DC: GPO.

_____ *Chapter 10* _____

# Actual Freedom

President Abraham Lincoln's Emancipation Proclamation noted the difference between what the document announced and what it termed "actual freedom." Understanding the difference was easy enough. It was the yawning gap between what law said and what people did. The Thirteenth Amendment did not close the gap. The distance separating blacks from whites in American society hardly changed simply because American Negro slavery became illegal. Outlawing slavery was not the same as stopping it. Actual freedom required more than a writ of law, for slavery was not simply a legal pronouncement; it was a way of life. It was a social system. It was a way of thinking. It was a way of treating people. More than words were required to change slavery in fact. Indeed, the change required no simple or single thing. Abolishing the law of slavery simply shifted the appearance and form of shackles; it did little to budge insistent social boundaries. So-called free Negroes had demonstrated that in and outside of the South for generations before 1865.

Slavery was part of a pervasive practice of white supremacy. It was part of the ideology of an American apartheid. It was one aspect of a many-faceted racial segregation imposed by law and practice. It was part of an American way of life organized to keep blacks in public and private spaces that restricted their choices. Slavery denied black autonomy, independence, and self-determination. Its deprivations were direct and formal, but it was hardly the only American institution to deny blacks access to "life, liberty, and the pursuit of happiness." Slavery was part of a system of black denial. Only ending the denial in all its forms in American custom, law, and practice promised blacks any fullness of actual freedom. As the one-time escaped slave Frederick Douglass noted in 1862 in anticipating the promise of the Emancipation Proclamation, "The work does not *end* with the abolition of slavery, but only *begins*" (Foner 1999, 523).

Grasping actual freedom was not a singular act or the act of a moment. Indeed, for African Americans reaching for what a poet described as "the place for which our fathers sighed" became a journey to an envisioned but elusive destination (Johnson, Still, and Johnson 1900, n.p.). No map designated the place, nor did any secure route lead to it. Indeed, not everyone located the destination in the same place. Many understandably marched to their own drummer, with their own sense of direction. Age, gender, experience, locality—everything in their life—varied their views and visions. Yet ex-slaves trod much common ground.

Many released from slavery with the Civil War's end immediately measured their progress toward actual freedom by their distance from their personal slavery. For tens of thousands freedom meant getting away from the place where they had slaved and from the people who had held them as slaves. Such a move meant leaving all that was familiar. But on the move they went. As slaves they could legally go only where their holders sent them. Going and coming as they pleased thus became one of the early tests of being free from slavery. "I want to take me off from this plantation, where I can be free," explained an ex-slave in 1865 outside Opelousas, Louisiana (Litwack 1979, 153–154).

For most moving meant facing the reality of having nothing and having to worry about everything, as Texas freedwoman Margret Nillin recalled in her narrative of her slavery and freedom. The recorder rendered Nillin's words in dialect. What she said was easy enough to put in common English. "Well, it's this way," she explained. "In slavery I owned nothing, never owned nothing. In freedom I own my home and my family. All that causes me worriment. In slavery I had no worriment. But I take freedom" (Litwack 1979, 229).

As Nillin noted, slaves had had title to nothing. Emancipation left them paupers. They left slavery owning only themselves. Being their own person, however, was their inestimable gain. They had title to themselves, and that meant title to their labor and its fruits. It meant also having claim to kin. Slaves had no legally recognized relations by blood or marriage, no legally recognized family. On their release from slavery, many joined in the lament of one man who cried "Where is my wife? Where are my children? Give me back the wife of my bosom, and give me back my poor children as were sold away" (Litwack 1979, 204). He was hardly alone in clamoring to reunite with kith and kin. Slavery had separated many who in freedom sought to rejoin their loved ones. Thousands upon thousands scoured the land in search of those they had lost. Circulars, handbills, and notices of all sorts flooded the ex-slave states and beyond to locate parents and children, mates, siblings, and lovers.

Some succeeded in finding lost loved ones. Ben Dodson sang hallelujahs on finding his wife Betty in a refugee camp after being sold apart 20 years earlier. "I found you at last," he exclaimed. "I hunted and hunted till I tracked you up here. I was bound to hunt till I found you, if you were alive," he cried (Litwack 1979, 229). Holding tight, ex-slaves such as Dodson demanded to have their families recognized. They insisted on law to accord them the status of husband and wife, of parents and children, of legal kith and kin that slavery had denied them. They wanted not simply to be married in the present; they wanted the fact of their marriages and relations in the past recognized as legitimate, making their children born in slavery legitimate so as to allow them the benefits of law. They wanted the facts of their nuclear and extended families recorded and protected against the intrusion of others that marked black families in slavery and in freedom as aberrant and dysfunctional. They wanted the strength of their extended kinship networks to enjoy the full sanction of law.

Gaining "the full and equal benefit of all laws" was in fact central to blacks' securing actual freedom, as Congress acknowledged in enacting the first federal civil rights act in April 1866 (United States 1866, 27). As slavery had demonstrated, blacks lived at the mercy of state law. Abolishing slavery did not abolish the power of state law over blacks, for the U.S. Constitution's system called "federalism" allowed states rights to determine most aspects of personal status—to determine, for instance, who could marry whom; who could vote; who could occupy, operate, or own what property; who could work where and when; and who could be punished for what and how.

On the ratification of the Thirteenth Amendment ex-slave states exercised their states' rights by enacting so-called Black Codes to define blacks' personal rights. Louisiana, Mississippi, and South Carolina immediately so restricted blacks' personal rights as to virtually reimpose slavery in a fresh guise. Throughout the South legislatures adopted codes to express the segregation slavery had overshadowed. Much of that segregation was not peculiar to the South. North and West, states had long segregated blacks. Law imposed some of that segregation in not allowing blacks to vote or to serve on juries or to attend school with whites. And the custom of segregation prevailed far beyond the law. Throughout the United States whites commonly shunned blacks. Dealing with such whites' attitudes, with their custom and practice, would prove even more difficult than changing the law's pronouncements and practices.

For many blacks and some whites the vision of blacks at large gaining actual freedom was for blacks to have the same rights and opportunities whites had. Congress projected that view in part in its 1866 act providing that "all persons . . . shall have the same right in every State and Territory . . . to the full and equal benefit of all laws and proceedings for the security of persons and property as is enjoyed by White citizens" (United States

1866, 27). The law acknowledged white status as the legal standard, but little in practice allowed blacks the same status as whites.

To begin, slavery had imposed destitution on slaves, and that was the condition of the millions of blacks released from slavery at the end of the Civil War. Congress in March 1865 followed private philanthropies such as the American Missionary Association (AMA) Freedmen's Aid Society, founded in 1861, to provide material aid to needy blacks. The U.S. Bureau of Refugees, Freedmen, and Abandon Lands (BRFAL) provided food, water, clothing, shelter, and some medical care. In time it did more, notably in providing schools. Congress created BRFAL to aid both displaced blacks and whites. It was not special legislation for blacks only. Yet it became popularly dubbed the Freedmen's Bureau as whites increasingly shunned its services, refusing to be treated with the same provisions as blacks. Critics lambasted the BRFAL as a government handout of white taxpayer money to pamper blacks too lazy or too inept to support themselves. The notion that blacks' were getting something for nothing, that they were getting something whites did not get, that whites were paying for something blacks got served long as political ammunition in conservative white campaigns against public policies to relieve blacks' destitution or discrimination.

Blacks such as Harriet Tubman scoffed at the idea that those who had been slaves were getting something for nothing from government assistance. Tubman and others argued that slaving as they had, blacks were due compensation for their labors. They had made many rich, and they deserved to be paid a part of that wealth. For blacks such as Tubman what came to be called "reparations" was a simple matter of social justice. Slavery was a wrong that needed to be righted by more than merely declaring it should not continue. The past called out for redress.

Others like Frederick Douglass had reservations about reparations. He did not demur on social justice grounds, for he fully acknowledged slavery's wholesale exploitation of blacks and their entitlement to the fruits of their past labors. "What class of people can show a better title to the land on which they live than the colored people of the South? They have watered the soil with their tears and enriched it with their blood and tilled it with their hard hands," he declared. But attuned to the American pulse, Douglass worried about how any perceived reparations would affect popular attitudes and practices. He expected backlash that would further denigrate rather than elevate blacks.

Douglass long projected the hope of blacks' standing on self-reliance. "Give the negro fair play and let him alone," he declared in 1872 (Foner 1999, 706). But as the years passed into failed Reconstruction, Douglass shifted to accept that ex-slaves would have been better off if staked to claims on the lands they had worked. U.S. Army General William Tecumseh Sherman

Frederick Douglass was the most recognized black man of the 1800s, working tirelessly to abolish slavery and to have blacks receive full citizenship and civil rights. (National Archives)

had offered such a stake with his January 1865 Special Field Orders, No. 15. Parceling out about 400,000 confiscated acres along the Atlantic coast in South Carolina, Georgia, and Florida, Sherman's order settled about 18,000 black families on plots of 40 acres or less—until President Andrew Johnson rescinded its effect (Cimbala 1989, 597–632). Such programs could have stabilized and shielded blacks by putting them in position to be "tilling the soil in comparative independence" rather than being mired in what Douglass further described in 1882 as "the terrible evils from which we now suffer" (Myers 2008, 239).

Reparations would persist as a theme as American society persisted in refusing to undertake any committed or concerted program to advance blacks from the degradations and deprivations of slavery. That refusal compounded blacks' deficit year after year, generation after generation. Chafing at the continued restraints on their progress, blacks such as Callie Guy House in the late 1890s would refresh the calls for reparations. Born a slave in Tennessee during the Civil War, House joined with others in 1897 to form the National Ex-Slave Mutual Relief, Bounty and Pension Association

(BPA) in Nashville. Campaigning throughout the ex-slave states with other BPA advocates, House would declare in 1899 "we are organizing ourselves together as a race of people who feels that they have been wronged." She would stand with a nationwide membership of 300,000 in 1900 as anti-reparations forces moved to suppress the movement. Federal prosecutors in 1901 indicted BPA leader Isaiah H. Dickerson for mail fraud and other charges to discredit the organization and the idea of reparations itself as a swindle (Berry 2005, passim).

Rejection of reparations was only part of what blacks suffered in the aftermath of the Civil War called Reconstruction. For many whites reparations to ex-slaves were ridiculous. Blacks had no legal claim for damages as slaves. Slavery had been wholly legal, after all. And while slaves may have received no wages, they had received compensation for their labor: they had been fed, clothed, sheltered, and otherwise cared for from birth to death in a social welfare system that made them better off than receiving wages, apologists said, extending arguments of proslavery social theorists. Moreover, some who scoffed at reparations insisted that blacks in general should be grateful for being in America, taken from the darkness of Africa to the enlightenment of the nation that nurtured and eventually emancipated them. Such misrepresentation or misunderstandings of American Negro slavery would long rankle blacks.

The Reconstruction years confronted blacks, with many whites dead set against their advancing from being slaves. Many whites had never welcomed blacks as slaves, and many also had not welcomed blacks at all. The black presence was troublesome throughout the nation from its beginning. The Thirteenth Amendment made the black presence even more worrying to many whites, particularly to those who felt physical or psychological needs to keep former slaves and blacks in general scraping at the bottom of society. Their ideology of white supremacy required blacks to forever be beneath whites, doing what they had done as slaves.

Almost in unison after the Thirteenth Amendment outlawed slavery, ex-slave state legislatures reconfigured their slave codes as Black Codes that aimed to confine blacks to positions slaves had held. Labor laws headed the design. What slaveholders personally and their society collectively had wanted from enslaved blacks, after all, was labor. And after the Thirteenth Amendment they continued to demand black labor on terms and conditions akin to slavery. They could not use the term *slavery*, but they could and did continue to use law to coerce black labor as slavery had.

Blacks in the ex-slave states found themselves stripped of choice in regard to labor. Mississippi, South Carolina, and Louisiana led the way in enacting laws to confine blacks to laboring as they had as slaves. "Every negro is required to be in the regular service of some White person, or former owner, who shall be held responsible for the conduct of said negro," declared the 1865 Black Code in St. Landry Parish, Louisiana, for example (Louisiana 1865, sec. 4). The racial subordination was undisguised. Although such laws applied to both sexes, they targeted those who in slavery were prime field hands—able-bodied males older than 14 and younger than 50 years of age. Contracts replaced slave titles, as laws required blacks to have labor contracts or be jailed as vagrants hired out to bidders who paid the town or county or state for any work done. Blacks thus faced take-it-or-leave-it contracts or a chain gang.

Blacks released from slavery had sought early to exercise their own choices by moving. But Black Codes clamped down on black mobility, as the slave codes had. Again in Louisiana, for example, laws required blacks to have special permits to travel from one place to another. Blacks resisted such laws as they had resisted slavery, and they protested bitterly that release from slavery had not delivered the rights of a free people but merely made them a *freed* people. They demanded the full rights of actual freedom. "We scorn and treat with contempt the allegations made against us that we understand Freedom to mean idleness and indolence," declared a group of blacks in Petersburg, Virginia, in June 1865, "We do understand Freedom to mean industry and the enjoyment of legitimate fruits thereof" (Aptheker 1951, 2: 538).

Blatant efforts in the ex-slave states to save or restore the slave system aggravated Northerners anxious about the South's willingness to accept its defeat and change its ways. Union Army commanders and Freedmen's Bureau officials such as Martin R. Delany, who rose to the rank of major in the U.S. Army and served as a Bureau agent in South Carolina, worked to counter local efforts to force blacks to work where they had slaved or to limit their mobility, as the slave codes had. For example, BRFAL agents refused to enforce ordinances that required blacks to have special permits to travel, but their efforts faced continuing opposition. Conservatives in the South insisted that matters such as labor laws and travel within the state were issues exclusively within state control. President Andrew Johnson championed that view. Congress adamantly disagreed.

Amid black protests for "such laws as shall secure us our rights as free-men," as a petition from Tennessee blacks put it in December 1865, Congress moved in the Civil Rights Act of April 1866 to provide blacks basic personal rights (Aptheker 1951, 2: 539). The legislation passed over President Johnson's veto. The statute opened by anticipating the Fourteenth Amendment in providing that "all persons born in the United States and not subject to any foreign power, excluding Indians not taxed, are hereby declared to be citizens of the United States." Blacks exulted at that provision as it confirmed their citizenship, a status they had long coveted, one that

Chief Justice Taney in the 1857 Dred Scott decision declared they had never had nor could they ever have. Further, the act enumerated basic civil rights "to make and enforce contracts, to sue, be parties, and give evidence, to inherit, purchase, lease, sell, hold, and convey real and personal property" (United States 1866, 27).

The difference between announcing rights and exercising rights was not lost on most blacks. North and South they faced resistance to the proposition of equal rights. In much of the South, in fact, blacks faced what essentially was a race war. Whites attacked blacks almost routinely to assert their dominance. The violence took the form of what were called riots in cities such as Memphis, New Orleans, and Charleston in 1866. Such white attacks on blacks had occurred in the North before the Civil War, and they would resume in time. The so-called draft riots in New York City in July 1863 were the worst of the early northern rash, leaving more than 100 dead and 2,000 injured, and torching black homes, churches, and institutions such as the Colored Orphan Asylum. But New York City had seen such violence earlier in 1834, for example, albeit on not so destructive a scale. Philadelphia, Cincinnati, and less populous northern communities also had antebellum antiblack violence.

The scale of antiblack violence in the postbellum South dwarfed anything outside of slavery. Throughout the countryside, white terrorists who dubbed themselves variously Knights of the Ku Klux Klan (KKK), Knights of the White Camelia, or the White League routinely murdered, raped, and assaulted blacks to keep them in what they described as "their place." The violence became so outrageous in South Carolina, where blacks were 60 percent of the population, that in 1871 President Ulysses S. Grant declared martial law in nine counties and dispatched U.S. Army troops to restore order.

Beset as they were, blacks persisted in building their lives, families, businesses, and communities as best they could. Almost en masse in the ex-slave states, they scrambled for schooling, craving literacy. Mastering the so-called Three Rs of reading, writing, and arithmetic as basic skills became a major badge of progress from slavery. Almost uniformly blacks clutched the belief that education was a leading avenue to success. They had poured into classes in contraband camps during the war, and after the war they crammed school rooms and classes wherever offered. The black churches springing up throughout the South were sites of Sunday schools and more. Nearly 50 private freedmen's relief agencies and the federal Freedmen's Bureau also sponsored schools. In time, the bureau started at least 4,000 schools with more than 250,000 students.

From the North and from the South, educated blacks hastened to teach their fellow blacks, as did more than a few northern and southern whites.

Southern blacks further contributed significantly to expanding their educational base. By 1870 they scraped together more than $1 million to fund their schooling—no small feat for a generally impoverished people (Taylor 1976, 198). Perhaps even more significant was blacks' insistence on creating public education systems throughout the South. Southern white conservatives, like the antebellum slaveholder oligarchy, were committed to privatization and opposed public spending for public goods such as public schools. Conservatives insisted that if you could not pay for it yourself, you should not have it; they preached that no one should pay for someone else to have anything. Blacks countered with a message of promoting the general welfare. Black Congressman Richard H. Cain (R-SC), for example, repeatedly pressed Congress to apply the precedent of the Northwest Ordinance of 1787 to the South by using public land sales to fund public education for blacks and whites.

Blacks' ambition for education drove school creation from the elementary level higher. It made the post–Civil War years the cradle of black colleges and universities opened in the first instance to train teachers and community leaders. Among the institutions that got their start then were Avery Institute (1865) in Charleston, South Carolina; Virginia Union University (1865) in Richmond; Fisk University (1866) in Nashville, Tennessee; Lincoln Institute (1866), in Jefferson City, Missouri; Howard University (1867) in Washington, D.C.; Morehouse College (1867) in Atlanta, Georgia; St. Augustine's University (1867) in Raleigh, North Carolina; Hampton Institute (1868) in Virginia; Tougaloo College (1869) in Jackson, Mississippi; Claflin Institute (1869) in Orangeburg, South Carolina; Benedict College (1870) in Columbia, South Carolina; and Alcorn A&M College (1871) in Lorman, Mississippi, the first state college for blacks. Private philanthropy from church groups such as the AMA largely funded such institutions.

Voting was also a priority among blacks. They had petitioned for the franchise repeatedly in the North before the war only to be repeatedly refused. New York, for example, steadfastly refused equal suffrage to blacks, voting down the proposition by popular referendum as late as 1869. Only in Maine, Massachusetts, New Hampshire, and Vermont—states with scant black populations—did blacks gain unrestricted suffrage before the Civil War. With general emancipation in 1865, the issue of black voting in the South became explosive. If voting by adult males were allowed without racial restrictions, blacks would have constituted statewide electoral majorities in South Carolina, Mississippi, Louisiana, Alabama, and Florida. They formed statewide majorities of the population in the first three states and throughout portions of all the ex-slave states, which frightened whites with the prospect of having their governments determined, if not directed, by black votes.

Many saw voting as a means to relieve blacks from oppressive laws. "Slavery is not abolished until the Black man has the ballot," Frederick Douglass insistently declared. Voting promised blacks a chance to control or at least contain public policy, to do away with laws harmful to their interests, and to promote their interests as part of the general welfare. Most blacks believed as Frederick Douglass said that as long as there were "laws making any distinction between Black and White, slavery still lives" (Aptheker 1951, 2: 549). The National Equal Rights League founded in 1864 to move the United States beyond slavery insisted that the Thirteenth Amendment outlawed legislation based on race or color.

From every view, allowing blacks in the South to vote presaged significant change—change of the sort blacks looked to embrace and whites looked to avoid. Ex-slave state legislatures refused to budge on black voting as it promised to undercut their own base. Congress forced the issue as the majority there hoped to oust the old southern regimes and eyed black voting as a lever to accomplish the task. Overriding obstructionist President Johnson, Congress in March 1867 required the former Confederate states with the exception of Tennessee, which former Tennessee Governor Johnson early exempted, to enfranchise adult black males. Congress would reiterate black men's voting rights in Section 2 of the Fourteenth Amendment in 1868 and then more directly with the Fifteenth Amendment in 1870.

The change black votes made was immediately evident. Black men were elected to public office en masse for the first time. Vermont in 1836 had elected Presbyterian minister Alexander Twilight as the first black in a U.S. legislature, but he was long alone. It was southern blacks who first opened wide doors to U.S. public office and seated blacks there.

The black majority in South Carolina immediately after receiving the vote in 1867 elected a black majority to the state House of Representatives. Two blacks would become speaker of the house—Samuel J. Lee (1872–1874) and Robert B. Elliott (1874–1876). Two also served as lieutenant governor—Alonzo J. Ransier (1870–1872) and Richard H. Gleaves (1872–1876). Another, Francis L. Cardozo, served as secretary of state (1868–1872) and as treasurer (1872–1876). Elliott served also as state attorney general (1876–1877) (Holt 1997, 43–71, 97).

The black majority in Louisiana also put blacks in office with 133 in the state legislature, starting in 1868 and ending in 1897, along with two notable black lieutenant governors—Oscar J. Dunn (1868–1871), the first black elected to that position in the United States; and P.B.S. Pinchback (1871–1872), who following the elected governor's impeachment succeeded from December 9, 1872, to January 13, 1873, to be the first black governor of a U.S. state (Vincent 1976, 71–97, 226–238).

Overall, nearly 700 black men served in the ex-slave state legislatures between 1868 and 1900, and another 120 served in western legislatures. More than 40 were elected sheriff. Tallahassee, Florida, and Little Rock, Arkansas, got a black as chief of police. The total tally of all black public officeholders during the period neared 1,500, with a high among the ex-Confederate states of 314 in South Carolina and a low of 20 in Tennessee (Foner 1993, xiv; Hine, Hine, and Harrold 2014, 268–269).

And beyond the local level, before the 1800s ended southern black voters saw 22 of their own seated in Congress, beginning in December 1870. In the U.S. House of Representatives, Joseph Rainey (R-SC, 1870–1879) was the first, followed by Jefferson F. Long (R-GA, 1871); Robert C. DeLarge (R-SC, 1871–1873); Robert B. Elliott (1871–1874); Benjamin S. Turner (R-AL, 1871–1873); Josiah T. Walls (R-FL, 1871–1876); Richard H. Cain (R-SC, 1873–1875, 1877–1879); John R. Lynch (R-MS, 1873–1877, 1882–1883); Alonzo J. Ransier (R-SC, 1873–1875); James T. Rapier (R-AL, 1873–1875); Jeremiah Haralson (R-AL, 1875–1877); John Adams Hyman (R-NC, 1875–1877); Charles E. Nash (R-LA, 1875–1877); Robert

Hundreds of blacks entered public office after the 1867 Reconstruction Acts, and the Fifteenth Amendment opened voting for black men. Among them were Senator Hiram R. Revels (R-MI) and U.S. Representatives Joseph Rainey (R-SC), Benjamin S. Turner (R-AL), Robert DeLarge (R-SC), Josiah Walls (R-FL), Jefferson Long (R-GA), and Robert B. Elliott (R-SC) who entered the U.S. Congress in 1870, forming the first Black Caucus. (Library of Congress)

Smalls (R-SC, 1875–1879, 1882–1883, 1884–1887); John E. O'Hara (R-NC, 1883–1887); Henry P. Cheatham (R-NC, 1889–1893); John Mercer Langston (R-VA, 1890–1891); Thomas E. Miller (1890–1891); George W. Murray (R-SC, 1893–1895, 1896–1897); and George Henry White (R-NC, 1897–1901). Also blacks in Mississippi saw their state seat the first black in the U.S. Senate, Hiram R. Revels (1870–1871), and the first to serve a full term in that body, Blanche K. Bruce (1875–1881).

To be clear, blacks nowhere gained control of state government. They became players rather than managers. They certainly were nowhere in charge of the state enterprise. The changes they wrought expanded the reach of state government more than ever before, but they hardly initiated unrestrained government of the people, by the people, and for the people. Women gained little, for example, except in the area of racial segregation. Sexism, along with other deep divisions, limited black officeholders' perspectives and programs. Their coalitions with whites often faltered as race displaced class and other common interests.

Blacks also split among themselves. Those free of slavery before general emancipation too frequently disdained those freed by the Civil War, and those who worked in the fields were further dismissed, as they were usually illiterate, woefully impoverished, and unmannered. Such bias spilled into disjointed views between northern blacks and southern blacks, those from the city and those from the countryside. Further, bourgeois pretensions reinforced class differences among blacks, and colorism or complexion consciousness also took a toll.

Infected by white supremacist ideology, some blacks succumbed to prejudices against dark skin and African features, preferring whiter complexions and European-like countenances. Indeed, in too many places descendants of Africa scorned being black, resisted being called "black," and segregated themselves from others of African descent on the basis of their looks. Preferences among African Americans for those with finer bones, flatter hips, lighter eyes, narrower noses, paler skins, straighter hair, and thinner lips reinforced divisions among blacks.

Black officeholders changed not only the face of government in the South, they altered public policy and perspective. An oligarchy had dominated government in the antebellum slave states. Black officeholders tilted government away from the rich and large landholding whites to focus more on the poor, the small landholders, and the landless. And, of course, they focused on personal rights, attacking racial segregation. They introduced public services such as public education and pushed to make such services available regardless of race. They were accused of fiscal mismanagement, and even fraud, as they necessarily raised taxes to pay for developing public services that conservatives unfailingly resisted with their philosophy of privatization, arguing for small government that concentrated its benefits on their elite at minimal cost to them. Black efforts advanced the general welfare principle in what perhaps the most astute student of black Reconstruction termed "the attempt to reconstruct democracy in America, 1860–1880" (Du Bois 1935, tp).

The black entry into U.S. electoral politics proved short lived. It had occurred largely because the federal government in 1867 insisted on it, and it continued so long as the federal government continued to insist on it. Conservative southern whites resisted black voting by any means they could manage. Terror campaigns plagued election seasons, and when the voting went against their wishes, whites simply stormed the government seat to oust the elected in favor of their own candidates, as illustrated in the so-called Colfax Massacre in Louisiana on Easter Sunday in April 1873 when paramilitary whites killed at least 100 blacks at the Grant Parish courthouse.

Disenfranchising blacks led the to-do list of whites who launched a counterrevolution termed "Redemption" to reverse what they deemed the untenable revolution Reconstruction ushered in with general emancipation and black enfranchisement and public officeholding. Redemptioners aimed to remove blacks from public life in the ex-slave states and to check black advances through terrorism that burned black churches and schools and murdered black leaders and sympathizers. The Fifteenth Amendment, prohibiting voting discrimination on the basis of "race, color or previous condition of servitude," and civil rights acts in 1870 and 1871 hardly halted the push against blacks.

Redemption proceeded apace in the 1870s as indicated by the resurgence of Democratic Party control in the southern states as the standard-bearer for conservative white rule, standing against the Republican Party of Lincoln that relied on black votes to maintain itself in the South. The Democrats' winning control of the U.S. House of Representatives in 1874 for the first time since 1860 furthered Redemption. The national parties' congressional compromise in 1877 to deny the presidency to Democratic candidate Samuel J. Tilden of New York despite his 250,000 vote victory at the polls over Rutherford B. Hayes of Ohio sealed a federal sanction for southern Redemption, as the deal provided for removing federal troops that remained in the South as something of a police force, thus effectively ending Reconstruction and making blacks' actual freedom a dream deferred.

## REFERENCES

Aptheker, Herbert. 1951. *A Documentary History of the Negro People in the United States*. New York: Citadel Press.
Berry, Mary Frances. 2005. *My Face Is Black Is True*. New York: Knopf.

Cimbala, Paul A. 1989. "The Freedmen's Bureau, the Freedmen, and Sherman's Grant in Reconstruction Georgia, 1865–1867." *Journal of Southern History* 55, no. 4 (November): 597–632.

Du Bois, W.E.B. 1935. *Black Reconstruction: An Essay toward a History of the Part Which Black Folk Played in the Attempt to Reconstruct Democracy in America, 1860–1880.* New York: Russel & Russel.

Foner, Eric. 1993. *Freedom's Lawmakers: A Directory of Black Officeholders during Reconstruction.* New York: Oxford University Press.

Foner, Philip S., ed. 1999. *Frederick Douglass: Selected Speeches and Writings.* Chicago: Lawrence Hill Books.

Hine, Darlene Clark, William C. Hine, and Stanley Harrold. 2014. *African Americans: A Concise History.* Upper Saddle River, NJ: Pearson Prentice Hall.

Holt, Thomas C. 1977. *Black over White: Negro Political Leadership in South Carolina during Reconstruction.* Urbana: University of Illinois Press.

Johnson, J. Rosamond, William Grant Still, and James Weldon Johnson. 1900. *Lift Ev'ry Voice and Sing.* Hollywood, CA: Cameo Music.

Litwack, Leon F. 1979. *Been in the Storm So Long: The Aftermath of Slavery.* New York: Knopf.

Louisiana, St. Landry's Parish. 1865. The Black Code of St. Landry's Parish. In U.S. Congress, Senate Executive Document No. 2, 93–94. Washington, DC.

Myers, Peter C. 2008. *Frederick Douglass: Race and the Rebirth of American Liberalism.* Lawrence: University Press of Kansas.

Taylor, Arnold H. 1976. *Travail and Triumph: Black Life and Culture in the South since the Civil War.* Westport, CT: Greenwood Press.

United States. 1866. "An Act to Protect All Persons in the United States in Their Civil Rights and Liberties, and Furnish the Means of Their Vindication" (the Civil Rights Act of 1866). 14 Stat. 27 (April 9, 1866).

United States. 1895. *Official Records of the Civil War: Military Operations.* Series 1. Washington, DC: GPO.

Vincent, Charles. 1976. *Black Legislators in Louisiana during Reconstruction.* Baton Rouge: Louisiana State University Press.

_____ *Chapter 11* _____

# A Dream Deferred

Blacks faced a national retreat as Reconstruction ended. During the Civil War and immediately afterward, they had reached high points in the ebb and flow of African American history. The era engendered hope and produced momentous gains. General emancipation with the Thirteenth Amendment in 1865 marked the Jubilee of American Negro slavery's end. Acknowledged personal rights had followed in federal civil rights acts from 1866 to 1875. The Fourteenth Amendment in 1868 confirmed blacks' status as U.S. citizens. Also it directed states to provide "equal protection of the laws," and it embraced blacks in the principle of adult male suffrage. The Fifteenth Amendment in 1870 introduced a historic antidiscrimination principle in suffrage, banning "race, color, or previous condition of servitude" as qualifications for voting. And blacks, indeed, had exercised their vote, sending their own in numbers to local, state, and national offices for the first time. Under changed state laws, blacks in the ex-slave states had legitimated their families. They had formed fresh communities, crowding into schools, building churches, starting businesses, and getting title to land where they could. Their gains were all hard won, for they faced adversity at every step, as their every advance met backlash.

Finding themselves increasingly isolated, particularly in the South where 9 in 10 continued to live during Reconstruction, blacks fought to defend themselves as best they could. But more and more they found themselves without recourse to the law's protection. State courts that had remained for the most part in conservative white hands in the ex-slave states offered blacks scant hearing, and federal courts did little better. Indeed, countervailing Congress's efforts, the U.S. Supreme Court routinely undercut federal protection of blacks' personal and political rights.

Rather than uphold blacks' fresh standing by accepting the Thirteenth, Fourteenth, and Fifteenth Amendments as enabling federal enforcement of civil rights, the Supreme Court repeatedly limited the reach of the Reconstruction amendments. In the *Slaughterhouse Cases* (1873) the Court reiterated the antebellum view that states alone held direct authority over personal rights, despite the provisions of the Fourteenth Amendment. It further restricted the Fourteenth Amendment in *United States v. Cruikshank* (1876), introducing the State Action doctrine that blocked federal reach to actions by private persons. That left crimes such as terrorist assault, murder, and rape outside federal punishment, along with lynchings and outrages such as the 1873 Colfax Massacre. The Court further elaborated that view in cases such as *United States v. Harris* (1883). Further, blacks found protections they had gained under state and federal law exposed. In *Hall v. DeCuir* (1877), for example, blacks witnessed the U.S. Supreme Court's ruling unenforceable in interstate travel Louisiana's 1869 antisegregation statute directing common carriers within the state to operate with "rules and regulations [that] make no discrimination on account of race or color" (Louisiana 1869, 37).

The Court in 1883 went further in *The Civil Rights Cases*, striking down Congress's 1875 provision for "full and equal enjoyment" of public accommodations regardless of race, color, or previous condition of servitude. Congress had introduced the principle on the basis that "it is essential to just government we recognize the equality of all men before the law" (United States 1875, 335). The Court held the provision unconstitutional. And not only did the Court rule again that except for state action Congress could not prohibit racial discrimination under the Fourteenth Amendment; it moreover limited the reach of the Thirteenth Amendment by essentially defining slavery as solely a chattel property relationship. "Mere discriminations on account of race or color are not regarded as badges of slavery," declared Justice Joseph P. Bradley for the Court in its *Civil Rights Cases* decision (United States 1883, 25).

Blacks took some solace in Justice John Marshall Harlan's vigorous dissent and repeatedly decried the virtual revocation of federal protection of their personal and civil rights. Almost uniformly black male leaders protested in the rhetoric of their day, demanding their "manhood rights," particularly the right to vote. But leaning on the vote offered blacks little support, for their franchise, itself, became increasingly fragile. Violence such as the massive Ku Klux Klan campaign in South Carolina in the early 1870s and the Colfax Massacre in Louisiana in 1873 pushed voting out of reach or made it a mockery. And the U.S. Supreme Court repeatedly diluted federal voting rights protections in *United States v. Reese* (1876) and following cases, as southern states moved from simple voter suppression to formal disfranchisement with dodges to circumvent the Fifteenth Amendment.

Blacks became rarer and rarer on southern voter registration rolls, particularly after 1890 when Mississippi pioneered an effective black disfranchisement plan with amendments to its state constitution to deploy a battery of measures such as property qualifications, poll taxes, literacy tests, and grandfather clauses. Such measures typically exempted whites who, for example, qualified to vote if their father or grandfather was qualified to vote before Congress first required the ex-Confederate states to enfranchise black men. Outside the South few other than blacks showed great concern about blacks voting, for it was an issue for the most part only in the South where blacks were numerous.

Mississippi's sister ex-slave states followed its lead in a rush after the U.S. Supreme Court dismissed black protests against the 1890 plan with rulings in *Mills v. Green* (1895), *Williams v. Mississippi* (1898), and *Giles v. Harris* (1903). The Court there sealed its partnership in black disfranchisement. It would take a turn in favor of blacks in striking down grandfather clauses in *Guinn v. United States* (1915), and it would continue with occasional decisions to restrain the most outrageous of state segregation laws until World War II (1939–1945) altered the political climate and turned the Court toward implementing the constitutional promises made in the Reconstruction amendments.

Disfranchisement was something of a last straw for southern blacks. They had suffered more and more segregation, as blacks in the North had suffered segregation following the First Emancipation. Northern states had segregated black schoolchildren, as famously illustrated in the 1850 Massachusetts court decision in *Roberts v. Boston*. Blacks in the antebellum North had faced segregated public transportation, accommodations, and housing. Typically restricted to black sections, they were relegated to menial jobs and seldom received the same pay as whites for the same work. The same occurred in the South with increased vigor following Reconstruction. The notable North–South difference was that for the most part custom and practice enforced segregation in the North, while the South used the force of law, creating segregation codes as it had created slave codes and Black Codes.

More and more cut off from public life and public spaces in the South, blacks persisted with self-help and seized opportunities for personal and community development. Mutual support organizations sprang up as they had in the North following the First Emancipation. Churches led all black institution-building. And Baptists led the way among denominations in the South with their early start reaching back to the 1770s with black Baptist preachers such as George Lisle in Savannah. By 1900 southern black Baptist churches counted about 1.3 million congregants, more than all other major sects combined. Various Methodist groups followed, led by the African Methodist Episcopal (AME) Zion (366,000), the African Methodist Episcopal (AME) (310,000), the Colored Methodist Episcopal (CME), founded in 1870 in Tennessee, and various other Methodists (125,000). Black Presbyterians numbered about 114,000 (Ayers 1992, 160–161).

As in the North following the First Emancipation, blacks in the South following general emancipation preferred churches they controlled and formed independent denominations of southern black Baptists, Methodists, and Presbyterians. But significant numbers of blacks worshiped also among Catholics and Episcopalians. As in the North desires for independence and differences in belief, as well as in social class, multiplied churches. A few large congregations grew as had "Mother" Bethel in Philadelphia, but small congregations of a few dozen or scores also grew. In Philadelphia, for example, between 1799 and 1897 the number of black churches grew from 3 to 55. The average congregation size among the six churches in 1813 was 394; in 1897 the average size was 234. Smaller congregations predominated particularly in the rural South, but newcomers to growing cities, North and South, formed their own little congregations from time to time, many of them transient (Du Bois 1897, 18–22, 197–199; Wortham 2009, 34–35).

Blacks North and South shared much, but as the First Emancipation earlier wedged differences between the enslaved and the unenslaved, general emancipation wedged differences also between northern and southern blacks. They would ever continue to share the basic discrimination and oppression of white supremacy and battle the same foe, but in different guises from time to time. Blacks in the North also faced resistance to Reconstruction's mandates of equal rights, for example. The work of civil rights activist Octavius Valentine Catto and his murder in the 1871 Philadelphia Election Day Riot illustrated the struggle in the North to secure voting rights, get quality public schooling, and desegregate streetcars.

Not only in the City of Brotherly Love, but throughout the North blacks battled in court and in the streets for the equal rights Reconstruction promised but white antagonism denied. They escaped the terrorism rampant in much of the South, yet the resistance they met was no less firmly rooted nor was their determination to overcome racial discrimination any less. They enjoyed little of the blush of political power blacks in the South enjoyed from their concentrated numbers, and perhaps that further fueled their insistent agitation for full and equal access to public life and public spaces. The massive horrors heaped on blacks in the South would long overshadow blacks' struggle for civil rights in the North, but overcoming white racism was daunting there too.

Public agitation persisted as a watchword among black activists in the North as they carried over their work against slavery to working against segregation. Conditions in the South dampened such public campaigning there as Reconstruction waned, leaving blacks for the most part to respond to white backlash by getting out of the way or by getting away. Blacks fled from the countryside into cities and towns, away from the reach of their former slaveholders. More urbanized areas had long attracted rural blacks as havens. Even before the Civil War, one in five to two in five of the residents of the typical southern city were black. Their numbers reflected urban slavery and, also, opportunities. After the war blacks clustered in cities throughout the South, from Augusta to Birmingham to Memphis to Savannah, for example. The black population in places of more than 4,000 residents in 1870 increased from 1860 levels by 80 percent on average—a rate six to seven times greater than for whites (Kellogg 1977, 310, 312).

Getting away became a much-discussed option as Reconstruction waned, and talk of colonization resumed, becoming again the hot topic it had been after the First Emancipation. Talking with a group of black leaders at the White House in 1862 President Lincoln, himself, had broached black colonization, repeating his earlier view that differences between blacks and whites "will probably forever forbid their living together upon the footing of perfect equality" (Basler 1953, 3: 16). What living together would mean for blacks and whites would be a continual question. The basic black answer to colonization, however, was consistently that the choice was not for others to make: it was a choice for blacks to make themselves. Staying where they were was a hard choice for many; leaving was no less a hard choice, as was deciding where to go if they left. Where would be better? Most black Americans had no desire to leave the United States. The brutal end of Reconstruction moved many, however, to want to leave the South. And many would for generations to come.

The first major black migration from the South started at the end of the 1870s. Flowing out from the Lower Mississippi Valley, pioneering blacks struck out for a better future, leaving Louisiana, Mississippi, and Tennessee for a place where their toil, tears, sweat, and blood could yield better harvests for themselves and their children and their children's children. They became "Exodusters," departing to have land of their own, escaping the landless laboring or tenancy or sharecropping that trapped most southern blacks in working in the fields as slaves had. Fewer than one in four (24.5%) blacks farming in the South in 1900 owned the land they worked (Painter 2006, 133).

The Exodusters went to Kansas. Clustering in the state's northeast corner, they formed sizable portions of the 1880 population in counties such as Wyandotte (23.9%), Shawnee (18.4%), Leavenworth (15.4%), Douglas (14.8%), and Atchison (12.8%). Georgia-born Union Army veteran Henry Adams encouraged Louisiana's early Exodusters. Finding the situation more

Like this black family walking away from the site of their continued oppression after Reconstruction failed, Exodusters in the late 1870s and 1880s quit the South for Kansas and other points West. (Courtesy Georgia Archives, Vanishing Georgia Collection, ben136)

and more hopeless after documenting almost 700 murders, whippings, and other assaults of blacks between 1866 and 1876 in the northern Louisiana area dominated by Shreveport in the west, he and others had formed a Colonization Council. Back-to-Africa was Adams's personal choice as he appeared to lose hope for America, yet he encouraged his fellow blacks to get away as best they could. Adams never went to Kansas himself, persisting with the idea that Liberia was a better place for blacks (Painter 1977, 71–201).

"The father of the Exodus," as he came to be called, was the Nashville-born Benjamin "Pap" Singleton. He preached a gospel of black landownership and recruited more than 20,000 blacks to Kansas at the end of the 1870s. Yet he, too, appeared to think emigration offered blacks better opportunity, setting his sights for a time on the Mediterranean island of Cyprus. Disheartening conditions did not, however, drive most black Americans to seriously consider moving from the United States so much as it moved them to consider moving within the United States. "We are Americans. We know no other country. We love the land of our birth," declared a group of black Virginians in Norfolk (Painter 1977, 71–201; Hine, Hine, and Harrold 2014, 257).

The Exodusters were not alone in heading West. The plains states and even the Far West witnessed phenomenal proportional surges in black population between 1870 and 1890. Granted most started from small bases. The black population in North Dakota, for example, grew more than 15-fold over the 20 years, but that was an increase from only 24 in 1870 to 373 in 1890. Colorado had a 13-fold increase from 456 to 6,215 at the same time. Other states trailed in increase: Nebraska (11-fold), Montana (8-fold); Washington (7-fold), South Dakota (7-fold), Wyoming (5-fold), Utah (5-fold), Minnesota (5-fold), Oregon (3-fold), Idaho (3-fold), and California (2.6-fold). Still Kansas led the West by far in black population in 1890 with almost 50,000, having had a 2.9-fold increase since 1870.

Before the Exodusters and the black move to the Great Plains in the late 1870s and 1880s, black U.S. Army veterans were making history in the West. Known collectively as "Buffalo Soldiers," they were the Indian fighters and settler escorts in the much of the post–Civil War Wild West. Their postwar units organized first in 1866 were the 9th and 10th cavalry and 24th and 25th infantry. The cavalry units had notable connections to the black Exodus to come, for the 10th was formed at Fort Leavenworth, Kansas; and the 9th drew heavily on recruits from Louisiana. The units formed the shock troops of the Indian wars, particularly in the Southwest, fighting the Apache, Kiowa, and Ute, for which 23 would receive the highest U.S. award for valor in combat, as had 32 blacks for service during the Civil War (Schubert 1997, 1–8).

The Buffalo Soldiers became emblems of a long African American tradition of service in arms that until the 1950s was in segregated American armed forces led almost exclusively by white officers. Major Martin R. Delany had become the first black field officer in the U.S. Army in 1865, but white opposition to black officers was long palpable and prevalent. Antipathy at the nation's officer academies early and often turned into ugly treatment of black candidates. James Webster Smith's entry to the United States Military Academy at West Point in 1870 proved short, as did that of his fellow South Carolinian Johnson Chestnut Whittaker 10 years later. Both were set upon by fellow cadets so that they could not graduate to commissions. Henry Ossian Flipper of Georgia became West Point's first black graduate in 1877, but once in the field he, too, was set upon, court-martialed, and in 1881 dismissed from the service. Kentucky-born Charles Young in 1889 became West Point's third black graduate. He reached the rank of lieutenant colonel and commanded a squadron of the 10th Calvary but was denied a command during World War I.

The United States Naval Academy at Annapolis proved even more hostile than West Point. John H. Conyers of South Carolina in 1872 became the first black midshipman but abuse forced him to resign in 1873. Not until 1949 did Annapolis graduate its first black, Wesley Anthony Brown, who rose to the rank of lieutenant commander. Even while being repulsed by whites who were in the same uniform, black soldiers and sailors persisted to do their duty with distinction. Black troops saved Theodore Roosevelt and his "Rough Riders" at San Juan Hill in 1898 during the U.S. War with Spain, earning four Congressional Medals of Honor. Yet as president, Teddy Roosevelt would cashier three companies of the 25th Infantry for the so-called Brownsville incident in Texas in August 1906. Rioting had broken out there between white townsmen and black troopers, exposing the aversion whites had when black men with guns appeared where they lived and even more to blacks in uniform with guns, as answering to blacks exercising authority was difficult for many whites.

Although segregated as they were, more and more blacks were rising to positions to be reckoned with and recognized in the mainstream of American life as the 1900s neared. The Reconstruction flurry of political power had put blacks in public office and in 1869 produced the first African American diplomat when Ebenezer Don Carlos Bassett became U.S. minister to Haiti. Black businesses developed to supply the needs and wants of black consumers confined to segregated communities. The black press continued to defend and inform black communities as journalists such as Timothy Thomas Fortune labored as equal rights advocates in newspapers such as the *New York Globe*, the *New York Freeman*, and the *New York Age*, and in organizations such as the National Afro-American League founded in 1889. And amid the rising tide of Social Darwinism with its message of survival of the fittest, black farmers and nonfarm laborers also banded together for self-protection and advancement in groups such as the Colored National Labor Union, founded in 1869, and the National Colored Farmers Alliance, founded in 1887.

For the most part blacks adhered to what was being called the Social Gospel, carrying forward the message of applying Christian ethics to social problems to reach social justice. From his center in Atlanta fiery AME Bishop Henry McNeal Turner insisted on blacks' believing in and belonging to religion relevant to their lives. A self-made man who ordained women as AME deacons and advocated women's suffrage, Turner preached the gospel of self-help and directed his ministry to black community development. And he was not alone. South and North, black churches everywhere served as community hubs, working with their own congregations and across congregations to advance mutual aid to encourage and sustain black businesses, employment, and personal development. Black churches were centers of activism. It was not that every black was a church member so much as it was that blacks recognized churches as places to go to get things done. In smaller communities social pressure pushed church membership and attendance as part of community cohesion. Churchgoing was perhaps even more social than it was religious, for church was a place to be close and share and stand with others.

Churches were places for black networking, and foremost in making and maintaining contacts were black churchwomen: they drove much of the outreach and directed and staffed much of the cultural, literary, and service work done in black communities. Particularly in the South moving out of Reconstruction, but not only there and then, black churchwomen spearheaded the thrust of the mass of blacks into the main currents of American life. Their work took nondenominational character in black women's clubs that flourished especially from 1880 to 1920 to advance black self-improvement and community uplift. The motto of the National Association of Colored Women's Clubs (NACWC) organized in 1896 expressed the overriding theme of black activist women: "Lifting as We Climb."

Activist black women advanced as models of personal self-improvement and of community involvement and development. They were leaders in black voluntarism and public relations. Aging abolitionist stalwarts such as Harriet Tubman and Frances E. W. Harper joined with younger black

Ida B. Wells-Barnett crusaded for black civil rights and particularly against antiblack violence exemplified in its ugliest form by lynching that ran rampant, particularly from the 1880s to the 1930s. Mississippi, Georgia, Texas, Louisiana, and Alabama led the nation in these horrors. (Private Collection/ Prismatic Pictures/Bridgeman Images)

women such as Mary Church Terrell in the common goal of advancing blacks' civil equality and self-development. They battled segregation in public policies that excluded blacks from public benefits and protections. Ida Bell Wells-Barnett exemplified black women pushing publicly in the 1880s for blacks' rights and for women's rights. Noted for her investigative journalism and organizing, Wells-Barnett was one of the foremost voices crying out against the national crime of lynching as it became epidemic in the 1880s and 1890s. In 1892 alone, the spectacle of mob murder of blacks claimed 160 victims, including 5 women; and the mayhem was not confined to the South. Mobs in Ohio lynched three blacks that year as did mobs in Kansas, and New York itself had one lynching (Wells-Barnett 1900, 15–24).

Black women such as Bostonian Josephine St. Pierre Ruffin joined Mississippi-born Wells-Barnett as journalists advancing black causes and as organizers of black women's clubs. Ruffin in 1884 began *Woman's Era* as the first newspaper published by and for African American women. Pushing for self-determination and self-improvement that began with education, Ruffin, Wells-Barnett, and Terrell performed multifaceted roles in uplift activities. They were prime examples of black women's emerging from traditional domestic sphere confines into roles as modern public figures. More and more were college-educated like Ruffin and Terrell—a graduate of Oberlin College in Ohio noted for being first in admitting blacks and women and for graduating Mary Jane Patterson in 1862 as the first recognized African American woman with a bachelor's degree.

Oberlin also graduated Matilda Arabella Evans, who in 1897 became the first African American woman licensed to practice medicine in South Carolina. She followed in the footsteps of Rebecca Davis Lee Crumpler, who in 1864 had graduated from the New England Female Medical College as the first African American female medical doctor. Other early black women physicians included Mary Britton in Lexington, Kentucky; Georgia E. Lee Patton in Memphis, Tennessee; and Georgia Dwelle in Atlanta, Georgia. Law had pioneers also: Valedictorian at the Central Tennessee College of Law in 1897, Lutie A. Lytle joined the faculty there as the first African American woman professor at a chartered law school.

Black women such as Maggie Lena Walker pioneered leading positions for black women in business. Moving from newspaper woman to organizer, at the turn of the century Walker became the first African American female bank president with the St. Luke Penny Savings Bank in Richmond, Virginia. Black women such as Sarah E. Goode and Miriam E. Benjamin would join the ranks of inventors like Lewis Howard Latimer, who worked with telephone pioneer Alexander Graham Bell and electrical pioneers Thomas A. Edison and George Westinghouse. The most successful black businesswoman moving into the turn of the century was the Louisiana-born Sarah

Breedlove. Best known as Madam C. J. Walker, she became America's first self-made female millionaire, manufacturing and distributing via mail order beauty products throughout the United States, the Caribbean, and Central America.

As black women were breaking into public leadership roles, U.S. public policy was sealing the limits of black public activity. In deciding *Plessy v. Ferguson* in 1896, the U.S. Supreme Court sanctioned legal segregation. Its Separate but Equal Doctrine became the law of the land. The decision was more confirmation than a commencement. It represented the culmination of the white conservative Redemption campaign that had begun during Reconstruction. It neither intended nor produced any equality. The decision arose in the area of public transportation, but it became most notorious in the area of public education. The inequity it confirmed was clear throughout the South but was perhaps most blatant in places like Mississippi and South Carolina. The Palmetto State in its 1908–1909 school year spent $1.70 per black pupil on average but $10.34 per white pupil. For its male teachers, South Carolina paid blacks on average $118.17 and whites $479.79 per year; it paid its black female teachers $91.45 and its white female teachers $249.13. That was the practice of separate but equal in the South (Hine, Hine, and Harrold 2014, 317).

Blacks bitterly protested the denial of equality, but separation was not so bothersome to some. Many, if not most, blacks were more interested in their fair share of public benefits and burdens than in sharing public or private spaces with whites. They wanted quality education for their children rather than necessarily having their children sit next to white children in schools or elsewhere. They wanted not to be excluded from public parks or other public recreation facilities. They wanted equal pay for equal work. They wanted the equal protection of the law the U.S. Constitution proclaimed.

The old abolitionist and equal rights advocate Frederick Douglass refused to yield on blacks' constitutional rights. The towering black figure of the 19th century, however, died in February 1895. A more conciliatory black leader rose as spokesman for a new era. Preaching a politics of accommodation rather than agitation, Alabama's Tuskegee Institute founder Booker T. Washington advised blacks and whites that "in all things purely social we can be as separate as the fingers, yet one as the hand in all things essential to mutual progress" (Washington 1901, 226–227).

Washington's signature address at the Atlantic Exposition in September 1895 received great acclaim among leading white conservatives eager to quiet angry black protest over hardening segregation. But leading blacks such as AME Bishop Henry McNeal Turner, *Washington Bee* newspaper publisher and lawyer W. Calvin Chase, and *Boston Guardian* publisher William Monroe Trotter condemned Washington as a sellout.

Washington preferred to avoid the confrontation of public politics in favor of confidential personal arrangements that produced practical results. His tact got him invited to dine at the White House with President Theodore Roosevelt in October 1901 and allowed him to raise millions for black causes, especially schools, from industrialist Andrew Carnegie and other white philanthropists. He pushed bread-and-butter issues, focusing on building economic foundations to advance blacks, particularly those in his native South. He advocated industrial education for blacks, arguing that "the masses of us are to live by the production of our hands." Skilled black craftsmen in the past—the blacksmiths, bricklayers, carpenters, and masons, for example—had sustained themselves and their families even during slavery, and industrial occupations would carry blacks to prosperity and social acceptance in the future, Washington insisted.

Washington's vision and the controversy it generated among blacks exposed a North–South, as well as a class, division. Washington advocated a strategy for blacks in what he called "the common occupations of life." Washington understood that the mass were not going to be doctors, lawyers, professors, or philosophers. So his approach differed from that of the leading black intellectual of the 20th century, W.E.B. Du Bois, with whom he would be contrasted, for Du Bois preached the gospel of the Talented Tenth.

Born in western Massachusetts in 1868 Du Bois enjoyed a privileged education at Fisk University in Nashville and at Harvard University in his native state where he earned a PhD in 1895 before going further to study at the University of Berlin in Germany. He shared the spirit of other black intellectuals such as the New York–born Episcopalian priest Alexander Crummell, educated in part at Cambridge University in England, and who in 1897 organized the American Negro Academy (ANA) in Washington, D.C., to bring together leading black thinkers.

In addition to Crummell and Du Bois, the ANA included eminents such as lawyer and historian John W. Cromwell; Presbyterian minister Francis J. Grimké, a Princeton Theological Seminary graduate; Howard University mathematics professor Kelly Miller, reputed as the first black student at Johns Hopkins University; Brown University graduate John Hope, who became the first black president of Morehouse College; and the internationally renowned poet Paul Laurence Dunbar. These men stood among 8.8 million blacks in the United States in 1900, when only about 2,220 blacks had graduated from college since 1860; and of that number a bit more than 1,100 had graduated in the 1890s.

Washington and Du Bois were posed as enemies, and an antagonism did develop between them before Washington died in 1915. The press and much public discussion highlighted their differences, as they would time and again contrast black leaders to emphasize discord and to dismiss one or another as disfavored in the quest for a single anointed black head. The search for such a leader often appeared more of a great white hope than any black desire for someone who would be the sole public face and voice articulating what blacks wanted and needed, directing their efforts and the efforts of those interested in helping them. Such a hope often appeared as one to quiet blacks. It ignored blacks' diversity, the differences in blacks' origins, experiences, locations, and expectations. Blacks shared in common a disdain for white supremacy that segregated and relegated them, and that denied their self-determination and refused to respect their abilities and accomplishments. But blacks were not singular. No uniform fit them all. African Americans had different voices and they desired to be heard both collectively and individually.

## PROFILE: IDA BELL WELLS-BARNETT (1862–1931)

A whirlwind in working to end violence against blacks and advance equal rights, Ida Bell Wells began life enslaved in Holly Springs, Mississippi, and rose to be one of the foremost investigative journalists of her day. She campaigned in print and on the lecture circuit to expose the brutality of lynching. Her 1892 *Southern Horrors: Lynch Law in All Its Phases* and 1895 *The Red Record* documented the dimensions of white terrorism to disfranchise and subjugate blacks.

Being displaced from her train seat on a ride between Memphis and Holly Springs, following Tennessee's 1881 Jim Crow law, triggered Wells's antisegregation activism. She sued the Chesapeake and Ohio Railroad Company and at trial in 1884 won damages of $500, but she lost that award on appeal and found herself having to pay court costs. Outrage at the episode turned her to journalism. She sent articles far and wide and purchased a share in the Memphis *Free Speech and Headlight* newspaper.

The Memphis Board of Education in 1891 dismissed Wells as a teacher, taking issue with her sharp writings. Her protesting black teachers being paid $30 a month while white teachers were being paid $80 particularly rankled the board. She infuriated more than the school board and bought a pistol for self-protection in the face of repeated threats, particularly after her incisive investigation of the 1892 lynching of three successful black business owners who also were friends of hers.

Terrorists wrecked Wells's *Free Speech and Headlight* newspaper offices in 1892 to quiet her. They did succeed in driving her from Memphis, but they hardly quieted her. She moved to Chicago for safety but refused to be silenced. She joined with leading blacks such as the venerable Frederick Douglass and fellow journalists I. Garland Penn and Ferdinand Barnett to boycott the 1893 World's Columbian Exposition in Chicago because of its exclusion of black exhibits. Her association there with Barnett led to their marriage in 1895: the couple would have two sons and two daughters (Giddings 2008, passim).

Wells-Barnett worked with others in 1896 to organize the NACWC and the National Afro-American Council, and in 1909 she was among the founders of the National Association for the Advancement of Colored People. Her unfinished autobiography, *Crusade for Justice*, chronicled her battle against racism and sexism. It was published after her death in Chicago on March 25, 1931. She was 68.

## REFERENCES

Ayers, Edward L. 1992. *The Promise of the New South: Life after Reconstruction.* New York: Oxford University Press.

Barnett, Ida Bell Wells, and Alfreda M. Duster. 1970. *Crusade for Justice: The Autobiography of Ida B. Wells.* Chicago: University of Chicago.

Basler, Roy P., ed. 1953. *The Collected Works of Abraham Lincoln.* New Brunswick, NJ: Rutgers University Press.

Du Bois, W.E.B. 1897. *The Philadelphia Negro: A Social Study.* Philadelphia: University of Pennsylvania Press.

Giddings, Paula. 2008. *Ida: A Sword among Lions.* New York: Amistad.

Hine, Darlene Clark, William C. Hine, and Stanley Harrold. 2014. *African Americans: A Concise History.* Upper Saddle River, NJ: Pearson Prentice Hall.

Kellogg, John. 1977. "Negro Urban Clusters in the Postbellum South." *Geographical Review* 67, no. 3 (July): 310–321.

Louisiana. 1869. An Act to Enforce the 13th Article of the Constitution of the State, and to Regulate the Licenses Mentioned in Said 13th Article (Common Carrier Act), 1869 La. Acts 37 (February 23, 1869).

Painter, Nell Irvin. 1977. *Exodusters: Black Migration to Kansas after Reconstruction.* New York: Knopf.

Painter, Nell Irvin. 2006. *Creating Black Americans: African-American History and Its Meanings, 1619 to the Present.* New York: Oxford University Press.

Schubert, Frank N. 1997. *Black Valor: Buffalo Soldiers and the Medal of Honor, 1870–1898.* Wilmington, DE: Scholarly Resources.

United States. 1875. The Civil Rights Act of 1875. 18 Stat. 335 (March 1, 1875).

United States. 1883. *The Civil Rights Cases*, 109 U.S. 3 (1883).

Washington, Booker T. 1901. *Up from Slavery: An Autobiography.* New York: Doubleday, Page & Co.

Wells-Barnett, Ida B. 1900. "Lynch Law in America." *The Arena* 23, no. 1 (January): 15–24.

Wortham, Robert A. 2009. "W.E.B. Du Bois and the Philadelphia Black Church: An Early Sociological Study." *Michigan Sociological Review* 23 (fall): 31–58.

_____ *Chapter 12* _____

# A New Negro

More and more blacks entered the 20th century determined to break the shackles of segregation that extended slavery's restrictions on their community and personal lives. Thousands and then tens of thousands fled the harshest of segregation in the South in what would become a more than half-century progression that changed the complexion of the United States and shifted what was called "the Negro Problem" from being a southern problem to being a national problem. In 1890 about 9 in 10 African Americans lived in the South. By 1930 the number would be just under 8 in 10. By 1970 it would be about 5 in 10 (53%). What came to be called the Great Migration moved blacks out of the South into the North, Midwest, and West.

Escaping the South had long been part of black visions of a better place. Colonial and antebellum runaways had traveled the path. The Exodusters of the 1870s and 1880s led the postbellum departure. At least 60,000 blacks moved from the South in the 1870s. Another 70,000 joined them in the 1880s. Then the southern outflow began streaming into a growing flood. In the 1890s and first decade of the 1900s the outflow reached 170,000. In the 1910s it swelled to more than 450,000, and it expanded again in the 1920s to almost 750,000. Close to 3 million blacks redistributed themselves from the South between 1890 and 1930. They created new communities and changed old communities, particularly in urban areas in the North and Midwest (Marks 1985, 148).

An insistent emergence of blacks in the mainstream of U.S. public life and culture accompanied their relocation. Not merely did their folkways migrate with blacks; their entertainments and expressions permeated more and more of American life. For example, their music became a soundtrack

Black women were a driving force in creating "A New Negro," exemplified by Madam C. J. Walker behind the wheel of a symbol of her success. Walker was among the first self-made female millionaires in America, representing a rising wave of black women advancing in public life as blacks surged to the cities in the early 20th century. (New York Public Library)

throughout much of America. It had been the soundtrack of much of the South from countryside to city. Enslaved blacks in the fields sang out with their work songs, field hollers, and shouts and chants. In the slave quarters they crooned with their ballads and spirituals and beat time with instrumentals. Enslaved and unenslaved, they entertained in the cities, fiddling, plucking, strumming, and singing. Postbellum sharecroppers, tenants, and chain gangs kept the beat going. Their hum permeated towns and cities, not only in segregated black sections but wherever blacks worked. Their diversions and amusements became entertainment, and not just for themselves. Black music became America's music.

The Mississippi River corridor, particularly the section from St. Louis through Memphis to New Orleans, produced the sounds of America's turn of the century. Ragtime emerged from black St. Louis with its unexpected varying and offbeat rhythms. Scott Joplin rose from the Arkansas–Texas border to a stint at the 1893 World's Fair in Chicago to stand as "the King of Ragtime" with his 1899 publication of "Maple Leaf Rag." Its harmonic progressions, metrics, and melody set a standard for the genre. His 1902 hit "The Entertainer" would be resurrected for the soundtrack of the 1974 Hollywood film *The Sting*, which contributed to his being awarded a posthumous Pulitzer Prize for music in 1976. All the rage from the mid-1890s to the end of World War I in 1919 Ragtime spun off the Cakewalk and honky-tonk.

With its piano-based up-tempo carried over to brass band and orchestra, Ragtime contrasted with the down Mississippi development of the same time, the Blues. Typically mournful with plucked guitar, bass, whining harmonica, and pain-filled voice, Blues spread from the Deep South's Delta and Black Belt. Telling stories of loss and suffering in a social history that reached back to general emancipation, the Blues grooved on personal troubles that moved from the fields to ramshackle juke joints at rural crossroads where Jim Crow left the tired and weary, the disappointed and disgruntled, to dance, drink, gamble, and shout away their anger and anxieties.

The Alabama-born William Christopher "W. C." Handy opened the Blues to wider audiences. Captivated by the folk form, he shifted from his formal music training and teaching displayed at the 1893 Chicago World's Fair and at Alabama's State Agricultural and Mechanical College for Negroes, to transcribe the folk sound into sheet music notably published in his 1912 *Memphis Blues* and in time garnering him the title "Father of the Blues." Tennessee-born Bessie Smith would rise as "the Empress of the Blues" to spread the form as the most popular songstress of the 1920s and 1930s with hits such as "Empty Bed Blues," "Nobody Knows You When You're Down and Out," and "A Good Man Is Hard to Find."

Beyond Blues and Ragtime, Jazz bubbled up from black New Orleans to spread not only across the United States but around the globe. It became an African American gift to international music. Flaunting various styles, Jazz would range throughout the 20th century and beyond without singular definition. Its polyrhythmic improvisation distinguished it from all else, facilitating and prompting its continual metamorphosis. Eclectic in its instrumentation, it embraced woodwinds, brass, reeds, trumpets, flutes, piano, organ, drums, stringed instruments, electronics, various vocal techniques, and more. In many senses, it became a form without boundaries. It spread with the black migration to so infuse the 1920s that many called the decade "the Jazz Age."

As Jazz became part of the Roaring Twenties, blacks became larger parts of urban America, especially in the North and Midwest, as they had rallied to the industrial demands of World War I (1914–1919). Moving into the steelworks in Gary, Indiana, for example, newcomers swelled that city's black population almost 13-fold between 1910 and 1920. New arrivals to the rubber works enlarged the black population in Akron, Ohio, more than sevenfold. The black population in Detroit expanded more than sixfold. By

1920 the United States for the first time had cities with populations of more than 100,000 blacks in New York City (152,467), Philadelphia (134,229), and Chicago (109,458).

Old connections with the Caribbean also contributed to the black flow North for, like southern blacks, West Indians came in search of a better life. A first wave came between 1900 and 1930, adding more than a quarter million blacks distributed mostly in northeastern urban areas. They came predominantly from English-speaking islands, with Jamaica leading. More settled in greater New York City than in any other locale; they made their mark with their own institutions, such as mutual benefit societies and clubs, and with their infusion into existing institutions such as churches, with St. Augustine's Episcopal Church in Brooklyn as a prime example.

West Indians made their mark also in arguments about how best to improve black circumstances and conditions. Indeed, as newcomers often did in relation to established communities, they shifted identities, images, and interactions. And often having higher levels of literacy and professional backgrounds, their visions of progress diverged from those of U.S.-born blacks. They voiced more radical ideologies, as seen from the likes of Jamaica-born Marcus M. Garvey in the 1910s and 1920s to Trinidad-born Stokely Carmichael in the 1960s and 1970s. Their differences with U.S.-born blacks produced disagreements as they had since the 1600s when blacks from the islands were considered "outlandish." Competition and attitudes on both sides produced friction between the two groups of blacks.

Any friction among blacks paled against whites' violent reaction to blacks' moving into cities and into the North and Midwest. Race riots characterized by whites attacking blacks, as had occurred infamously in the New York Draft Riots in 1863, flared across the nation at the turn of the century. The shocking race riot in Springfield, Illinois, that leveled much of the black section in August 1908 quickened the Niagara Movement's call for equal protection and equal rights. More notably, in response to the Springfield riot a biracial but predominantly white group of about 60 prominent Americans announced on Abraham Lincoln's birthday in February 1909 their formation of the National Association for the Advancement of Colored People (NAACP). W.E.B. Du Bois emerged as director of publications and research, in charge of the official publication *The Crisis*, which he edited until 1934, but he was the only black among the NAACP's initial leadership. It was not a black organization but an interracial organization aimed at advancing nonwhites to constitutional rights and protections.

The NAACP joined various other organizations focused on blacks' circumstances and conditions. Black women had come together in July 1896 in the National Association of Colored Women's Clubs. Booker T. Washington led development of the National Negro Business League in 1900.

Other groups organized to focus directly on blacks' problems arising from the Great Migration's start. Blacks in Detroit, for example, had in 1897 established the first Phillis Wheatley Home, joining the settlement house movement Jane Addams and Ellen Gates Starr pioneered with their Hull House in Chicago in 1889. The harsh and seedy situations black women encountered moved activist black Baptist women's leader Shirley W. Layten to collaborate in founding the National League for the Protection of Colored Women in 1905 with headquarters in New York City and units in other major cities such as Baltimore, Philadelphia, and Washington, D.C. Black social scientist George E. Haynes was a prime mover in founding the Committee for the Improvement of Industrial Conditions among Negroes in New York. In 1910 Layten's and Haynes's organizations merged into the National League on Urban Conditions among Negroes (later simply the National Urban League).

Joining in the Progressive push to uplift the downtrodden and accepting a duty to advance not only themselves but others of their race, black college students and graduates in the early 1900s initiated fraternities and sororities that would become the basis of the so-called Divine Nine of the National Pan-Hellenic Council. Black college graduates in Philadelphia organized *Sigma Pi Phi* (the Boulé) in 1904. Black students at Cornell University in Ithaca, New York, in 1906 formed *Alpha Phi Alpha* fraternity. Students at Howard University formed *Alpha Kappa Alpha* (AKA) sorority in 1908. *Kappa Alpha Psi* fraternity was organized in 1911 at Indiana University. Students at Howard University formed *Delta Sigma Theta* sorority in 1913, *Phi Beta Sigma* in 1914, and *Zeta Phi Beta* sorority in 1920. Blacks in Indianapolis in 1922 organized the *Sigma Gamma Rho* sorority.

Such organizations joined the black push for racial advancement in the social activism and political reform of the Progressive Era. Recently arrived poor black migrants shared similarities with poor whites, and particularly with recently arrived poor European immigrants, but racial discrimination cleaved most efforts at collaborating in common cause. The Progressive Era war against poverty and for reform of urban conditions only slightly budged the burden of color weighing down blacks in areas from housing to employment to education. In places, Progressivism added to the burden as the elitist movement assumed elements of an ideology of genetic superiority and upper white middle-class values. While some blacks passed progressive tests, the mass remained mired in public disdain. Indeed, irrespective of personal achievement or resources, blacks commonly found themselves steered into segregated housing, jobs, and public spaces, forming the base of enduring ghettos.

Blacks again found liberating opportunities in war. Europe's descent into horrific slaughter in August 1914 quickened southern blacks' outflow. As the war cut off northern industry's supply of European immigrants, blacks became an alternative labor source for whom employers paid labor agents $2 to $3 a head to recruit from the South (Marks 1985, 151–152). In a push–pull dynamic, southern blacks hastened to escape oppressive rural confines blighted by the boll weevil and hurried to embrace higher pay in shifting from low-wage work in the South, averaging $.75 per day for agricultural workers and $1.25 to $3.00 for nonagricultural workers.

Georgia-born Robert Sengstacke Abbott's *Chicago Defender* led northern black newspapers in campaigning to draw blacks to opportunities outside the South. Promoting a version of the American dream, the *Defender* and other black newspapers pressed for relocation with new realities in a North free of rampant lynching and full of jobs in contrast to the South where unemployment among blacks stood at about 13 percent in 1910, rising to 20 percent by 1920.

When the United States entered the World War I in April 1917, blacks split in their response to President Woodrow Wilson's call to arms "to make the world safe for democracy." "Let us have a real democracy for the United States and then we can advise a house cleaning over on the other side of the water," the *Baltimore Afro-American* chided (Williams 2011, n.p.). Black labor leaders A. Philip Randolph and Chandler Owen in their newspaper *The Messenger* joined socialists and others in denouncing the war and urging blacks to resist military service.

What would it prove if blacks fought or did not fight for the United States? That question generated heated discussion as it had from the nation's beginning and as it would long after. More than a few blacks asked themselves how appropriate it was to fight to support a nation that so suppressed them. The ugly four-day race riot in East St. Louis, Illinois, in June 1917 that slaughtered 125 blacks accentuated the question. The thousands marching in New York City with banners asking "Mr. President, why not make America safe for democracy" in the NAACP-sponsored Silent Protest Parade in July 1917 further stressed the question.

Yet black men were employed under arms, voluntarily and involuntarily. About 370,000 black draftees under the Selective Service Act of 1917 joined the approximately 10,000 black regulars in the U.S. Army. Black doctors volunteered for service to care for the 40,000 men of the Army's sole black combat units, the 92nd and 93rd divisions (Fisher and Buckley 2016, 3–5). The 369th, 370th, 371st, and 372nd regiments won France's highest military honor, the *Croix de Guerre*, for their gallantry in combat in the American Expeditionary Force.

Blacks in uniform faced resentment from whites in and out of the armed services, abroad and at home, as illustrated in Houston, Texas, in August 1917. In something of a repeat of the 1906 Brownsville incident,

black troopers in the 24th Infantry's 3rd Battalion at Camp Logan beset
by local police and white residents responded in a melee that left 16 whites
and 4 of the black troopers dead. White outrage produced three sets of
courts-martial that convicted 110 of the troopers, sentenced 63 to life terms,
and hanged 13 whose bodies were then buried in unmarked graves.

Blacks needed to do little to incur white wrath. But their growing numbers competing for social space and perhaps especially the no-nonsense
bearing of black veterans returning from Europe made the aftermath of the
November 1918 armistice a touchy time. Bloody race rioting smeared the
U.S. map throughout 1919. Charleston, South Carolina, Elaine, Arkansas,
Knoxville, Tennessee, Omaha, Nebraska, Waco and Longview, Texas, and
even Washington, D.C., experienced notable white attacks on blacks. The
worst of the rash of at least two dozen major riots in what became known
as the Red Summer hit Chicago. The city was in an uproar from July 27 to
August 3. The South Side housing most blacks suffered the most damage.
Blacks lost not only their homes but also their jobs in rioting that resulted in
an official death toll of 38–23 blacks and 15 whites.

Governmental and nongovernmental investigations studied how to
avoid such large-scale racial violence and promote greater harmony, but
deep-seated attitudes and popular practices weighed against meaningful
reforms. The segregation white supremacy imposed nationwide under-
lay the violence. For the most part blacks refused to accept it, and whites
refused to alter it. To many whites black uplift meant white displacement;
it meant blacks having what whites had, which were things many whites
thought blacks should not have. It meant reducing the privileges of being
white, for it reduced the differences between being white and being black.
The Tulsa race riot in 1921 illustrated how black advancement triggered
white rage.

In the early move West, blacks built a thriving community in Oklahoma's
second-largest city. By the time of World War I, Tulsa's Greenwood District
stood in the oil boom town as what many referred to as "the Negro Wall
Street." Its 12,000 residents featured affluent and ambitious blacks whose
wealth elevated the district to being what many reputed as the richest black
community in the United States. Black professionals abounded—attorneys,
bankers, clergy, dentists, insurers, physicians, and real estate agents, for
example.

White attackers devastated "Deep Greenwood," as locals called the district's center, destroying 191 black businesses. They burned down nearly
1,300 black homes and looted more than 200 others. They burned the local
black hospital, various black churches, and a black junior high school.
Blacks got little substantial help from authorities. In fact, local police and
state militia corralled more than 6,000 blacks as if they were vigilantes

rather than victims. The rioting left at least 176 dead (Ellsworth 1982, 45–70; Brophy 2002, 24–68).

Florida's Rosewood Massacre in January 1923 further illustrated the extended season of white violence determined to put blacks back in their place. Whites murdered eight in Rosewood, burning down the black town and essentially erasing it from the map. Such violence reached beyond escalated black lynchings—38 in 1917 and 58 in 1918—and rioting of the World War I years. Whites throughout the United States had campaigned at least since the Civil War's end to rid themselves of blacks. A brutal pattern akin to ethnic cleansing from the late 1860s through the 1930s turned about 1 in 12 of the 3,100 U.S. counties into white-only enclaves. White rampages between 1918 and 1927 lynched at least 416 blacks, 47 of them in Florida (Jaspin 2007, passim).

For blacks Rosewood, Tulsa, and the World War I riots marked fresh notches in a rising backlash. The Great Migration had quickened attacks across a broad front as assaults occurred not only in person but in popular media and from those considered scientists and scholars. North Carolina–born Baptist preacher Thomas Dixon's 1905 best-selling novel *The Clansman*, for example, recast post–Civil War antiblack violence for popular adulation. New Jersey–born Columbia University professor William A. Dunning offered reactionary accounts applauding black repression, disfranchisement, and segregation in his 1907 *Reconstruction, Political and Economic, 1865–1877*. He launched the so-called Dunning-School of historical apologists for slavery, Redemption, and segregation. Further popularizing such defenses, adapting *The Clansman* for the big screen, Kentucky-born filmmaking pioneer D. W. Griffith boosted the heroic portrayal of the Ku Klux Klan (KKK) and other white terrorists with his immensely popular 1915 *The Birth of a Nation*, with its stark stereotyping of blacks as idle, ignorant, rapacious, and incapable of civilization.

New York–born lawyer Madison Grant added pseudoscientific racism to the mix with his 1916 immediate best seller *The Passing of the Great Race*. Preaching theories of white supremacy, particularly of Nordic superiority, Grant advanced eugenics almost as a moral imperative that would suppress lesser civilized and undesirable peoples such as blacks. Georgia-born historian U. B. Phillips, a PhD student of Dunning's at Columbia, recast black bondage in his long-applauded 1918 *American Negro Slavery* as a blessing that advanced savages toward civilization. Blacks needed repression, Phillips suggested, to save them from themselves and also to save society from them.

Blacks countered the onslaught as best they could without access to mainstream organs of communication. The most widely circulated medium was the black press, and it persisted in its struggle against hateful black stereotypes.

The *Chicago Defender, California Eagle, Baltimore Afro-American, New York Amsterdam News, Norfolk Journal and Guide, Pittsburgh Courier,* and others worked to bring facts to popular attention. At least 275 black newspapers published between 1900 and 1910. They pressed issues for debate not only to raise black consciousness but to reach whites as *Freedom's Journal* had aimed to do when launched in 1827 as the first black newspaper and as Frederick Douglass had sought to do with his *North Star* and other publications. Yet black newspapers operated as a confined forum, attended almost exclusively by blacks. White readers saw almost no "black news" except for sensationalized crimes or other negative items, which was almost exclusively what the mainstream press published about blacks.

In terms of scholarship, blacks again for the most part had to publish their own. The American Negro Academy that Rev. Alexander Crummell and others had begun in Washington, D.C., in 1897 produced its occasional papers to limited circulation. That same year John E. Bruce and Arthur A. Schomburg in New York founded the Negro Society for Historical Research. Blacks in Philadelphia preceded both organizations, forming in 1892 the American Negro Historical Society. All three were collectors of materials and relatively self-contained. Virginia-born Harvard PhD Carter G. Woodson dedicated himself to widening the reach of facts about blacks' communities and contributions. With Ohio-born Congregational minister and Howard University graduate Jesse Moorland, Carter in 1915 established the Association for the Study of Negro Life and History (Harris 1998, 109–119).

Woodson established the Associated Publishers to print and distribute scholarly studies, but in 1916 the *Journal of Negro History* became his centerpiece. Appearing quarterly, it carried foundational works by foremost scholars in black history, such as Charles Wesley, Alrutheus A. Taylor, Rayford W. Logan, Lorenzo J. Greene, Lawrence D. Reddick, and John Hope Franklin. The research and writing that appeared in the *Journal* established what would grow into the interdisciplinary field of black studies. The *Journal* provided publication opportunities unavailable elsewhere and became an entry for black scholars as professional academics and public scholars, as well as a major forum for discovery and discourse about black life and development in America and around the world.

While Woodson worked with his fellow scholars to correct and expand facts about blacks, black writers in other forms came to enjoy wider readership. They had their start with the early black writing that had expanded with increasing breadth after the 1760s, following Briton Hammon, Jupiter Hammon, and Phillis Wheatley. The ex-slave narrative genre, with examples such as the 1789 *Interesting Narrative of the Life of Olaudah Equiano,* contributed to a tradition of black autobiography, providing witness to black

lives and also serving white curiosity about black lives. The form opened
to black women as the 1831 *History of Mary Prince, A West Indian Slave*
became an early autobiography by a black woman enslaved in the Americas.
The 1836 *Life and Religious Experiences of Jarena Lee, a Coloured Lady,
Giving an Account of Her Call to Preach the Gospel* furthered African
American female autobiography, as did Harriet A. Jacobs's 1861 *Incidents
in the Life of the Slave Girl*; Elizabeth Hobbs Keckley's 1868 *Behind the
Scenes, or, Thirty Years a Slave and Four Years in the White House*; and
Julia A. J. Foote's 1879 autobiography, *A Brand Plucked from the Fire*.

The form launched Frederick Douglass with his 1845 *Narrative of an
American Slave* and William Wells Brown with his 1847 *Narrative of a
Fugitive Slave*. Brown initiated black fiction in 1853 with his novel *Clotel;
or, the President's Daughter*. Brown also produced in 1858 *The Escape; or,
A Leap for Freedom*, the first stage play by an African American. His oldest
daughter Elizabeth Josephine Brown would also be among leaders in writ-
ing black biography with her 1856 portrait of her father, *Biography of an
American Bondman*.

Black women produced a goodly amount of reading for popular audiences in the late 1800s. Perhaps foremost was Frances E. W. Harper. Best
known for her 1892 novel *Iola Leroy: Or, Shadows Uplifted*, Harper got
her start with three novels—*Minnie's Sacrifice* (1869), *Sowing and Reaping:
A Temperance Story* (1876–1877), and *Trial and Triumph* (1888–1889)—
first serialized in the AME Church's *Christian Recorder*. She produced collections of poetry also, and she was hardly alone at the time as a black
female poet or novelist.

Before Harper's first published poems in 1872, Adah Isaacs Menken produced her 1868 collection *Infelicia*. Josephine D. Heard in 1890 published
her 72-poem collection *Morning Glories*. H. Cordelia Ray offered her 1893
collection *Sonnets* and Mary Weston Fordham her 1897 poetry collection
*Magnolia Leaves*. Alice Ruth Moore gained acclaim with her 1895 poetry
collection *Violets and Other Tales* but became better known later as Alice
Dunbar Nelson after her 1898 marriage to the most famous black poet of
his day, Paul Laurence Dunbar. Gertrude Bustill Mossell's 1894 collection of
essays and poems documented the contributions of many of her day under
the title *The Work of the Afro-American Woman*.

A literary blooming accompanied the Great Migration. From the first
decade of the 20th century into the 1930s African American writers thrust
their work into public attention. Georgia Douglas Johnson emerged as a
leading playwright and poet with work such as *The Voice of the Negro*
(1905) and *The Heart of a Woman* (1916). Among her 28 stage dramas,
her "Lynching Plays" attested to her outspoken civil rights advocacy. Jessie Redmon Fauset also emerged as a major early 20th-century writer with

her four novels—*There is Confusion* (1924), *Plum Bun* (1928), *The China-berry Tree* (1931), and *Comedy, American Style* (1933). She was perhaps even more influential as literary editor of *The Crisis*, where she nurtured black writers including Countee Cullen, Claude McKay, Jean Toomer, and Langston Hughes.

Fauset's editing earned her the title "midwife" in some circles, as she gave birth to the careers of writers who became giants in the black artistic blossoming called "the New Negro Renaissance." The production preceded the title that settled on the movement with publication of Howard University philosophy professor Alain Locke's 1925 anthology titled *The New Negro*. Many came in time to call the movement "the Harlem Renaissance," as New York City's Manhattan district had become something of a black Mecca in growing to lead the nation in black population. But the New Negro Renaissance was bigger and broader than Harlem.

Chicago, Washington, D.C., Atlanta, St. Louis, New Orleans, Baltimore, Philadelphia, and other cities with major black populations all served as sites of the New Negro Renaissance. It was a dispersed cultural phenomenon transported in the experience of the black migration northward and city-ward. Locke explained it "primarily in terms of a new vision of opportunity, a social and economic freedom, of the spirit to seize, even in the face of an extortionate and heavy toll, a chance for the improvement of conditions." It was part of "a mass movement toward a larger and more democratic chance," Locke noted. It was "a deliberate flight . . . from medieval America to modern" (Locke 1925, 6).

The black spirit was unyielding. Particularly returning World War I veterans were militant for change. Du Bois described the spirit in the May 1919 issue of *The Crisis*: "We return. We return from fighting. We return fighting. Make way for Democracy! We saved it in France, and by the Great Jehovah, we will save it in the United States of America, or know the reason why," he wrote. That assertive attitude clashed with the white status quo and the results showed in the eruptions of the Red Summer and more white-on-black mob violence throughout the 1920s.

The backlash against blacks was clear throughout the 1920s as it became a signal decade for a revitalized KKK. Spectacular rallies across the nation displayed the Klan's fresh appeal, with members reaching into mainstream America and reportedly numbering 3 to 8 million. Ohio was said to have 300,000 KKK members and Pennsylvania 200,000. No longer just a group of night riders, the KKK campaigned openly and captured public offices. It elected mayors in 1924 in Portland, Maine, and Portland, Oregon. It reportedly had pivotal control of state government in Colorado and Indiana. In their white robes with peaked hoods, Klansmen proudly paraded more than 50,000–60,000 strong in Washington, D.C., in 1925 with President

Calvin Coolidge's go-ahead, as *The Literary Digest* chronicled in its August 22 issue.

Blacks were not backing down, however. In a virtual anthem of the times, Jamaican-born poet Claude McKay had declaimed in July 1919, "If we must die, let it not be like hogs/. . . but fighting back!" And blacks had begun to exercise their own electoral muscle built in part from being steered into northern ghettos. In Chicago, Alabama-born Oscar Stanton De Priest in 1915 had become the city's first black on the city council. William Henry Lewis had won election in 1899 to the city council in Cambridge, Massachusetts, but De Priest's election marked a budding black political machine. Earlier De Priest served as a Cook County Commissioner, and in 1929 he would become the first black outside the ex-Confederate states to be elected to the U.S. Congress, where he served three consecutive terms, and he would be followed by successive black representatives (Davis 1992, 142).

And more than local thinking was going on among blacks. Not only was a new national outlook taking hold, a fresh Atlantic connection was at work as focus on Africa and the Caribbean migration renewed external perspectives. Jamaican-born Marcus M. Garvey stirred black nationalism

Marcus M. Garvey rallied a mass black movement in the 1920s to reshape black self-image and public perception through communal pride and self-help. (Library of Congress)

and Pan-Africanism on coming to the United States in 1916 with his Universal Negro Improvement Association (UNIA). Impressed by Booker T. Washington's industrial education approach to uplift the masses, Garvey focused on broad-based appeal that resonated with common folk blacks. Exposure to Harlem socialism and radicalism in the likes of St. Croix-born Hubert Harrison and others moved Garvey further to eschew any Talented Tenth approach. He condemned the NAACP as the National Association for the Advancement of *Certain* People and became a nemesis to Du Bois, as Du Bois had been a nemesis of Booker T. Washington until his death in 1915.

Garvey built perhaps the broadest black mass movement in U.S. history. Millions flocked to his banner. The UNIA's weekly newspaper, *Negro World*, reached a peak circulation of about 500,000, easily outselling all other black publications. It carried Garvey's message of black pride and universal black collaboration to empower blacks economically and politically in self-realization. He organized business enterprises to employ blacks and to service their needs. His Negro Factories Corporation, for example, launched a grocery store chain; it ran a restaurant; and operated a tailor, dressmaker, hat maker, and steam laundry. Also it started a publisher, the Universal Printing House. Like Booker T. Washington, Garvey believed economics was the basis of black advancement. "Be not deceived, wealth is strength, wealth is power, wealth is influence, wealth is justice, is liberty, is real human rights," he insisted (Clarke 1974, 346).

Much in the headlines and later history was Garvey's Black Star Line. A shipping company launched to provide cargo and passenger connections among blacks, it would have four ships—the first a leaky coal tub rechristened the *SS Frederick Douglass*. The line sailed primarily between U.S. ports and the West Indies. Many took it as the primary vehicle for Garvey's Back-to-Africa campaign, commonly misunderstanding both the line and the campaign. Garvey was no colonizationist and issued no call for wholesale black removal from the United States or any place else in the Americas. He called for black unity to uplift Africa in uplifting blacks globally. His call to Africa that "we are coming" was a call to collective aid, not a call for mass relocation.

Garvey's Back-to-Africa was primarily about consciousness. It was about how blacks perceived themselves individually and collectively, and about how they might best think of themselves to realize their individual and collective potential. It was about Africa being no place of shame and about black being beautiful. Garvey preached that rather than rejecting their common African heritage or despising their African features blacks should embrace their heritage and themselves. "Up, you mighty race, you can accomplish what you will!" he exhorted (Clarke 1974, 329).

Garvey focused positive attention on Africa and the connections of the African Diaspora with the motto "One Aim, One God, One Destiny" (Garvey and Garvey 1923, 38). He carried forward the late 1700s black nationalism of Prince Hall and that of Martin Delany in the late 1800s and Edward Wilmot Blyden's of the turn of the century. And his influence would reach forward into the 1960s and 1970s with the Nation of Islam (NOI). The NOI 1960s' firebrand Malcolm X learned Garvey's precepts at the knee of his father, Earl Little, a staunch Garveyite. Further, Garvey extended the Pan-Africanism popular among leading West Indian immigrants such as Blyden, Henry Sylvester Williams, Hubert Harrison, and Cyril Briggs.

Pan-Africanism was hardly new when Garvey advanced it in the 1920s. The idea of all African peoples being joined in struggle reached back to resistance against the transatlantic slave trade. Equiano had notions of it in his 1789 *Narrative*. His fellow African Quobna Ottobah Cugoano elaborated it further in his 1791 *Thoughts and Sentiments on the Evil of Slavery*. Rev. Alexander Crummell and other African American missionaries, including the likes of AME Bishop Henry McNeal Turner, preached the unity of African peoples throughout the 1800s. The accelerated European colonization of Africa following the Berlin Congress of 1884–1885 incited further black organized action to aid Africa.

A Pan-African Congress convened in London in 1900. Trinidad-born Henry Sylvester Williams was the organizing force from his base in London. W.E.B. Du Bois was also a prime figure, serving as chairman of the Committee on the Address to the Nations of the World. The conference was the first of a series that quickened with the 1919 Treaty of Versailles's redrawing maps and redistributing territory in Europe and around the globe. Indeed, a second Pan-African conference convened in Paris in the shadow of Versailles in 1919. Pan-Africanists and other anti-colonialists lobbied hard for decolonization and self-determination in Africa, Asia, and the Caribbean. Pan-African Congresses would follow at London and Brussels in 1921. Two convened also in 1923 at London and at Lisbon. Another convened in New York in 1927. The meetings would go on to 1945, with lobbying at the freshly created United Nations. Their theme was singular in focusing the world's eyes on self-determination for peoples of the African Diaspora.

While Pan-Africanism could connect Du Bois and Garvey in common cause, it could not join them on U.S. domestic issues. Garvey's Black Nationalism sounded too much like separatism, too much like Booker T. Washington's concession to segregation, to suit the likes of Du Bois. The clash between elite focus and mass focus approaches also played a part in dividing leaders such as Du Bois and Garvey. And black-on-black leadership conflicts would not subside. Differences in background and class stoked competition of egos, personalities, and positions. As money to sustain organization activity and reach was ever an issue, the competition was sometimes cut-throat. Mainstream media contributed to the competition by virtually insisting on there being only a single black voice worthy of attention and by thus elevating some voices to diminish others.

Internal divisiveness among blacks paled against organized white disruption. Government agents at the federal and local levels repeatedly targeted black leaders to limit their appeal and effectiveness. In an effort to hobble the National Ex-Slave Mutual Relief, Bounty and Pension Association (BPA), for example, the U.S. Department of Justice (DOJ) in 1901 prosecuted BPA leader Isaiah H. Dickerson, getting a conviction that was overturned on appeal. Similarly, in his rise to Chicago City Council, Oscar Stanton De Priest found himself indicted for fraud in 1917 but represented by noted attorney Clarence Darrow won acquittal. Throughout World War I numbers of blacks found themselves under federal surveillance and investigation of their U.S. loyalties. Socialists such as A. Philip Randolph and Chandler Owen were particularly suspect.

As his popularity soared, Garvey fell under scrutiny by the DOJ's anti-radical division. Marking Garvey in a series of blacks he would find dangerous over time, J. Edgar Hoover led the forerunner of the Federal Bureau of Investigation to hound the UNIA leader. Hoover hoped for grounds to deport Garvey as an undesirable alien, but settled for prosecuting him for mail fraud. Convicted in 1923 and sentenced to five years in prison, Garvey was deported to Jamaica in 1927 when President Calvin Coolidge commuted his sentence. That effectively flattened the Garvey movement in the United States. He went the way of many other blacks whom officials saw as radicals or disturbers of the racial peace. He was one of multiplying blacks increasingly seen as troublesome in the rise of the New Negro.

## REFERENCES

Brophy, Alfred L. 2002. *Reconstructing the Dreamland: The Tulsa Riot of 1921*. New York: Oxford University Press.

Clarke, John Henrik. 1974. *Marcus Garvey and the Vision of Africa*. New York: Vintage Books.

Davis, Thomas J. 1992. "De Priest, Oscar Stanton." In *Encyclopedia of African-American Civil Rights: from Emancipation to the Present*, ed. Charles D. Lowery and John F. Marszalek, 142. New York: Greenwood Press.

Ellsworth, Scott. 1982. *Death in a Promised Land: The Tulsa Race Riot of 1921*. Baton Rouge: Louisiana State University Press.

Fischer, W. Douglas, and Joann H. Buckley. 2016. *African American Doctors of World War I: The Lives of 104 Volunteers*. Jefferson, NC: McFarland.

Garvey, Marcus, and Amy Jacques Garvey. 1923. *Philosophy and Opinions of Marcus Garvey*. New York City: Universal Pub. House.

Harris, Janette Hoston. 1998. "Woodson and Wesley: A Partnership in Building the Association for the Study of Afro-American Life and History." *Journal of Negro History* 83, no. 2: 109–119.

Jaspin, Elliot. 2007. *Buried in the Bitter Waters: The Hidden History of Racial Cleansing in America.* New York: Basic Books.

Locke, Alain. 1925. *The New Negro: An Interpretation.* New York: A. & C. Boni.

Marks, Carole. 1985. "Black Workers and the Great Migration North." *Phylon* 46, no. 2 (2nd qtr): 148–161.

Williams, Chad. 2011. "African Americans and World War I." In *African Age: African & African Diasporan Transformations in the 20th Century*, The Schomburg Center for Research in Black Culture, accessed at http://exhibitions. nypl.org/africanaage/essay-world-war-i.html.

_____ *Chapter 13* _____

# A Great Depression

The New Negro of the Great Migration grew as blacks continued to stream out of the South, driven by Jim Crow's violent racial subordination and drawn particularly by the industrial boom in the Northeast and Midwest. The flow from the Caribbean virtually halted, however, as a wave of nativism closed U.S. entry to almost all who were not northern Europeans. Only about 75,000 from the Caribbean entered the United States in the 1920s, and most of those arrived before the Immigration Act of 1924's severe national origins quotas. In 1925 immigrants from the Caribbean barely topped 2,000, and their numbers fell to about 15,000 for all the 1930s. In contrast, more than 900,000 blacks left the South in the 1920s. But the boom of that decade turned to bust in the 1930s as the Great Depression sank the United States and economies around the globe. Diminished opportunities for migrants and dwindling resources cut southern black outmigration to fewer than 500,000 in the 1930s.

The Great Depression confronted the New Negro with old problems. The common black experience of being last-hired-first-fired cut deeply into black families and communities as official nationwide unemployment soared from 8.9 percent in 1930 to peak at 24.9 percent in 1933, and black unemployment more than doubled that. In 1934 when the official count put white unemployment about 17.0 percent, black unemployment was at least 38.0 percent. Blacks in 1920s migration boom cities suffered even worse unemployment: Chicago (40%), Pittsburgh (48%), New York City (50%), Philadelphia (56%), Detroit (60%), and Atlanta (65%). Hard times hit everywhere (Myrdal 1944, 300–303).

Even where blacks had jobs, their family incomes seldom reached half of white family incomes. A typical black husband–wife family in Chicago

Blacks endured the utmost destitution during the Great Depression. Last-hired-and-first-fired, they suffered more than 50 percent unemployment in some areas of the United States during the 1930s. (Everett Collection Historical/Alamy Stock Photo)

in 1935–1936 earned roughly $726, about 43 percent of a typical white husband–wife family's income of $1,687. Disparities were generally higher in southern cities: in Atlanta and Mobile typical black family income was 34 percent of a white family's, and in Columbia, South Carolina, a black family earned about 31 percent of a white family's income. The disparities reflected numerous factors from education to employment sector to skill levels, but most of all it reflected racial segregation (Myrdal 1944, 364–369).

Also blacks found themselves pushed out of positions as domestics, porters, and waiters, and other positions often thought of as "Negro jobs," as desperate whites grabbed whatever work they could take (Sundstrom 1992, 420–422). Wherever competition tightened, whites usually sought to displace blacks, for white intolerance historically hardened during hard times as whites sought to further restrict blacks so as to maintain white privilege and supremacy. So while blacks worked to close the racial gap, whites worked to maintain, if not widen, separation.

Relegated to deepening poverty, blacks experienced the Great Depression as another disruptive episode in their quest to share fully in the American Dream. Yet they responded with characteristic perseverance. Black women led the way as they typically did with their ingenuity and personal networks. Striving to keep their families and themselves together, to weather the conflicts and tensions of the Depression, black women drew on all available resources from their connections of concern and cooperation. Such contacts helped them through daily life, but more than kinship communities sustained them. Their wages made up larger portions of family income, even at a time when they were being elbowed out of their paid positions by white women seeking to secure their own family incomes. They increased as heads of households by at least 20 percent during the 1930s in places such as Chicago, Cleveland, and Philadelphia. At least one in six black households in such cities were female-headed by 1940 (Helmbold 1987, 651).

Black women characteristically reached beyond themselves to help one another and their larger communities. Fannie B. Peck organized the Housewives League of Detroit in 1930, for instance, and pushed to create the National Housewives League of America (NHLA) in 1933 to help black women help themselves and their communities with the motto "Buying, Boosting, Building." The NHLA worked with the National Negro Business League and others to promote self-help and community development by circulating what money there was within black communities. It promoted the positive side of "Don't Buy Where You Can't Work" campaigns, encouraging blacks to spend money to advance and build their own communities.

The "Don't Buy" thrust aimed to open opportunities for blacks in their own neighborhoods and beyond, boycotting and picketing businesses that had no black workers, particularly businesses located in black areas. Linking spending to hiring, the campaign enjoyed considerable support in New Negro boom cities. Chicago was a primary site. Black newspapers such as the *Chicago Whip* early championed the cause. At least 35 cities mounted major "Don't Buy" operations. From Cleveland and Toledo in Ohio, to Detroit and New York City, down to Baltimore and Washington, D.C., the campaign had effect. It had some successes in Newport News and Richmond, Virginia, in St. Louis, and in a few other southern cities, but it succeeded mostly in northern urban centers. Rev. Adam Clayton Powell Jr. led Harlem's Greater New York Coordinating Committee, for instance, to significant gains for blacks in white-collar retail positions, and the National Urban League in Chicago gained jobs for black drivers and salesmen. Exercising their strength as consumers was an old lesson blacks would continue to learn, particularly after the U.S. Supreme Court in 1938 sustained blacks' boycotts against discrimination in *New Negro Alliance v. Sanitary Grocery Co.*

Blacks did not simply draw in on themselves during the Depression; they continued to reach out to share equally in public benefits. They agitated to get benefits being distributed in President Franklin D. Roosevelt's New Deal programs. Beginning with FDR's National Recovery Act of 1933, federal spending rushed to relieve hunger and homelessness and especially to boost employment and overall economic production and stability. Blacks hardly got a fair share of benefits, but thousands did get more than a little of value. As many as 200,000 black youths got positions in the Civilian Conservation Corps between 1933 and 1942, improving their job skills as well as their 3Rs. They benefited also from National Youth Administration (NYA) projects. Federal Emergency Relief Administration initiatives reached black sharecroppers, as well as black colleges and their students. The Works Progress Administration (WPA), Public Works Administration, and National Recovery Administration provided benefits in one way or another to about one in seven black families by 1940 (Sears 1976, 94–95). The Social Security program, begun in 1935, provided continuing benefits.

Public benefits hardly offset blacks' destitution. They agitated for their full fair share, and their frustration at the discrimination that limited their lives was in many places palpable. Indeed, in many places Depression desperation aggravated race relations. Harlem flared as the most visible site of blacks' refusing to continue quietly in oppressive conditions. Thousands took to the streets in March 1935 at rumors of police brutality, and a rampage ensued along Harlem's main thoroughfare, W. 125th Street. From Fifth to Eighth Avenues blacks vented their anger primarily against white-owned businesses, ransacking many. One of New York City's leading tabloids, the *Daily News*, on March 20 carried the headline "4,000 Riot in Harlem; One Killed." Critical outcries immediately blamed Communist agitators for the violence, but it was in fact a spontaneous outburst that signaled a new form of race riot. It was not the traditional whites' mobbing blacks. It was blacks attacking property as the reachable symbols of the system oppressing them. A panel New York Mayor Fiorello H. LaGuardia commissioned to study the riot concluded that its causes arose from "injustices of discrimination in employment, the aggressions of the police, and . . . racial segregation" (Roberts 1935, 3).

In running riot in Harlem's streets blacks joined a tradition of protest central to American history since its colonial beginnings. Rioting was an old part of the American political process. It forcefully focused popular attention on problems and tended to produce flurries of activity, if not solutions. Taking to the streets was something blacks would do more and more of after 1935. They were moving also to bring pressure by other political means. New Negro advances in northern cities built political muscle. Electing Oscar Stanton De Priest to Congress in 1928 showed black strength. They could muster at least swing votes in city or county elections, and they leveraged that in hard bargaining that increasingly shifted black allegiance from Republicans to Democrats.

Impressed by FDR, longtime Republican Mary McLeod Bethune switched to being a Democrat. The party shift replaced black Republican congressman

FDR's so-called Black Cabinet, chaired by Mary McLeod Bethune (center), advised the president on responding to black destitution and demands during the 1930s' Great Depression. (Archives Center, National Museum of American History, Smithsonian Institution)

De Priest in 1935 with the black Democrat Arthur W. Mitchell. And blacks gained visibility as officeholders and advisors in FDR's administration. Indeed, a so-called Black Cabinet developed with Mary McLeod Bethune and Robert C. Weaver in the forefront. Bethune directed the NYA's Division of Negro Affairs. Weaver was a special assistant in the U.S. Housing Authority. Other notable members of what was sometimes called the "Black Brain Trust" included Sterling Brown, editor for Negro affairs in the WPA's Federal Writers Project; James P. Davis, Agricultural Adjustment Administration head field officer; Crystal Bird Fauset, WPA director of women and professional projects; William H. Hastie, U.S. Department of the Interior assistant solicitor; Eugene K. Jones, U.S. Department of Commerce advisor on Negro affairs; and Robert Vann, assistant to the U.S. attorney general. Formally referred to as the Federal Council on Negro Affairs, the members acted as conduits for the interests and needs of black communities. They were tapped to be black voices usually unheard at high levels of national policymaking.

How much FDR's New Deal program helped blacks was hotly contested at the time and later. Complaints arose about focus and benefits going to a black elite rather than to the bulk of blacks. Overall, critics offered perennial complaints that government interference with the economy hurt blacks. Without question, federal programs frequently discriminated against blacks. The Federal Housing Administration (FHA), for example, excluded blacks from loans and other programs from which whites greatly benefited. The U.S. Department of Agriculture systematically dispossessed black farmers, as documented generations later in court action such as *Pigford v. Glickman* (1999).

Black radicals assailed the New Deal and the overall U.S. system. Indeed, the radicalism of the Great War and its aftermath escalated from the Pan-Africanism of Marcus Garvey's UNIA or Cyril Briggs's more radical African Blood Brotherhood's calls for black liberation everywhere to blacks approaching fellow travelers in the Communist call for worldwide revolution against capitalist oppression. Relatively few blacks fully embraced the Communist Party (CP) as enrolled card-carrying members. Distrust and suspicion marked most African Americans' views of the CP with its Moscow-based agenda and class- rather than race-based ideology. But the degree to which the CP championed antiracism, attacked Jim Crow, crusaded against lynching, and promoted other black causes led to at least wary association.

West Indian immigrants were prominent in the African American socialist forefront. The Jamaican-born poet Claude McKay, for example, attended the 1922 Fourth Congress of the Comintern, the international Communist organization. Other black immigrants were also active. Surinam-born Otto Huiswoud in 1922 became a charter member of the Communist Party of America. Homegrown blacks also joined the party. Nebraska-born African Blood Brotherhood member Harry Haywood, for example, joined the Young Communist League in 1923 and then in 1925 the CP, going off to study in Moscow, as he would explain in his 1978 autobiography *Black Bolshevik*. Georgia-born Grace P. Campbell was among the CP's first black members; she also was the first black woman to run for statewide office in New York, campaigning in 1919 and 1920 on the Socialist ticket for the 19th Assembly District seat. Virginia-born Williana Jones Burroughs joined the CP in 1926, visited the Soviet Union, and in the 1930s ran as CP candidate for New York controller and also for lieutenant governor.

Amid the agitation of the 1930s, various blacks found themselves linked with the CP in common cause. Notable examples arose in the early years of the decade from outrageous miscarriages of justice. The most noted was the infamous Scottsboro Boys case in Alabama. Nine black males ranging in age from 12 to 19 years, hoboing down from Tennessee on a Southern Railroad freight in March 1931, found themselves charged in Scottsboro with raping two white female hobos on the train. News of the alleged sexual assault incited white lynch mobs, and hastily arranged trials before all-white juries convicted the blacks. All except 12-year-old Roy Wright faced death sentences.

The CP's International Labor Defense (ILD) immediately appealed on the boys' behalf, initially edging out National Association for the Advancement of Colored People (NAACP) lawyers to handle the cases with their worldwide publicity. The CP organized a massive demonstration in New York City's Union Square on August 1, 1932, to protest Alabama's handling of the Scottsboro Boys. Extended legal maneuvering eventually got the cases to the U.S. Supreme Court, which in *Powell v. Alabama* (1932) and *Norris v. Alabama* (1935) overturned the convictions. Alabama persisted, nevertheless. Although the state dropped charges against four of the nine, further prosecution put all but two in prison.

Angelo Herndon's case a year after the Scottsboro Boys' arrest also produced black outrage and collaboration with the CP. Ohio-born labor organizer Herndon was arrested in Atlanta in July 1932 on charges of inciting insurrection. Earlier authorities had arrested black labor organizers who became known as "the Atlanta Six," charging them in 1930 with distributing insurrectionary literature, as unionism to some was akin to socialism or communism and clearly subversive. The Atlanta Six received nowhere near the notice of Herndon, as the ILD came to his defense and drew national and international attention to his case. Georgia courts sentenced Herndon to an 18- to 20-year term. The U.S. Supreme Court initially refused Herndon's appeal, but finally in 1937 in the 5–4 decision in *Herndon v. Lowry* the Court overturned Herndon's conviction, holding Georgia's insurrection statute violated the First Amendment. Herndon was released after serving two years in prison.

Blacks seemed ever in the position of needing to push back against America's criminal justice system as it functioned to repress them as part of the white supremacist system of racial control. Angelo Herndon and the Scottsboro Boys stood as points going back to slavery in a drive particularly against black males deemed dangerous, aiming to cut them off from others and to show the consequences of stepping beyond the color line. NAACP lawyers worked criminal cases such as *Brown v. Mississippi* (1936), the *Scottsboro Boys*, and others to highlight systemic racial discrimination. And they made important law treating criminal defendants' rights.

But landmark black victories in court arose primarily in civil cases treating discrimination. The NAACP campaigned almost from its start to get the Supreme Court to recognize and enforce blacks' constitutional rights to equal protection of the laws. The Court proved itself reluctant at best to rule for blacks. Yet it did from time to time. In *Guinn v. United States* the Court in 1915 had held so-called Grandfather Clause voting rights prohibitions violated the Fifteenth Amendment. In *Buchanan v. Warley* in 1917 the Court held that residential segregation imposed by law violated the Fourteenth Amendment.

Furthering its long campaign for voting rights in the 1920s, the NAACP pressed a series of cases that came to be called the Texas White Primary Cases. It won initial victories in 1927 in *Nixon v. Herndon* and in 1932 in *Nixon v. Condon*, as the Supreme Court held Texas Democratic Party primaries' excluding black voters violated the Fourteenth Amendment. But Texas continued to thwart the efforts of blacks such as El Paso physician Lawrence A. Nixon to vote.

Texas changed its law to declare the Democratic Party a private entity without connection with the state, and the Supreme Court in 1935 unanimously upheld that position in *Grovey v. Townsend*, allowing exclusion of blacks such as Houston barber and civil rights activists Richard Randolph Grovey. Again in 1937 in *Breedlove v. Suttles*, upholding Georgia's poll tax as a valid qualification for registering to vote, the Court effectively agreed to curtail blacks' rights. A long hard road stretched toward the 1964 Twenty-Fourth Amendment outlawing poll taxes in the seemingly endless struggle that moved forward to the Voting Rights Act of 1965 and beyond.

The NAACP had an ongoing campaign also against segregated public education. Southern states woefully underfunded their separate primary and secondary schools for blacks and also excluded blacks in areas of public higher education. Equalizing educational opportunity promised a protracted battle, but not so exclusion which clearly violated *Plessy v. Ferguson*'s "Separate but Equal" doctrine, as Howard University School of Law (HUSL) graduate Thurgood Marshall insisted in his first major case. Working with HUSL dean Charles Hamilton Houston and the NAACP in state court, Marshall in 1936 won Donald Gaines Murray entry to the University of Maryland Law School. The Maryland Court of Appeals ruled that the Fourteenth Amendment's Equal Protect Clause prohibited the state law school from excluding blacks solely because of their color in the absence of any separate facility for them. NAACP lawyers moved the U.S. Supreme Court to adopt the Maryland ruling as national law in 1938, winning Lloyd Gaines's entry to the School of Law at the University of Missouri. Such battles would continue into the 1950s.

Relief seemed not close at hand at any turn for blacks as the Depression deepened, and various black artists depicted the struggles of the day. Throughout the 1930s writer Langston Hughes portrayed the black plight, opening with his 1930 novel *Not without Laughter* describing the poverty and abuse blacks suffered and moving to his 1939 drama *Angelo Herndon Jones* treating the labor organizer's tribulations. Arna Bontemps wrote of the ups and downs of black success in his 1931 novel *God Sends Sunday* and of black radicalism and revolt in his 1936 novel *Black Thunder: Gabriel's Revolt, Virginia 1800* and in his 1939 novel *Drums at Dusk* treating the Haitian revolution. Zora Neale Hurston contributed collections of southern black folklore in *Mules and Men* (1935) and spotlighted black women and their sexuality in her 1935 novel *Their Eyes Were Watching God*. Richard

Wright's 1938 novellas published together as *Uncle Tom's Children* laid bare the ugliness of the Jim Crow South, and his 1940 masterwork *Native Son* displayed the persistent black plight amid the changed scenery of the Great Migration. Wright's central character Bigger Thomas was no New Negro; he was the perennial black boy caught in white America's maw without prospect of salvation from Communist intervention or any other source. The novel's social dynamics featured racist-induced self-hatred and more.

Somber notes sounded also in black music. Billie Holiday's 1939 rendition of "Strange Fruit" with its protest against lynching captured white terrorism's ugliness. "Lady Day," as Holiday was popularly known, joined the likes of Ella Fitzgerald and Sarah Vaughan in following Bessie Smith from blues to jazz as record companies increasingly recognized profits in black music, producing "race records." Their popularity seldom made black performers rich, but their reach was ever widening as radio and recordings carried their sounds everywhere. "It Don't Mean a Thing If It Ain't Got That Swing," bandleader and composer Duke Ellington noted in one of his signature songs, and that swing was as much black as anything. It entertained as it exhibited black talent.

In classical forms, Mississippi-born William Grant Still pioneered black recognition in the Philharmonic world with more than 150 classical compositions and performances around the world. He worked for a while as an arranger for W. C. Handy and played with Noble Sissle and Eubie Blake and also arranged music for such Hollywood films as *Pennies from Heaven* (1936) and *Lost Horizon* (1937). Still's *Symphony No. 1 in A-flat*, "*Afro-American*" (1930) became the first symphonic composition by a black performed in the United States when the Rochester Philharmonic Orchestra premiered it in 1931. Also, Still became the first black to conduct a major U.S. orchestra when he led the Los Angeles Philharmonic in 1936. His work earned him the title "the father of African American classical music."

Contralto Marian Anderson also earned acclaim in classical music during the 1930s, especially after her 1939 Easter Sunday Lincoln Memorial concert drew more than 75,000, following the Daughters of the American Revolution's excluding her from performing at the national capital's Constitutional Hall.

As Still was arranging scores for Hollywood, blacks were finding entrée on the big screen. Black jazz stars such as Louis Armstrong, Cab Calloway, and Duke Ellington appeared in musicals such as *I Will Be Glad When You Are Dead* (1932), *Minnie the Moocher* (1932), *Rhapsody in Black and Blue* (1932), and *Jitterbug Party* (1935). Blacks danced on screen, too. Fayard and Harold Nicholas were sensations known for their acrobatic "flash dancing" and tap dancing. They starred as the Nicholas Brothers in films such as *Barbershop Blues* (1933) and the *Black Network* (1936).

Mostly blacks in film appeared in stereotyped roles. Hattie McDaniel won an Academy Award, popularly called an "Oscar," for best support-ing actress for her role as "Mammy" in the 1939 blockbuster *Gone with the Wind*. Such subservient roles and portrayals of blacks behaving badly prompted critics to scold actors who played such parts. McDaniel famously retorted to critics of the role that won the first Oscar for a black actor say-ing, "I can be a maid for $7 a week or I can play a maid for $700 a week" (Watts 2005, 139).

Blacks hustled to produce their own films. Oscar Micheaux stood atop pioneer black filmmakers. He was a "Mr. Everything" scripting, produc-ing, and directing at least 48 films from the silent era into the talkies. His first movie was *The Homesteader* (1917). His 1919 film *Within Our Gates* depicted lynching and mob violence, although he generally shied away from confronting American racism. He aimed to entertain with his "race mov-ies," as people called them. And entertainment was much desired during the Depression. Blacks flocked to Micheaux movies featuring blacks billed as versions of popular white actors of the time: romantic lead Lorenzo Tucker became the "Black Valentino" and Bee Freeman the "sepia Mae West." Alfred "Slick" Chester was known as the "colored Cagney." Micheaux movies also featured the multitalented Paul Robeson and Robert Earl Jones, father of the later award-winning stage and screen actor James Earl Jones.

Complaints arose that race movies, like race records, exploited both black artists and black audiences, contributing to ongoing arguments about the politics and purpose of black arts. But blacks in the public eye could not escape racial politics as race attached to whatever they did. Langston Hughes, for example, was not simply a writer or even an American writer; he was a *Negro* writer. There was no escaping race for blacks. That was part of white supremacist segregation. Talent could not transcend color. There was no need with whites as their color was invisible in the American mainstream. Whites themselves did not notice themselves as having color. They were not *white* Americans, they were simply Americans. But not so for nonwhites: their color was noted. They were not simply Americans or persons or performers. Paul Robeson was not simply a great performer; he was a *Negro* performer. First and foremost was his color not his talent. That was a black reality in everyday American life.

Blacks faced the color line everywhere—where they lived, where they worked, and even where they played. But moving through the Depression, the New Negro was becoming an increasing presence in American sports. The boxer Joe Louis, popularly known as the "Brown Bomber," was the towering black sports figure of the era. His fights took on a double edge amid domestic and international politics. Fighting fascist Italy's Primo Car-nera and Nazi Germany's Max Schmeling, Louis stood not only as a Negro but as an American. He became world heavyweight champion in 1937 and would reign until 1949. Many would rank him in history as the Number One heavyweight of all time ending with a record of 66–3–1. Whatever else he was, in the 1930s and 1940s he was the pride of black America, demonstrating that matched by the same rules, head to head, blacks were no inferior people. They could do more than hold their own, given a level playing field.

The track and field phenom Jesse Owens joined Louis in the 1930s as an American hero. At the Summer Olympics in Berlin in 1936, Owens won four gold medals in the face of Germany's Adolf Hitler and his vaunted Aryan superiority. Owens was world record holder at 100 and 220 yards, at the 220-yard low hurdles, and in the long jump. He followed a short list of other black Olympians. University of Wisconsin graduate George Poage won two bronze medals in the hurdles in 1904 as the first African American to participate in the Olympic Games. University of Pennsylvania 400-meter runner John Taylor on the medley relay team in 1908 became the first black to win an Olympic gold medal. University of Michigan long jump star DeHart Hubbard in 1924 was the first black to win an individual Olympic gold medal.

Owens and Louis competed in individual sports in which blacks had come to the fore from time to time. Marshall "Major" Taylor—nicknamed "the black cyclone"—became world champion in 1899 in pro track cycling. The boxer known as Joe Gans was the first black world boxing champion as a lightweight from 1902 to 1908. Boxer Jack Johnson followed as a sensation before World War I, becoming the first black world heavyweight champion in 1908. His July 4, 1910, thrashing of great white hope James J. Jeffries in what was billed as "the fight of the century" triggered white rioting against blacks throughout the United States.

Blacks played major team sports just about from their beginnings in the United States, and for a time after the 1860s they played in many areas as professionals. John W. "Bud" Fowler was reputed as the first black professional baseball player and field manager, pitching and playing in the East and Midwest in the 1870s and 1880s, when Moses Fleetwood Walker caught for the Toledo Blue Stockings in the American Association, after playing for the University of Michigan. Blacks played collegiate and pro football, too. William H. Lewis in the 1890s played at Amherst College and was an all-American at Harvard, where he captained, coached, and wrote a pioneering work on the fundamentals of the sport, the 1896 *Primer of College Football*. Fritz Pollard played football for Brown University and in 1916 became the first black in the Rose Bowl game. Pollard went on with Bobby Marshall in 1920 to be the first black players in the National Football League; and with the Akron Pros in 1921, Pollard became the first black

NFL coach. Harry "Bucky" Lew played in the New England Professional Basketball League in the early 1900s. By the time of the Depression, however, blacks suffered exclusion from most major team sports.

Segregation pushed blacks into their own separate leagues from the late 1880s to the 1940s as pro team sports in America became mostly "whites only" until after World War II. Blacks then fielded their own pro teams. In baseball the Negro Leagues opened with the 1885 Cuban Giants in New York. Black Chicagoan Frank Leland and then Rube Foster organized and promoted the business of all-black baseball, with Foster earning the title "father of black Baseball" for his playing, managing, and promoting from the 1900s to the 1930s. Such leagues developed players that would go on after World War II to star in American sports such as Major League Baseball. In fact, a generation after the Great Depression, blacks would be major players in almost all major team sports in America.

## PROFILE: MARY MCLEOD BETHUNE (1875–1955)

Born in Maysville, South Carolina, the 15th of 17 children of former slaves, Mary Jane McLeod became a leading black educator, organizer, and administrator. In her family, only she and two of her siblings got any formal education, and seeing the difference it made from her early attendance at a local Presbyterian mission school set McLeod on a quest to bring the benefits of education to as many blacks as she could.

On graduating in 1894 from North Carolina's Scotia Seminary for Girls (later Barber-Scotia College), McLeod set out to bring "Christ and school" to blacks in America. She taught in Georgia, South Carolina, Florida, and Illinois before opening her Daytona Normal and Industrial Institute for Negro Girls in 1904. Along the way, she married Albertus Bethune in 1898 and had a son. In 1923 her school merged with the Jacksonville-based Cookman Institute for Men, creating Bethune-Cookman College, and she became the school's president.

While developing her school, Bethune engaged also in organizing and leading black women to advance themselves and their communities. Elected president of the Florida Federation of Colored Women in 1917, she went on in 1924 to become president of the National Association of Colored Women. Her standing and acquaintance with First Lady Eleanor Roosevelt gained Bethune appointment as director of the National Youth Administration (NYA) that trained tens of thousands of blacks for jobs during President Franklin D. Roosevelt's New Deal and into World War II. She chaired FDR's informal Black Cabinet and also served in 1951 on President Harry S Truman's Committee of Twelve for National Defense that among other things examined the pace of desegregation in the armed forces.

Bethune exulted at the 1954 U.S. Supreme Court decision in *Brown v. Board of Education* that outlawed Jim Crow public schools. After a lifetime of dedicating her political activism and civil service to empower education for racial and gender equality, she died on May 18, 1955, at age 79.

## REFERENCES

Bethune, Mary McLeod, Audrey Thomas McCluskey, and Elaine M. Smith. 1999. *Mary McLeod Bethune: Building a Better World: Essays and Selected Documents*. Bloomington: Indiana University Press.

Helmbold, Lois Rita. 1987. "Beyond the Family Economy: Black and White Working-Class Women during the Great Depression." *Feminist Studies* 13, no. 3 (autumn): 629–655.

Myrdal, Gunnar. 1944. *An American Dilemma: The Negro Problem and Modern Democracy*. New York: Harper & Brothers.

Roberts, Charles H. 1935. *The Negro in Harlem; A Report on Social and Economic Conditions Responsible for the Outbreak of March 19, 1935*. New York: Mayor's Commission on Conditions in Harlem.

Sears, James M. 1976. "Black Americans and the New Deal." *The History Teacher* 10, no. 1 (November): 89–105.

Sundstrom, William A. 1992. "Last Hired, First Fired? Unemployment and Urban Black Workers during the Great Depression." *Journal of Economic History* 52, no. 2 (June): 415–429.

Watts, Jill. 2005. *Hattie McDaniel: Black Ambition, White Hollywood*. New York: HarperCollins.

_____ *Chapter 14* _____

# Conquer Hate

War again lifted blacks' positions and prospects. Nazi fuehrer Adolf Hitler's blitzkrieg of Poland in September 1939 changed the world and with it the place of African Americans. As the United States became what President Franklin D. Roosevelt called the "Arsenal of Democracy," the Great Depression dissipated, and booming industrial production revived the Great Migration, drawing more blacks out of the South than ever before. The percentage of blacks living in the South between 1940 and 1950 fell from 77 percent to 68 percent. And whether in the South or not, blacks became increasingly urban.

The movement many called the "Second Great Migration" as it continued from 1940 to 1970 redistributed more than 5 million blacks throughout the United States, bringing more than 8 in 10 to live in cities. It moved blacks from farming into nonfarm jobs as assembly lines and heavy industry claimed an unprecedented share of black labor. Almost half (47%) of all black men employed in April 1940 worked on farms; by 1944 the proportion had fallen to almost a quarter (28%). Blacks employed in manufacturing more than doubled (135%) between April 1940 and January 1946. Most of that increase came in heavy industry. By 1945, for instance, one in four foundry workers were blacks, and about one in eight workers in blast furnaces, steel mills, and shipbuilding were blacks (Anderson 1982, 84–85). But their headway was hardly uniform.

Black women increasingly found paid employment as the war progressed, and more than ever they shifted out of domestic service. Between 1940 and 1944, at least 15 black women in 100 engaged as domestics left for better positions. They also left farm work for factories as the percentage of black women in industrial occupations rose from 6.5 to 18 during the war. "Rosie the Riveter" became a cultural icon representing working women's wartime

U.S. mobilization for World War II required the nation's full resources, opening doors for blacks in the military and civilian arenas for men and women, as illustrated by the black counterparts to the famed "Rosie the Riveter" character. (Library of Congress)

contribution, and while the image was usually white, black women came to make up 6 in 10 (60%) of the 1 million blacks who entered work for pay during the war (Anderson 1992, 82).

Nevertheless, many, if not most, wage-earning black women remained underemployed. They lay at the bottom of the "last-hired-first-fired" pecking order. Race and sex persisted in limiting blacks in general and black women in particular, but in the rising economic tide their lot rose, too, mostly from prodigious black effort. Many of the jobs blacks got in the war industry to start resulted from pressure mounted by the March on Washington Movement (MOWM). Black labor leader A. Philip Randolph organized the effort in 1940–1941 to protest discriminatory hiring and training. When quiet negotiating for nondiscriminatory public policy failed, Randolph called for 10,000 blacks to march on Washington as had other disgruntled groups such as Jacob Coxey's Army of unemployed in 1894 and the Bonus March of veterans in 1932.

The prospect of thousands of blacks from around the United States protesting in the capital's streets unnerved officials. To head off such a scene, President Franklin D. Roosevelt issued Executive Order 8802 in June 1941, prohibiting discrimination in defense industries and creating a Fair Employment Practices Committee to monitor compliance. But there was no rush to hire blacks. A year after Executive Order 8802, only about 3 in 100 war industry workers were blacks. And in many places the numbers were lower. One count in late 1942 found only 142 blacks among 29,215 defense contract workers in and around New York City. In St. Louis 56 defense factories averaged three blacks each (Ottley 1943, 289–290).

Randolph kicked off his MOWM campaign by declaring "we loyal Negro-American citizens demand the right to work and fight for our country" (Welky 2012, 224). Getting to fight in the U.S. armed forces, however, was in itself a fight. From even before the War for U.S. Independence, blacks found their services spurned among America's regular fighting forces. Time after time, military necessity made the nation take blacks in arms, but even then it kept them segregated, as illustrated with the U.S. Colored Troops of the Civil War era and the continuing black units led by white officers.

The U.S. Army entered World War II with 4,450 black troops in six segregated units and a small black officer corps, with Brigadier Benjamin O. Davis Sr. in 1940 becoming the Army's first general officer. Perhaps its major innovation with blacks was the Army's training the first black military

Given a chance for the first time to be U.S. fighter and bomber pilots, blacks commonly called "Tuskegee Airmen" won prestige for their proficiency and valor in the U.S. Army Air Forces. (U.S. Air Force)

aviators. Called the Tuskegee Airmen because of their training at the black institute in Alabama and later nicknamed "Red Tails" because of markings on their planes' vertical stabilizers, the pilots formed the 332nd Fighter Group and the 477th Bombardier Group in the U.S. Army Air Forces.

The U.S. Navy shunned blacks except as steward's mates. Only about 2 in 100 (2.3%) of the Navy's 170,000 men in 1940 were black, and that changed little during the war. Only in March 1944 did the Navy get its first regularly commissioned black officers referred to as the "Golden Thirteen." The U.S. Marine Corps was lily white until June 1942 when it admitted Howard P. Perry among the initial 13 so-called Montfort Point Marines, trained in segregated facilities in Jacksonville, North Carolina. They remained in units that were all black except for white officers. Only in November 1945 did the Corps commission its first black officer, Frederick C. Branch (MacGregor 1985, passim; Davis 2008, 28–31).

By World War II's end in 1945, 1.1 million blacks had served the nation under arms, distinguishing themselves from the moment of Japan's attack on Pearl Harbor in December 1941. Navy Messman Dorie Miller rushed topside to man an anti-aircraft machine gun on the sinking battleship USS West Virginia during the attack. Cited for "extraordinary courage," he became the first black awarded the Navy Cross. In November 1943 he gave his life in battle at Kiribati in the South Pacific Gilbert Islands.

Clear discrimination denied any blacks the nation's highest military honor for valor during World War II until long after its end. Seven black veterans finally received the Congressional Medal of Honor in 1997 from President Bill Clinton as an upgrade of their Distinguished Service Cross, the nation's second-highest military award. In addition to individual honors, distinctions went to such vaunted black units as the 761st Tank Battalion, the 452nd Antiaircraft Artillery Battalion, and the Tuskegee Airmen who in 2007 received a Congressional Gold Medal for "an achievement that has an impact on American history and culture" (Kruzel 2007, n.p.).

Black women also served in uniform with distinction during World War II. They battled even more severe discrimination than black men, and like them were denied entry into certain services. The WASPS (Women Airforce Service Pilots), for example, barred black women. Similarly, the Naval WAVES (Women Accepted for Volunteer Emergency Services) excluded black women until December 1944 when it commissioned Lieutenant (junior grade) Harriet Ida Pickens and Ensign Frances Wills.

As with black men, the Army employed the most black women in the armed forces. Black nurses had fought their way into service during World War I when 18 of them did duty beginning in December 1918. In 1941 the Army Nurse Corps again opened itself to black women but limited their number to an initial 56 led by Della Raney Jackson, the U.S. Army's first commissioned black nurse who eventually rose to the rank of major. At Japan's surrender in September 1945, only 479 of the 50,000 Army Nurse Corps were black. Phyllis Mae Dailey in March 1945 became the first black commissioned U.S. Navy nurse, one of four blacks among the 6,000 in the U.S. Navy Nurse Corps.

The Women's Army Auxiliary Corps (WAAC) and its successor Women's Army Corps (WAC) enlisted the most black women, beginning in May 1942 with 440 trainees at Fort Des Moines, Iowa, and growing to about 4,000 by war's end. They, too, were severely restricted in number, never accounting for more than 6 percent of WAACs. Persevering against racism and sexism, they dealt with condescending commanding white male officers, limited job opportunities, and doing dirty work. Charity Edna Adams Earley was among the first black WAACs and rose to the rank of lieutenant colonel, commanding the 6888th Central Postal Directory Battalion. The first in overseas service were 800 in the 6888th working in England and France (Putney 1992, passim; Hine, Brown, and Terborg-Penn 1993, 3: 385).

Blacks' struggles to serve in uniform and their trials while in uniform pointed up America's racial abyss. To protest the intransigence of military segregation, William H. Hastie Jr. in January 1943 resigned as advisor to Secretary of War Henry L. Stimson. Having to "fight to fight" was but one part of blacks' many-sided battles during the war. Not everyone, of course, was ready or willing to take up arms for the nation. Some blacks asked again "what are you fighting for?" Standing against war, black pacifists such as Bayard Rustin and black nationalists such as Elijah Muhammad went to jail rather than join the U.S. armed forces.

And in uniform blacks encountered intolerable conditions that reached the breaking point, not only for individuals but for units. In the long-suppressed largest incident, racist treatment boiled over in May 1942 in the Townsville Mutiny in Australia, where about 600 blacks of the 96th Battalion's A and C companies faced off with shots fired against white officers and troops in two days of fighting. Only a single fatality resulted as Australian troops cordoned off the area with orders to shoot to kill any blacks leaving the base called Kelso Field (McKerrow 2013, 160–161).

Stateside in 1944 the so-called Port Chicago Mutiny occurred. Black sailors assigned as cargo loaders at the Naval Munitions Depot along California's Suisun Bay, about 30 miles northeast of San Francisco, refused to continue loading munitions after a July cargo ship explosion killed at least 320 sailors and civilians and wounded nearly 400 others. The Navy court-martialed leading insubordinate blacks called the "Port Chicago 50" and sentenced them to prison, but their protests pointed up the disparities in naval assignments, duties, standards, and treatment.

Even antiwar activists could applaud the "Double V" campaign the *Pittsburgh Courier* launched in 1942 to gain blacks' equal treatment in the face of an announced international war against an ideology of racial superiority. The most widely circulated black newspaper of its day, the *Courier* pressed for "Democracy: Victory at Home, Victory Abroad" in its February 7, 1942, issue. The theme resounded throughout the nation. The NAACP magazine *Crisis* had declared "We Return Fighting" at the close of World War I; the *Courier* campaign declared that in World War II blacks were committed to victory over racism everywhere.

Fighting racism on the home front spilled into the streets in 1943 as racial violence erupted across the nation from May through August. The old pattern of whites attacking blacks reappeared in May in Mobile, Alabama, where drydock and shipping workers rioted against blacks being hired to work on mixed welding crews. Later that month and into June, Los Angeles suffered the so-called Zoot Suit Riots, with whites, including servicemen in uniform, attacking Latinos and blacks. In mid-June shipyard and other industrial workers rioted against blacks being hired in Beaumont, Texas.

The deadliest of the 1943 events struck Detroit in late June. White youths at Belle Isle Park attacked black youths and then invaded black neighborhoods like Paradise Valley, where blacks counterattacked. In the midst of World War II, 6,000 federal troops occupied the Motor City to restore order. The rioting left 34 persons dead and 433 wounded. In the opening days of August, Harlem again erupted much as it had in 1935 at rumors of white police brutality. Over two days, six persons were killed amid a rampage that put nearly 600 in jail. Such sights unsettled any national sense of unity.

African Americans appeared intent on deep change in America, insisting throughout World War II that things were different now. The cataclysm in Europe and the Pacific had ushered in a New World order, and blacks determined that there be a new domestic order in the United States. Friend and foe during the 1930s and 1940s noted the hypocrisy of American racism. Swedish political economist Gunnar Myrdal's 1944 Carnegie Corporation–funded study *An American Dilemma: The Negro Problem and American Democracy* further exposed the measurable depths of antiblack discrimination. Not only was a black agenda for change clear by the war's end in September 1945, but a fresh attitude among blacks everywhere challenged segregationist society.

Blacks such as James Farmer moved increasingly during the war in common cause with whites and others for interracial justice. Farmer in 1942 became coleader of the Committee (later Congress) of Racial Equality (CORE). Members overlapped with the pacifist Fellowship for Reconciliation that promoted India's "Mahatma" Gandhi's nonviolent strategies for social change. CORE expanded from Chicago into a nationwide movement protesting segregation particularly in public accommodations. It adopted the industrial labor tactic of sit-ins to make its presence seen and felt. Also it sponsored integrated demonstrations such as its 1947 two-week Journey of Reconciliation with matched black-and-white teams riding together in interstate public transportation in light of the U.S. Supreme Court's 1946 decision in *Morgan v. Commonwealth of Virginia* outlawing racial segregation on interstate buses: that would be a prelude to CORE's 1960s "Freedom Rides."

The NAACP's Legal Defense and Educational Fund (LDF) continued to build on its successes. Incorporated in 1940 to separate liability from its parent, the LDF campaigned to certify segregation as unconstitutional. Thurgood Marshall headed the LDF. With Constance Baker Motley and others, the LDF pushed against Jim Crow across a broad front. It especially targeted voting rights, public education, and fair housing, but it also supported actions against economic discrimination such as *Taylor v. Georgia* (1942) and *Pollock v. Williams* (1944), in which the U.S. Supreme Court reiterated that debt peonage was illegal as a form of slavery or involuntary servitude.

In *Smith v. Allwright* (1944), the LDF finally won the campaign since the 1920s to have Texas's all-white Democratic primaries declared unconstitutional. It celebrated Mexican Americans' victory against segregated schools in *Mendez v. Westminster School District* (1946). In *Sipuel v. Board of Regents of the University of Oklahoma*, the LDF won law school admission for Ada Lois Sipuel, reinforcing the doctrine that states had to provide blacks the same educational opportunities it provided whites. Also the LDF made strides against housing discrimination in 1948 in *Shelley v. Kraemer*, when the Supreme Court reversed its 1926 decision in *Corrigan v. Buckley* to rule restrictive covenants legally unenforceable. Such contracts had barred rental or sale of real estate to blacks and others not white or Christian. Further the NAACP moved its arguments to the court of world opinion. Black abolitionists had done much the same in the mid-1800s, touring Britain and Europe to relate the horrors of American Negro slavery. The post–World War II era offered fresh opportunities for blacks to raise international pressure to influence U.S. domestic policies and practices. Indeed, the war and its aftermath put race relations on the international stage. The US-USSR Cold War battle for hearts and minds would feature blacks' treatment as a test of America's character.

The newly created United Nations with its Universal Declaration of Human Rights drafted between 1946 and 1948 provided blacks an international stage to protest American apartheid. In June 1946 the National Negro Congress was the first black organization to petition the UN. The NAACP followed in October 1947 with a petition titled "An Appeal to the

World." The radical Civil Rights Congress would in December 1951 deliver to the UN a third black petition: titled "We Charge Genocide," it carried a litany of U.S. human rights abuses since the UN's birth, exhibiting lynchings and documenting 153 killings and 344 crimes of violence against blacks between 1945 and 1951.

The NAACP addressed its October 1947 petition also to fresh U.S. President Harry S Truman, for blacks found the southern Democrat a surprising and welcome ally. He had in June 1947 become the first U.S. president to address a NAACP Annual Convention, speaking at the Lincoln Memorial to an audience of 10,000. With Executive Order 9808 the Missourian had in December 1946 created a presidential committee to recommend reforms of federal law, policy, and practice to end segregation. In October 1947 the President's Committee on Civil Rights returned its recommendations in a report titled "To Secure These Rights," using a phrase from the Declaration of Independence.

Blacks cheered Truman's initiatives and backed him as he suffered considerable political backlash for his civil rights initiatives. His political party split as white southern Democrats, segregationists, and civil rights foes launched the States' Rights Democratic Party, popularly known as Dixiecrats, to oppose Truman's 1948 election. The *Chicago Defender* early endorsed Truman: "No president in modern history has shown more courage and more determination in the face of great controversy," it declared in its August 7 issue.

History was in the making as blacks thrust forward in a postwar surge like that following the War for Independence, the Civil War, and World War I. At home and abroad, African Americans won virtually unprecedented recognition for their abilities and achievements. William H. Hastie, for example, continued his succession of firsts. He had become in 1937 the first black federal judge, and in 1950 he would become the first black to serve on the U.S. Court of Appeals, sitting in the Third Circuit. Amid his government service, Hastie taught at the Howard University School of Law and for a time was dean, mentoring Thurgood Marshall and other key black civil rights lawyers.

In the international realm, Howard University political scientist professor Ralph J. Bunche in 1950 became the first African American to receive a Nobel Prize, winning for Peace with his Mideast mediation. Bunche's international diplomacy aided blacks in the U.S. diplomatic service, too. In 1949 President Truman appointed NAACP lawyer Edward R. Dudley as the first black to hold the rank of U.S. ambassador. Ebenezer Don Carlos Bassett had become the first black U.S. diplomat in 1869 when President Ulysses S. Grant appointed him as minister to Haiti at a time when the rank of U.S. ambassador did not exist. Like Bassett, Dudley also represented the United

States in a black nation—Liberia. Also Edith S. Sampson joined the U.S. delegation at the United Nations in 1950 as its first African American.

As before and during the war, blacks led much of postwar America's music. Indeed, black artists, entertainers, and sports figures determinedly persisted to gain worldwide recognition in the postwar world. The big bands of Duke Ellington, Count Basie, Cab Calloway, and Fletcher Henderson became ever more popular in the 1940s. Live and on the airwaves and in records, black musicians reached out to ever wider audiences and garnered undeniable recognition. And a fresh group of blacks were also revolutionizing jazz. Billy Eckstine pushed forward what Coleman Hawkins had introduced with his 1939 Bluebird recording "Body and Soul," with its fresh quick jump, double-time themes. Eckstine carried the sound with his 1944 band featuring Art Blakey on drums, Dizzy Gillespie on trumpet, Charlie "Bird" Parker on alto sax, and Budd Johnson on clarinet and sax.

"Bebop" or simply "bop" broke out with "Bird" leading the way. The 1947 Charlie Parker Quintet with Miles Davis on trumpet, Max Roach on drums, Duke Jordan on piano, and Tommy Potter on bass produced soon classic sounds. With others such as Bud Powell and Thelonious Monk on piano, and John Coltrane and Sonny Rollins on tenor sax, and Kenny Clarke on drums, these artists created fast-tempo chord progressions with improvised changes in harmonic structures that introduced what many came to call "modern jazz."

Black women supplied the voice of jazz. Carrying on from Bessie Smith, Ella Fitzgerald rose as the "Queen of Jazz" or "First Lady of Song," along with Billie Holiday, "Lady Day." Lena Horne added her voice, along with her dancing and acting on stage and screen. Sarah Vaughan, Dinah Washington, Betty Carter, and later Etta James produced captivating melodies and tones that added incomparable vocals to jazz. They excelled in making their voice an instrument of melody and rhythm with improvisational nonsense, wordless syllables of scatting, and Ella was the "Queen of Scat."

Radio extended the reach of great black female jazz vocalists and black music broadly. With the growing recording industry, radio further popularized black gospel music. Mahalia Jackson with her powerful contralto influenced music worldwide, producing million sellers mostly for Columbia records, and rising as the "Queen of Gospel Music" ahead of Shirley Caesar, the "First Lady of Gospel," with her 11 Grammy Awards from the National Academy of Recording Arts and Sciences.

Jackson and Caesar both followed "Georgia Tom," as Thomas A. Dorsey was early called. His fresh compositions transposed standard Christian hymns to personalized divine praise in the rhythm of blues and jazz, elevating Dorsey to being called the "father of black gospel music." His 1932 composition "Take My Hand, Precious Lord" became his best-known work and a much-demanded standard by Mahalia Jackson. Albertina Walker, Della Reese, Cissy Houston, and Dorothy Norwood followed in a cohort that would move from gospel to soul, as perhaps best illustrated by Aretha Franklin, the "Queen of Soul," and also by Cissy Houston's daughter Whitney.

Radio not only expanded the reach of black music but also extended the presence of black characters. Initially, it typically aired caricatured voices, with whites mimicking blacks in demeaning and disparaging positions as notoriously illustrated in *Amos 'n' Andy*. It had whites playing the equivalent of blackface radio voices from the comic series that began in 1928 on Chicago's WMAC. Eddie Anderson was in 1937 the first black to have a recurring radio role with his portrayal of "Rochester" on *The Jack Benny Program*. He and Hattie McDaniel, with her title role of *Beulah* starting in 1947, both played domestics in white households, but they were blacks, not whites playing blacks.

"Rochester" had notable substance as he played the role of foil rather than fall man. Anderson continued the role into television, and his portrayals contrasted with those of the controversial black actor known for stereotypic shuffling as "Stepin Fetchit" and referred to as the "laziest man in the world." The actor named Lincoln Perry played in at least 60 films from the 1925 *The Mysterious Stranger* to the 1976 *Won Ton, the Dog Who Saved Hollywood*; the Fetchit character made Perry reputedly the first black actor to become a millionaire.

Only relatively limited roles appeared on radio or on stage, on the big screen, and on the expanding little screen of television, for strong black personalities. Blacks broke in as leads in the new medium of television in 1948, with pianist and vocalist Bob Howard in *The Bob Howard Show* and Amanda Randolph in *The Laytons*. On stage Juanita Hall in 1950 became the first black to win a Tony Award for excellence in theater for her performance as "Bloody Mary" in the Rodgers and Hammerstein musical *South Pacific*. Paul Robeson and particularly Canada Lee also made headway on stage and screen. Lee provided a memorable starring role as a black religious minister in South Africa in the 1952 British film *Cry, the Beloved Country*—one of rising black star Sidney Poitier's early films.

Lee broke into the public eye as an athlete. He was a jockey to start and then a welterweight boxer. The athletic arena was a place where personal ability could not be denied except by exclusion. And increasingly in the postwar world black talent broke out of segregationist exclusion. The National Football League got its first black players in 1946 as Kenny Washington and Woody Strode joined the Los Angeles Rams and Marion Motley and Bill Willis joined the Cleveland Browns. Strode's UCLA backfield running mate Jackie Robinson made the more historically noted move in

1947 in Major League Baseball (MLB), joining the National League (NL) Brooklyn Dodgers. Larry Doby joined the American League (AL) Cleveland Indians later in 1947, becoming with Robinson MLB's first black players. Doby with teammate Satchel Paige in 1948 became the first blacks to be MLB World Series champions.

Robinson was 1947 MLB Rookie of the Year and 1949 NL Most Valuable Player, both black firsts. The list of MLB firsts soon included Hall of Famers Monte Irvin with the NL New York Giants and Ernie Banks with the NL Chicago Cubs. Other firsts on teams around the league included Elston Howard with the AL New York Yankees. Pumpsie Green in July 1959 would be a first with the AL Boston Red Sox, the last MLB team to field a black player. Most of the firsts played in the Negro leagues, as did others who would star in MLB such as Roy Campanella, Junior Gilliam, Willie Mays, Don Newcomb, and Hank Aaron.

UCLA's Don Barksdale in 1947 became the first black college basketball all-American. In 1948 he became the first black on the U.S. Olympic basketball team and was among the first blacks in the National Basketball Association (NBA). The firsts were in 1950 when Earl Lloyd and Harold Hunter joined the Washington Capitols, "Sweetwater" Clifton joined the New York Knicks, and Chuck Cooper joined the Boston Celtics. Playing for the Celtics, Barksdale in 1953 became the first black to play in an NBA All-Star game.

Black women had no major pro-sports, but they made strides in individual sports. Tuskegee Institute high jumper Alice Coachman in 1948 became the first black woman to win an Olympic gold medal, leaping a world-record height that stood for 12 years. Also a world-class sprinter, Coachman was five-time USA national champion at 50 meters. She led the way for generations of black women in track and field that would yield Olympic champions such as Wilma Rudolph, Wyomia Tyus, and Jackie Joyner-Kersee.

Althea Gibson broke the color line in tennis and golf. She became in 1950 the first black to play in the U.S. Nationals (later Open) championship and would win in 1957 and 1958. In winning the French Open in 1956 Gibson became the first black Grand Slam winner in tennis and would win 11 Grand Slams in all, including Wimbledon in 1958. She was the first African American to play Wimbledon, and she became an inspiration to many, including later black female tennis multiple Grand Slam champs Venus and Serena Williams. Gibson in 1964 became the first black player on the Ladies Professional Golf Association (LPGA) tour.

Black women also gained increasing recognition in arts and letters. Margaret Walker in 1942 became the first black woman to receive a national prize for writing, winning the Yale Series of Younger Poets competition for her collection *For My People*. Gwendolyn Brooks in 1950 became the first black to win a Pulitzer Prize with her 1949 poetry collection *Annie Allen*. Both Walker and Brooks were part of the continued artistic flowering of the New Negro Renaissance that flourished in black Chicago or "Bronzeville," as it was sometimes known. Brooks titled her first published book of poetry *A Street in Bronzeville* (1945). Brooks and Walker were part of the South Side Writers Group that included Arna Bontemps, Langston Hughes, Willard Motley, and Richard Wright. In connection, John H. Johnson began his magazine publishing empire in black Chicago with his 1942 *Negro Digest* (later titled *Black World*), adding *Ebony* in 1945 and *Jet* in 1951.

Black women in the plastic arts followed in the footsteps of Edmonia Lewis, whose sculptures such as *The Wooing of Hiawatha* (1866) won international acclaim even as U.S. segregation forced her to work in Rome. The multitalented Meta Vaux Warrick Fuller became a protégé of French sculptor Auguste Rodin and in 1921 created *Ethiopia Awakening*, which the New Negro Renaissance took as a symbol of black independence. In painting, Howard University's first fine arts graduate (1924) Alma Woodsey Thomas introduced her exuberant, expressionist large canvas bright color abstracts.

Howard University graduate and professor Lois Mailou Jones produced stunning watercolors and oils such as *Les Fétiches* (1938) with its Afrocentric inspiration that incorporated into the visual arts themes of the Négritude movement Aimé Césaire, Léon Damas, and Léopold Sédar Senghor pioneered in their writings. Jones's work would reach from the New Negro Renaissance into the Black Arts (Aesthetics) Movement in the 1960s. Elizabeth Catlett's graphic arts and sculpting similarly expressed social themes, vibrant, for example, in her 1952 painting *Sharecropper*, with its central female figure wearing the toil and travail of black life in her features. "I'm not thinking about doing things new and different," Catlett famously explained about her art. "I'm thinking about creating art for my people," she declared (Brenson 2003, 35). And her people were on the move, continuing to push to conquer hate white supremacy inculcated against black equality.

## PROFILE: PAUL ROBESON (1898–1976)

A black man for all seasons, Paul Leroy Robeson excelled in multiple talents: he was a singer, actor on stage and screen, all-American and pro football player, law school graduate, and tireless anti-capitalist advocate for social justice.

Born in Princeton, New Jersey, in 1898 to a Presbyterian minister and a mother steeped in Quakerism, Paul was the last of five children. His household stressed education and also independence, a trait that forced his father's resignation as pastor of Princeton's Witherspoon Street Presbyterian

Church and the family's move to St. Thomas AME Zion Church in Somerville, New Jersey, where Paul attended high school and starred in chorus and stage productions and at football, basketball, baseball, and track and field.

Robeson won an academic scholarship to Rutgers, the State University of New Jersey, where he again starred in athletics and debate, earning admission to the national academic honor society *Phi Beta Kappa* and becoming his 1919 class valedictorian. He went on to Columbia Law School and played pro football while earning his law degree.

He early spoke out against American racism, questioning even as a teenager the propriety of black men going to battle in World War I (1914–1919) "to make the world safe for democracy," as President Woodrow Wilson declared, while they suffered no democracy at home. He also denounced fascism in supporting Republican forces during the Spanish Civil War (1936–1939) and became an active member of the anti-colonial Council on African Affairs. In 1946 he founded the American Crusade Against Lynching.

While his political positions put him under government surveillance, his roles on stage and screen won him accolades. He drew rave reviews for his London performance in the musical *Show Boat*, and his West End performance as Shakespeare's Othello became a classic standard. His early films included *The Emperor Jones* (1933), *Sanders of the River* (1935), *Song of Freedom* (1936), *Show Boat* (1936), *Big Fella* (1937), and *King Solomon's Mines* (1937), mostly British productions.

Robeson's visits to the Soviet Union in the 1930s and his continuing political activism put him under House Un-American Activities Committee (HUAC) scrutiny, and in 1950 he suffered the State Department's rescinding his passport. He became blacklisted, having his name expunged even from college football records. His receiving in 1952 the Soviet Union's International Stalin Prize further darkened his prospects during the McCarthy era.

In his 1958 autobiography *Here I Stand*, Robeson persisted in denouncing racism, colonialism, and capitalist exploitation. The 1958 U.S. Supreme Court decision in *Kent v. Dulles* allowed Robeson to reclaim his passport, and moving to London, he resumed his worldwide travels and performances, often in support of causes such as rights for Australian aborigines and for colonial freedom.

Declining health curtailed Robeson's activities, and he died on January 23, 1976, at age 77.

## REFERENCES

Anderson, Karen Tucker. 1992. "Last Hired, First Fired: Black Women Workers during World War II." *Journal of American History* 69, no. 1 (June): 82–97.

Brenson, Michael. 2003. "Form That Achieves Sympathy: A Conversation with Elizabeth Catlett." *Sculpture* 22, no. 3 (April): 28–35.

Davis, Thomas J. 2008. *Race Relations in the United States, 1940–1960.* Westport, CT: Greenwood Press.

Duberman, Martin B. 1988. *Paul Robeson.* New York: Knopf.

Hine, Darlene Clark, Elsa Barkley Brown, and Rosalyn Terborg-Penn. 1993. *Black Women in America: An Historical Encyclopedia.* Brooklyn, NY: Carlson Publishers.

Kruzel, John J. 2007. "President, Congress Honor Tuskegee Airmen." American Forces Press Service, March 30. Accessed at http://www.army.mil/article/2476/President__Congress_Honor_Tuskegee_Airmen/.

MacGregor, Morris J., Jr. 1985. *Integration of the Armed Forces 1940–1965.* Washington, DC: Center of Military History, United States Army.

McKerrow, John. 2013. *The American Occupation of Australia, 1941–1945: A Marriage of Necessity.* Newcastle upon Tyne UK: Cambridge Scholars Publishing.

Ottley, Roi. 1943. *"New World A-Coming": Inside Black America.* Boston: Houghton Mifflin.

Putney, Martha S. 1992. *When the Nation Was in Need: Blacks in the Women's Army Corps during World War II.* Metuchen, NJ: Scarecrow Press.

Welky, David. 2012. *America between the Wars, 1919–1941: A Documentary Reader.* Malden, MA: Wiley-Blackwell.

_____ *Chapter 15* _____

# Keep on Pushing

Worldwide blacks entered the 20th century's second half aggressive and confrontational in their insistence on self-determination. W.E.B. Du Bois's prescient statement at the 1900 Pan-African conference that "the problem of the Twentieth Century is the problem of the color-line" appeared more and more to being realized as colonized people of color around the world girded themselves to battle for independence in the aftermath of World War II (Du Bois 1903, vii). In the United States blacks showed themselves increasingly ready to march and do more in the long struggle against segregation that excluded them from opportunities and rights whites enjoyed as their exclusive privilege.

Desegregation loomed as the next giant step toward the civil rights the U.S. Constitution promised and the human rights the United Nations' international community declared the common and equal heritage of humanity. And conditions appeared favorable for accomplishing the leap as African Americans entered the 1950s. Adolf Hitler's Aryan superiority rants and outrages, especially in the genocidal Holocaust, had so disgraced the ideology of white supremacy that it had become reprehensible. Only increasingly marginalized diehards appeared publicly willing to espouse such beliefs as the basis for American social order. Open and intentional exclusion of blacks on the basis of race seemed ebbing as accepted official policy and public practice in much of the United States. Jim Crow segregation in the 1950s looked more and more as American Negro slavery had in the 1850s. It was under attack as international opinion condemned it; and while domestic opinion remained split, most Americans outside the 1860 slave states rejected it, even if unready or unwilling to embrace blacks.

For blacks the former slave states and the District of Columbia—referred to collectively as "the South"—stood solidly as the most obvious and immediate antagonists. Jim Crow segregation sat as a southern mainstay. It formed the core of the South's designated social order, replicated and reinforced in state action and public practice. The South's public school systems operated as glaring Jim Crow examples. Entering the 1950s, all 15 states that had maintained slavery in 1860 mandated Jim Crow public schools. So did the southern offshoots of West Virginia and Oklahoma and the District of Columbia. Four other states—Arizona, Kansas, New Mexico, and Wyoming—allowed Jim Crow schools as local options. Sixteen states positively prohibited officially segregated schools; the other 11 had no official policy on the matter.

Blacks had attacked Jim Crow schools since the early 1800s. They took the matter to court in Massachusetts in the notable 1850 case of *Roberts v. Boston*. They lost there and long continued to lose, although brief respites appeared during Reconstruction, as when Louisiana prohibited racially segregated schools. *Plessy v. Ferguson* (1896), which arose in Louisiana, while treating transportation rather than education, provided the notorious Separate but Equal doctrine used to sanction Jim Crow schools.

Racially separate schools were the dominant order of the day all over the United States throughout the 1900s. Even where they were not imposed by law, they were common in practice as many whites simply refused to have their children schooled with blacks. Many blacks were themselves not opposed to separate schools, but they were insistent on equal schools, and they persisted in suing for equal educational opportunity in public schools. In the face of *Plessy v. Ferguson* sanctioned segregation, blacks had immediately battled exclusion from public schools as a violation of the Fourteenth Amendment's Equal Protection Clause. In *Cumming v. Richmond County Board of Education* (1898), Georgia blacks lost the initial bid for a separate but equal high school, but blacks persisted in agitating for equal access and funding, for where Jim Crow systems did provide public schools for blacks the funding was woefully unequal.

The National Association for the Advancement of Colored People (NAACP) enjoyed a string of successes against exclusion in graduate and professional public education beginning with Thurgood Marshall and Charles Hamilton Houston's 1936 victory in *Murray v. Pearson*, winning a black man's admission to the University of Maryland School of Law. *Missouri ex rel. Gaines v. Canada* followed in 1938, gaining admission of a black man to the law school of the University of Missouri. Ten years later *Sipuel v. Board of Regents of the University of Oklahoma* won law school admission for a black woman.

In 1950 the NAACP's Legal Defense Fund won two cases—*Sweatt v. Painter* and *McLaurin v. Oklahoma State Regents*—that capped the campaign against exclusion in graduate and professional public education. *Sweatt* proved especially influential for it not only gained Heman Marion Sweatt admission to the School of Law of the University of Texas but also dismissed the defense that creating a separate black law school would provide equal legal education. The ruling thus moved beyond exclusion to weigh and consider equal access to public education. But court action would remain necessary, as illustrated in blacks gaining admission to the law school by court order at the University of Virginia in September 1950 and at the University of Florida in March 1956.

As blacks made headway in court, they found Congress opposed to civil rights, led by a phalanx of southern Democrats committed to segregation under the banner of states' rights. Blacks then had a champion in President Harry S Truman. Persisting in campaigning for civil rights after winning election in 1948, he appointed in 1950 the President's Committee on Equality of Treatment and Opportunity in the armed forces, which in a report titled "Freedom to Serve" measured compliance with his 1948 desegregation order. He pushed further in 1951 in establishing the Committee on Government Contract Compliance to enforce antidiscrimination in federal contracts. Congress blocked the president's civil rights initiatives, however, and the armed forces appeared at best dragging their feet on desegregation. During their deployment in the Korean War (1950–1953), U.S. forces fought almost exclusively in segregated units as they long had.

Blacks took heart in the U.S. Supreme Court's increasing turn to favor challenges against segregation. Its June 1950 decision in *Henderson v. United States*, for example, used the 1887 Interstate Commerce Act to declare segregation in interstate railroad dining cars illegal. That built on Irene Morgan's 1946 victory when the Court ruled segregation on interstate buses unconstitutional. The Court would grow throughout the 1950s and into the 1960s to champion blacks' civil rights.

Momentum was building for blacks' full frontal assault on Jim Crow. While too often unsung in annals that preferred to focus on lone male leaders, black women persisted as activists and organizers who rallied their communities and sustained resistance against segregation. And in the 1950s black women were more and more making their presence seen and felt in local and state politics. Michigan Democrat attorney Cora Brown in 1952 became the first black woman elected to a state senate. She followed Charles Diggs Sr. who in 1937 had become the first black elected to Michigan's state senate and the driving force for Michigan's 1938 Equal Accommodations Act. His son U.S. Representative Charles Diggs Jr. would in 1969 become the first chairman of the Congressional Black Caucus, then known as a "Democratic Select Committee." Also in 1952 the Progressive Party nominated *California Eagle* newspaper publisher Carlotta Bass as its vice presidential candidate, making her the first black woman selected to run for national office on a national party ticket.

Black church women carried on as activists and organizers as black churches continued to be hubs of black community life. Particularly in the South, black churches were the sites for organizing fresh challenges to Jim Crow, as illustrated in June 1953 in Baton Rouge, Louisiana. With Mount Zion Baptist Church pastor T. J. Jemison as their spokesperson, blacks mounted a boycott against segregated seating on city buses. Such protests to segregation on public transportation went back to antebellum days as blacks had decried so-called Jim Crow cars when they first appeared in Massachusetts in the 1840s. In *Jennings v. Third Avenue Railroad* (1854), the black schoolteacher Elizabeth Jennings had won a noted public transportation desegregation suit in New York City.

Immediately after the Civil War blacks in New Orleans had protested and won desegregation of streetcars in 1867 in what was then Louisiana's capital. They and other southern blacks rose up again against the wave of streetcar segregation arising in the 1890s and washing over public transportation in general, as contested in the 1896 Louisiana case of *Plessy v. Ferguson*. Between 1891 and 1912 blacks across the South repeatedly boycotted segregated streetcars. They organized in more than two dozen cities from New Orleans to Little Rock to Montgomery to Mobile to Jacksonville to insist on blacks' right to ride public transportation without racial restrictions. The Baton Rouge bus boycott rekindled those protests in Louisiana's capital.

The most noted black bus boycott occurred in Alabama's capital, Montgomery. Again black women led the way. Local Women's Political Council (WPC) President Jo Ann Robinson campaigned for a boycott to end abuse of blacks for sitting in so-called white seats or sections on city buses. While the WPC bided its time, teenage black females moved to the fore. In March 1955 Claudette Colvin, a 15-year-old NAACP Youth Council member, refused to yield her city bus seat to a white man and suffered arrest. Four others—Aurelia S. Browder, Susie McDonald, Jeanette Reese, and Mary Louise Smith—followed Colvin in ensuing months and together would take the Jim Crow practice to federal court in *Browder v. Gayle* (1956).

In December 1955 local NAACP chapter secretary Rosa Parks famously refused to yield her Montgomery city bus seat to a white man and was arrested and fined. Parks's arrest ignited further outrage that the WPC fueled with circulated flyers urging blacks to boycott city buses. Black community leaders came together to form the Montgomery Improvement Association (MIA) to coordinate the boycott and chose local black pastors as spokespersons. The 26-year-old recently installed pastor of the Dexter Avenue Baptist Church, Rev. Martin Luther King Jr., became MIA president and Rev. Ralph

David Abernathy, senior pastor of Montgomery's largest black congregation, the First Baptist Church, became secretary.

The Montgomery Bus Boycott ran for 381 days, beginning in December 1955 and ending in December 1956 and thrust the young Reverend King into national and international attention. The boycott demonstrated blacks' determined to mobilize against Jim Crow, and it won another court victory. *Browder v. Gayle* in July 1956 ruled legally mandated segregated city bus seating violated the Fourteenth Amendment's Equal Protection Clause. The U.S. Supreme Court affirmed that ruling in December 1956 in *Gayle v. Browder*.

Seating on a first-come first-served basis on public transportation hardly killed Jim Crow, but it cut away another piece of the monster. An even larger piece had been cut away as blacks battled to victory against Jim Crow schools in the historic May 1954 U.S. Supreme Court decision in *Brown v. Board of Education*. Chief Justice Earl Warren pronounced for a unanimous Court that "in the field of public education, the doctrine of 'separate but equal' has no place. Separate educational facilities are inherently unequal" (United States 1954, 495).

The 1954 *Brown v. Board of Education* victory against segregated public schools arose from generations of black challenges to Jim Crow, and triggered escalating confrontations over racial segregation. (Bettmann/Getty Images)

Blacks exulted. Thurgood Marshall, the lead NAACP lawyer in *Brown*, said he expected whites to follow the law and not "resist the Supreme Court" (Huston 1954, 14). He was very wrong, and blacks' jubilation over *Brown* proved sadly premature, as such rejoicing had proved so often in the past. Their victory of the moment proved just that. It was not to be lasting as blacks faced infuriated segregationists.

Southern white leaders denounced the *Brown* decisions, with J. Strom Thurmond leading the assault. The South Carolina governor had been the 1948 Dixiecrat presidential candidate opposing President Truman on civil rights. As U.S. senator from South Carolina Thurmond continued to head segregationists, leading southern congressmen in March 1956 to issue what they titled a "Declaration of Constitutional Principles," popularly published as the *Southern Manifesto*. It cast the *Brown* decision as unconstitutional and recast the desegregation mandate in terms of long-reviled racial integration.

Massive white resistance to desegregation was at hand, and it encouraged more antiblack violence. President Dwight D. Eisenhower in September 1957 reluctantly had to order troops from the U.S. Army's 101st Airborne Division—without its black troopers—to Arkansas's capital of Little Rock to escort to the city's Central High School black students called the "Little Rock Nine." White mobs confronted the black schoolchildren there and elsewhere.

Venom-spitting whites were not merely rabble. As with the *Southern Manifesto*, the call to resist blacks and federal civil rights efforts came from many of America's highest elected white officials. Virginia's Democrat U.S. Senator Harry F. Byrd Sr., for example, led the campaign that shut down public schools rather than desegregate. In 1956 Virginia, with other states following, adopted various ruses, such as vouchers and tax credits, to fund all-white schools with public monies, while declaring such schools were private so as to avoid desegregation mandates.

Black students in Prince Edward County, Virginia, became poster children for blacks' predicament in light of whites' defying desegregation mandates. They and others were essentially locked out of school. In contempt of the U.S. Supreme Court's further desegregation order in September 1958 in *Cooper v. Aaron*, Arkansas Governor Orval Faubus closed Little Rock's four public high schools. The governors of Virginia and North Carolina also ordered public schools closed rather than desegregated. *Brown* was proving of little benefit to black children who had gone from woefully unequal public schools to having no public schools.

Long before *Brown*, it was evident that Jim Crow would not go quietly. White backlash met black advances at almost every turn. As they had during Reconstruction and long afterward, southern white vigilantes sought to suppress civil rights agitation as the 1950s opened. Ku Klux Klansmen rampaged again, targeting NAACP leaders and other black activists. In December 1956 Alabama KKK members bombed Rev. Fred Shuttleworth's Birmingham home. They later beat him with chains and stabbed his wife Ruby Keeler Shuttlesworth as the couple sought to enroll their children in a previously all-white school (Mills 2006, 95–96, 199–200).

In June 1958 KKK members bombed Shuttlesworth's Birmingham Bethel Baptist Church, headquarters of the Alabama Christian Movement for Human Rights. That proved a prelude to the September 1963 KKK bombing of Birmingham's 16th Street Baptist Church which killed 11-year-old Carol Denise McNair and three 14-year-olds—Addie Mae Collins, Carole Robertson, and Cynthia Wesley. Similar violence met the Montgomery Bus Boycott. Snipers fired on two city buses and separately shot a pregnant black woman in both her legs. Also white men pummeled a black teenage female bus rider. Shotgun blasts exploded into Martin Luther King Jr.'s front door, and in January 1957 bombs destroyed five black Montgomery churches.

Blacks remained undaunted as white diehards decried desegregation as indiscriminate racial mixing that promised miscegenation with the age-old cry against black men abusing white women sexually. Such outcry did not carry to white men abusing black women. Rape was a color-coded charge, as 19-year-old Celia's 1855 case in Missouri demonstrated. Yet black males faced death at even hints of sex with white women, as 14-year-old Emmett Till discovered in August 1955 in Money, Mississippi. He was murdered, mutilated, and dropped in the Tallahatchie River reportedly for whistling at a white woman. The state indicted no one for that outrage as the age-old legal and extralegal assault on black males persisted.

As they had in battling slavery, in battling segregation blacks found themselves confronting state action. Reviving antebellum nullification doctrines, for example, Mississippi's legislature in February 1956 declared federal desegregation rulings "invalid" in that state. Georgia went further a year later in declaring the Fourteenth and Fifteenth Amendments void in that state. Alabama's legislature voted in March 1956 to request federal funds to deport blacks from the state, proposing in part to relocate them in northern states so northern whites would have first-hand experience with how it felt to live with large numbers of blacks. Further, Alabama in 1956 outlawed the NAACP, prosecuting it as a foreign corporation doing business in violation of state law. A unanimous U.S. Supreme Court in *NAACP v. Alabama* (1958) denounced Alabama's actions as unconstitutional in violating due process. Also the Court ruled the NAACP's civil rights "advancement of beliefs and ideas" constitutionally protected under rights of free speech and freedom of association.

Blacks took advantage of southern recalcitrance to make headway finally in Congress. Emphasizing southern defiance as the challenge to federal authority that it was, blacks helped to move Congress for the first time since 1875 to pass a Civil Rights Act over a Strom Thurman-led filibuster. The September 1957 statute revived Reconstruction-era prohibitions against voter intimidation and added federal oversight by authorizing a Civil Rights Division in the Justice Department and by creating an independent U.S. Commission on Civil Rights to investigate and report on the condition of civil rights and also to recommend improvements. The legislation passed more as a measure to vindicate federal authority being embarrassed than as a measure to vindicate blacks' civil rights. Yet it was unquestionably a response to blacks' long protests (Berry 2009, 9–37).

Battles in Congress and in the courts would long persist. The more immediate and telling battles were for hearts and minds. To fight American Negro slavery, blacks had importuned public opinion. And in the 1950s they found television a powerful ally to show all America and all the world Jim Crow's tyranny. The increasingly popular medium produced invaluable pictures as undeniable proof of the horribly separate and unequal lives forced on blacks, particularly in the South. As blacks recognized television's power to dramatize their plight, segregationists early recognized television as an enemy that could undermine their preferred benign image of white supremacy and broadcast alternative social visions segregationists found subversive.

Not only television but stage, screen, and other media also put blacks more and more in the public eye. Juanita Hall in 1950 became the first black to win a Tony award for her performance in the musical *South Pacific*. Starring in the 1954 film *Carmen Jones*, Dorothy Dandridge garnered the first best actress Oscar nomination of a black. She also became in November 1954 the first black woman featured solo on the cover of *Life* magazine. Major cultural institutions also began featuring blacks. In 1955 contralto Marian Anderson became the first black at New York City's Metropolitan Opera; dancer Arthur Mitchell became the first black male at the New York City Ballet; and the National Broadcasting Company (NBC) featured Leontyne Price as the first black to star in a telecast opera. NBC in 1956 also broadcast the *Nat King Cole Show* as the first nationwide network program starring a black.

The flow of postwar "firsts" grew. Ralph Ellison won the National Book Award for fiction in 1952 for his novel *Invisible Man*. Black students were admitted to the University of Oklahoma in June 1955. Amid rioting in February 1956 Autherine Lucy enrolled at the University of Alabama only to be expelled for taking legal action against the university's segregation. Charlayne Hunter and Hamilton E. Holmes entered the University of Georgia under court orders in January 1961, amid rioting. They, too, were expelled for causing disruption, but a federal court ordered them readmitted. In sports, Willie O'Ree became the first black in the National Hockey League, playing for the Boston Bruins in 1958. Charlie Sifford joined the Professional Golf Association of America tour in 1961, the same year Syracuse University All-American Ernie Davis won the Heisman Trophy as the nation's outstanding college football player.

Still in many places blacks appeared only as tokens. They were often not so much being included as they were being put on display as supposed gestures of goodwill. They were expected to act as totems to ward off accusations of discrimination. Frequently they occupied entry levels where they could be seen but not heard or felt at the heart of things. They were for show, not for substance. Frequently they were not allowed to mix and mingle. They were not actually sharing the same space. They were present but still separated, often standing in glaring spotlights.

And their presence was sometimes only fleeting. *The Nat King Cole Show*, for example, lasted only 13 months as national advertisers shrank from challenging segregation, unready or unwilling to be identified with a black presence on national television. Further, television images of black–white interaction were at times not what they seemed, as illustrated by the nationally televised *American Bandstand* program. While host Dick Clark from 1956 onward touted the show as racially integrated, its cameras reproduced the segregated reality of Philadelphia where WFIL-TV broadcast only white-on-white, black-on-black teens (Delmont 2012, 1–10).

Even where blacks proved disruptors, their presence early represented a distraction more than fundamental change, for desegregation was not simply a top-down or a one-off proposition. Eradicating Jim Crow called for radical revolution, and that was not happening in 1950s America. At best, an evolution was unfolding. And it was happening at no single site. Concentrated as it was in the South in the 1950s and early 1960s, the drive against black exclusion and devaluation was everywhere in motion, as it ever had been. It was a daily and ongoing part of black life in America as successive generations had experienced since the beginning of American Negro slavery.

Each generation of African Americans bought fresh energies and perspectives to protest for full recognition of their humanity, and so it was moving from the 1950s into the 1960s. Black youth proved to have significantly different views and tolerances than their elders. Perhaps characteristic of youth, they were less patient; they were less interested in negotiating and more interested in demonstrating. They wanted change now, and they were eager in pushing for it. As NAACP Youth Council members moved in the forefront of what became the Montgomery Bus Boycott, so too did young blacks move in the forefront of sit-in campaigns. "We do not want our freedom gradually, but we want our freedom now," SNCC's John Lewis would declare (Lewis 1963, 230).

  Sit-ins developed from labor's sit-down strikes of the 1930s. Black attorney Samuel Wilbert Tucker in August 1939 directed an early sit-in to protest blacks' exclusion from public libraries in Alexandria, Virginia. Morgan State college students in January 1955 joined CORE members in a lunch counter sit-in campaign in Baltimore. In the summer of 1958 NAACP Youth Council members in Wichita, Kansas, and Oklahoma City launched lunch counter sit-ins, insisting on getting food and beverage service like any other customers. Black North Carolina Agricultural and Technical State College students in February 1960 launched the much-noted six-month-long Greensboro sit-ins that reached throughout the South with campaigns in Richmond, Houston, and Nashville, for example. Shepherded by NAACP field secretary Ella Baker, the Student Nonviolent Coordinating Committee (SNCC) organized in Raleigh, North Carolina, in April 1960 to facilitate and coordinate such activities.

  While their elders seemed more inclined to await negotiated developments, black youth seemed more inclined to force change. Thirty-one years old in 1960, Rev. Martin Luther King Jr. stood not quite at the midpoint between black youth such as twentysomething SNCC leaders Diane Nash, Stokely Carmichael, or Bob Moses and fifty- or sixty-something old guard black

The black sit-in campaign that captured headlines in 1960 when North Carolina A & T college students protested "whites-only" lunch counter service illustrated the escalating battles against Jim Crow that followed the 1954 *Brown v. Board* decision. (Bettmann/Getty Images)

leaders such as the NAACP's Roy Wilkins or the National Urban League's Whitney Young. As others had before him, King led his own umbrella organization, the Southern Christian Leadership Conference (SCLC). Founded in 1957 in the aftermath of the Montgomery Bus Boycott, the SCLC advocated and engineered Gandhian massive nonviolent protest against Jim Crow. At its founding, SNCC incorporated the "nonviolent" element but would drop it in the late 1960s, changing its name to the Student *National* Coordinating Committee.

Activism everywhere became the watchword of black protest. As the 1960s opened, gradualism prevailed among many blacks but radicalism was on the rise. The Civil Rights Act of 1960, extending the two-year life of the U.S. Civil Rights Commission and providing for federal inspection of voter registration, placated few blacks. Their push for more became part of the 1960 presidential campaign as Democrat John F. Kennedy, largely through his brother Robert F. Kennedy, wooed black voters as they were rising as forces to be reckoned with.

Black ballots were making a difference. Blacks in Georgia in 1962 sent attorney Leroy Johnson to their state senate as one of their own for the first time since the early 1900s. Gus Hawkins in 1962 won election to the U.S. House of Representatives from a Los Angeles district, becoming California's first black in Congress. And in Massachusetts, Republican Edward W. Brooke in 1963 became the state's attorney general. In 1966 Brooke won election to the U.S. Senate as the first black since Reconstruction.

The appearance of more and more black public officeholders reflected not only their personal achievements but collective accomplishments. The paths to public office and changes in public policy were being opened by creative and courageous blacks and their allies out on the streets, highways, and byways organizing and pressing for change. Captivated by the distracting cult of personality, news of the day and later writing too often simply lauded individual leaders. Fundamentally, however, the persistent black thrusting that too many with short historical perspectives came to call *the* Civil Rights Movement or *the* Civil Rights Era arose from the black many not the black few. The quest for black civil rights was a centuries-old cultural production of the masses not merely of an elite. It drew on resources and relied on resilience from ordinary black women, men, and children who were doing extraordinary deeds as foot soldiers turning the tide in battling for civil rights.

The surging black movement's force rushed into the 1960s. Riding public transportation again was a major demonstration site, following the U.S. Supreme Court's December 1960 ruling in *Boynton v. Virginia*. CORE in May 1961 organized teams of black and white "Freedom Riders" to travel on interstate buses from Washington, D.C., southward to test compliance with the *Boynton* ruling. They met violence. A mob in Anniston, Alabama, attacked and burned a bus carrying Freedom Riders. In Birmingham a mob pummeled Freedom Riders. Officials in Jackson, Mississippi, sent Freedom Riders to Parchman Penitentiary.

SNCC joined the Freedom Riders' movement to press the point for seating and service regardless of race or color. A showdown developed over white defiance at Georgia's Albany Union Railway Terminal in November 1961. Mass demonstrations followed in what became known as the Albany Movement. Thousands mobilized as desegregation of public transportation spilled over into voter registration in a campaign to capture and change local and state public policy.

Aggressively pushing voting rights grew as a primary goal of SNCC and a focus for civil rights protests in the South as the ballot box again took precedence as an object of violent contention. Black Southerners like Mississippian Fannie Lou Hamer showed themselves ready to do battle to register and vote even while white terrorists were burning black churches in places such as Sasser, Georgia, in September 1962 because they were places for black voter education.

Blacks at the grassroots were organizing and pressing for change across America. The movement was not evenly paced. Blacks in the South, North, West, and Midwest had different tempos. Except in broad outline, in fact, they had different agenda. Discrimination and inequality reached everywhere but not to all in the same ways. Everywhere blacks confronted segregation's bulwarks, but their groundbreaking movements took different paths in different places and times. From the Baton Rouge Bus Boycott in 1953 into the 1960s, southern black communities led the way against Jim Crow, but as they reached the mountaintop in their quest, the horizon of black protest spread nationally as never before.

## PROFILE: ELLA BAKER (1903–1986)

A tireless crusader for what she called "participatory democracy," Ella Josephine Baker did unstinting service in grassroots organizing for the NAACP, SCLC, and SNCC. She was a giant in the 20th-century civil rights movement.

Born in Norfolk, Virginia, on December 13, 1903, Baker grew up in rural North Carolina hearing horrors of American Negro slavery from her maternal grandmother. Baker graduated as class valedictorian in 1927 from Shaw University in Raleigh and moved to New York City amid the New Negro Renaissance. Plunging into journalism and politics, she wrote for the *American West Indian News* and the *Negro National News* (NNN), and with early socialist and later conservative George S. Schuyler she cofounded the Young Negroes Cooperative League (YNCL).

Her organizational skills got Baker appointed NNN office manager and YNCL secretary-treasurer, as well as the YNCL's New York Council chairman and national director. At the onset of the Great Depression, she taught in the Works Progress Administration's Worker's Education Project. In 1938 she joined the NAACP as a field office organizer, but she continued ever active in the Harlem community on local and national issues. She protested Alabama's railroading of the Scottsboro Boys, Italy's invasion of Ethiopia, and fascism's rise in Spain. She became NAACP New York branch president in 1952, focusing on police brutality and school desegregation, and she ran in 1953 as a Liberal Party candidate for a New York City Council seat.

Baker believed in people summoning their inner strength. "My theory is, strong people don't need strong leaders," she instructed. She rejected messianic leadership styles with their male bias. She recruited networks throughout the South, particularly in rural areas. People related to her because she was down with them. Movement success flowed up from the people, for they were the real force and did the real work, Baker insisted. She saw herself as a facilitator who got people together. The In Friendship group she organized in 1956 to raise money for the Montgomery Bus Boycott illustrated her style, as did her SCLC recruitment work from 1957 to 1960 (Crawford, Rouse, and Woods 1990, 51; Ransby 2003, 173–175).

Baker's shepherding the founding and development of SNCC perhaps best demonstrated her organizational genius, mentoring youth who became major forces throughout the 1960s. She worked also with the Mississippi Freedom Democratic Party and voter registration drives, as well as with the Southern Conference Education Fund, aimed at interracial cooperation. Further in the 1970s she worked to advance social solidarity with the Mass Party Organizing Committee, as she campaigned also against South African apartheid and joined the "Free Angela" protest supporting the outspoken Angela Davis.

Baker's passion and presence permeated the civil rights movement from the 1930s into the 1970s. She shunned headlines for herself as she pressed to make headway for people's causes. She died on her 83rd birthday, December 13, 1986.

## REFERENCES

Berry, Mary Frances. 2009. *And Justice for All: The United States Commission on Civil Rights and the Continuing Struggle for Freedom in America.* New York: Alfred A. Knopf.

Crawford, Vicki L., Jacqueline Anne Rouse, and Barbara Woods. 1990. *Women in the Civil Rights Movement: Trailblazers and Torchbearers, 1941–1965.* Brooklyn, NY: Carlson Publishing.

Delmont, Matthew F. 2012. *The Nicest Kids in Town: American Bandstand, Rock 'n Roll, and the Struggle for Civil Rights in 1950s Philadelphia.* Berkeley: University of California Press.

Du Bois, W. E. Burghardt. 1903. *The Souls of Black Folk: Essays and Sketches.* Chicago: A. C. McClurg.

Huston, Luther A. 1954. "1896 Ruling Upset: 'Separate but Equal' Doctrine Held Out of Place in Education High Court Bans Public Pupil Bias." *New York Times*, May 18, 1954, 1, 14.

Lewis, John. 1963. Speech at the March on Washington for Jobs and Freedom. Excerpted in "For Jobs and Freedom: The Leaders Speak." *Crisis* 80, no. 7 (August/September 1973): 228–240.

Ransby, Barbara. 2003. *Ella Baker and the Black Freedom Movement: A Radical Democratic Vision.* Chapel Hill: University of North Carolina Press.

Thornton, J. Mills. 2006. *Dividing Lines: Municipal Politics and the Struggle for Civil Rights in Montgomery, Birmingham, and Selma.* Tuscaloosa: University of Alabama Press.

United States. 1954. *Brown v. Board of Education,* 347 U.S. 483 (1954).

*Chapter 16*

# The Revolution *Was* Televised

Hundreds of thousands thronged the U.S. capital's Lincoln Memorial on Wednesday, August 28, 1963. Rallying to organizer A. Philip Randolph's call to March on Washington for Jobs and Freedom, they demanded more than Randolph's 1941 March on Washington Movement that had secured FDR's Executive Order 8802, prohibiting discrimination by defense contractors receiving federal money. Blacks in 1963 demanded affirmative action for jobs at living wages that would lift them from poverty and open economic opportunity that would finally furnish black freedom 100 years after President Abraham Lincoln signed the Emancipation Proclamation. They also demanded federal action to make real for blacks the civil rights the U.S. Constitution announced for all Americans.

Rev. Martin Luther King Jr. delivered his "I Have a Dream" speech that later became the March's signature, but he was no single star coming into the day. His work since the Montgomery Bus Boycott of 1955–1956 and his Southern Christian Leadership Conference's Birmingham campaign in April and May 1963 had elevated him among national black leaders. His April *Letter from Birmingham Jail* further established him as a voice of constructive moderation with his declarations such as "Injustice anywhere is a threat to justice everywhere," calling for unity to realize American ideals of justice regardless of race (King 1963, n.p.). But at the Lincoln Memorial, the Reverend King was but one of the black leaders some called "the big six." He stood in the shadow of the venerable A. Philip Randolph, then vice president of the American Federation of Labor and Congress of Industrial Organizations. The other "big" four were CORE leader James Farmer, SNCC leader John Lewis, National Urban League leader Whitney Young, and NAACP leader Roy Wilkins.

With broadcast images of baton-wielding police and attack dogs besetting peaceful protesters as in Birmingham, Alabama, in April 1963, television made real to millions of Americans the brutality of Jim Crow oppression of blacks in the South. (AP Photo/Bill Hudson)

The marchers avoided any civil disobedience as a show of good faith with President John F. Kennedy's administration and its support for stronger civil rights legislation. They were not all blacks. Whites from varied backgrounds joined in pushing for economic security and social justice. Indeed, for many whites the March's goal of federal job training and public works to boost employment was a major attraction. Black women made up the bulk of marchers, as they had from time immemorial formed the greater part of the black body moving onward and upward as the everlasting fiber and sinew of black advancement.

Male chauvinism elbowed black women from center stage at the March, providing them scant public recognition. They got to sing but hardly to speak in the official program, despite longtime activist Anna Arnold Hedgeman's arguments in organizing the March alongside Randolph and Bayard Rustin. The internationally known entertainer Josephine Baker spoke in the preliminaries, but women's appearance in the official program was largely in the form of singers Mahalia Jackson, Marian Anderson, and Camilla Williams. A brief segment paid tribute to "Negro Women Fighters for Freedom," introducing Maryland activists Gloria Richardson, SNCC's Diane

Nash, Little Rock's Daisy Bates, and Myrlie Evers and Prince E. Lee—the widows of slain NAACP activists Medgar Evers in Mississippi and Herbert Lee in Louisiana. Being relegated to backstage or out of the limelight was hardly new for black women. So often anxious in public to show a sense of manliness defined by public control and domination, black men—like the leaders at the March—persistently preferred black women in public only as background. But a new day was dawning.

The Reverend King's call for judgment based on the content of a person's character weighed on more than race. It reached gender also. Black women increasingly refused to take a backseat to anyone, just as Rosa Parks had refused to give up her seat in 1955 in Montgomery. Black women had their own issues to march for, and they refused to be denied. They had their say in private, and they would have their say in public, for they were more than singers and dancers or performers of any kind or out-of-sight-out-of-mind scut workers.

Being black and female had ever complicated their lives. Their experiences were not the same as those of black males or the same as white females. They experienced a peculiar, indeed a unique, triple bind, suffering from being black, from being female, and from being black *and* female. The perspectives of that experience informed the outlook of many black women activists long before the 1963 March on Washington, moving them to embrace human rights initiatives against classism, racism, and sexism. Ella Baker's lifelong grassroots organizing to press for radical democracy that embraced fundamental human equality, for example, reflected the goals of the largely behind-the-scenes black women organizers and activists who built black civil rights successes of the 1950s and 1960s.

Marked among the March's successes was the Civil Rights Act of 1964. President Kennedy's assassination in November 1963 contributed to passing the legislation, as it sympathetically inclined the national attitude. The landmark statute reprised almost 100-year-old Reconstruction efforts to realize blacks' rights to vote, to have equal access to public accommodations, education, and facilities, and not to be discriminated against in employment.

President Lyndon B. Johnson championed the 1964 measure. Indeed, the Texan became a major champion of black civil rights, as the Missourian Harry Truman had in the 1940s. But while these sons of the South joined to enforce the Constitution's provisions against discrimination, many of their white brethren refused to yield. Newly elected Alabama Governor George C. Wallace, for example, on taking office in 1963 had pledged "segregation now, segregation tomorrow, segregation forever" and defiantly stood in the door at the University of Alabama to prevent Vivian Malone and James Hood from entering as the first black students (Davis 2006, 185–186).

Voting took center stage in blacks' desegregation campaign in 1964. The Alabama Voting Rights Project and the Mississippi Freedom Summer Project exemplified efforts to register southern blacks to vote. The umbrella Council of Federated Organizations, with SNCC field secretary Bob Moses as its codirector, coordinated the Mississippi campaign. Among other things it produced a host of "freedom schools" and the Mississippi Freedom Democratic Party (MFDP).

Violent white backlash met the MFDP as state and local vigilantes attacked black efforts. Mississippi terrorists bombed or burned 37 black churches and at least 30 black businesses or residences in 1964. Blacks were pummeled in the streets, evicted from homes, and fired from jobs for advocating for the MFDP or associating with those who did. Police arrested almost 1,100 MFDP volunteers and sympathizers. The most noted terrorism left James Chaney, Andrew Goodman, and Michael Schwerner dead. The murders of the one black and two Jewish MFDP volunteers occurred outside Philadelphia, Mississippi, in June 1964. But blacks and their supporters pressed on, notably in the MFDP's challenge to be recognized and seated at the 1964 Democratic National Convention in New Jersey's Atlantic City, with Fannie Lou Hamer pressing blacks' case as Mississippi's loyal Democrats in contrast to white segregationists set to turn Republican (McAdam 1988, passim; Dittmer 1994, passim).

Worse violence was coming. What came to be called "Bloody Sunday" at the Edmund Pettus Bridge outside Selma, Alabama, in March 1965 provided worldwide pictures of the brutality that beset civil rights marchers in the South. Organized as a 50-mile trek from Selma to the state capital at Montgomery to press for black voting rights, the March became a symbol throughout the South. The horrifying attack killed white Boston Unitarian minister James Reeb, sent 16 other marchers to the hospital, and injured more than 50 others. Also KKK members outside Selma later in March shot dead Viola Liuzzo, a white marcher from Michigan.

Such terrorism shocked many and multiplied the marchers' numbers from about 500 to 2,500. With the Reverend King, fresh from his December 1964 award of the Nobel Peace Prize, in the lead, the Selma-to-Montgomery March resumed with careful compromises. The scene moved President Johnson to stand before Congress to urge passing of what became the Voting Rights Act of 1965 with his adopting a black rallying cry in declaring "We Shall Overcome."

The Voting Rights Act of 1965 capped a long campaign to recoup a federal commitment to realize rights the Reconstruction amendments announced. Indeed, with the act's passage in August 1965, many throughout the nation considered that blacks had finally achieved their civil rights goals. The act outlawed traditional barriers to black voting, such as discriminatory literacy

tests and poll taxes. The Twenty-Fourth Amendment ratified as part of
the U.S. Constitution in January 1964 had earlier outlawed poll taxes for
voting in federal elections. The Civil Rights Act of 1964 had extended federal reach to protect blacks' rights to equal access to public education and
accommodations, and the Supreme Court continued to sustain that reach.
In *Heart of Atlanta Motel v. United States* in December 1964, the Court
restored the 1875 principles its predecessor struck down in the *Civil Rights
Cases* of 1883. From some perspectives, the developments of 1964 and 1965
appeared a move back to a future of repeated promises nearly 100 years old.

Enforcing the 1965 Voting Rights Act made a clear difference throughout
the South, as illustrated in rates of black voter registration. The percentage
of black voters in Mississippi went from 5 percent in 1960 to 59 percent
by 1970, from 14 percent to 55 percent in Alabama, and from 16 percent
to 46 percent in South Carolina, for example. More than a million blacks
enlisted on the Deep South's voter registration rolls by 1968. And the number of black elected officials increased impressively throughout the South
and, indeed, throughout the nation. From fewer than 100 before the 1965
act, black elected officials increased to 1,469 in 1970; by 1998 their number
would stand at 8,868 nationwide (Hine, Hine, and Harrold 2014, 498, 527).

The battle against Jim Crow appeared won, at least on paper. As large a
fight as it was, however, it was hardly the entire struggle. Just as the battle
against slavery was only part of blacks' struggle for recognition of their
humanity, so too was the battle against Jim Crow. It was part of a larger
confrontation and had never been blacks' exclusive target. Jim Crow was
identified with the South, as slavery had been identified with the South.
But the pervasive segregation that bedeviled blacks pervaded more than the
South. And it was more than public policy reached by changes in law. It was
public practice, and it permeated white attitudes as part of their acknowledged and unacknowledged sense of white privilege. Its persistence beyond
the travesty of Jim Crow became painfully clear less than a week after President Johnson signed into law the Voting Rights Act of 1965.

The black section of California's South Central Los Angeles called Watts
erupted on August 11–17, 1965, in rioting against brutal discrimination.
Residential segregation created Watts as it had long created black ghettos in
major cities throughout the nation. Policed largely by white officers as if it
were a reservation to confine and discipline blacks, the area smoldered with
resentments—as did other such districts across America. Black residents suffered mass unemployment and underemployment, poor public schools, public facilities, and public services, and exploitation by businesses that exacted
premium prices for substandard services. Persistent police brutality ignited
Watts, as it had ignited black rioting earlier and as it would ignite black
rioting later.

As blacks and others around America and the world had recoiled from television shots of southern whites viciously suppressing blacks during civil rights protests, they recoiled also from television shots of rampaging blacks. The California National Guard, along with Los Angeles city and county police, quelled the violence—arresting more than 3,400 persons and killing at least 31. Many asked what would move blacks to do such things. Official studies examined the causes that sent more than 30,000 people to run riot in the streets and that resulted in more than $40 million in property damage. The findings differed little from those in reports from the 1919 Chicago riot or the 1943 Harlem riot or future black riots. The conclusions boiled down to hopeless anger arising from oppressive living conditions and impoverished prospects.

What do blacks want now? The naïve and the relieved may have embraced the Civil Rights Act of 1964 and the Voting Rights Act of 1965 as solving blacks' problems. Or they supposed that at least solutions were certainly at hand with the addition of President Johnson's declared War on Poverty, with its community-based development, education, and job training programs flowing from the Economic Opportunity Act of 1964. To such persons the Watts rioting was more than jarring as it clashed with the symbols of civil rights success. For blacks living the reality of America's debasement and devaluation, however, Watts highlighted their daily challenges distant from idealism or legal pronouncements.

Fostering black economic growth, as President Johnson's War on Poverty proposed in his larger Great Society program, proved much less popular than desegregation. Federal programs such as Head Start and the Jobs Corps might have seemed unobjectionable in concept. Providing preschool children health care, nutrition, and early education was surely something all parents wanted for their children. Similarly, vocational education for late teenagers and early adults, aged 16 to 24 years, appeared a sensible approach to improving the nation's human capital. But critics disparaged such programs as they had the post–Civil War Bureau of Refugees Freedmen and Abandoned Lands (BRFAL).

Labeling BRFAL the "Freedmen's Bureau," opponents had cast it as a boondoggle for blacks despite its feeding, clothing, sheltering, and tending to tens of thousands of needy whites. Similar criticisms arose in the 1960s to label antipoverty program handouts for blacks despite the benefits to millions of whites. Denunciation of antipoverty programs disingenuously ignored the fact that most poor people in America were white and that in terms of overall expenditures most benefits went to whites not to blacks or other people of color. Much of the attack reflected an age-old strategy of dividing blacks and whites with shared economic interests. And its success would be further illustrated in the Poor People's Campaign the Reverend

King organized before his 1968 assassination. While formed to transcend race in reaching the problem of American poverty, the campaign and its June 1968 March on Washington reflected limits to the civil rights movement's continuing appeal. The campaign drew mostly marginalized people of color as many whites rejected its call for expanded federal antipoverty programs as an extension of the so-called welfare state.

The War on Poverty and the Watts riots reflected an increasing shift of attention to blacks beyond the South, where desegregation remained the primary focus. Watts exposed to worldview the severity of black problems outside the South, and such problems were emerging from the shadows of the long focus on Jim Crow. While the laws of slavery and segregation had constantly demanded most attention, blacks outside the South had persistently demanded attention to the extralegal, popular practices of white supremacy that beset blacks. They had long complained about discrimination in education, employment, and housing, and their rhetoric often carried a non-southern accent.

The focus on Jim Crow often obscured sharp differences in perspective between blacks inside and outside the South. The opposition projected between W.E.B. Du Bois and Booker T. Washington in the early 1900s exhibited that divide. In the early 1960s it became embodied in the contrast between Nation of Islam minister Malcolm X and the Reverend King, the one taken as the voice of black radicalism and the other as a voice of reason; the one preaching nonviolence and the other declaring "I am not against using violence in self-defense," and explaining "I don't call it violence when it's self-defense, I call it intelligence" (McKelvey 1994, 163). Like Du Bois and Booker T., Malcolm and Martin shared similar goals. They differed primarily on means, not ends. They exemplified the growing debate over the direction of black liberation that increasingly arose as a question following the civil rights successes of 1964 and 1965.

The enduring scenes for the Reverend King were those of whites attacking nonviolent blacks in the South, but a new scene was dawning with blacks fighting back. The Black Panther Party for Self-Defense (BPP) that Merritt College students Huey P. Newton and Bobby Seale founded in October 1966 in Oakland, California, showed blacks' more radical direction. In part a generational shift was occurring in the black liberation movement. The Reverend King had bridged a gap between old-line black backroom and courtroom negotiations and massive black action. As the 1960s went on, however, King more and more appeared part of the old guard as a more radical SNCC illustrated younger blacks' and whites' impulses for far-reaching results sooner rather than later.

Black urban rioting further demonstrated blacks' changing mood. Watts proved only an initiation as more black anger and frustration in 1967 spilled into the streets in Newark and Detroit. The violence in the New Jersey and

Michigan cities flared from police brutality. The kindling was long laid in continual neglect and under-servicing. From public schooling to housing to employment and across the social landscape, many urban blacks had had enough of being short-shrifted. Their sense that no one was paying attention to their plight stoked resentment and rage that erupted on July 12–17 in Newark. The outbreak officially left 26 dead, at least 750 others injured, and nearly 1,500 arrested. Property damage reached $10 million. In Detroit the outbreak on July 23–27 officially left 33 blacks and 10 whites dead, with more than 450 injured and more than 7,200 arrested. Estimates of the property damage there ranged from $40 to $80 million.

The prophet of nonviolence would himself become the occasion of a nationwide black eruption. News of the Reverend King's assassination in Memphis on April 4, 1968, ignited a rampage among tens of thousands of blacks. Sometimes referred to as the "Holy Week Uprising," black rioting struck at least 150 U.S. cities. Baltimore, Chicago, Detroit, Kansas City, Louisville, and Washington, D.C., were among the hardest hit. Estimates put the property damage across the nation in the billions of dollars. More than 35,000 persons were injured and 46 were officially listed as killed.

The King assassination riots came one month after a presidential commission impaneled to study urban rioting from Watts in 1965 to Detroit in 1967 released its report calling for sweeping changes in the racial structure of U.S. cities and the nation itself. The *Report*'s oft-quoted conclusion that "our nation is moving toward two societies, one Black, one White—separate and unequal," sounded to many blacks not simply as old news but as fact too patent to provide any meaningful responses or solutions to their complaints (United States 1968, 1). Left unsaid in the *Report* was the clear and obvious fact for most blacks that the nation suffered systemic racism as white supremacy infected every element of America, as it had from the nation's birth.

The urban rioting exposed the nationwide reach of the divide Jim Crow had symbolized. The nation *was* at least "two societies, one Black, one White—separate and unequal." Residential segregation exhibited the gulf. Many, if not most, whites simply refused to live in proximity to blacks. By many measures, in fact, the Jim Crow South displayed more close interaction between blacks and whites than places outside the South. Whites' flight to the suburbs in the 1950s and 1960s in many places displayed their displeasure at blacks moving into the nation's cities on the last leg of the Great Migration.

Whites in Cicero, Milwaukee, and other Midwestern and northern suburbs and cities rebuffed open housing movements and displayed their rejection of any black presence, and the Fair Housing Act section of the 1968 Civil Rights Act changed few attitudes. Homeowners and condominium associations, cooperatives, and gated communities replaced restrictive covenants as barriers to blacks' moving in where whites did not want them. California's 1964 referendum to repeal the state's Fair Housing Act of 1963, with the cry of "property owner rights," unmistakably demonstrated the degree of white resistance to ending racial discrimination in public and private housing.

If whites refused to yield place and privilege, blacks were no less insistent on having their share of place and privilege. So the age-old confrontation persisted. The difference in the 1960s was that blacks were in revolt, as the urban rioting suggested. The BPP was a vanguard for some. But black unrest represented only a part of America in revolt in the late 1960s. The escalating U.S. war in Vietnam and a developing youth counterculture merged with black anger to threaten social revolution. The black civil rights drive of the 1950s and 1960s gave further direction to widespread social protest evident in the 1968 Democratic National Convention protests in Chicago.

The black civil rights movement had become a beacon for many Americans in quest of fundamental changes in America, and the social protest synergy showed on college campuses. Deadly results in February 1968 hit the South Carolina State University campus in Orangeburg. State Highway Patrol officers there killed three black men and injured at least 28 others among approximately 150 protesting continued segregation. At Brandeis University outside Boston white students joined blacks in January 1969 to demand an Afro-American studies program. No violence occurred there, but similar protests for black studies in February 1969 at the University of Wisconsin at Madison and at Duke University in North Carolina resulted in clashes between students and police.

Armed black students at Cornell University in Ithaca, New York, seized the student union building in April 1969 to demand an Afro-American studies program. In May 1969 a student takeover closed the City College of New York for two weeks until securing agreement for programs in Afro-American studies and Puerto Rican studies. Harvard University in September 1969 initiated an Afro-American studies program, signaling academic acceptance of the field. The most noted on-campus incident occurred at an antiwar protest in May 1970 at Kent State University in Ohio, where National Guard troopers shot dead four white students and wounded nine others, setting off sympathetic protests on campuses around the nation.

The violence student protests attracted paled against the continuing terrorist onslaught against desegregation activists. Beatings and bombings persisted, as did official repression. Perhaps more than ever before, black activists were tagged as radicals. BPP members particularly found themselves at risk as FBI director J. Edgar Hoover and state and local law enforcement agencies targeted them for infiltration and disruption. Hoover had from early days dogged the Reverend King, considering him "the most dangerous Negro in America," as A. Philip Randolph and others were tagged before and after King in official campaigns against black militancy (Kornweibel 1998, 77; King and West 2014, x). Police simply assassinated BPP leaders such as Fred Hampton and Mark Clark in Chicago in December 1969. Between January 1968 and December 1969 police in various locales killed at least 28 BPP members (Epstein 1971, 45).

Public campaigns smeared the BPP and other black organizations not merely as radical but as criminal. Few in mainstream U.S. media reported positive programs of groups such as the BPP. Even a cursory review of the BPP's charter Ten Point Program laying out "what we want, what we believe" showed the BPP's fundamental focus on black self-determination with community control of public services and with full employment, decent housing, and quality education for blacks. Unyielding in opposing police brutality, the BPP called also for reform of the U.S. criminal justice system that persisted in disproportionately executing and incarcerating black men. It popularized the slogan "the only good pig is a dead pig," identifying police as enemies of the people. Its advocacy and armed in-your-face attitude cast the BPP as the most visible Black Power group in the late 1960s and early 1970s.

Blacks pressing for liberation stood in many eyes as radicals needing to be cut down. U.S. track and field athletes Tommie Smith and John Carlos became such symbols at the 1968 Olympic Games in Mexico City. Each saluted with a raised black-gloved fist during the national anthem at their 200-meter-dash medals award ceremony. U.S. officials dismissed them from the team, and they became a disgrace to some and heroes to others. Their salute became iconic. They explained their gesture as a call for recognition of human rights. Others took it as a signal of "Black Power." And, indeed, the raised fist had become a symbol for pushing beyond civil rights to black self-determination. The slogan "Black Power" sounded in various voices that simultaneously attracted many blacks and alienated many whites.

Harlem's flamboyant Democrat U.S. Representative Adam Clayton Powell Jr. raised the phrase "Black Power" to popular notice in 1966. Addressing a Howard University audience that May, Powell declared that "Human rights are God-given. . . . To demand these God-given rights is to seek Black power" (Lincoln 1984, 107). SNCC made the phrase its own during its 1966 Mississippi Freedom Summer, and SNCC leader Stokely Carmichael became frequently pictured with the Black Power slogan and raised fist salute. Carmichael and black political scientist Charles V. Hamilton produced a notable 1967 book titled *Black Power: The Politics of Liberation America*.

Black Power increasingly became a rallying cry among younger blacks such as SNCC leader Stokely Carmichael, impatient with the pace of change to improve black lives even after the 1964 Civil Rights Act and the 1965 Voting Rights Act. (AP Photo)

Old guard black leaders tended to denounce the Black Power slogan. "It is absolutely necessary for the Negro to gain power, but the term Black power is unfortunate because it tends to give the impression of Black nationalism," the Reverend King explained cautiously. Black Republican Massachusetts U.S. Senator Edward Brooke worried that the "slogan has struck fear in the heart of Black America as well as in the heart of White America." Blacks could not go it alone, suggested practical politician Brooke. "The Negro has to gain allies—not adversaries," he explained. President Johnson himself rejected the slogan while continuing to press for civil rights. "We're not interested in Black power and we're not interested in White power, but we are interested in democratic power with a small d," Johnson said (Lincoln 1984, 107).

Black Power was, in fact, afoot politically. Gary, Indiana, Democrat Richard G. Hatcher and Cleveland, Ohio, Democrat Carl B. Stokes in 1967 became the first blacks elected mayor of any major U.S. city. Walter E. Washington had become mayor of the District of Columbia earlier in 1967, but he was appointed: when the post became elected in 1975, he would become Washington's first elected mayor. SNCC activists Julian Bond in

1967 won election in Atlanta to the Georgia House of Representatives. Longtime NAACP lead attorney Thurgood Marshall in 1967 became the first black to sit on the U.S. Supreme Court. Democrat Shirley Chisholm in 1968 became the first black woman elected to the U.S. Congress, representing a Brooklyn, New York, district; and as she took her seat in the 91st Congress (1969–1971) the number of blacks in the House doubled from 5 to 10. They would in 1983 again double, reaching 20; and in 1993 they would double yet again, reaching 40 (Manning and Shogan 2012, 2).

Others soon joined Hatcher and Stokes as black mayors. Howard Lee in 1969 became mayor of Chapel Hill, North Carolina, the first black mayor of a predominantly white city in the South. Kenneth Gibson in 1970 became mayor of Newark. Tom Bradley in Los Angeles, Clarence Lightner in Raleigh, North Carolina, and Coleman Young in Detroit became mayors in 1973. That same year Doris A. Davis in Compton, California, became the first black woman mayor of a U.S. metropolitan city. Maynard Jackson became mayor of Atlanta in 1974, succeeded in 1982 by Andrew Young. Dutch Morial became mayor of New Orleans in 1978. SNCC's first chairman Marion Barry became mayor of Washington, D.C., in 1980. Harold Washington became mayor of Chicago in 1983. David Dinkins would become mayor of New York City in 1990, and Willie Herenton in 1991 became mayor of Memphis. Black Power thus appeared as a real force in the nation's cities moving from the late 1960s into the 1990s.

Blacks rose also to significant ranks in the federal executive. FDR black unofficial cabinet member Robert C. Weaver in 1966 became the first black on a president's official cabinet, heading the Department of Housing and Urban Development (HUD). Also in 1966 Constance Baker Motley became the first black female federal judge, and Andrew Brimmer became the first black Federal Reserve Board governor. Barbara Watson in 1968 became U.S. assistant secretary of state. Dr. Louis Sullivan in 1975 became U.S. surgeon general. Patricia Roberts Harris in 1977 became the first black woman cabinet member, heading HUD, as Robert Weaver had.

Georgia Democrat President Jimmy Carter appointed Harris and several other notable blacks to posts in 1977: Andrew Young became U.S. ambassador to the United Nations and Wade McCree became U.S. solicitor general, following Thurgood Marshall who in 1965 had been the first black to hold the position. Eleanor Holmes Norton became chair of the U.S. Equal Opportunity Employment Commission, and Clifford Alexander became the first black secretary of the U.S. Army. Other notable black Carter appointees included Mary Frances Berry, assistant secretary for education and later a member and chair of the U.S. Commission on Civil Rights; Drew Days III, assistant U.S. attorney general for civil rights and later solicitor general; and Ernest Green, assistant secretary of labor.

Blacks became more prominent also in popular culture. Television showed more and more blacks, and not simply in the background. In *I Spy* comedian Bill Cosby in 1965 became the first black to star in a U.S. television series. Portraying a nurse rather than a stereotypic domestic, Diahann Carroll in 1968 became the first black woman to star in her own television series, *Julia.* Sammy Davis Jr. and Nancy Sinatra kissed on network television in 1967, and in 1968 black actress Nichelle Nichols shared a kiss with William Shatner on the *Star Trek* series, the first black–white kisses on U.S. television.

Movies such as *In the Heat of the Night* (1967) and *Guess Who's Coming to Dinner* (1967), both starring Sidney Poitier, presented blacks as forceful characters, as did *The Great White Hope* (1967), starring James Earl Jones as boxer Jack Johnson. Both *Guess Who's Coming to Dinner* and *The Great White Hope* also flew in the face of the hoary taboo of miscegenation, as they featured not only intimate relations between a black man and a white woman but their marriage. And national policy was not far behind screen fiction as the U.S. Supreme Court in 1967 decided *Loving v. Virginia,* finally and fully overturning *Plessy v. Ferguson* in declaring state laws banning racial intermarriage unconstitutional.

The black civil rights movement of the 1950s and 1960s had ignited a fresh phase of America's ongoing cultural war. From the earliest English colonization of North America, a racial struggle for dominance had ensued with Native American genocide and American Negro slavery. The American Civil War itself was a phase of the struggle to define America as a white man's land. The campaign of white redemption in the post–Civil War South extended the battle. White supremacist stepped up the battle in the face of the Black Power challenge and energized a reactionary movement they called American conservatism.

## PROFILE: SHIRLEY CHISHOLM (1924–2005)

Born in Brooklyn, New York, on November 30, 1924, and educated at its Girls' High School in Bedford-Stuyvesant, at Brooklyn College (BA 1946), where she won prizes for debate, and Teachers College at Columbia University (MA 1952), Shirley Anita St. Hill Chisholm won election as a Democrat from a Brooklyn district to the New York State Assembly beginning in 1965 and in 1968 won election from Brooklyn to the U.S. House of Representatives, becoming the first black congresswoman.

Chisholm proudly campaigned as "unbought and unbossed," and her political career demonstrated her independence and insistence on advancing public programs to reach people's needs. She helped expand the federal food stamp program, for example, as well as education and labor programs such as minimum wage and health care. A fierce advocate of women's rights, she hired only women for her congressional office staff and in 1971 became a founder of the National Women's Political Caucus. She was also in 1971 a founding member of the Congressional Black Caucus.

Chisholm in 1972 campaigned for the Democratic Party nomination for U.S. president, becoming the first black major-party presidential candidate. She followed Maine's Republican U.S. Senator Margaret Chase Smith as the second female major-party presidential candidate. Chisholm ran on an inclusive call for a "bloodless revolution" that turned away from the war in Vietnam and toward domestic development. She found many unwilling, however, to hear or see her as other than a black candidate or a woman candidate. She was simply stereotyped. Much of the public reduced her campaign to symbolic status rather than treating it substance. Yet her running marked a milestone in both African American and U.S. political development.

Personal tragedy and the nation's political shift moved Chisholm from office as she resigned her seat in 1982 to care for her husband who had been severely injured in an automobile accident. Also her faith in change drained with the rising conservative tide of Ronald Reagan's presidency and the ebbing tide of liberal agendas.

Chisholm returned to teaching, as Purington professor at Massachusetts's Mount Holyoke College and as a visiting scholar at Spelman College in Atlanta. Remaining politically active, she joined in 1990 in forming the African-American Women for Reproductive Freedom. She retired to Florida 1991 and was inducted that year into the National Women's Hall of Fame. Declining health continually curtailed her further activities. After a series of strokes she died on New Year's Day 2005 at age 80.

## REFERENCES

Carmichael, Stokely, and Charles V. Hamilton. 1967. *Black Power: The Politics of Liberation in America*. New York: Random House.

Chisholm, Shirley. 1970. *Unbought and Unbossed*. Boston, MA: Houghton Mifflin.

Davis, Thomas J. 2006. *Race Relations in America*. Westport, CT: Greenwood Press.

Dittmer, John. 1994. *Local People: The Struggle for Civil Rights in Mississippi*. Urbana: University of Illinois Press.

Epstein, Edward Jay. 1971. "The Black Panthers and the Police: A Pattern of Genocide?" *New Yorker*, February 13, 45–77.

Hine, Darlene Clark, William C. Hine, and Stanley Harrold. 2014. *African Americans: A Concise History*. Upper Saddle River, NJ: Pearson.

King, Martin Luther, Jr. 1963. *Letter from a Birmingham Jail*. Stanford University: The Martin Luther King Jr. Research and Education Institute. Accessed at https://kinginstitute.stanford.edu/king-papers/documents/letter-birmingham-jail.

King, Martin Luther, Jr., and Cornel West. 2014. *The Radical King.* Boston, MA: Beacon Press.

Kornweibel, Theodore. 1998. *Seeing Red: Federal Campaigns against Black Militancy, 1919–1925.* Bloomington: Indiana University Press.

Lincoln, C. Eric. 1984. *Race, Religion, and the Continuing American Dilemma.* New York: Hill and Wang.

Manning, Jennifer E., and Colleen J. Shogan. 2012. *African American Members of the United States Congress: 1870–2012.* Washington, DC: Congressional Research Service.

McAdam, Doug. 1988. *Freedom Summer.* New York: Oxford University Press.

McKelvey, Charles. 1994. *The African-American Movement: From Pan Africanism to the Rainbow Coalition.* New York: General Hall.

United States. 1968. *Report of the National Advisory Commission on Civil Disorders.* Washington, DC: GPO.

_____ *Chapter 17* _____

# Fight the Power

Translating legal decrees into everyday realities became primary challenges for blacks in what many came to call the post–civil rights era. What was on paper did not necessarily reflect what blacks lived. Changing their lived realities meant more than changing their legal status; it meant changing whites' lived realities, for it meant changing blacks and whites' daily and fundamental relations throughout America. Such change reached to public accommodations, residences, schools, and workplaces. More than access was at issue; acceptance and interaction were in question.

Truly desegregating America as implied in the civil rights successes of the 1950s and 1960s meant shifting basic social constructions of identity in America. It struck at long-held American beliefs and customs; indeed, it struck at many whites' self-identity, for many had come to see themselves, consciously or not, in contrast to blacks. They knew who they were and where they stood because they knew who blacks were and where they stood. Changing how whites saw and treated blacks meant changing how whites saw and treated themselves. For many whites such change meant surrendering what they had come to think of as their deserved rights, what blacks saw as white privilege that needed to be removed to eliminate systemic racism and reach a just and equitable society.

Even whites who considered themselves not unwilling to see blacks advance were not necessarily willing to see blacks advance at what they considered their own expense. And there lay the perennial rub. Changing blacks' status came at a cost. Who was to pay that cost was a point at issue, as illustrated as early as the American Revolution's First Emancipation that essentially shifted to blacks themselves the cost of releasing them from slavery. Bearing the cost of blacks' post–Civil War General Emancipation was a price imposed on the South for its insurrection. But white Southerners resisted paying the price of releasing blacks from slavery, fighting tooth and nail to preserve slavery in fact but not name.

Conservative southern whites and others persistently minimized the meaning of slavery from the Civil War onward. They declared slavery merely a property relation, not a system of social or racial relations. Once the law declared no property relation existed, slavery ended in their view. Nothing more needed to be done. Blacks were on their own to do whatever they could, the argument went. And so it was again when segregation was outlawed. Conservative southern whites and others argued that once segregation was outlawed, nothing more needed to be done. Blacks' prospects were their personal responsibility, not issues of public concern or properly a subject for public policy; and they were certainly not items for public monies or other support. Such arguments attached themselves to antiwelfare state, privatization, and small government ideologies.

Segregation had secured to whites unshared public benefits and exclusive control and use of public facilities. Directed to share such benefits, many preferred for government to provide no such benefits. They preferred privatization, restricting public goods across the board. Where once they had supported state and local recreation facilities such as golf courses, parks, beaches, and swimming pools, directed to share such public facilities with blacks, many whites preferred private facilities. Moreover, they no longer favored having such public facilities as they declined to pay for what they no longer exclusively used. They could keep private facilities segregated by choice, and price could impose sufficient segregation in public accommodations. They preferred paying for their own facilities, and they preferred that blacks pay for their own. To each their own extended segregation.

Blacks confronted shrinking public goods and services as whites withdrew in the face of desegregation. The challenge blacks faced appeared early in the aftermath of the U.S. District Court decision in *Law v. Baltimore* (1948). Whites in Maryland's premier city largely stopped attending public recreational facilities to which they had once flocked. White attendance at Baltimore public pools, for example, dropped by more than 47 percent a year after desegregation. The city closed some pools for lack of attendance, and at other sites white visits "dropped almost to the vanishing point," according to a 1960 report (Wells, Buckley, and Boone 2008, 167). Whites fled not only from public facilities but from the city itself, clearly unwilling to share space with blacks. Consistent with trends in other major cities, as blacks moved into Baltimore whites moved out. From 1950 to 2000 Baltimore's white population declined by 71.5 percent, falling from 723,655 to 205,982; at the same time the city's black population increased 86.1 percent, growing from 225,099 to 418,951 (ibid.).

Blacks' quest for quality public education perhaps suffered most in whites' reaction to desegregation. To great local consternation and protest *Morgan v. Hennigan* (1974) initiated court-ordered busing to desegregate public schools in Boston. The violent response displayed that antibusing sentiment in the 1960s and 1970s among whites outside the South ran no less deep than the Massive Resistance to desegregation of the 1950s and 1960s in the South. Whites' withdrawal from public schools fueled private school growth; and with their flight went public funding. An American Council on Education study described state school budget appropriations as "a race to the bottom" since the 1980s (Mortenson 2012, n.p.). The Center on Budget and Policy Priorities also reported long-term declines in per-pupil funding for kindergarten through 12th grade. At the same time, public monies for alternatives to traditional public schools increased through charter schools, voucher programs, and tax credits.

By most, if not all, measures blacks found U.S. public schools more segregated going into the 21st century than they had been before the 1954 *Brown v. Board of Education* decision. As before *Brown*, segregation reflected income as much as race, and that changed little after *Brown*. The antipoverty efforts of the 1960s made brief headway, but backlash stifled development. Indeed, backlash fought to a standstill most advances under programs many tagged as "affirmative action." The phrase became a rallying cry as opponents cast it as a preference program, and proponents cast it as an anti-preference program aimed to end traditional white privilege.

Blacks insisted that government and the society generally do more than simply say blacks were no longer being segregated or that they now had access to jobs, housing, or whatever. Blacks demanded results more than lip service. They wanted not merely to hear employers would hire blacks. They wanted to see employers actually hire blacks and advance them through the ranks of the workplace. In short, they wanted to avoid the situation blacks found themselves in at General Emancipation when they had been declared no longer slaves but left slavery with nothing of their own. The same had happened after the *Brown* decision when school systems such as that in Virginia's Prince Edward County closed public schools rather than desegregate them. From suffering in separate public schools, blacks went to suffering with no public schools.

The black push for positive results showed in the title of the 1963 March on Washington for Jobs and Freedom. The press for jobs demanded material progress. A. Philip Randolph strongly advocated having substantial, quantifiable outcomes. The 1941 March on Washington Movement had demonstrated the need for that. FDR's Executive Order 8802 announced antidiscrimination principles but produced relatively few jobs that market demands would not otherwise have opened. Again in 1953 President

Eisenhower's issue of Executive Order 10479 had provided for a watchdog committee to monitor federal contractors' equal employment opportunity practices, but that did relatively little to secure actual equal employment. President Kennedy's 1961 Executive Order 10925 first officially used the phrase *affirmative action* in directing federal contractors to ensure nondiscriminatory employment.

President Johnson's 1965 Executive Order 11246 required federal contractors receiving $50,000 or more or employing 51 or more employees "to take affirmative action to ensure" they did not discriminate in employment on the basis of race, color, religion, sex or national origin. That mandate fit with the 1964 Civil Rights Act prohibitions and the direction of the federal Equal Employment Opportunity Commission (EEOC). And under LBJ the Office of Federal Contract Compliance moved to establish goals and time-tables for black hiring, notably in what came to be called the Philadelphia Plan. President Richard Nixon's Department of Labor in 1969 implemented timetables in a Revised Philadelphia Plan, much to consternation and challenge from white trade unionists.

The Congressional Black Caucus (CBC) organized in 1971 from a 1969 Democratic Select Committee of 10 pushed in 1972 for more than declarations of principles. Boosted by the election of Barbara Jordan (D-TX) and Andrew Young (D-GA) in 1972 as the first blacks in Congress from the South since George White (R-NC) in 1898, the CBC called for a guaranteed annual income for federal welfare recipients, proportional black representation in federal appointments, and "redistribution of educational wealth and control" (Johnson 2007, 126).

The CBC 1972 "Black Declaration of Independence and the Black Bill of Rights" paled against the *Black Agenda* the National Black Political Convention issued from its March 1972 meeting in Gary, Indiana. Representing strong black nationalist elements, the Gary convention leaned toward creating a separate black political party to leverage black voting power into a force that produced material results for black people.

Congresswoman Shirley Chisholm (D-NY) took up the challenge of advancing the agenda for an equitable and inclusive nation by campaigning for the 1972 Democratic presidential nomination. The first black on the highest level of a national party stage, Chisholm explained the civil rights movement as not merely a black movement, but as one for principles of nondiscrimination and self-determination beyond race, gender, or class. Despite her message calling for real democracy in America, Chisholm could not escape being labeled *merely* a black candidate. Moreover, much of her message was washed away amid a wave of popular anxiety about black radicalism.

Sights and sounds of Black Power and Black Nationalism had captured much of America's popular imagination by the 1970s. Perhaps ironically the

Brooklyn-born Shirley Chisholm in 1968 became the first black woman elected to the U.S. Congress. She represented her native New York neighborhood, fusing her Caribbean ancestry with local community building that spread to her becoming, in 1972, the first major-party black candidate for the U.S. presidency. (Library of Congress)

public smear campaign against groups such as the Black Panthers and the Nation of Islam (NOI), vilified for black radicalism, heightened the public sense of the pervasiveness and power of such groups. In some circles black radicalism became chic. Also it drew a certain commercialism. Black Panther Party (BPP) leader Eldridge Cleaver's 1968 collection of essays published as *Soul on Ice* circulated as a best seller, describing his transformation from drug dealer to revolutionary. It evoked attention the 1964 *Autobiography of Malcolm X* had received. And, indeed, Cleaver held NOI minister Malcolm X as one of his heroes. Writings such as one-time SNCC member Julius Lester's 1968 *Look Out, Whitey! Black Power's Gon' Get Your Mama!* played up shock value in recollecting black resistance to oppression throughout American history. Intentionally inflammatory, Lester's book stoked fears among many with lines such as "It is clear that America must be destroyed."

Ex-convict Cleaver's and others' writings increased attention on blacks in prison. Along with the NOI, the BPP was, in fact, a leading force in the Black Power movement in U.S. prisons and portrayed many black convicts as political prisoners. The shockingly disproportionate rates of black male imprisonment showed the U.S. criminal justice system's traditional bias, which appeared only worsening as the 20th century lengthened. Black males were the face of U.S. prisoners, and their radicalization became more and more worrying for readers of works such as *Soledad Brother: The Prison Letters of George Jackson* (1970) and Jackson's posthumous *Blood in My Eye* (1972).

Murderous prison incidents intensified focus on blacks in prison. George Jackson was at the center of notable events in the early 1970s. His younger brother Jonathan's August 1970 attempt to free him and other prisoners at California's Marin County Courthouse resulted in a shootout that killed four persons, including the younger Jackson. His association with radical black Marxist UCLA professor Angela Yvonne Davis led to her being charged as an accomplice in the shootout. Her flight from arrest landed her on the FBI's Ten Most Wanted Fugitives List and set off a nationwide hunt for Davis, whom President Nixon branded as a "dangerous terrorist" (Carrier 2015, 39). She was acquitted of all charges in June 1972. But a San Quentin prison guard shot George Jackson dead in August 1971, triggering black inmate riots throughout the country. The worst occurred in September 1971 at New York's Attica Correctional Facility where more than 2,000 inmates seized control for four days. The brutal suppression of the riot left 43 persons dead.

Public focus on what was cast as black radicalism contributed to more conservative backlash that made many whites unwilling to hear what Shirley Chisholm was saying in her 1972 presidential campaign or to listen to blacks' calls for reform to establish justice and insure domestic tranquility. With the civil rights successes of the 1950s and 1960s in mind and with the rising appearance of prominent blacks in public media, many whites felt blacks had found sufficient place and space in American life and needed no more than they already had.

Blacks witnessed an almost palpable fatigue among many whites who wanted to hear no more black complaints. Continued black criticisms of the American system angered more than a few whites who considered blacks ungrateful for advantages and benefits of living in America. They resented blacks such as Muhammad Ali. Under his birth name Cassius Clay, he had upset Sonny Liston in 1964 to become world heavyweight boxing champion, before announcing his new name and faith in the NOI. Ali set off a furor in 1967 by refusing for religious reasons to be drafted into the U.S. armed forces as the war in Vietnam escalated.

Being ungrateful was an old charge against blacks. It rejected basic claims of civil equality and suggested, instead, that blacks compare their lot not to their fellow Americans but to peoples outside America, specifically to other blacks or Third World peoples. The notion extended the theme that blacks should have been grateful for slavery's dragging them from Africa's darkness to America's progress.

But it was not as if African Americans recognized no advances. Significant strides had been made as blacks reached positions never before touched. The black presence in professional and collegiate sports, for example, was growing more and more. Arthur Ashe in 1968 had won the U.S. Open men's singles tennis title, joining Althea Gibson's 1957 feat on the women's side as the first black champions. Boston Celtics 11-time NBA champion Bill Russell in 1975 became the first black player inducted into the Basketball Hall of Fame. Also in 1975 Lee Elder became the first black to play in The Masters golf championship.

And outside sports blacks were appearing more prized than ever. *Ebony* magazine's Moneta Sleet Jr. in 1969 won the Pulitzer Prize in photography. Black model Beverly Johnson in 1971 graced the cover of *Glamour* magazine, signaling a shift in accepting black beauty amid traditional white standards, leading in 1984 to Vanessa Williams becoming the first black "Miss America." Cicely Tyson won a Primetime Emmy as outstanding lead actress in the 1974 miniseries *The Autobiography of Miss Jane Pittman*. Also in the world of academics, blacks were receiving recognition as programs in African and African American studies were spreading across college campuses, stimulated by a 1969 Ford Foundation million-dollar curriculum development grant and Harvard University's boosting the stature of the field by initiating an Afro-American studies program.

U.S. popular culture resonated with black music. Black performers such as guitarist Jimi Hendrix were headliners. The rhythm and blues pumped out by Berry Gordy Motown Records in Detroit, Stax Records in Memphis, and Atlantic Records in New York City covered America with "soul" music. Moving from the late 1950s and running to the 1970s America echoed with black voices such as Brook Benton, James Brown, Sam Cooke, Roberta Flack, Aretha Franklin, Marvin Gaye, Isaac Hayes, Curtis Mayfield, Otis Redding, Diana Ross, Nina Simone, Carla Thomas, Rufus Thomas, and Stevie Wonder. Groups such as Booker T. & the MGs, Earth, Wind & Fire, Gladys Knight & the Pips, the Jackson Five, Sly and the Family Stone, Smokey Robinson & the Miracles, the Staples Singers, and the Temptations serenaded America.

The Black Arts Movement—also called the Black Aesthetic Movement, both abbreviated BAM—accompanied the surging black presence in popular culture. A fresh generation joined with continuing practitioners from the New Negro Renaissance and postwar eras. They struggled to reach the very soul of America, presenting themselves as true voices and visions of the nation's character and culture. Prize-winning author Margaret Walker described blacks as the creators of a new paradigm showing America the way "forward into a new and humanistic age." African Americans provided exceptional contributions to the nation and the world, Walker said. "Our Black culture is aware of human needs and human values," she explained. "It is not only that we are singers and dancers, poets and prophets, great athletes and perceptive politicians—but we are also a body of charismatic and numinous people," she insisted (Walker 1981, 70).

A spirit pressing forward their essential humanity in protest and prophecy had ever appeared among blacks' work in print and in the visual arts, no less than in music. Pianist and singer Nina Simone's 1964 composition and performance of her song "Mississippi Goddam," with its cry "just give me my equality!" echoed vibrations of black artists long before and long after. The dynamic featured in jazz and blues, gospel and soul music, in the choreography and performance of Katherine Dunham, "Queen Mother of Black dance," and on stage and screen with Paul Robeson, Canada Lee, Ossie Davis, Ruby Dee, and other black actors. It was in James Baldwin's essays and novels, in Elizabeth Catlett's prints and sculptures, on the canvases of Charles White, Vincent Smith, and Jacob Lawrence.

LeRoi Jones and others in the 1960s accelerated the tempo and radicalized the tenor of black arts. Jones's 1963 book *Blues People: Negro Music and White America* and his 1969 *Black Magic Poetry* anticipated and joined the Black Power movement in calling for Afrocentric artistic production. Jones's 1965 poem "Black Art" became BAM's manifesto. Renaming himself Imamu Amiri Baraka, his plays and poetry advanced revolutionary elements joined by many, including black nationalist and secular humanist Maulana Karenga, creator of *Kwanzaa*. Such efforts defined BAM as a long step toward African American cultural sovereignty.

BAM inspired inward-focused writing among blacks and also among other peoples of color, particularly Latinos and Asians. Rosa Guy, Hoyt Fuller, Maya Angelou, Sonia Sanchez, Nikki Giovanni, Toni Cade Bambara, Alice Walker, August Wilson, and Ntozake Shange explored and expanded understanding of the social realities of race, sex, poverty, and class. They empowered blacks and fed whites both fascinated by and fearful of glimpses into black life. Sometimes overtly political but always socially engaged, the work of such writers also received acclaim. Toni Cade Bambara's novel *The Salt Eaters* won the 1980 American Book Award. Alice Walker's epistolary novel *The Color Purple* won the 1983 Pulitzer Prize for fiction. August Wilson's play *Fences* won the 1987 Pulitzer Prize for drama and he repeated in 1990 for his play *The Piano Lesson*. And in 1993 Toni Morrison became the first African American to win a Nobel Prize in literature.

Blacks' rising public stature produced notable white backlash as it had in Reconstruction and other eras of notable advance. Richard Nixon's presidency (1969–1974) signaled a conservative ascendancy. Interrupted by his fall from the Watergate scandal, a rising call for "law and order" recoiled against black marches and riots. The ascendancy reigned in Ronald Reagan's presidency (1981–1989), which in many ways not only capped but reversed black gains, retrenching civil rights successes. Reagan's minions worked, for example, to discredit affirmative action as reverse racism. Reaching back to post-Reconstruction days, their rhetoric echoed Supreme Court Justice Joseph P. Bradley's put down in the 1883 *Civil Rights Cases*, accusing blacks of wanting to be "the special favorites of the law" and of "running the slavery argument into the ground."

Blacks progressively groaned as the U.S. Supreme Court under 1969 Nixon appointee Chief Justice Warren Burger retreated incrementally on advances under the Warren Court. Equal employment opportunity advocates welcomed the Burger Court's 1971 decision in *Griggs v. Duke Power Co.*, outlawing discriminatory job tests. But that decision opened argument about the legal standard for proving discrimination: was impact or intent sufficient to establish a violation of the 1964 Civil Rights Act or constitutional equal protection? Was it enough to show a far greater proportion of blacks than whites suffered from a job test, for example? Or was it necessary to show that the job test intended to discriminate against blacks? Conservative whites insisted on discriminatory intent. Blacks and equal opportunity employment advocates insisted on disproportionate or disparate impact.

In pressing to see actual results in increased numbers of blacks hired and promoted, blacks found themselves increasingly stymied as the Supreme Court shifted to its more traditional position as barrier rather than benefactor in blacks' struggle to advance to equality. The primary sites of conflict were the usual—jobs, schools, and public funding. Through much of the 1970s federal courts accepted affirmative action arguments to allow and in some cases order programs that showed actual increases in black hiring, placement, and promotion. Into the 1980s, however, federal courts necessarily followed the Supreme Court in declining to accept arguments of systemic racial discrimination against blacks as justification for affirmative action.

As so much of their lives rested on the economic foundation their workplaces provided or proscribed, blacks persisted in their protest against job discrimination. When they were not simply excluded from jobs, they suffered from being underemployed and trapped in the last-hired-first-fired syndrome. To overcome such conditions required workplace changes that whites immediately argued illegally disadvantaged them on the basis of their race. Thus, the meaning and application of the antidiscrimination principles in the 1964 Civil Rights Act and in the Fourteenth Amendment's Equal Protection Clause became contested terrain in the 1970s and 1980s.

*United Steelworkers v. Weber* in 1979 illustrated issues arising when a private employer such as Kaiser Aluminum and Chemical Corporation and its principal union admitted past patterns and practices of discriminating against blacks and in their collective bargaining agreement (CBA) provided for training programs in which blacks and whites would be admitted on a one-to-one basis. As there were more whites than blacks in the pool, whites had lower chances than blacks of being accepted into the CBA program. Not having an equal chance was unfair, claimed Brian Weber, a white who sued when he was not admitted to the training program, asserting his rejection was based on race in violation of the 1964 Civil Rights Act.

The Supreme Court in *Weber* sanctioned the CBA program as legitimate to rectify black underrepresentation, but Chief Justice Burger and Justice William Rehnquist vigorously dissented. *Quotas* and *qualifications* became watchwords in the public debate that ensued, as did *merit*. Critics argued that counting-by-race remedies violated principles dictating that positions be awarded by accomplishment, regardless of race. Rehnquist held firmly to that position, arguing in *Local 93 of the International Association of Firefighters v. City of Cleveland* (1986) that affirmative action programs impermissibly allowed for "leapfrogging minorities over senior and better qualified Whites." Rehnquist lost the argument in *Cleveland*, but he had prevailed in two earlier cases pitting seniority against affirmative action. In *Memphis Firefighters v. Stotts* (1984) and *Wygant v. Jackson Board of Education* (1986), the Court disapproved plans that sought to adjust last-hired-first-fired principles that grandfathered whites in the face of layoffs, ruling in essence to uphold seniority systems despite their perpetuating blacks' historical disadvantages.

Another line of cases traced affirmative action challenges in the area of government funding called "set-asides." Seeking to ensure that blacks and other minorities received a share of public contracting monies, selectively federal, state, and local governments provided for direct contract awards to minority-owned business. *Fullilove v. Klutznick* (1979) upheld as a legitimate exercise of Congress's spending powers 1977 federal appropriation provisions that directed 10 percent of public works program funding to minority businesses. But that proved a high point for blacks and other minorities on that track as the Court shifted personnel and position, narrowing what governments could lawfully do in directing public monies.

In *Richmond v. J. A. Croson* (1989), the Court required any state funding using suspect classifications such as race to show that such means were substantially related to serving an important state interest. The next year, the Court in *Metro Broadcasting v. FCC* (1990) held federal funding to the same heightened scrutiny. In *Adarand Constructors, Inc. v. Peña* (1995) the Court in essence disallowed minority set-asides, holding all government spending to the same standard of strict scrutiny that required narrow tailoring of the least restrictive means to reach a compelling governmental interest. Writing for the majority Justice Sandra Day O'Connor insisted, as she had in an earlier case, that "it is not true that strict scrutiny is 'strict in theory, but fatal in fact.'" Affirmative action proponents in the area, however, correctly saw *Adarand* as the end of the line as Justice Thurgood Marshall had predicted before retiring from the Court in October 1991.

Affirmative action in public education provoked even more argument than the workplace and public funding. For generations race had been used to exclude blacks from public higher education and to trap them in inferior elementary and primary schools. The degree to which race might be used to afford blacks access where they had earlier been excluded became much contested. That showed early in federal court–ordered busing cases following the unanimous 1971 decision in *Swann v. Charlotte-Mecklenburg Board of Education* upholding busing as a constitutional tool to remedy segregation. Ordering busing outside the South as the Court did in Detroit and its suburbs in *Milliken v. Bradley* (1974) and as the district court did in Boston and its suburbs in *Morgan v. Hennigan* (1974) produced further furor.

Public higher education took the fore in 1976 with *Regents of University of California v. Bakke*, which in essence disallowed a set-aside program for minority admission to the UC Davis School of Medicine, yet allowed race to be considered as an element of "diversity" in public higher education admission processes. The diversity rationale settled little. Arguments only intensified about qualifications, standards, and merit. Blacks became tainted in higher education, as they were in workplaces, with suspicions that they were not "truly qualified" for the spots they occupied and that their presence was denying their spots to "truly deserving" whites.

Two notable cases at the University Michigan (UM) carried the higher education affirmative action arguments into the 21st century. *Gratz v. Bollinger* and *Grutter v. Bollinger* decided on the same day in 2003 provided no clarity on the role race might play in admissions policies. In *Gratz* the Court struck down the UM undergraduate admission policy that awarded points to applicants because they were blacks or other racial minorities. Yet in *Grutter* the Court upheld the UM law school admission policy that gave special consideration to blacks and other racial minorities. The Court continued without clear direction in the ongoing arguments in *Fisher v. Texas*, which started in 2008 and extended into 2016 in considering the University of Texas at Austin's using race as one of various factors in its undergraduate admission process.

For many blacks affirmative action issues concerned their systemic lack of equal access to social benefits. In a world of finite and fixed resources, however, increased black access almost necessarily meant decreased white access that simply colored such change as unpopular. Political pushback responded with state campaigns to outlaw affirmative action. Black University of California regent (1993–2005) Ward Connerly rose as an anti-affirmative action champion in heading a state ballot campaign titled the "California Civil Rights Initiative" (CCRI) that voters passed in 1996, with Proposition 209 to prohibit the state from recognizing race, sex, or ethnicity in deciding public employment, public contracting, and public education. Similar campaigns rolled across the nation. In 2006 Michigan voters amended their state's constitution to prohibit its discrimination or preference based on race, sex, color, ethnicity, or national origin in public contracting, employment, and education. A U.S. Supreme Court plurality in *Schuette v. Coalition to Defend Affirmative Action* (2014) upheld the affirmative action ban as constitutionally permissible.

The appearance of blacks such as Ward Connerly in the vanguard of opposition against affirmative action reflected significant differences among blacks. Such differences were not new. Indeed, they reached back to antebellum and postbellum arguments about colonization or disagreements such as those among Booker T. Washington, W.E.B. Du Bois, and Marcus Garvey. From the 1970s forward diverging black opinions often focused on a group called "Black conservatives" and considered as dissidents from the black majority. Political economist and social theorist Thomas Sowell led such conservatives whom the Republican Party embraced. President Reagan appointed black conservative Clarence Pendleton in 1981 to head the U.S. Commission on Civil Rights.

Other black conservatives such as economist Walter E. Williams and political sociologist Shelby Steele advanced an agenda in writings promoting free-market principles stressing personal responsibility for a person's lot in life in line with a framework Sowell outlined. Considering himself more a libertarian than a conservative, Sowell dismissed the efficacy of government policies or programs to uplift blacks and instead emphasized individual initiative and voluntary association as true means for black improvement. Stressing individualism, Sowell and other black conservatives scoffed at what they considered continued black group-think that shackled them to race-based programs.

Black Republicans enjoyed a resurgence with the Conservative ascendancy. Edward Brooke's election in 1966 as U.S. senator from Massachusetts brought fresh notice, but it was in the Reagan presidency that black conservatives rose to national prominence. General Colin Powell in 1987 became national security advisor. Other black Reagan appointees included Clarence Thomas at the EEOC, Alan Keyes at the State Department, Louis Wade Sullivan at Health and Human Services, Condoleezza Rice at the National Security Council, and Constance Berry Newman at the Office of

Personnel Management. President George H. W. Bush continued the parade in 1991, appointing Clarence Thomas to the U.S. Supreme Court. President George W. Bush made further elevations in 2001, appointing Colin Powell secretary of state and Condoleezza Rice national security advisor and later secretary of state.

Blacks became notable figures in Republican circles moving into the 21st century. Several rose to run for the Republican Party presidential nomination. Alan Keyes entered the 1996, 2000, and 2008 races. Businessman Herman Cain entered the 2012 race, as a Tea Party favorite. Pediatric neurosurgeon Ben Carson ran for the 2016 presidential nomination. And blacks were prominent also in the party apparatus, illustrated by former Maryland lieutenant governor Michael Steele in 2009 becoming the first black to chair the Republican National Committee. Tea Party favorite Tim Scott (R-SC) won a special election in 2014 to the U.S. Senate after being appointed to an unexpired term in 2013. Also Utah's Mia Love in 2014 became the first black woman elected to the U.S. Congress as a Republican.

Moving from the 20th to the 21st century for African Americans was about more than a divide over political party affiliation. It was about the cyclical ennui that appeared to envelop white America when blacks appeared

Among growing mass protests of persisting injustices, Rev. Al Sharpton and Rev. Jesse Jackson join in the outpouring at the August 2014 funeral of 18-year-old Michael Brown, killed by police in Ferguson, Missouri. (Scott Olson/Getty Images)

too prominent. Much white headshaking accompanied the so-called Rodney King riots in Los Angeles in 1992, for example. Negative views persisted with the media spectacle of former NFL-star running back O.J. Simpson's 1994 trial for double homicide or even the 1995 Million Man March NOI minister Louis Farrakhan led in Washington, D.C. The cycle of negative black stereotyping seemed to have returned to popularity.

More and more deaf ears appeared as blacks continued to rail for remedies of social ills. Rev. Jesse Jackson, Al Sharpton, and other blacks became almost constant media fixtures protesting incidents of injustice, but an increasing number of whites took such complaints and criticisms as continual whining. Blacks in their view stood as persistent naysayers and ne'er-do-wells blaming society for their own faults. Richard Herrnstein and Charles Murray's 1994 book *The Bell Curve: Intelligence and Class Structure in American Life* captured a prevalent antiblack mood in reverting to old Social Darwinism's survival of the fittest theory in submitting that blacks' plight and position resulted from their own nature and nurture. Like others in American society, blacks were where their abilities, ambitions, and aptitudes fit them, Herrnstein and Murray asserted.

## PROFILE: JESSE JACKSON (1941–)

The son born Jesse Louis Burns on October 8, 1941, in Greenville, South Carolina, took the surname of his adoptive father Charles Jackson and rose from being a student activist at North Carolina Agricultural and Technical College in Greensboro, North Carolina, where he became a protégé of the college president, Rev. Dr. Samuel DeWitt Proctor, to being the most recognized face of black civil rights in the 1970s and 1980s.

Jackson was in the forefront of 1962 A&T sit-in demonstrators in Greensboro and joined in the 1965 Selma-to-Montgomery March for voting rights. He left the Chicago Theological Seminary in 1966 to engage full-time in civil rights activism as a lieutenant of Rev. Dr. Martin Luther King Jr. in the Southern Christian Leadership Conference (SCLC). He headed the SCLC's Operation Breadbasket, expanding its reach through consumer boycotts to gain blacks jobs and market share. Ordained a Baptist minister in 1968, he carried on SCLC's Poor People's Crusade in Washington, D.C., in the wake of the Reverend King's assassination in April 1968. Many touted him as MLK's eventual successor.

Jackson made impressive inroads in Chicago, establishing a future base for himself on the South Side. His removing Operation Breadbasket's headquarters from Atlanta to Chicago and his October 1971 Black Expo in Chicago cemented his base there. His success also opened rifts in the SCLC, and in December 1971 he withdrew to form Operation PUSH. Initially the acronym stood for People United to *Save* Humanity but changed to People United to *Serve* Humanity. It aimed to galvanize political pressure to change economic and social conditions for blacks and others dispossessed.

Organizing what he dubbed the "Rainbow Coalition" in 1984, Jackson launched a campaign for the Democratic Party's presidential nomination, following in the footsteps of Shirley Chisholm's 1972 run. He proved more successful than she, winning primaries in five states. He ran again in 1988, garnering more than 7 million votes in the primaries. International activism added to his public attention as he undertook private rescue missions to Syria in 1983 and Cuba in 1984.

After his presidential runs, popular attention often focused on Jackson as a voice of black interests and of humanitarian concerns. He won the District of Columbia symbolic post of shadow senator in 1991, but did not run for reelection in 1996. Throughout the 1990s and into the 2000s, he undertook trips abroad to ease tensions or extract hostages, as he did in going to Iraq in 1991 and Kosovo in 1999. He became something of an elder statesman and political power broker, recognized for his legacy of contributions.

## REFERENCES

Carrier, Jerry. 2015. *Hard Right Turn: Assassination of the American Left—A History*. New York: Algora Publishing.

Johnson, Cedric. 2007. *Revolutionaries to Race Leaders: Black Power and the Making of African American Politics*. Minneapolis: University of Minnesota Press.

Mortenson, Thomas G. 2012. *State Funding: A Race to the Bottom*. Washington, DC: American Council on Education. Accessed at http://www.acenet.edu/the-presidency/columns-and-features/Pages/state-funding-a-race-to-the-bottom.aspx.

Walker, Margaret. 1981. "Black Culture." In *On Being Female, Black, and Free: Essays by Margaret Walker, 1932–1992*, ed. Maryemma Graham. Knoxville: University of Tennessee Press, 1997.

Wells, James E., Geoffrey L. Buckley, and Christopher G. Boone. 2008. "Separate but Equal? Desegregating Baltimore's Golf Courses." *Geographical Review* 98, no. 2 (April): 151–170.

_____ *Chapter 18* _____

# Challenges, Dreams, and Hopes

Rev. Martin Luther King Jr. in 1967 asked, "Where do we go from here?" It was an old question for blacks. Yet it was no less relevant entering the 21st century. Blacks had come a long way since Africans entered American shores in slavery. Those with forebears from slavery times had trod a stony road. Later arrivals brought different experiences and perspectives. Through it all, much individual black success permeated America as the 2000s began, but what that meant for the bulk of blacks and their place and prospects remained in question.

Black stars glittered throughout popular culture in the early 2000s. The chanted and spoken rhymes of rap had taken over from the spoken word poetry of early geniuses such as reputed "Godfather of Rap" Gil Scott-Heron and blended into hip-hop to rise from subculture to a genre of American music with global penetration, making millionaires of boys from the block or out of the 'hood and making legends of Tupac Shakur, Dr. Dre, Snoop Dogg, and others. Ice-T, LL Cool J, and Ice Cube became household names in suburbs as well as inner cities. So did Queen Latifah, Janet Jackson, and Nicki Minaj. Will Smith and Diddy translated their rap and hip-hop hits into broader careers and business success, as did Russell Simmons, cofounder of hip-hop label Def Jam Recordings, and producer Nile Gregory Rodgers. Rapper Jay-Z built a business empire with his success. A performer and personality beyond category with his singing, songwriting, multi-instrumentalism, and record-producing, the artist known as Prince set the edge of extravagant and innovative flamboyance that made him an image leader. And with his singing, dancing, innovative fashions, and extravagant stage productions, Michael Jackson entered the 21st century as a global figure some hailed as "the King of Pop"; in many minds he was clearly the biggest pop star of the 20th century.

Blacks stood among major sports icons from Muhammad Ali in boxing to Jackie Robinson, Hank Aaron, and Willie Mays in baseball to Carl Lewis, Florence Griffith Joyner, and Jackie Joyner-Kersee in track and field to Arthur Ashe and Althea Gibson in tennis to Bill Russell, Oscar Robertson, and Wilt Chamberlain in basketball. Charlie Sifford had been inducted into the World Golf Hall of Fame. Tiger Woods had followed to take the pro golf world by storm. Serena and Venus Williams were dominating women's pro tennis. Magic Johnson and Michael Jordan had transcended basketball to become not only sports icons but also business moguls.

The *Bill Cosby Show* had broadcast blacks as a model American family in the Huxtables with a physician father, lawyer mother, and overachieving children. Oprah Winfrey was dominating television and moving beyond talk show host to become a media proprietor, producer, and social trendsetter, as illustrated in the influence of her book club. Denzel Washington and Halle Berry were winning best actor Oscar awards. They followed in the footsteps of black pioneers such as Butterfly McQueen, Lena Horne, Ethel Waters, Dorothy Dandridge, Canada Lee, Sidney Poitier, and Harry Belafonte. And into the narrow window Hollywood allowed black stars, notable figures crossed into the 21st century. Among them were Louis Gossett Jr., Morgan Freeman, Phylicia Rashad, Samuel L. Jackson, Alfre Woodard, Whoopi Goldberg, S. Epatha Merkerson, Debbi Morgan, Angela Bassett, Forest Whitaker, Laurence Fishburne, Wesley Snipes, Viola Davis, Regina King, and Kerry Washington.

And in 2008 an earlier almost unthinkable success occurred as African American Barack Hussein Obama won election as president of the United States. With his inauguration talk proliferated that blacks had entered a new day and new place that some called a "post-racial" society. The theme extended anti-affirmative action rhetoric to insist that if a black person could rise to the highest political office in the land, then no barriers to black achievement continued to exist. The old obstacles had finally been overcome, declared post-racial society advocates who pointed also to the host of black stars across the nation as shining examples of access, achievement, and opportunity. Blacks could do whatever their individual determination and talents allowed, like any others in America, such advocates insisted. Choices of personal responsibility alone were all blacks faced in their efforts to secure and improve their lives, as historical racism had receded to being a relic of some distant past, post-racial advocates proclaimed.

Individual black successes, especially being elected U.S. president, hardly reflected the daily realities most blacks lived entering the 21st century. Racial disparities remained stark as gaps between blacks and whites not only persisted but were widening in crucial areas such as education, employment, health, housing, income, and wealth. PEW Research Center studies showed the black–white gap in median household income of a family of three as $19,360 in 1969 but growing to $27,414 by 2011. At the same time the black–white gap in median household wealth for such families grew from $75,224 to $84,960. And the recession of 2007–2008 took a bigger bite out of black median household net worth, as blacks' dropped 53 percent in contrast to 16 percent for whites. In 2013 the median net worth of white households was 13 times greater than that of black households. For some such gaps represented progress because it was less than in 1989, when the black–white gap had peaked 17 times (Kochhar and Fry 2014, n.p.).

The 2007–2008 recession magnified historical patterns of disinvestment in black households, resulting from their being funneled into residential areas with declining values. Collapsing real estate prices in places such as the St. Albans in Queens, New York, or Detroit or Baltimore illustrated the pattern. While whites traditionally enjoyed significant appreciation in the common American family's largest investment—their home, blacks tended to suffer significant depreciation (Pietila 2010, 47–60). The firm economic footing blacks had long prayed and worked for appeared no closer in the 2000s than it had generations before.

The dream of a better life for his children that Martin Luther King Jr. expressed at the 1963 March on Washington and that of generations of black parents before and since appeared more and more dim moving into the 2000s. Intergenerational upward mobility was not the constant among blacks that it was for many whites in America. The much-touted American dream envisioned rising from crude beginnings to at least middle-class comfort, but realizing such a transition appeared increasingly rare for blacks in the early 21st century.

The 1950s and 1960s civil rights successes had made a difference for blacks. Their median family incomes had risen, but not to the same degree or at the same rates as for whites. More important, blacks realized less passing on of success from parents to children to build intergenerational progress, moving from the late 1960s into the early 2000s. U.S. Census data on income and other economic indices revealed that since the 1960s white children had tended to exceed their parents in income, but almost half (45%) of black children born in solidly middle-class families fell below their parents in economic status and income, while the rate for whites in the same cohort was 16 percent (Isaacs 2011, 1).

Blacks' overall economic position had stagnated at best entering the 21st century. Moreover, cohorts of blacks suffered significant slippage. Perennially endangered black males, particularly thirtysomethings, suffered actual income declines. That connected also to widening black–white incarceration rates as the United States more and more became a carceral state with expanding prison populations. At the end of 2011 federal, state, and local prisons and jails held 2.2 million incarcerated, and African American males headed all prisoners. The U.S. Justice Department reported in 2014 that black males were at least one in three of all persons in the nation's jails or prisons. Moreover, a 2013 report to the United Nations Human Rights Committee projected that "one in every three Black American males born today can expect to go to prison in his lifetime" (The Sentencing Project 2013, 1).

Already in 2000 the Justice Department noted that U.S. prisons held more black men (791,600) than were enrolled (603,032) in U.S. colleges. To some such statistics perpetuated a myth. But even given discrepancies in the data and manipulation of counts, that the numbers were anywhere comparable indicated black male incarceration persisted as a real and profound problem. In his 2008 presidential campaign, then Senator Obama (D-IL) called attention to the issue. "We have more work to do when more young Black men languish in prison than attend colleges and universities," he said (Bouie 2013, n.p.).

Mass incarceration of black men represented for some a renewed segregation and suppression strategy to systematically assert the comprehensive social control over blacks that had existed in slavery and its aftermath. The racial complexion of America's prison population demonstrated beyond doubt that race was not only alive but exercising brutal power over black lives. It offered a poster image to belie the rhetoric of 21st-century America being or becoming a post-racial society. Further, rising incarceration rates reached beyond prison walls to disrupt and disfigure black life on the outside, reducing the number of black voters, blacks' income, consumption, and cohesion by depriving black communities of members and black families of fathers and sons and brothers, of wage earners and helpmates.

The constants of prison and poverty joined with ever-present health problems for blacks as a whole. From birth to death, African Americans continued to trail other Americans in measures of health. Entering the 21st century black infant mortality rates were 2½ times those of white newborns. And black life expectancy trailed that of whites and other Americans. Yet some gains showed as African American life expectancy grew from 71.7 years in 2000 to 75.1 years by 2010, as white life expectancy rose from 77.4 to 79.0 years. Yet the distinct dangers of black life showed in unintentional accidents and homicide ranking as the fifth and sixth leading causes of death among blacks at the beginning of the century. Blacks struggled also with HIV/AIDS as the seventh leading cause of death overall, but as the leading cause of death for black men aged 35 to 44 (NetWellness 2016, n.p.).

The state of black health embodied choices and conditions of the 37 million self-identified blacks in the United States in 2010 census statistics. Limited access to health care had long been a chronic problem among blacks and other impoverished Americans. The federal Affordable Healthcare Act (ACA) of 2010, often called ObamaCare, significantly improved blacks' access to medical services as it reached out to the more than one in five blacks who had no health insurance in 2010–2011. Low income was a primary cause of blacks being uninsured, but the ACA's expansion of Medicaid promised to reach at least 9 in 10 of low-income uninsured blacks. Nevertheless, blacks would remain significantly more likely to be uninsured than whites, and the quality of their health care was not assured (Duckett and Artiga 2013, n.p.).

The black–white divide in health care and in many other areas reflected a persistent residential divide. Blacks and whites for the most part tended not to occupy the same residential space. That was true not only in neighborhoods but also in a broader national sense. Since the development of American Negro slavery, whites and blacks tended to concentrate in different places. Where whites were most numerous, blacks were least numerous; in contrast, where blacks were most numerous, whites were least numerous. During the antebellum period, for example, as the number of blacks increased in the slave states, the relative proportion of whites decreased. In 1820, for instance, the South had 36.8 percent of whites in the U.S. population. By 1860, it had fallen to 30.0 percent, as 94.9 percent of all blacks lived in the South.

The Great Migration redistributed the black population during the first half of the 1900s, but after 1970 another redistribution developed. In 2010 more than half of all blacks in the United States lived in eight states—Delaware, Maryland, North Carolina, South Carolina, Georgia, Alabama, Mississippi, and Louisiana—and District of Columbia, all of which had maintained slavery in 1860. Those were the only places in the United States where blacks constituted more than 20 percent of the total population. In 18 states blacks ranged from 6 to 20 percent. In 12 states blacks ranged between 2 and 6 percent; and in 11 states they were less than 2 percent of the total population. The distribution perpetuated much of the North–South divide, but also an East–West divide. Of the 11 states where blacks were less than 2 percent of the population, 8 were in the West. Nevada alone in the West had a black population greater than 6 percent (Duckett and Artiga 2013, n.p.).

Not only geographic distribution marked the position of African Americans at the start of the 21st century. The black population stood out also as notably younger than the white population. About 4 in 10 blacks in 2010 were under the age of 26 years; for whites the number was 3 in 10. And while 1 in 10 blacks were over the age of 65, almost 2 in 10 whites were over age 65 (Duckett and Artiga 2013, n.p.). Being younger translated into less time to accumulate wealth and also less time to rise in income on the occupational ladder. Thus, the age distribution influenced income and wealth. Also it emphasized the continuing importance of education for blacks at a time when the proportion of whites in public education continued to decline.

Wide gaps in black–white educational attainment persisted, carrying forward legacies of racial segregation. Across the range of school levels, blacks significantly trailed whites in 2013 data, sometimes at rates of two to one. For example, 16 percent of blacks had no high school diploma in 2013, in contrast to 8 percent of whites. At the college level, while 21 percent of whites had bachelor's degrees, only 13 percent of blacks did; 12 percent of whites had advanced degrees, but only 6 percent of blacks did. Such attainments trickled down from parents to children as household literacy has had a demonstrable effect on early childhood development and educational attainment. Being read to, told stories, and taught the alphabet, and arts and crafts at home, for example, significantly advances child learning proficiency. Hearing stories builds vocabulary and imagination. Early counting also builds skills with numbers, and matching colors and shapes adds to dimensional skills. Parents with less education tend to have less access to materials for their children, and because they also tend to have more consuming working obligations, they have less time for their children (Cook 2015, n.p.).

So even before formal schooling has begun, black children have tended to find themselves in a hole when compared to their white counterparts. And while in school, the hole has tended to widen and deepen. The black–white gap in National Assessment of Educational Progress (NAEP) eighth-grade reading scores in 2013 was 26 points (276 – 250), for instance. Black scores had risen from 236 in 1994, when white scores were 267. So improvements were afoot, as scores overall were rising. Yet the gap remained notable and disheartening for blacks (NAEP 2015, n.p.).

Moreover, black students were more likely to be held back in school, on average at a rate three times higher than their white peers, leading them to be more likely to drop out before finishing high school, which also tended to make them more likely to be cited for juvenile delinquency. And for black students who made it past high school, they tended to experience lower four-year-college graduation rates than whites (Cook 2015, n.p.). Such inequities in the educational landscape continued to feed enduring negative images of blacks in popular culture.

Visual media especially has continued to feed the American public a steady diet of images of black males as dangerous ne'er-do-wells. So-called reality television, talk shows, regular programming—whether comedic or drama series or news—music videos, and film have continued to portray black males as less than hard-working, sensible, regular, responsible folk. Rather their projected image most typically has appeared as irresponsible or, at worst, as immoral and violently criminal. Black male drug dealers or gangsta thugs have persisted as prevalent characters. Accompanying them have been the office or unit token or the comic relief sidekick. Black males can appear as great athletes but by natural ability, not by dint or disciplined work ethic, prevailing through athleticism, not intelligence. Black men can make appearances as absentee fathers but seldom as steady role models.

Black men have rarely appeared as heroes. At best they can be portrayed as offering crucial emotional or moral support as Morgan Freeman did in his 1989 breakthrough role in *Driving Miss Daisy* and again in the 1994 *Shawshank Redemption* or in the 2004 *Million Dollar Baby*, for which he won the 2005 Oscar for best supporting actor. Freeman has been cast as speaker of the House of Representatives or vice president in movies such as *Olympus Has Fallen* (2013) and *London Has Fallen* (2016), standing close enough to the top man to act as the top man when disaster strikes. His being in charge, however, has tended to reinforce the fact that disaster has struck. Freeman can even play God as in the 2003 film *Bruce Almighty*, but that was for laughs. Even films such as the 2012 *Red Tails*, portraying the exploits of the Tuskegee airmen of the 332nd Fighter Group of the U.S. Army Air Force, veered off into the common portrayal of blacks as the over-sexed ladies' men engaged in the ultimate no-no of chasing white women.

Black men have seldom been the main characters in serious general release feature films. Will Smith often has stood as an exception, insisting from time to time on roles in which he as protagonist leads triumphant forces of good as in *Independence Day* (1996), *Enemy of the State* (1998), or *Concussion* (2015). In contrast, Denzel Washington's portrayal of corrupt LAPD Detective Alonzo Harris in the 2001 film *Training Day*, for which he won an Academy Award as best actor, exploded with violence and a depravity deepened by its contrast with the film's innocent white protagonist played by Ethan Hawke.

On Hollywood's margins director-producer Spike Lee has offered mixed images of black men as not necessarily doing the right thing but working to stand strong on their own ground. Lee's 1992 biographical drama *Malcolm X*, with Denzel Washington in the title role, best illustrated that direction. But other productions also fit the form, including *He Got Game* (1997), *A Huey P. Newton Story* (2000), *Jim Brown: All-American* (2002), the television documentary *Kobe Doin' Work* (2009), and *Michael Jackson's Journey from Motown to Off the Wall* (2016). Granted, much of Lee's early work and more commercially successful productions, from his initial 1986 *She's Gotta Have It* and 1988 *School Daze* to his 2006 top grosser to date, *Inside Man*, traffics in stereotypes.

In the search for commercial success through comedy, Tyler Perry's productions have tended to collect and even exaggerate stereotyped characters. That was clear at the outset in his television sitcom *Tyler Perry's House of Payne* on TBS from 2006 to 2012. It outran other predominantly black cast television series such as *The Jeffersons, Family Matters*, and *The Cosby Show*, but it hardly outdid them in quality content nor did it match the progressiveness of the 1970s' *Good Times*. And on the big screen Tyler Perry's Madea series and productions such as *Tyler Perry's Diary of a Mad Black Woman* (2005), while perhaps sometimes reaching for outrageous humor, at times simply became outrageous in presenting blacks in dysfunctional families and relationships.

The tough elderly woman Tyler portrayed in his Madea character illustrated too well that black women have fared little better than black men on the big screen. Their traditional positions as domestics have persisted in such films as *The Help* (2011). In roles such as Leticia Musgrove in the 2001 *Monster's Ball*, for which Halle Berry won an Academy Award as best actress, black women have appeared as worse than vamps. Their sexual attractiveness worked as a tool for manipulation and seduction, leaving them outside the scope or standards of morality. Kerry Washington's role as Olivia Pope in the much-touted television series *Scandal* that began in 2012 reproduced the vamp image in her successive sexual escapades.

Washington received nominations as best or lead actress as *Scandal* won a Peabody Award for Excellence in Television. But what image of black women did Washington's role offer the viewing public? Was the behavior depicted what blacks would or should want their daughters, sisters, or young people in general to emulate? Similarly, Viola Davis's role as law professor Annalise Keating on the television drama series *How to Get Away with Murder*, which premiered in 2014, projected a black woman at an exalted point of professional success, as a high-profile defense lawyer teaching law at a prestigious university. Yet her personal life appeared a shambles. Davis's superb performance in her role garnered her deserved critical acclaim, and she became in 2015 the first black woman to win a Primetime Emmy Award for outstanding lead actress in a drama series. *Time* magazine listed her in 2012 among the 100 most influential persons in the world. Yet how real was her role for black women? What was art saying about black life?

American popular culture has long been entertained by images of blacks behaving badly. That has been the preferred image, representing blacks in fiction as it preferred to represent them in fact. And perhaps too often for purposes of commercial success, blacks have adopted such representations. Oscar Micheaux's so-called race films from the 1920s into the 1940s illustrated that path. The so-called Blaxploitation films of the 1970s introduced with the 1971 duo of Melvin Van Peebles's *Sweet Sweetback's Baadasssss*

*Song* and Gordon Parks's *Shaft* played race to the hilt, pandering to both black and white fantasies. Violence predominated as the theme, whether the type was action/martial arts, crime, horror, or Westerns. The characteristically rich soundtracks—perhaps best illustrated by Isaac Hayes's *Shaft* recording that won a Grammy Award for best score soundtrack album for motion picture, with the "Theme from Shaft" winning the Academy Award for best original song—failed to elevate the usually empty action and irresponsibility that not only reinforced rejection of current social constructions and conventions but appeared an embrace of anarchism or even nihilism.

Granted the license of entertainment to alter reality for effect, persistent negative popular images have historically and continuously taken a toll on blacks individually and collectively. Such images have tended to seep into the consciousness of blacks and whites, channeling their expectations and evaluations. They have tended to embed racialized reactions that create both calluses and sores and create muscle memories that move blacks and whites often in polar directions that have prevented any meaningful conversation or other interaction.

The August 2014 tragedy in the Ferguson suburb of St. Louis, Missouri, the horror of the June 2015 multiple homicides at Mother Emanuel African Methodist Episcopal Church in Charleston, South Carolina, and the July 2016 police shootings of Philando Castile in a St. Paul, Minnesota, suburb and of Alton Sterling in Baton Rouge, Louisiana; and Micah Xavier Johnson's shooting of police in Dallas terribly illustrated the persisting deep black–white divide African Americans have continued to confront in the 21st century. Many blacks saw the events as the-same-old-same-old. A black boy or man being gunned down by a white cop, as 18-year-old Michael Brown was in Ferguson, was no new thing. Long memories recalled blacks slaughtered without public notice in the gloomy past of slavery and Jim Crow. More recent but somewhat distant memory recalled the 1955 lynching of Emmett Till; the 1960s assassinations of Medgar Evers, Malcolm X, and Martin Luther King Jr.; the Orangeburg Massacre of 1968; and the Jackson State killings of 1970.

Fresh memories fixed on much-publicized police assaults on black men such as that on Rodney King in Los Angeles (1991), Abner Louima (1997) and Amadou Diallo (1999) in New York City, Laquan McDonald in Chicago (2014), Eric Garner in New York City (2014), Tamir Rice in Cleveland (2014), Walter Scott in North Charleston (2015), Samuel DuBose in Cincinnati (2015), and Freddie Gray in Baltimore (2015). Not that black women had ever been spared, as Joann Little's 1974–1975 North Carolina prison ordeal reminded and as Sandra Bland's 2015 death in a Texas jail cell demonstrated.

The attack at Mother Emanuel was another in the long line of bombings, torchings, and killings at black churches. A gun-toting 21-year-old white supremacist shooting dead Rev. Clementa Pinckney and eight of his black parishioners was another in a long line of white rage and terrorist attacks on religious and social hubs of black communities. Violence against blacks was a historical commonplace. Another incident meant more of the same to some. It put the lie to post-racial society rhetoric for anyone having eyes to see or ears to hear. The fact that more than 1,100 blacks in 2015 died at the hands of police at a rate almost three times that of whites was to too many mere coincidence or a sign of blacks' bad behavior, not proof of any pattern or practice of official and public disregard for black lives.

Commenting on the early July 2016 shootings, former Arkansas Governor Mike Huckabee, an early candidate for the 2016 Republican presidential nomination, insisted that police killings of black males were exaggerated, saying that "more white people have been shot by police officers this year than minorities" (Lowery 2016, n.p.). The British national daily newspaper *The Guardian*'s full-year study of 1,134 deaths at the hands of U.S. law enforcement officers in 2015 noted, however, that "young black men were nine times more likely than other Americans to be killed by police officers." Breaking down the 2015 data, *The Guardian* study noted that while "making up only 2% of the total US population, African American males between the ages of 15 and 34 comprised more than 15% of all deaths logged this year by . . . the use of deadly force by police. Their rate of police-involved deaths was five times higher than for white men of the same age," the story concluded (Swaine 2015, n.p.).

The drumbeat of law-and-order rhetoric has resounded throughout America's history when blacks have appeared out of their place. Blacks' popular image as dysfunctional and violent has continually risen to support repetitive police focus on blacks not because of their behavior but because of their appearance. Blacks, particularly black males, getting stopped, questioned, searched, arrested, indicted, tried, convicted, and incarcerated at disproportionate rates has throughout U.S. history triggered very different responses between blacks and whites, relief on the one hand and resentment on the other.

The Black Lives Matter (BLM) movement organized in 2013 to heighten public awareness of the chronic condition of black–white relations throughout America. BLM's street demonstrations and other protests appeared, however, not so much to raise understanding of blacks' feelings about public abuse and police brutality as to aggravate many whites' ingrained sense that blacks wanted special treatment to cover for their lack of personal responsibility. The disparate response reflected old views of who or what needed to change to improve America. The cry that police were doing what they

The rising tide of public assaults against blacks, particularly cases of police brutalizing and murdering blacks, produced surging mass protests exemplified by the Black Lives Matter (BLM) movement. These protests not only filled streets nationwide, but used social media to bring to light incessant socially sanctioned violence against blacks and other marginalized people. (Mustafa Caglayan/Anadolu Agency/Getty Images)

should not be doing clashed with shouts that police were doing exactly what they should be doing. The confrontation regenerated timeworn arguments about whether it was America that needed change or blacks that needed to change.

As ever, blacks were in fact changing as America pressed into the 21st century. Traditionally a people on the move, as were Americans generally, blacks were repositioning themselves regionally and being repositioned locally, both as concentrations within inner cities such as in Detroit and in being moved out to the suburbs as in Washington, D.C. Most notably, refreshed diversity was altering African American character, complexion, and community. The continuing flow of fresh immigration from the Caribbean and Africa, following the Immigration and Naturalization Act of 1965, significantly changed those in America counted as black.

Entering the 21st century, the foreign-born population among blacks grew as the foreign-born in the general U.S. population also grew. Indeed, moving toward 2020 the U.S. foreign-born population approached new highs in number (41.3 million) and climbed to 13.1 percent of the total U.S. population.

In that surge, the number of foreign-born blacks also increased, as the black immigrant population more than quadrupled since 1980, climbing to 3.8 million in 2013 and reaching 8.7 percent of the U.S. black population (Anderson 2015a, n.p.).

Blacks from the Caribbean and the West Indies contributed most to the surge, accounting for just over half (50.3%) of all foreign-born blacks in the U.S. population in 2013, with Jamaica (18.0%) and Haiti (15.0%) as leading sources. Africa contributed next most (35.9%), trailed at a distance by South America (4.9%) and Central America (3.6%). Nevertheless, Africa provided the most rapid growth in number of immigrants. From about 80,000 in 1970, Africa contributed 830,000 in 2013. Africans were, in fact, the fastest-growing group of U.S. immigrants between 2000 and 2013, increasing by about 41 percent over those years (Anderson 2015b, n.p.). Nigeria (228,000), Ethiopia (195,000), Egypt (183,000), Ghana (150,000), and Kenya (121,000) constituted the leading birthplaces among Africans in the United States in 2013. On arrival, black immigrants tended to congregate in urban areas that had older black communities. About one in three (34.0%) of the blacks living in Florida's Miami-Fort Lauderdale-West Palm Beach metro area in 2013, for example, were immigrants. Similarly, a bit more than one in four (28.0%) of the blacks living in the New York-Newark-Jersey City metro area were immigrants, as were about one in seven (15.0%) in the Washington, D.C., metro area (Anderson 2015b, n.p.).

The shifting demographics emphasized blacks' diverse characteristics. Foreign-born blacks tended, for example, to be significantly older than U.S.-born blacks, with a median age of 42 years as opposed to 29. The age difference contributed to foreign-born blacks having higher educational attainments: for example, among those 25 years and older, about one in four (26.0%) had a bachelor's degree in contrast to about one in five (19.0%) among U.S.-born blacks. That differential further contributed to foreign-born blacks having lower poverty rates (20.0% vs. 28.0%) and household incomes on average $10,000 higher than that of U.S.-born blacks (Anderson 2015b, np).

The fresh black immigration and increased numbers of blacks of mixed parentage moving deeper into the 21st century have more and more displayed African Americans as peoples of a worldwide diaspora. The reach of that diversity was illustrated in the son of a Kenyan being elected U.S. president and in the daughter of Haitians being elected to the U.S. Congress as a Republican from Utah. That diversity has expressed itself also in increasing distance among blacks, shown in increasingly less community than among earlier generations.

National origin and individualism have isolated blacks evermore among themselves as they have recognized less and less in common. Deep differences

An African Day Parade in New York's Harlem illustrates the surge of new black immigrants from Africa, the Caribbean, and elsewhere in the Americas, acknowledging common heritage while refreshing diversity among 21st-century African Americans. (Richard Levine/Alamy Stock Photo)

have carved their way through peoples commonly collected as blacks. From language to culture to lifestyle, Francophone Haitians, Spanish speakers from the Dominican Republic and elsewhere, and Anglophone Jamaicans, for example, often have shared little with each other or with African-born or U.S.-born blacks.

Identification by skin color has increasingly proved too thin to bring together many of these peoples in common cause or concerted action over a broad range. Local events have sometimes galvanized common response to join neighborhoods in community, as in protests over outrages such as those that have propelled the BLM movement. Enduring connections of common community, however, have become tenuous at best among the mass of African Americans.

Martin Luther King's full question for blacks coming from the civil rights' successes of 1964 and 1965 was "Where do we go from here: chaos or community?" Chaos has not appeared in the offing nor has community moving deeper into the 21st century. Blacks in America have never been a singular people or a singular community. Their reactions to white supremacy have pushed them to share in common cause from time to time, but their differences have always been patent and palpable.

The shades of black have multiplied, and many blacks have come to see themselves as not all the same or even similar. Nods of acknowledgment and recognition that were once commonplace among blacks, even passing by, have become a thing of the past. In the 21st century more and more averted eyes have signaled to others of dark skin not only I-do-not-know-you but I-do-not-necessarily-want-to-know-you. Individualism and small group solidarity have appeared to replace larger black community.

Part of the apparent distance among blacks arose from another element of demographics—age, and with it memory. Generation gaps have typically separated younger and older blacks, as the New Negro movement of the 1920s and 1930s illustrated. Moving deeper into the 21st century, the generation gap has appeared to separate many younger blacks from the starker realities of their elders such that they seemed unable to understand what 2015 National Book Award winner Ta-Nehisi Coates took pains to explain to his then 14-year-old son Samori about the hateful heritage of America continuing to confine and define peoples of African descent.

An African American history has developed no singular question, but two have prominently persisted for blacks from of old and they have remained urgent in the 21st century: What is America for me? What is America to be?

## PROFILE: MAYA ANGELOU (1928–2014)

Publication of her 1969 autobiographical *I Know Why the Caged Bird Sings* put Maya Angelou on the *New York Times* best-seller list and got her nominated for the 1970 National Book Award. Long before then the woman born Marguerite Annie Johnson in St. Louis, Missouri, on April 4, 1928, had displayed her multiple talents in various ways, moving from childhood in Stamps, Arkansas, and Oakland, California, to world stages. She went from being an elective mute to being called "the black woman's poet laureate" for her poem "On the Pulse of Morning" delivered at President Bill Clinton's 1993 inauguration.

Her life of adventure and adversity informed her writing, particularly her seven serial autobiographies that ended in 2013 with *Mom & Me & Mom*. Taking as her professional name the combination "Maya," the nickname her older brother Bailey had given her in childhood, and the changed spelling of her first husband's family name, "Angelos," she worked early as a modern dancer and singer who produced a 1957 album titled *Miss Calypso* and performed on tour in Europe and Africa. Angelou worked also as a journalist and editor with publications such as Cairo's weekly *Arab Observer*, the South African-based *African Review* magazine, and the Accra-based *Ghanian Times* daily newspaper. An activist against Jim Crow segregation and South African apartheid, she served for time as northern coordinator of the Martin Luther King–led Southern Christian Leadership Conference.

Using music and dance as an introduction to examining the influence of African American culture on American behavior, history, and society in 1968, Angelou wrote, produced, and narrated the 10-part documentary series *Blacks, Blues, Black!* She wrote screenplays such as *Georgia, Georgia* (1972), composed songs and movie scores, acted on Broadway and on television, for example, in the 1977 miniseries *Roots*, and became a theater director. She later directed the 1996 feature film *Down in the Delta* focused on her often treated themes of family, identity, race, and redemption. She won the 1994 "Best Spoken Word" Grammy Award for her recording of her Clinton inaugural poem "On the Pulse of Morning" and made the 2000 Billboard chart with her collaboration with R&B artists Ashford & Simpson.

While she described herself as "a teacher who writes," after accepting a lifetime appointment as Reynolds Professors of American Studies at Wake Forest University in Winston-Salem, North Carolina, in 1981 Angelou continued to make her life itself a work of performance art replete with remarkable productivity. Her creative work as an autobiographer, poet, civil rights activist and organizer, composer, choreographer and dancer, journalist, screenwriter, singer, stage and screen actor, film and theater director, and teacher was recognized in 2011 in her receiving the Presidential Medal of Freedom, the highest U.S. civilian award. She moved beyond promise to production, consistently testifying in her actions and intonations, in her ironic understatement and natural metaphors that life was to be lived to the fullest without hesitation in the face of horrors and with expressive and gracious joy. She died on May 28, 2014, at age 86.

## REFERENCES

Anderson, Monica. 2015a. "6 Key Findings about Black Immigration to the U.S." *FactTank: News in the Numbers* (April 9): n.p. Accessed at http://www.pew research.org/fact-tank/2015/04/09/6-key-findings-about-Black-immigration/.

Anderson, Monica. 2015b. "African Immigrant Population in US Steadily Climbs." *FactTank: News in the Numbers* (November 2): n.p. Accessed at http://www. pewresearch.org/fact-tank/2015/11/02/african-immigrant-population-in-u-s-steadily-climbs/.

Bouie, Jamelle. 2013. "More Black Men in College Than in Prison." *The American Prospect*, February 28. Accessed at http://prospect.org/article/more-Black-men-college-prison.

Cook, Lindsay. 2015. "U.S. Education: Still Separate and Unequal." *U.S. News & World Report*, January 28. Accessed at http://www.usnews.com/news/blogs/data-mine/2015/01/28/us-education-still-separate-and-unequal.

Duckett, Philethea, and Samatha Artiga. 2013. "Health Coverage for the Black Population Today and under the Affordable Care Act." Disparities Policy, The Henry J. Kaiser Family Foundation. Accessed at http://kff.org/

disparities-policy/fact-sheet/health-coverage-for-the-Black-population-tod
ay-and-under-the-affordable-care-act/.

Isaacs, Julia. 2011. *Economic Mobility of Black and White Families*. Washington, DC: Economic Mobility Project, an initiative of The PEW Charita-
ble Trusts. Accessed at http://www.brookings.edu/~/media/research/files/
papers/2007/11/BlackWhite-isaacs/11_BlackWhite_isaacs.pdf.

Kochhar, Rakesh, and Richard Fry. 2014. "Wealth Inequality Has Widened on
Racial, Ethnic Lines since End of the Great Recession." *Fact Tank: News in
the Numbers*, Pew Research Center, December 12. Accessed at http://www
.pewresearch.org/fact-tank/2014/12/12/racial-wealth-gaps-great-recession/.

Lowery, Wesley. 2016. "Aren't More White People Than Black People Killed by Police?
Yes, but No." *Washington Post*, July 11. Accessed at https://www.washing
tonpost.com/news/post-nation/wp/2016/07/11/arent-more-white-peopl
e-than-black-people-killed-by-police-yes-but-no/?utm_term=.616de2160ae7

NAEP. 2015. "The Nation's Report Card: 2015 Mathematics and Reading Assessments."
Washington, DC: National Assessment of Educational Progress. Accessed at
http://www.nationsreportcard.gov/reading_math_2015/#?grade=4.

NetWellness. 2016. "African American Health: Statistics on Health Disparities among
African Americans." Accessed at http://www.netwellness.org/healthtopics/
aahealth/currentstats.cfm.

Pietila, Antero. 2010. *Not in My Neighborhood: How Bigotry Shaped a Great
American City*. Chicago: Ivan R. Dee.

The Sentencing Project. 2013. *Report of the Sentencing Project to the United Nations
Human Rights Committee: Regarding Racial Disparities in the United States
Criminal Justice System*. Washington, DC: The Sentencing Project Research
and Advocacy for Reform.

Swaine, Jon, et al. 2015. "Young Black Men Killed by U. S. Police at Highest Rate in
Year of 1134 Deaths." *The Guardian* (UK), December 31. Accessed at https://
www.theguardian.com/us-news/2015/dec/31/the-counted-police-killing
s-2015-young-black-men.

# Selected Bibliography

Aberjhani West, Sandra L. *Encyclopedia of the Harlem Renaissance*. New York: Facts on File, Inc., 2003.

Alkebulan, Paul. *The African American Press in World War II: Toward Victory at Home and Abroad*. Lanham, MD: Lexington Books, 2014.

Anderson, Noel S., and Haroon Kharem. *Education as Freedom: African American Educational Thought and Activism*. Lanham, MD: Lexington Books, 2009.

Andrews, William L. Foster, Frances Smith, and Trudier Harris. *The Oxford Companion to African American Literature*. New York: Oxford University Press, 1997.

Appiah, Anthony, and Henry Louis Gates. *Africana: Civil Rights: An A-to-Z Reference of the Movement That Changed America*. Philadelphia: Running Press, 2004.

Appiah, Anthony, and Henry Louis Gates. *Africana: The Encyclopedia of the African and African American Experience*. New York: Basic Civitas Books, 1999.

Astor, Gerald. *The Right to Fight: A History of African Americans in the Military*. Novato, CA: Presidio, 1998.

Balgooy, Max van. *Interpreting African American History and Culture at Museums and Historic Sites*. Lanham, MD: Rowman & Littlefield, 2015.

Baraka, Amiri. *Blues People; Negro Music in White America*. New York: W. Morrow, 1963.

Barber, John T. *The Black Digital Elite: African American Leaders of the Information Revolution*. Westport, CT: Praeger, 2006.

Bearden, Romare, and Harry Henderson. *A History of African-American Artists: From 1792 to the Present*. New York: Pantheon Books, 1993.

Bell, Derrick. *And We Are Not Saved: The Elusive Quest for Racial Justice*. New York: Basic Books, 1987.

Bell, Derrick. *Race, Racism, and American Law*. Boston: Little, Brown, 1973.

Bell, Derrick. *Silent Covenants: Brown v. Board of Education and the Unfulfilled Hopes for Racial Reform*. New York: Oxford University Press, 2004.

Berlin, Ira. *The Destruction of Slavery*. Cambridge; New York: Cambridge University Press, 1985.

Berlin, Ira. *Free at Last: A Documentary History of Slavery, Freedom, and the Civil War*. New York: The New Press, 1992.

Berlin, Ira. *Generations of Captivity: A History of African-American Slaves*. Cambridge, MA: Belknap Press of Harvard University Press, 2003.

Berlin, Ira. *The Making of African America: The Four Great Migrations*. New York: Viking, 2010.

Berlin, Ira. *Many Thousands Gone: The First Two Centuries of Slavery in North America*. Cambridge, MA: Harvard University Press, 1998.

Berlin, Ira. *The Wartime Genesis of Free Labor: The Lower South*. New York: Cambridge University Press, 1990.

Berlin, Ira, Marc Favreau, and Steven F. Miller. *Remembering Slavery: African Americans Talk about Their Personal Experiences of Slavery and Emancipation*. Washington, DC: New Press, 1998.

Berry, Mary Frances. *And Justice for All: The United States Commission on Civil Rights and the Continuing Struggle for Freedom in America*. New York: Alfred A. Knopf, 2009.

Berry, Mary Frances. *Black Resistance, White Law: A History of Constitutional Racism in America*. New York: A. Lane, Penguin Press, 1994.

Berry, Mary Frances. *Military Necessity and Civil Rights Policy: Black Citizenship and the Constitution, 1861–1868*. Port Washington, NY: Kennikat Press, 1977.

Berry, Mary Frances, and John W. Blassingame. *Long Memory: The Black Experience in America*. New York: Oxford University Press, 1982.

Blackmon, Douglas A. *Slavery by Another Name: The Re-Enslavement of Black People in America from the Civil War to World War II*. New York: Doubleday, 2008.

Boehm, Lisa Krissof. *Making a Way Out of No Way: African American Women and the Second Great Migration*. Jackson: University Press of Mississippi, 2010.

Bolster, W. Jeffery. *Black Jacks: African American Seamen in the Age of Sail*. Cambridge, MA: Harvard University Press, 2009.

Booker, Bryan D. *African Americans in the United States Army in World War II*. Jefferson, NC: McFarland, 2008.

Bowser, Benjamin P., and Louis Kushnick. *Against the Odds: Scholars Who Challenged Racism in the Twentieth Century*. Amherst: University of Massachusetts Press, 2002.

Bracey, John H., August Meier, and Elliott M. Rudwick. *Black Workers and Organized Labor*. Belmont, CA: Wadsworth Pub. Co., 1971.

Bracks, Lean'tin L. *The Complete Encyclopedia of African American History: 400 Years of Achievement*. Westport, CT: African American Publications, 2014.

Bracks, Lean'tin L., and Jessie Carney Smith. *Black Women of the Harlem Renaissance Era*. Lanham, MD: Rowman & Littlefield, 2014.

Broadnax, Samuel. *Blue Skies, Black Wings: African American Pioneers of Aviation*. Westport, CT: Praeger, 2007.

Brown, Lois. *The Encyclopedia of the Harlem Literary Renaissance*. New York: Checkmark Books, 2006.

Brown, Tamara, Gregory Parks, and Clarenda M. Phillips. *African American Fraternities and Sororities: The Legacy and the Vision*. Lexington: University Press of Kentucky, 2005.

Brundage, W. Fitzhugh. *Beyond Blackface: African Americans and the Creation of American Popular Culture, 1890–1930*. Chapel Hill: University of North Carolina Press, 2011.

Buckley, Gail Lumet. *American Patriots: The Story of Blacks in the Military from the Revolution to Desert Storm*. New York: Random House, 2001.

Burnim, Mellonee V., and Portia K. Maultsby. *African American Music: An Introduction*. New York: Routledge, 2006.

Carey, Charles W. *African Americans in Science: An Encyclopedia of People and Progress*. Santa Barbara, CA: ABC-CLIO, 2008.

Clark, Kenneth Bancroft. *Dark Ghetto: Dilemmas of Social Power*. New York: Harper & Row, 1965.

Colburn, David R., and Jeffrey S. Adler. *African-American Mayors: Race, Politics, and the American City*. Urbana: University of Illinois Press, 2001.

Collier-Thomas, Bettye, and V. P. Franklin. *Sisters in the Struggle: African American Women in the Civil Rights-Black Power Movement*. New York: New York University Press, 2001.

Combs, Rhea L., Deborah Willis, and Lonnie G. Bunch. *Through the African American Lens*. Washington, DC: National Museum of African American History and Culture, Smithsonian Institution, 2014.

Conniff, Michael L., and Thomas J. Davis. *Africans in the Americas: A History of the Black Diaspora*. Caldwell, NJ: Blackburn, 2002.

Curry, George E., and Cornel West. *The Affirmative Action Debate*. Reading, MA: Addison-Wesley, 1996.

Dandridge, Rita B. *Black Women's Blues: A Literary Anthology, 1934–1988*. New York: G. K. Hall, 1992.

Danky, James Philip, and Maureen E. Hady. *African-American Newspapers and Periodicals: A National Bibliography*. Cambridge, MA: Harvard University Press, 1998.

Davis, Charles T., and Henry Louis Gates Jr., eds. 1985. *The Slave's Narrative*. New York: Oxford University Press.

Davis, David Brion. *Inhuman Bondage: The Rise and Fall of Slavery in the New World*. New York: Oxford University Press, 2006.

Davis, Thomas J. *A Rumor of Revolt: The "Great Negro Plot" in Colonial New York*. Amherst: University of Massachusetts Press, 1990.

Davis, Thomas J. *Plessy v. Ferguson*. Santa Barbara, CA: Greenwood, 2012.

Davis, Thomas J. *Race Relations in America: A Reference Guide with Primary Documents*. Westport, CT: Greenwood Press, 2006.

Davis, Thomas J. *Race Relations in the United States, 1940–1960.* Westport, CT: Greenwood Press, 2008.

Davis, Thomas J. *When Is Labor Free? Federal Freedmen's Policy, Freedom of Contract, and Free Labor Theory.* Chicago: American Bar Foundation, 1994.

Dawson, Michael C. *Black Visions: The Roots of Contemporary African-American Political Ideologies.* Chicago: University of Chicago Press, 2001.

dele, jegede. *Encyclopedia of African American Artists.* Westport, CT: Greenwood Press, 2009.

Diawara, Manthia. *Black American Cinema.* New York: Routledge, 1993.

Dickson-Clark, Darryl. *The Columbia Guide to Contemporary African American Fiction.* New York: Columbia University Press, 2005.

Dierenfield, Bruce J., and John White. *A History of African-American Leadership.* Harlow, England; New York: Pearson, 2012.

Du Bois, W.E.B. *Black Reconstruction: An Essay toward a History of the Part Which Black Folk Played in the Attempt to Reconstruct Democracy in America, 1860–1880.* New York: Russel & Russel, 1935.

Earle, Jonathan Halperin. *The Routledge Atlas of African American History.* New York: Routledge, 2000.

Early, Gerald Lyn. *A Level Playing Field: African American Athletes and the Republic of Sports.* Cambridge, MA: Harvard University Press, 2011.

Ellett, Ryan. *Encyclopedia of Black Radio in the United States, 1921–1955.* Jefferson, NC: McFarland, 2012.

Ellis, Mark. *Race, War, and Surveillance: African Americans and the United States Government during World War I.* Bloomington: Indiana University Press, 2001.

Falola, Toyin, and Amanda Warnock. *Encyclopedia of the Middle Passage.* Westport, CT: Greenwood Press, 2007.

Farrington, Lisa E. *Creating Their Own Image: The History of African-American Women Artists.* New York: Oxford University Press, 2005.

Finkelman, Paul. *Encyclopedia of African American History.* 2 vols. New York: Oxford University Press, 2006–2009.

Finkelman, Paul. *Milestone Documents in African American History: Exploring the Essential Primary Sources.* Dallas, TX: Schlager Group, 2010.

Fisch, Audrey A. *The Cambridge Companion to the African American Slave Narrative.* Cambridge: Cambridge University Press, 2007.

Flamming, Douglas. *African Americans in the West.* Santa Barbara, CA: ABC-CLIO, 2009.

Ford, Tanisha C. *Liberated Threads: Black Women, Style, and the Global Politics of Soul.* Chapel Hill: University of North Carolina Press, 2015.

Franklin, John Hope, and Evelyn Brooks Higginbotham. *From Slavery to Freedom: A History of African Americans.* 9th ed. New York: McGraw-Hill, 2011.

Freedman, Lew. *African American Pioneers of Baseball: A Biographical Encyclopedia.* Westport, CT: Greenwood Press, 2007.

Gates, Henry Louis Jr. *Life upon These Shores: Looking at African American History, 1513–2008.* New York: Alfred A. Knopf, 2011.

Gates, Henry Louis Jr. *The Oxford Handbook of African American Citizenship, 1865–Present*. New York: Oxford University Press, 2012.

Gates, Henry Louis Jr., and Evelyn Brooks Higginbotham. *The African American National Biography*. New York: Oxford University Press, 2008.

Gatewood, Willard B. *Black Americans and the White Man's Burden, 1898–1903*. Urbana: University of Illinois Press, 1975.

Gavins, Raymond. *The Cambridge Guide to African American History*. New York: Cambridge University Press, 2016.

Genovese, Eugene D. *Roll, Jordan, Roll; the World the Slaves Made*. New York: Pantheon Books, 1974.

Gill, LaVerne McCain. *African American Women in Congress: Forming and Transforming History*. New Brunswick, NJ: Rutgers University Press, 1997.

Graham, Maryemma, and Jerry Washington Ward. *The Cambridge History of African American Literature*. New York: Cambridge University Press, 2011.

Hall, Kermit L. *Race Relations and the Law in American History: Major Historical Interpretations*. New York: Garland Publishing, 1987.

Harris, Robert L., and Rosalyn Terborg-Penn. *The Columbia Guide to African American History since 1939*. New York: Columbia University Press, 2008.

Higginbotham, A. Leon. *In the Matter of Color: The Colonial Period*. New York: Oxford University Press, 1978.

Hill, Errol, and James V. Hatch. *A History of African American Theatre*. Cambridge; New York: Cambridge University Press, 2003.

Hine, Darlene Clark. *Black Women in American History*. Brooklyn, NY: Carlson Publishing, 1990.

Hine, Darlene Clark, Elsa Barkley Brown, and Rosalyn Terborg-Penn. *Black Women in America: An Historical Encyclopedia*. Brooklyn, NY: Carlson Publishing, 1993.

Hine, Darlene Clark, William C. Hine, and Stanley Harrold. *African Americans: A Concise History*. Upper Saddle River, NJ: Prentice Hall, 2004.

Hine, Darlene Clark, and Kathleen Thompson. *Facts on File Encyclopedia of Black Women in America*. 11 vols. New York: Facts on File, 1997.

Holt, Thomas C. *Children of Fire: A History of African Americans*. New York: Hill and Wang, 2010.

Hornsby, Alton. *A Companion to African American History*. Malden, MA: Blackwell Publishing, 2005.

Horton, James Oliver. *Chronology of African American History: From 1492 to the Present*. Detroit, MI: Gale Research, 1997.

Horton, James Oliver. *Free People of Color: Inside the African American Community*. Washington, DC: Smithsonian Institution Press, 1993.

Horton, James Oliver, and Lois E. Horton. *In Hope of Liberty: Culture, Community, and Protest among Northern Free Blacks, 1700–1860*. New York: Oxford University Press, 1998.

Howard, John R. *The Shifting Wind: The Supreme Court and Civil Rights from Reconstruction to Brown*. Albany: State University of New York Press, 1999.

Iverem, Esther. *We Gotta Have It: Twenty Years of Seeing Black at the Movies, 1986–2006*. New York: Thunder's Mouth Press, 2007.

Jackson, Cynthia L. *African American Education: A Reference Handbook*. Santa Barbara, CA: ABC-CLIO, 2001.

Jacobs, Ronald N. *Race, Media, and the Crisis of Civil Society: From Watts to Rodney King*. New York: Cambridge University Press, 2000.

James Van DerZee Institute. *The Black Photographer (1908–1970): A Survey*. New York: James Van DerZee Institute, 1971.

Johnson, Sylvester A. *African American Religions, 1500–2000: Colonialism, Democracy, and Freedom*. Cambridge: Cambridge University Press, 2015.

Jordan, William G. *Black Newspapers and America's War for Democracy, 1914–1920*. Chapel Hill: University of North Carolina, 2001.

Joseph, Peniel E. *Waiting 'Til the Midnight Hour: A Narrative History of Black Power in America*. New York: Henry Holt and Co., 2006.

Kaplan, Sidney. *The Black Presence in the Era of the American Revolution, 1770–1800*. Greenwich, CT: New York Graphic Society, 1973.

Katz-Hyman, Martha B., and Kym S. Rice. *World of a Slave: Encyclopedia of the Material Life of Slaves in the United States*. 2 vols. Santa Barbara, CA: Greenwood, 2011.

Kelley, Blair Murphy. *Right to Ride: Streetcar Boycotts and African American Citizenship in the Era of Plessy v. Ferguson*. Chapel Hill: University of North Carolina Press, 2010.

Kelley, Robin D. G., and Earl Lewis, eds. *A History of African Americans since 1880*. 2 vols. New York: Oxford University Press, 2005.

Kelley, Robin D. G., and Earl Lewis. *To Make Our World Anew: A History of African Americans*. New York: Oxford University Press, 2000.

King, Stewart R., and Beverly C. Tomek. *Encyclopedia of Free Blacks and People of Color in the Americas*. New York: Facts on File, 2012.

King-Meadows, Jeni Tyson McRay. *African American Leadership: A Reference Guide*. Santa Barbara, CA: Mission Bell Media, 2015.

Kitwana, Bakari. *The Hip Hop Generation: Young Blacks and the Crisis in African American Culture*. New York: Basic Civitas Books, 2002.

Klein, Herbert S. *The Middle Passage: Comparative Studies in the Atlantic Slave Trade*. Princeton, NJ: Princeton University Press, 1978.

Knauer, Christine. *Let Us Fight as Free Men: Black Soldiers and Civil Rights*. Philadelphia: University of Pennsylvania Press, 2014.

Kusmer, Kenneth L. *African American Urban History since World War II*. Chicago: The University of Chicago Press, 2009.

Lazerow, Jama, and Yohuru R. Williams. *In Search of the Black Panther Party: New Perspectives on a Revolutionary Movement*. Durham, NC: Duke University Press, 2006.

LeFlouria, Talitha L. *Chained in Silence: Black Women and Convict Labor in the New South*. Chapel Hill: University of North Carolina Press, 2015.

Lemann, Nicholas. *The Promised Land: The Great Black Migration and How It Changed America*. New York: Knopf, 1991.

Lentz-Smith, Adrienne Danette. *Freedom Struggles: African Americans and World War I*. Cambridge, MA: Harvard University Press, 2011.

Levine, Lawrence W. *Black Culture and Black Consciousness: Afro-American Folk Thought from Slavery to Freedom.* New York: Oxford University Press, 1977.

Lewis, Samella S. *African American Art and Artists.* Berkeley: University of California Press, 2003.

Lomotey, Kofi. *Encyclopedia of African American Education.* 2 vols. Los Angeles, CA: Sage, 2010.

Lowery, Charles D., John F. Marszalek, and Thomas Adams Upchurch. *The Greenwood Encyclopedia of African American Civil Rights: From Emancipation to the Twenty-First Century.* Westport, CT: Greenwood Press, 2003.

Mance, Ajuan Maria. *Inventing Black Women: African American Women Poets and Self-Representation, 1877–2000.* Knoxville: University of Tennessee Press, 2007.

Marable, Manning, and Kristen Clarke. *Barack Obama and African American Empowerment: The Rise of Black America's New Leadership.* New York: Palgrave Macmillan, 2009.

Marable, Manning, Nishani Frazier, and John Campbell McMillian. *Freedom on My Mind: The Columbia Documentary History of the African American Experience.* New York: Columbia University Press, 2003.

Martin, Waldo E. *No Coward Soldiers: Black Cultural Politics and Postwar America.* Cambridge, MA: Harvard University Press, 2005.

Martin, Waldo E., and Patricia Sullivan. *Civil Rights in the United States. Volume 1.* New York: Macmillan Reference USA, 2000.

Massood, Paula J. *Black City Cinema: African American Urban Experiences in Film.* Philadelphia: Temple University Press, 2003.

McCann, Bob. *Encyclopedia of African American Actresses in Film and Television.* Jefferson, NC: McFarland & Co., 2010.

McCaskill, Barbara, and Caroline Gebhard. *Post-Bellum, Pre-Harlem: African American Literature and Culture, 1877–1919.* New York: New York University Press, 2006.

McNeil, W. K. *Encyclopedia of American Gospel Music.* New York: Routledge, 2005.

Meier, August, and Elliott M. Rudwick. *From Plantation to Ghetto; An Interpretive History of American Negroes,* New York: Hill and Wang, 1966.

Merelman, Richard M. *Representing Black Culture: Racial Conflict and Cultural Politics in the United States.* New York: Routledge, 1995.

Meyers, Marian. *African American Women in the News: Gender, Race, and Class in Journalism.* New York: Routledge, Taylor & Francis Group, 2013.

Mitchell, Angelyn, and Danille K. Taylor. *The Cambridge Companion to African American Women's Literature.* New York: Cambridge University Press, 2009.

Mjagkij, Nina. *Loyalty in Time of Trial: The African American Experience in World War I.* Lanham, MD: Rowman & Littlefield, 2011.

Moss, Hilary J. *Schooling Citizens: The Struggle for African American Education in Antebellum America.* Chicago: University of Chicago Press, 2009.

Muhammad, Khalil Gibran. *The Condemnation of Blackness: Race, Crime, and the Making of Modern Urban America.* Cambridge, MA: Harvard University Press, 2011.

Murphy, Larry G., J. Gordon Melton, and Gary L. Ward. *Encyclopedia of African American Religions.* New York: Garland Publishing, 1993.

Nordin, Dennis Sven. *From Edward Brooke to Barack Obama: African American Political Success, 1966–2008.* Columbia: University of Missouri Press, 2012.

Painter, Nell Irvin. *Creating Black Americans: African-American History and Its Meanings, 1619 to the Present.* New York: Oxford University Press, 2006.

Palmer, Colin A. *Encyclopedia of African-American Culture and History: The Black Experience in the America*s. Detroit, MI: Macmillan Reference USA, 2006.

Palmer, Colin A. *Passageways: An Interpretive History of Black America.* Belmont, CA: Wadsworth/Thomson Learning, 2002.

Parent, Anthony S. *Foul Means: The Formation of a Slave Society in Virginia, 1660–1740.* Chapel Hill: Published for the Omohundro Institute of Early American History and Culture, Williamsburg, Virginia, by the University of North Carolina Press, 2003.

Patterson, James T. *Brown v. Board of Education: A Civil Rights Milestone and Its Troubled Legacy.* Oxford; New York: Oxford University Press, 2001.

Pederson, Jay P., and Jessie Carney Smith. *African American Breakthroughs: 500 Years of Black Firsts.* New York: U X L, 1995.

Peretti, Burton W. *Lift Every Voice: The History of African American Music.* Lanham, MD: Rowman & Littlefield, 2009.

Piersen, William Dillon. *From Africa to America: African American History from the Colonial Era to the Early Republic, 1526–1790.* New York: Twayne Publishers; Prentice Hall International, 1996.

Pinn, Anthony B., Stephen C. Finley, and Torin Alexander. *African American Religious Cultures.* Santa Barbara, CA: ABC-CLIO, 2009.

Prahlad, Anand. *The Greenwood Encyclopedia of African American Folklore.* Westport, CT: Greenwood Press, 2006.

Price, Emmett George, Tammy L. Kemodle, and Horace Joseph Maxile. *Encyclopedia of African American Music.* 3 vols. Santa Barbara, CA: ABC-CLIO, 2011.

Quarles, Benjamin. *Black Mosaic: Essays in Afro-American History and Historiography.* Amherst: University of Massachusetts Press, 1988.

Quarles, Benjamin. *The Negro in the Making of America.* New York: Collier Books, 1969.

Reagon, Bernice Johnson. *If You Don't Go, Don't Hinder Me: The African American Sacred Song Tradition.* Lincoln: University of Nebraska Press, 2001.

Reagon, Bernice Johnson. *We'll Understand It Better By and By: Pioneering African American Gospel Composers.* Washington, DC: Smithsonian Institution Press, 1992.

Reid, Debra Ann, and Evan P. Bennett. *Beyond Forty Acres and a Mule: African American Landowning Families since Reconstruction.* Gainesville: University Press of Florida, 2014.

Riech, Steven A. *The Great Black Migration: A Historical Encyclopedia of the American Mosaic.* Westport, CT: Greenwood, 2014.

Riech, Steven A. *A Working People: A History of African American Workers since Emancipation.* Lanham, MD: Rowman & Littlefield, 2013.

Riley, Sam G. *African Americans in the Media Today: An Encyclopedia.* Westport, CT: Greenwood Press, 2007.

Robinson, Donald L. *Slavery in the Structure of American Politics, 1765–1820.* New York: Harcourt Brace Jovanovich, 1970.

Rucker, Walter C., and James N. Upton. *Encyclopedia of American Race Riots: Greenwood Milestones in African American History.* Westport, CT: Greenwood Press, 2006.

Rutkoff, Peter M., and William B. Scott. *Fly Away: The Great African American Cultural Migrations.* Baltimore, MD: Johns Hopkins University Press, 2010.

Sanders, Robert B. *Contributions of African American Scientists to the Field[s] of Science, Medicine, and Inventions.* New York: Nova Science Publishers, 2010.

Sarat, Austin. *Civil Rights in American Law, History, and Politics.* New York: Cambridge University Press, 2016.

Schneider, Richard C. *African American History in the Press, 1851–1899: From the Coming of the Civil War to the Rise of Jim Crow as Reported and Illustrated in Selected Newspapers of the Time.* Detroit, MI: Gale Research, 1996.

Shockley, Evie. *Renegade Poetics: Black Aesthetics and Formal Innovation in African American Poetry.* Iowa City: University of Iowa Press, 2011.

Sidbury, James. *Becoming African in America: Race and Nation in the Early Black Atlantic.* Oxford; New York: Oxford University Press, 2007.

Simmons, Charles A. *The African American Press: A History of News Coverage during National Crises, with Special Reference to Four Black Newspapers, 1827–1965.* Jefferson, NC: McFarland & Co., 1998.

Skocpol, Theda, Ariane Liazos, and Marshall Ganz. *What a Mighty Power We Can Be: African American Fraternal Groups and the Struggle for Racial Equality.* Princeton, NJ: Princeton University Press, 2006.

Smith, Jessie Carney. *Encyclopedia of African American Popular Culture.* Santa Barbara, CA: Greenwood, 2011.

Smith, Jessie Carney, and Shirelle Phelps. *Notable Black American Women.* Detroit, MI: Gale Research, 1992.

Smith, Robert C. *Encyclopedia of African American Politics.* New York: Facts on File, 2003.

Sokol, Jason. *All Eyes Are upon Us: Race and Politics from Boston to Brooklyn.* New York: Basic Books, 2014.

Sollors, Werner. *Interracialism: Black-White Intermarriage in American History, Literature, and Law.* New York: Oxford University Press, 2000.

Sotiropoulos, Karen. *Staging Race: Black Performers in Turn of the Century America.* Cambridge, MA: Harvard University Press, 2008.

Southern, Eileen. *The Music of Black Americans: A History.* New York: W. W. Norton, 1971.

Stewart, Earl L. *African American Music: An Introduction.* New York; London: Schirmer Books; Prentice Hall International, 1998.

Streitmatter, Rodger. *Raising Her Voice: African-American Women Journalists Who Changed History.* Lexington, KY: University Press of Kentucky, 1994.

Sutherland, Jonathan D. *African Americans at War: An Encyclopedia.* 2 vols. Santa Barbara, CA: ABC-CLIO, 2004.

Tadman, Michael. *Speculators and Slaves: Masters, Traders, and Slaves in the Old South.* Madison: University of Wisconsin Press, 1989.

Taylor, Quintard. *In Search of the Racial Frontier: African Americans in the American West, 1528–1990.* New York: W. W. Norton, 1998.

Taylor, Quintard, and Shirley Ann Wilson Moore. *African American Women Confront the West: 1600–2000.* Norman: University of Oklahoma Press, 2003.

Thompson, Gordon E. *Black Music, Black Poetry: Blues and Jazz's Impact on African American Versification.* Farnham: Ashgate, 2014.

Trotter, Joe William. *The African American Experience.* Boston, MA: Houghton Mifflin, 2001.

Trotter, Joe William, and Earl Lewis. *African Americans in the Industrial Age: A Documentary History, 1915–1945.* Boston, MA: Northeastern University Press, 1996.

Trotter, Joe Willliam, Earl Lewis, and Tera Hunter. *African American Urban Experience: Perspectives from the Colonial Period to the Present.* New York: Palgrave Macmillan, 2004.

Turner-Sadler, Joanne. *African American History: An Introduction.* New York: Peter Lang, 2006.

Vorenberg, Michael. *Final Freedom: The Civil War, the Abolition of Slavery, and the Thirteenth Amendment.* Cambridge: Cambridge University Press, 2004.

Walker, Juliet. *Encyclopedia of African American Business History.* Westport, CT: Greenwood Press, 1999.

Walters, Kerry S. *American Slave Revolts and Conspiracies: A Reference Guide.* Santa Barbara, CA: ABC-CLIO, 2015.

Washburn, Patrick Scott. *The African American Newspaper: Voice of Freedom.* Evanston, IL: Northwestern University Press, 2006.

Weir, William. *The Encyclopedia of African American Military History.* Amherst, NY: Prometheus Books, 2004.

Westheider, James E. *The African American Experience in Vietnam: Brothers in Arms.* Lanham, MD: Rowman & Littlefield, 2008.

Whelchel, L. H. *The History & Heritage of African-American Churches: A Way Out of No Way.* St. Paul, MN: Paragon House, 2011.

White, John. *Black Leadership in America: From Booker T. Washington to Jesse Jackson.* London: Longman, 1990.

Wilkerson, Isabel. *The Warmth of Other Suns: The Epic Story of America's Great Migration.* New York: Random House, 2010.

Williams, David. *I Freed Myself: African American Self-Emancipation in the Civil War Era.* New York: Cambridge University Press, 2014.

Williams, Heather Andrea. *Help Me to Find My People: The African American Search for Family Lost in Slavery.* Chapel Hill: University of North Carolina Press, 2012.

Williams, Heather Andrea. *Self-Taught: African American Education in Slavery and Freedom.* Chapel Hill: University of North Carolina Press, 2005.

Williams, Kidada. *They Left Great Marks on Me: African American Testimonies of Racial Violence from Emancipation to World War I*. New York: New York University Press, 2012.

Willis, Deborah. *Reflections in Black: A History of Black Photographers*. 2 vols. New York: W. W. Norton, 2000.

Willis, Deborah. *An Illustrated Bio-Bibliography of Black Photographers*. 2 vols. New York: Garland Publishing, 1985–1989.

Willis, Deborah, and Howard Dodson. *Black Photographers Bear Witness: 100 Years of Social Protest*. Williamstown, MA: Williams College Museum of Art, 1989.

Wilson, Dreck Spurlock. *African American Architects: A Biographical Dictionary, 1865–1945*. New York: Routledge, 2004.

Wynn, Neil A. *The African American Experience during World War II*. Lanham, MD: Rowman & Littlefield, 2010.

Young, Harvey. *The Cambridge Companion to African American Theatre*. Cambridge: Cambridge University Press, 2013.

# Index

## About the Author

Thomas J. Davis, PhD, JD, is professor of history at Arizona State University, Tempe. He is coauthor with Michael L. Conniff of *Africans in the Americas: A History of the Black Diaspora* and author of *Race Relations in America: A Reference Guide with Primary Documents, Race Relations in the United States, 1940–1960*, and *Plessy v. Ferguson* among other works. An historian and lawyer, he focuses on issues of race, identity, and law, particularly U.S. constitutional issues of civil rights.